Steffen Becker

Coupled Model Transformations for QoS Enabled Component-Based Software Design

The Karlsruhe Series on Software Design and Quality

Volume 1

Chair Software Design and Quality
Faculty of Computer Science
Universität Karlsruhe (TH)

and

Software Engineering Division
Research Center for Information Technology (FZI), Karlsruhe

Editor: Prof. Dr. Ralf Reussner

Coupled Model Transformations for QoS Enabled Component-Based Software Design

by
Steffen Becker

universitätsverlag karlsruhe

Dissertation, University of Oldenburg,
Department of Computer Science, 2008

Impressum

Universitätsverlag Karlsruhe
c/o Universitätsbibliothek
Straße am Forum 2
D-76131 Karlsruhe
www.uvka.de

Universitätsverlag Karlsruhe 2008
Print on Demand

ISSN: 1867-0067
ISBN: 978-3-86644-271-9

Contents

1 Introduction **1**

1.1 Motivation 1
1.2 Application Scenario 7
1.3 Scientific Contributions 8
1.4 Structure 11
1.5 Context of this Thesis 14
1.6 Abstract 14
1.7 Abstract (in German) 15

2 Foundations and Related Work **17**

2.1 Components, Architecture and Component Models 19
2.1.1 Software Component 19
2.1.2 CBSE Developer Roles 22
2.1.3 Software Architecture 24
2.1.4 Component Models 26
2.2 Model-Driven Software Development 34
2.2.1 Model / Meta-Model / MOF 35
2.2.2 Transformations: MDA / Generative Programming 41
2.2.3 Platforms and Platform Specific Models 46
2.3 Performance Modelling and Prediction 49
2.3.1 Influence Factors on Software Performance 50
2.3.2 Performance Prediction Process 52
2.3.3 Performance Prediction Methods 55
2.3.4 Performance Simulations 58
2.3.5 Prototyping 59
2.3.6 CBSE Performance Prediction 60
2.3.7 Model-Driven Methods 62

2.3.8 Platform Completions 65
2.4 Discussion of the Existing Approaches 66
2.4.1 Requirements for Model-Driven, CBSE Predictability . . . 66
2.4.2 Resulting Deficiencies 70

3 The Palladio Component Model **75**
3.1 Palladio Development Process 77
3.1.1 PCM Development Process 77
3.1.2 Introducing MDSD into the Palladio Development Process 80
3.2 PCM Core Concepts 85
3.2.1 Random Variables and Stochastic Expressions 86
3.2.2 Context Model 88
3.3 Interfaces and Datatypes 92
3.4 Components and Component Types 94
3.4.1 Provided and Required Roles 94
3.4.2 PCM Component Types 95
3.4.3 Basic Components 96
3.4.4 Composite Components 96
3.5 Resource Demanding SEFF 98
3.5.1 External Calls 99
3.5.2 Service Parameters 100
3.5.3 SetVariableAction 103
3.5.4 Inner Elements of Collections 103
3.5.5 InternalActions 104
3.5.6 Parametric Resource Demands 105
3.5.7 Resource Acquisition and Release 106
3.5.8 Control Flow 106
3.5.9 Concluding remarks 110
3.6 Systems 110
3.6.1 System QoS Annotations 111
3.6.2 Component Parameters 112
3.7 Allocation 112
3.7.1 Resource Environment 113
3.7.2 Allocation Contexts 114
3.8 Usage 115
3.8.1 Usage Model and Usage Scenarios 115

3.8.2 UsageBehaviour 116
3.8.3 Usage Context 117
3.9 Tool support 117
3.10 Assumptions and Limitations 120

4 Transformations **123**
4.1 Coupled Transformations Method 124
4.1.1 Motivation 124
4.1.2 Formalisation of Coupled Transformations 129
4.2 Modular Transformations 137
4.3 Mapping Overview 140
4.4 Simulation Mapping 142
4.4.1 SimuCom Overview 144
4.4.2 Evaluating Stochastic Expressions 146
4.4.3 Simulated Resources 150
4.4.4 Usage Model 158
4.4.5 Composite Structures 160
4.4.6 Resource Demanding SEFFs 162
4.4.7 Allocation 171
4.4.8 Component Context in SimuCom 172
4.4.9 Semantics of the Simulation 173
4.4.10 Assumptions and Limitations 173
4.4.11 Simulation Time Estimation 174
4.5 Coupled Transformations 176
4.5.1 CBSE Platform Transformations 177
4.5.2 Mark Meta-Models 179
4.5.3 Methods to Parametrise Analysis Transformations 181
4.6 Technological Java EE Mapping 186
4.6.1 Components 189
4.6.2 ComposedStructures 202
4.6.3 Assembly Connectors 204
4.6.4 Add-Ons 217
4.6.5 Limitations and Discussion 218
4.7 Prototype Mapping 220
4.7.1 Combining Mappings 221
4.7.2 Simulation of Load 222

4.7.3 Assumptions and Limitations 224

5 Validation **227**

5.1 Type I Validation 228

5.1.1 Mark Model Independent Predictions 229

5.1.2 Mark Model Dependent Predictions 231

5.2 Type II Validation: Controlled Experiment 239

5.2.1 Influence factors 239

5.2.2 PCM Tool Suite 240

5.2.3 Study Design 243

5.2.4 Evaluation 246

5.2.5 Validity 252

5.2.6 Summary 253

6 Conclusions **255**

6.1 Summary 255

6.2 Limitations 259

6.3 Open Questions and Future Work 259

6.4 Visions 265

A Appendix **269**

A.1 Contributions and Imported Concepts 269

A.2 Generated RD-SEFFs for Connector Completions 273

A.3 Detailed QVT Transformations 274

A.4 Detailed Experiment Results 274

List of Figures

2.1 Research Areas Involved in this Thesis 18
2.2 CBSE Developer Roles and their Artefacts 22
2.3 UML2 Syntaxtical Notations for a Component and its Interfaces . 29
2.4 The parts of a meta-model 37
2.5 The ECORE meta-model 40
2.6 Example for a Feature Diagram 42
2.7 Function of a MDSD-Transformation Engine 43
2.8 PIM to PSM Transformations 48
2.9 Influence Factors on the Performance of CB-Software Systems . . 51
2.10 Model-based Performance Prediction Process 52
2.11 An example Queuing Network 55

3.1 The PCM Developer Roles and the Transformation Artefacts . . . 78
3.2 Process Model of the PCM 79
3.3 MDSD-Refined Specification Workflow 82
3.4 MDSD-Refined QoS Analysis Workflow 83
3.5 The same Component in different Assembly Contexts 89
3.6 The same Component in different Allocation Contexts 91
3.7 *Interfaces* and *DataTypes* 93
3.8 Different Component Types in the PCM 95
3.9 The meta-model of a ComposedStructure 97
3.10 The RD-SEFF and its Relationship to *BasicComponents* 98
3.11 *ExternalCallAction* and passing of Parameter Characterisations . 100
3.12 *VariableUsages* and Characterisations 100
3.13 *InternalActions* and their *ParametricResourceDemand* 105
3.14 Resource Acquisition and Release 106
3.15 Control Flow concepts in the PCM 107

3.16 The PCM's *ResourceEnvironment* 113
3.17 *UsageModel*, *UsageScenario* and Workloads (Becker et al., 2007) . 115
3.18 Different *UserActions* 117
3.19 PCM Tools - Modelling Perspective 118
3.20 PCM Tools - Analysis Perspective 119

4.1 Motivating Example for Coupled Transformations 125
4.2 Model Abstraction and Model Refinement 126
4.3 Using Transformation Knowledge in Coupled Transformations . . 127
4.4 Example using Static Decisions 128
4.5 Example using Parametric Decisions 128
4.6 Template Methods used to Implement Coupled Transformations . 139
4.7 Overview on SimuCom's Transformation Structure 145
4.8 Overview on SimuCom's Parts 145
4.9 An example for a Simulated Stack 149
4.10 Stackframe with Proxy for Late Evaluation 150
4.11 Queue Events and State Changes 154
4.12 Mapping of ActiveResources 157
4.13 Activity diagram showing the generic closed user behaviour 158
4.14 Activity diagram showing the behaviour of the open workload driver 159
4.15 Example for Component Paramter Stack Frames 162
4.16 Example for an ExternalCallAction and its Stack Frames 164
4.17 Example for Conditional Branch Transitions 169
4.18 Activity Diagram for the Generated Fork Simulation Code 170
4.19 An Example for an Allocation Mapping 172
4.20 An Example for General and Decorator-based Feature Mark Models 180
4.21 Example for Structure Changing Options 182
4.22 Completions Meta-Model 185
4.23 Completion Types 186
4.24 Transformation of a Component using Dependency Injection . . . 192
4.25 Transformation of a Component using the Context Pattern 193
4.26 Sequence Diagram for the Interaction in the Broker Pattern . . . 193
4.27 Feature Diagram for Required Role Resolution 195
4.28 Structural Change to add a Broker 198
4.29 Example for Adding the Broker Lookup 198
4.30 Broker Allocation Alternatives 198

4.31 Mapping of Provided Roles to Ports 201
4.32 Exemplary Feature Diagram for *AssemblyConnectors* 205
4.33 Replacing a Connector with a ConnectorCompletion 206
4.34 Inner Structure of the Generated *ConnectorCompletion* 207
4.35 Example for a Generated RD-SEFF on the Client's Side 208
4.36 Composed Completions 214
4.37 Allocated Connector Completion Example 215
4.38 Composed RD-SEFF of the Connector Completion 215
4.39 An Example for the ProtoCom Mapping Strategy 221

5.1 Architectural overview on the Web Audio Store (Becker et al., 2007) 230
5.2 Web Audio Store PCM Model 231
5.3 Web Audio Store PCM Model 232
5.4 Prediction and Measurements without Encoder 233
5.5 Prediction and Measurements with Encoder 233
5.6 Architecture of the Media Store (Koziolek et al., 2007) 234
5.7 Prediction Error without Coupled Transformations 235
5.8 RMI Mapping with and without Authentication 236
5.9 Adding Encryption to an RMI Connector 237
5.10 Different Marshalling Strategies: SOAP vs. RMI 237
5.11 Adding Encryption to the Comparison of SOAP and RMI 238
5.12 Experiment Design 245
5.13 Durations for the Complete Task (Martens, 2007, p.102) 247
5.14 Breakdown of the Activity's Durations 248

A.1 PCM Packages and their Creators 270
A.2 PCM Transformations and their Creators 271
A.3 PCM Editor Support and their Creators 272
A.4 Generated RD-SEFFs in Connector Completions 273
A.5 Adding Broker Calls 274

List of Tables

3.1 The PCM's Context Model 90

4.1 Overview on the Mappings 141
4.2 Overview on Mapping Aspects For Mapping PCM Instances to EJB177
4.3 Examples for Calculating the Type and Amount of Data to be Marshalled 210

5.1 Mean Value Comparison 238
5.2 Deviation of the predicted response times 246
5.3 Subjective advantages and disadvantages of the automated transformation 251

A.1 Relative deviation of the predicted response times for Palladio . . 275
A.2 Relative deviation of the predicted response times for SPE 276
A.3 Subjective evaluation of the comprehensibility of the Palladio concepts 277
A.4 Relative number of Palladio related problems (p.92) 278

List of Listings

4.1 Simulation Loop 139
4.2 Code Skeleton Loop 140
4.3 EntryLevelSystemCall: generated simulation code 160
4.4 InternalAction: code generation template 164
4.5 SetVariableAction: code generation template 165
4.6 Example EJB Code 178

List of OCL Fragments

4.1 Deriving the Parameter Sets 211
4.2 Recursively Deriving Instance Formula for DataTypes 211
4.3 Derving the Final Instance Number 212

Acknowledgements

During the development and writing of this thesis, I have had support by numerous persons. Without their help, this thesis would not have the broad scope it finally got by looking at different fields of research, i.e., component-based software development, model-driven software development, and early, design-time performance predictions.

Taking the risk of forgetting important persons, I explicitly want to name the involved persons. First, I thank Heiko Koziolek and Jens Happe for their intensive discussions on the topic, their collaboration in the development of the PCM's meta-model, their help for formalising things, very intensive proof-reading, and directing me at improvements of the presented material.

Furthermore, I thank all current and former members of the DFG research group Palladio, the chair for Software Design and Quality (SDQ) at the University of Karlsruhe (TH), and the members of the associated group at the Forschungszentrum Informatik (FZI) for their discussions in numerous PhD seminars and private sessions. They are (in chronological order of them joining the groups) Ralf Reussner, Viktoria Firus, Heiko Koziolek, Jens Happe, Klaus Krogmann, Michael Kuperberg, Anne Martens, Thomas Goldschmidt, Henning Grönda, Chris Rathfelder, and Johannes Stammel.

My special thanks also goes to all students who contributed to this PhD thesis in individual projects, study theses, diploma theses, or master theses. They are Marko Hoyer, Matthias Ufflacker, Rico Starke, Andreas Kostian, Klaus Krogmann, Niels Streekmann, Reiner Schaudl, Matthias Biehl, Anne Martens, and Roman Andrej. Additionally, I have to thank all members of the project group RIDE.NET in Oldenburg for implementing early editor support for the PCM and discussing the flaws in the meta-model. Finally, I thank all research students (HiWis) for their support in discussing and implementing the PCM's tools. They are Marko Hoyer, Jens Happe, Sascha Olliges, Klaus Krogmann, Philipp Maier, and Roman Andrej.

The conducted experiment required intensive preparation and planning. It would not have had its success without the support by Anne Martens, Heiko Koziolek, Ralf Reussner, Roman Andrej, and last but not least all the participants who took part in the experiment in their spare time. Also, I would like to thank Walter Tichy and Lutz Prechelt for their review of the experiment's design.

I thank my supervisors Ralf Reussner and Willi Hasselbring for their fruitful comments, discussions, and support during my studies. Additionally, I thank the DFG graduate school "Trustsoft" and its members for their support.

Several people helped my in forming an extensive view on components, model-driven software development, or design time performance predictions. I especially like to thank Sven Overhage, Ralf Reussner, Clemens Syzperski, Wolfgang Weck, Frantisek Plasil, Achim Baier, Karsten Thoms, Rafaella Mirandola, Vincenzo Grassi, and Dorina Petriu for their inspiring comments and discussions on these topics.

I also like to thank my parents for their personal and financial support during my studies and while preparing this thesis.

Finally, I thank my girlfriend Sina Schäfer for her support during the time I was working on this thesis. I specially note her patience during several time-intensive phases in the course of preparing this thesis. I dedicate this thesis to her.

Chapter 1

Introduction

1.1 Motivation

Performance-aware Component-based Software-Development A characteristic of an engineering discipline is the ability to predict the impact of design decisions. For example, in civil engineering accurate predictions of the impact of adding an additional floor on a construction's statics are available. Having a similar ability in software engineering requires software development processes and methods, in which the impact of design decisions on the resulting software system is predictable. While this is important for functional requirements such as developing a web shop, it is even more important for *extra-functional requirements* like the ability to serve 10.000 users simultaneously under acceptable response times. Among these extra-functional requirements, the Quality of Service (QoS) requirements of a system like performance, reliability, or availability are directly experienced by the end-user of a system explaining their importance.

However, despite this importance, software developers validate whether a software system fulfils its extra-functional requirements only during late development stages when the software is available. At these stages, testing teams can install and test the software system to detect violated extra-functional requirements. Smith and Williams (2002) name this practice 'fix-it-later' approach. This approach can cause significant costs to correct violated extra-functional requirements, which may even lead to project failure (Glass, 1998), especially in cases, where the cause of not meeting extra-functional requirements are design flaws in the software architecture.

A solution based on the introduced engineering idea is offered by *design-time QoS prediction methods.* They *predict* the impact of design decisions based on design documents *before* implementing them. This allows early reasoning on design decisions while in parallel not violating the software's extra-functional requirements. Those methods increase up-front development costs but save costs in cases where insufficient QoS would otherwise have caused major refactorings of the software's architecture.

Component-based software engineering (CBSE) is a development paradigm initially developed to support reuse, but which is also expected to support the engineering approach to software development. It aims at constructing systems by composing software components into larger components and finally into complete systems. In an engineering approach to CBSE, software architects derive extra-functional characteristics of systems using compositional reasoning based on the properties of the constituting components and their assembly (Hissam et al., 2002). Using components produced by independent developers allows a distribution of development effort for creating a complete system. In such a scenario, a necessary prerequisite is the existence of extensive specifications of each component as the software architect relies on component specifications to assess, select and finally compose components.

For the prediction of extra-functional properties, software architectures built from composed components offer advantages. The reduced degree of freedom introduced by limiting the design to composing pre-build components increases the predictability of the resulting architecture as it can be based on the components and their composition. Additionally, the already existing extended specifications of components lower the additional costs to create component specifications suited for QoS predictions. For QoS predictions, component developers often simply need to extends their existing (functional) component specifications with certain QoS annotations.

Despite the wide-spread industrial use of components in component-based middleware technologies like Java Enterprise Edition (Java EE) with its Enterprise Java Bean (EJB) component model, the prediction of extra-functional properties of software architectures in early design phases is performed seldomly. Focusing on performance as an important QoS attribute, a major issue preventing the wide-spread use of performance predictions during architectural design is the high effort and expertise needed to create a system's performance model using classical performance prediction models like queuing networks or stochastic petri nets. Even using a more abstract high level approach like Software Performance Engineering (SPE) by Smith and Williams (2002) is often infeasible as their design is focused on monolithic systems. For component-based systems however, limited knowledge on component internals due to the black box nature of components hinders the construction of input models needed by monolithic approaches. As an additional problem, assumptions made by these approaches on properties of the behaviour of the whole system cannot be guaranteed or even checked in a component-based setting. This is again a consequence of the black-box nature of components: a component's behaviour is only visible when interacting with other components but its internals are hidden.

Furthermore, the component's behaviour (including their resource demands needed for performance predictions) depends on the *context* in which the component is used. For example, when connecting a book-keeping component to a small size company database it will react much faster than when it is connected to the database of a large scale enterprise. Factors influencing the performance of a component are its implementation, performance characteristics of components it calls, the hard- and software environment it runs on, and the degree of concurrent use and the size and complexity of processed data. All these factors are *unknown* to the developer of a component. As a consequence, the developer can not provide fixed numbers for the performance attributes of his components, but he has to provide them *parameterised* by all factors listed besides the implementation which is under his control. As a final issue, when deriving a complete performance model for a given component-based system, the set of parameterised component specifications and their connections have to form a consistent model with all parameterisations being solvable. This usually requires the use of the same modelling language including a common understanding of its concepts.

A subset of the existing performance prediction methods directly targets component-based software systems instead of monolithic systems by approaching the introduced issues. A survey on existing component-based performance prediction methods by Becker et al. (2006b) revealed that all investigated methods target a certain subset of the identified influence factors on the performance of software components (component implementation, external services, hardware platform, component usage), but none of them yet respects a comprehensive set. Either some influence factors are missing like in the CB-SPE approach by

Bertolino and Mirandola (2004) which assumes that the software architect adds the missing information or the scope of the model is focused resulting in a reduced information need like in the RoboCop (Bondarev et al., 2004) model which is directed at embedded systems showing limited hard- and software modelling complexity than for example web applications.

As a solution approach, this thesis introduces the Palladio Component Model (PCM) as modelling language to specify component-based software systems. The PCM is a meta-model for performance-aware component-based software modelling which explicitly tackles the introduced issues of early design time performance prediction in a component-based context. It supports parameterised component specifications including support for parameterisation over the externally connected components, the hardware execution environment, and usage dependencies including abstractions of the inter-component data flow. The PCM provides distinct modelling languages for each developer role participating in a component-based development process. It allows performance specifications with arbitrary distributed stochastic performance annotations thus lowering the risk of violating model assumptions when composing components from different sources. Its initial development started in the context of this work, but meanwhile extensions by other PhD theses, e.g., for parameterisations based on component usage, exist (Koziolek, 2008).

Model-Driven Software Development and Performance Prediction When using modelling languages, it is desirable to gain an advantage of the effort spent on model construction during later development phases. A paradigm targeting this issue is *model-driven software development* (MDSD). MDSD aims at leveraging the role of models in the software development process from documentation- and communication-oriented artefacts to artefacts equally important as source code. For reasons of flexibility, MDSD allows developers to define their own problem-oriented modelling languages using meta-models. Transformations then take instances of these meta-models and transform them into models of lower abstraction levels and finally source code. Advantages of the transformation-based approach are the ability to deal with increased problem complexities because of model abstractions, model-based reasoning on software properties, or improved communication- and management activities. In addition, the use of models and transformations ensures a synchronisation between models of a software and its implementation, i.e., the model reflects the implementation in a consistent way at any time. Especially for architectural models, MDSD offers a way to transform the system's abstract architectural model into an implementation. In this usage scenario, transformations add technical details of an implementation like middleware specific code fragments commonly omitted in architectural models for reasons of abstraction.

MDSD already demonstrated its advantages in industrial software development practice (Pietrek et al., 2007) to generate implementations of systems based on models. In research one application of MDSD is transforming software system models into performance prediction models. The automated execution of such transformations allows using a high level software system specification for performance predictions without the need for performance experts to construct prediction models. However, while several approaches exist which realise such transformations, they are based on the abstract system model. While it is desirable from the viewpoint of the software architect to use this model and not an additional one, this model intentionally omits details of the implementation like used design patterns or used features offered by a particular middleware platform like a Java EE application server. This information is also missing from the prediction model, however, it contains information which might by relevant for more accurate predictions.

Existing model-based performance prediction methods as those surveyed by Balsamo et al. (2004a) base their predictions solely on abstract architectural models, i.e., models that do not contain information on the realisation of the software. As a consequence, their predictions are inaccurate in cases where the implementation diverts from the original architectural model. For example, this happens if developers implement the system differently and do not update the models accordingly or in cases where they add implementation details intentionally omitted in abstract models. Such information is commonly the mapping to middleware technologies like Java EE. As a consequence, the performance impact of such realisation decisions is not part of the prediction model. Some paper deal with the problem on an ad hoc basis. The work by Verdickt et al. (2005) automatically includes details of a CORBA middleware platform into the performance prediction model. Grassi et al. (2006) automatically include details of component connectors into instances of their KLAPER performance prediction model.

Finally, Woodside et al. (2002) already raised the issue of including details omitted from a system model into a performance model by manually adding so called completions reflecting performance relevant system details into the performance prediction model.

A solution approach to this problem presented in this thesis is based on the assumption, that the abstract system model is not transformed manually into an implementation but also by using model-driven techniques, i.e., so called platform transformations. If they are used, there is a *defined relationship* between the abstract system model and its implementation which can be exploited to refine the performance prediction model in order to gain more accurate predictions.

The idea is demonstrated using model transformations in the context of the PCM. Transformations introduced in this thesis map instances of the PCM either to a newly developed simulation-based prediction model called SimuCom, architectural prototypes called ProtoCom (both serving as prediction models) or code skeletons for EJB (serving as realisation environment). In order to get more accurate prediction models, a method called Coupled Transformations is introduced, which automatically exploits the fact that parts of the application code are generated by transformations. As a result, the software architect can still model on an abstract level but gets a refined performance prediction model which includes details of the realisation.

The method uses for each code generation transformation an additional, *coupled* transformation that alters the prediction model in a way which adds the performance impact of the generated code to the prediction model. The coupled transformations use the aforementioned concept of completions introduced by Woodside et al. (2002) by leveraging the general concept of completions to completions based on special components thus fitting them into the overall CBSE setting.

Additionally, Coupled Transformations support transformations that can be parameterised. Parameterised transformations use so-called mark models to make user options available in the transformation explicit, e.g., the choice between different types of component implementations offered by the component middleware (for example stateful vs. stateless in EJB). The mapping of PCM instances to Java EE applies the Coupled Transformations method for the generation of aspects of component deployment and communication to demonstrate its application and increase CBSE based performance prediction accuracy.

This thesis contains a validation of the presented concepts on two levels. The first level shows the prediction accuracy of the introduced simulation and its increase when using Coupled Transformations. The second level shows the applicability of the modelling language for model-driven performance predictions as introduced by the PCM and its transformations. For this, this thesis presents results of a replicated case study performed with students using the PCM's toolsuite.

1.2 Application Scenario

The application scenario targeted in this thesis is a forward engineering process for constructing a component-based software system by using model-driven techniques with early incorporation of the performance impact of design and implementation decisions. The PCM supports this by design time models which allow early estimates of the performance. Especially, it is assumed that different design alternatives for realising the system or its implementation exist. This thesis supports answering two types of questions: First, which alternative has the best performance compared to a given performance goal? Second, which of these alternatives do not violate given performance requirements?

The PCM and the transformations introduced in this thesis support a development process where the development tasks may be distributed among several developer roles. In the forward engineering approach, component developers take requirements for needed components and create PCM models for them. The PCM supports this component refinement task by its component type hierarchy. Finally, the refinement process yields implementation component types, i.e., a specification of the realisation of a component. Component developers can use transformations to generate code skeletons for this type of components. The transformation may offer parameters. After completing the generated skeletons, component developers package the implemented components and the PCM model containing the chosen transformation options and deposit it into a repository.

Software architects retrieve these components and their models. They use the models and create alternative designs for their system. The alternatives can vary in the composition of the components but also in the way the components and their connectors are mapped to realisations, e.g., setting of middleware features offered for component connectors. Coupled Transformations add the impact of the latter mapping automatically into the prediction model. Adding PCM sub models of the soft- and hardware environment and the usage of the system by its users, the software architect analyses the different design alternatives and finally decides for one. For the selected design alternative model transformations generate component adapters, middleware configuration files like deployment descriptors and skeleton load test drivers.

For the analysis model, the focus of this thesis lies on performance. However, the Coupled Transformations method also helps when evaluating other properties using different model transformations with different analysis models as target, i.e., other QoS attributes, development costs, or functional analysis. Additionally, the PCM may be extended in future work to support additional QoS attributes like reliability.

1.3 Scientific Contributions

The main contributions of this thesis are twofold:

1. The Palladio Component Model, a meta-model for the specification of component-based software systems which allows both, the transformation of models into (partial) implementations and the transformation of the same model instance into a performance prediction model. The introduced meta-model deals with requirements specific to a CBSE development process like separated developer roles.

2. The Coupled Transformations method which aims at exploiting the defined relationships between an abstract system model and its implementation as defined by the transformation that maps the model to implementations. This method uses performance relevant decisions encoded into the implementation transformation to refine the performance prediction model and increase its accuracy.

The following gives details on both contributions.

Palladio Component Model and Transformations Each model-driven process has to define its meta-model. In this thesis, the PCM is introduced and used as meta-model. It defines a modelling language for a component-based development process which allows early performance predictions.

In the PCM, each developer role has a domain-specific modelling language (DSL) to formalise the information available to them (Becker et al., 2007). Component developers model components and their resource demands with parametric dependencies on influence factors unknown to them like the behaviour of external service, the hard- and software environment, and the usage. Especially the usage dependencies have been added to the PCM by Koziolek (2008) and is not part of this thesis' contribution. However, this thesis' transformations rely on the added concepts. Other roles supported by the PCM are the software architect who builds systems by composing components, the deployer who specifies and maintains the execution environment, and the domain expert who models the expected behaviour of the system's users.

The PCM follows a normative approach (Reussner et al., 2007). It defines components and their properties in terms of its meta-model's syntax and static semantics via OCL constraints. Thus, it captures the component concept for automated processing by transformations. As a normative approach, the PCM's component concept is not based on existing industrial component platforms, but on properties available in literature like explicit, contractually specified provided and required interfaces or the ability to compose components into composite structures like composite components or systems.

A central concept introduced by the PCM is the use of contexts (Becker et al., 2006c). By using a component in a composition of other components, a developer puts a component in a context. The PCM's meta-model contains these context dependencies explicitly to capture all component external influence factors on the component's QoS attributes. Currently, the PCM supports *AssemblyContext*s to store connections and differentiate several bindings of the same component type, *AllocationContext*s to model the mapping of components to execution environments, and *UsageContext*s to model dependencies on input parameters of component services.

The PCM's meta-model contains information from the functional design of systems like interfaces, data types, components, or connectors as well as non-functional attributes like performance annotations or resource environment modelling. As such, it can be used as source for code generation and for performance analysis.

This thesis introduces SimuCom (Becker et al., 2007, 2008b), a transformation of PCM model instances into a Java based, event-discrete simulation environment for predicting performance. The simulation approach is necessary, as the PCM's expressiveness allows the specification of models with no known analytical solution. The simulation's hardware model is based on queuing network theory (Bolch et al., 1998a). For its evaluation of component contexts it adapts the idea of stack frames used in compiler construction (Muchnick, 1997).

Mapping instances of a normative meta-model like the PCM to an implementation platform like Java Enterprise Edition and EJB requires to bridge mismatches in the underlying concepts. For example, as EJB uses classes for components, it has no explicit support for required interfaces. Several options exist to reflect this concept. This thesis makes the options for bridging mismatches explicit and allows a selection by the transformation user. For this, the transformations use feature diagrams (Czarnecki and Eisenecker, 2000) to parametrise the transformation.

Finally, this thesis introduces a third transformation to generate a prototype whose behaviour mimics the resource demand of PCM instances (Becker et al., 2008a; Koziolek et al., 2008). Prototyping is an established approach for early testing whether a system meets extra-functional requirements (Bardram et al., 2005). The generated prototype supports early validation of predictions made by the simulation. It is not bound to assumptions made by the simulation on the systems' execution environment. Especially for complex distributed and highly concurrent systems, the simulation model's assumptions might be unrealistic.

Coupled Transformations The Coupled Transformations method (Becker, 2008) is based on the observation that code generation reduces the degree of freedom available to developers. For the prediction of extra-functional properties this reduction in the degree of freedom can lead to an increased prediction accuracy as it is sufficient for the prediction method to deal with the reduced output that the generator can produce instead of arbitrary code fragments.

The use of generators becomes popular by the increasing adoption of model-driven software development techniques in industry. For example, in the OMG's MDA process, transformations map an abstract model to different platform specific implementation, e.g., one transformation can map an UML model to a .NET realisation and another one maps it to EJB. If it is known *how* a model is transformed into an implementation, i.e., the transformation is given, this knowledge can be used to derive a second transformation that reflects this knowledge in an analysis model, e.g., a performance prediction model. This second transformation is called a *coupled transformation* to the first one, as it reflects the impact of the first transformation. In the example above, coupled transformations would reflect the different performance properties of a mapping to .NET versus a mapping to EJB.

Coupled Transformations also help in cases where a system is modelled using a non-technical DSL. As in such a process, there may not even exist technical design documents like UML2 diagrams if transformations generate code directly from instances of the DSL. In such cases the performance of the final implementation depends mainly on the transformation. Coupled Transformations is a method which is not restricted to performance modelling. Coupled Transformations offers the advantage for developers to model their systems on higher abstraction level without loosing details of lower abstraction levels necessary for accurate analyses of system properties. An automated coupled transformation includes these details into the analysis model making its results more accurate.

This thesis uses Coupled Transformations to include the impact of mapping PCM instances to EJB implementations. The focus in this thesis is on the mapping of components and connectors. This thesis' coupled transformations introduce so called completion components to include the impact. Completion components leverage the completion concept introduced by Woodside et al. (2002) to component-based software modelling (Wu and Woodside, 2004). The Coupled Transformations in this thesis directly modify a PCM instance with in-place transformations to include the performance impact. This allows reusing the expressiveness of the PCM and the existing simulation transformation to solve the modified model.

1.4 Structure

This thesis is structured in six chapters:

Chapter 2 introduces foundations and work related to the concepts presented in this thesis. Its basic structure follows the three main areas involved in this thesis: CBSE, model-driven software development, and performance prediction. Section 2.1 discusses concepts from the domain of component-based software engineering. Besides introducing the concepts of component, the developer roles involved in a CBSE process, and software architecture, it also contains a survey on existing component models and their capabilities. Section 2.2 gives a brief overview on the concepts available in model-driven software development. It contains definitions for the terms model, meta-model and transformation, an introduction to the most important technical concepts, and a brief overview on the platform term as coined by the OMG's MDA paradigm. Section 2.3 gives an introduction on early design time performance prediction methods. It presents a process giving an overview on performance prediction activities, influence factors on software performance, and required input models for performance prediction methods. A brief survey on simulation-based performance prediction methods and performance prototyping serves as discussion of related work for the analysis methods introduced in this thesis. The chapter closes in section 2.4 with a list of requirements for a combined CBSE, MDSD, and performance prediction enabled method.

Chapter 3 introduces the Palladio Component Model (PCM). After an introduction to the development process including the CBSE developer roles envisioned by the PCM in section 3.1, section 3.2 describes fundamental concepts used in various places in the PCM's meta-model like modelling using random variables and component contexts. Sections 3.3 to 3.8 give a brief introduction to the different parts of the PCM's meta-model. Interfaces and Datatypes introduced in section 3.3 are prerequisites for the definition of the various component types supported in the PCM (section 3.4). Resource Demanding SEFFs (section 3.5) describe the behaviour and resource interaction of single component services in the PCM. Section 3.6 explains the meta-model used when describing systems composed from components. Section 3.7 focuses on the allocation of components in run-time environments. Finally, instances of the meta-model presented in section 3.8 model the interaction of users with a system. Section 3.9 gives a brief overview on the current PCM's tool suite and its status. Chapter 3 concludes with assumptions and limitations restricting the application of the PCM in its current state in section 3.10.

Chapter 4 starts with an introduction of Coupled Transformations in section 4.1. It provides a motivating example and an abstract formalisation of the central idea. Before using Coupled Transformations, section 4.2 introduces modular transformation, i.e., transformations with a common part and output specific parts. After giving an overview on this thesis' transformations in section 4.3, section 4.4 elaborates on SimuCom, which is a transformation of instances of the PCM into a performance prediction simulation. SimuCom is a native simulation tool for PCM instances and thus supports the full set of model elements of a PCM instance. It relies on generated Java code which is embedded into SimuCom's platform based on Desmo-J. Based on the PCM as CBSE performance model, section 4.5 introduces the two techniques used in this thesis to couple transformations, i.e., structural changes and completion components. The transformation of PCM instances into an EJB- or POJO-based realisation presented in section 4.6 uses Coupled Transformations and the techniques introduces in section 4.5 to modify SimuCom's transformation to include knowledge of the code mapping into the simulation model. The presented code mapping focuses on component assembly and uses identified design options which arise when mapping PCM components to EJBs as case study for transformation coupling. Finally, section 4.7 shows how a combination of SimuCom and the code mapping leads to ProtoCom, a mapping to generate performance prototypes from PCM instances useful in later development stages to validate and refine performance prediction models.

Chapter 5 shows in case studies the validity of the contributions of this thesis. Section 5.1 demonstrates that predictions made by SimuCom reflect reality in an appropriate way. For this, it presents two different case studies. In the first case study, SimuCom produces predictions for a web-based music store. The second case study elaborates on the impact of Coupled Transformations on prediction accuracy. It uses a mark model to predict different kinds of realisations of a component connector. Section 5.2 reports on an experimental setting to validate the PCM's applicability by third parties for doing performance analyses.

Chapter 6 concludes this thesis. It gives a summary of the results of this thesis in section 6.1 and references the assumptions and limitations in section 6.2. Sections 6.3 and 6.4 discuss opportunities for future work. While section 6.3 lists questions which remained unanswered in this thesis, section 6.4 points to other application areas for the PCM and Coupled Transformations.

1.5 Context of this Thesis

Three areas form the context of this thesis. The first area is component-based software engineering, especially component models. The PCM uses several concepts common in component-meta models as surveyed by Lau and Wang (2006). Its concept of parameterised specifications of context-dependent, extra-functional properties builds on the concept of parametric contracts introduced by Reussner (2001).

The second area is model-based and model-driven performance prediction methods as surveyed by Balsamo et al. (2004a). The presented simulation relies on queuing network theory (Bolch et al., 1998b), however, the PCM's semantics is more related to queued petri nets (Bause and Kritzinger, 1996). The idea to automatically include details on performance relevant parts of a system to the design model is based on the completion idea introduced by Woodside et al. (2002).

The third area is model-driven software development (Völter and Stahl, 2006) and generative programming (Czarnecki and Eisenecker, 2000). Especially the use of feature diagrams to parameterise transformations is based on the domain analysis concept introduced by Czarnecki and Eisenecker (2000).

Additionally, the PhD thesis by Koziolek (2008) is closely related to this thesis. It extends the PCM's meta-model with parameteric usage dependencies. This thesis' transformations already use the extended version of the PCM's meta-model.

1.6 Abstract

Component-based software engineering aims at developing software systems by assembling pre-existing components to build applications. Advantages gained from this include a distribution of the development effort among various, independent developer roles, and the predictability of properties, e.g., performance, of the resulting assembly based on the properties of its constituting components. Especially, during software design, system models abstract from system implementation details. These abstract models are the input of automatic, tool supported architecture-based performance evaluation methods. However, as performance is a run-time attribute, abstracting from implementation details might remove performance-relevant aspects resulting in a loss of prediction accuracy.

Existing approaches in this area have two drawbacks: First, they insufficiently support the specifics of a component-based development process like distributed developer roles and second, they disregard implementation details by focusing on design-time models only. The solution presented in this thesis introduces the Palladio Component Model, a meta-model specifically designed to support component-based software development with predictable performance attributes. Transformations map instances of this model into implementations resulting in a deterministic relationship between the model and its implementation. The introduced Coupled Transformations method uses this relationship to significantly increase prediction accuracy by an automatic inclusion of implementation details in predictions. The approach is validated in several case studies showing the increased accuracy as well as the applicability of the overall approach by third parties for making performance-related design decisions.

1.7 Abstract (in German)

Beim Entwurf komponentenbasierter Software-Systeme werden bereits existierende Software-Komponenten zu neuen Anwendungen kombiniert. Durch dieses Vorgehen entstehen unter anderem Vorteile durch die effiziente Verteilung der Arbeitslast auf mehrere Entwicklerrollen oder durch eine erhöhte Vorhersagbarkeit des neu gebildeten Systems. Letzteres basiert auf der Annahme, dass die Eigenschaften der bereits existierenden Komponenten bekannt und spezifiziert sind, damit aus ihnen die Eigenschaften des Gesamtsystems hergeleitet werden können. Hierzu werden zur Entwurfszeit abstrakte Modelle der Komponenten genutzt, um werkzeuggestützte Vorhersagen durchzuführen. Viele der derzeit verwendeten Modelle abstrahieren von Implementierungsdetails, die Laufzeiteigenschaften wie Performance oder Zuverlässigkeit entscheidend beeinflussen können. Als Konsequenz ergibt sich, dass Vorhersagen über diese Eigenschaften unpräzise werden. Existierende Arbeiten im Bereich der Vorhersage komponentenbasierter Systeme gehen bisher unzureichend auf die Spezifika des komponentenbasierten Systementwurfs und seiner Rollenteilung ein. Ferner basieren sie ihre Vorhersagen bisher alleine auf den abstrakten Modellen und verlieren so die angesprochene Vorhersagepräzision. In dieser Dissertation wird eine Lösung für die geschilderten Probleme im Rahmen des Palladio Component Models (PCM) präsentiert. Das PCM ist ein Meta-Modell, das speziell für die modellgetriebene Performance-Vorhersage komponentenbasierter

Software-Systeme entworfen wurde. Durch die Verwendung von Transformationen zur Abbildung der Instanzen des PCM auf Implementierungen wird dabei ein deterministischer Zusammenhang zwischen dem Entwurfsmodell und der späteren Implementierung geschaffen. Die Nutzung dieses definierten Zusammenhangs zur Verbesserung der Vorhersagemodelle im Rahmen der Coupled Transformations-Methode stellt dabei den zentralen Beitrag dieser Dissertation dar. Das PCM sowie die Coupled Transformations-Methode wird in verschiedenen Fallstudien validiert, die zeigen, wie die Vorhersagegenauigkeit durch das Einfügen performance-relevanter Details der Implementierung ins Vorhersagemodell gesteigert werden kann. Da dieser Prozess durch Transformationen automatisiert ist, können Dritte von der Verbesserung der Vorhersagepräzision profitieren, ohne Fachkenntnisse im Gebiet der Performance-Modellierung besitzen zu müssen.

Chapter 2

Foundations and Related Work

Today, software development processes still offer many challenges. They span from management issues like time and budget estimations, over choosing the right development processes and selecting the right methods and tools, to managing the quality of the resulting system. Software engineering aims to deal with these problems by leveraging software development to an engineering discipline. A characteristic of an engineering discipline is the availability of a catalogue of methods and practices with guidelines for their systematic selection. Applying these methods leads to products which ideally have predictable functional and extra-functional properties and processes with determinable time frames and costs.

Component-based software engineering (CBSE) is a mean for software engineering to become an engineering discipline. In CBSE, developers compose basic building blocks, so called components, into more complex structures like composed components and finally complete systems. Basing software development processes on component composition helps breaking the development process systematically down into smaller parts. Time and budget management based on components allows more accurate predictions. Additionally, reasoning on the extra-functional properties of a composition of components can rely on the properties of the basic components plus a theory for deriving attributes of composed structures from their basic constituting parts.

Such an extra-functional attribute, that is often of high importance during software development, is the *performance* of the resulting system. If systems offer an insufficient performance, they are usually not applicable causing projects to fail. Therefore, early design time performance predictions help to take the right decisions to create systems which fulfil their performance requirement. This avoids cost intensive redesigns of systems in late development phases. In a component-based development process estimating the performance of design alternatives usually involves estimating the performance characteristics of different compositions of components based on the performance of single components.

To reduce the complexity of reasoning on components based on their source code, developers use *models* of components and their composition. Models of basic components specify their basic attributes, and models of component compositions describe their collaboration. Using both types of models, methods derive the attributes of composed structures. Additionally, the created models may serve as basis for code generators reliving developers from the burden to implement the structures designed in their models manually. A programming paradigm which supports the described transformation steps is *model-driven software development* (MDSD) which aims at leveraging the role of models in the development process by making models the primary development artefacts.

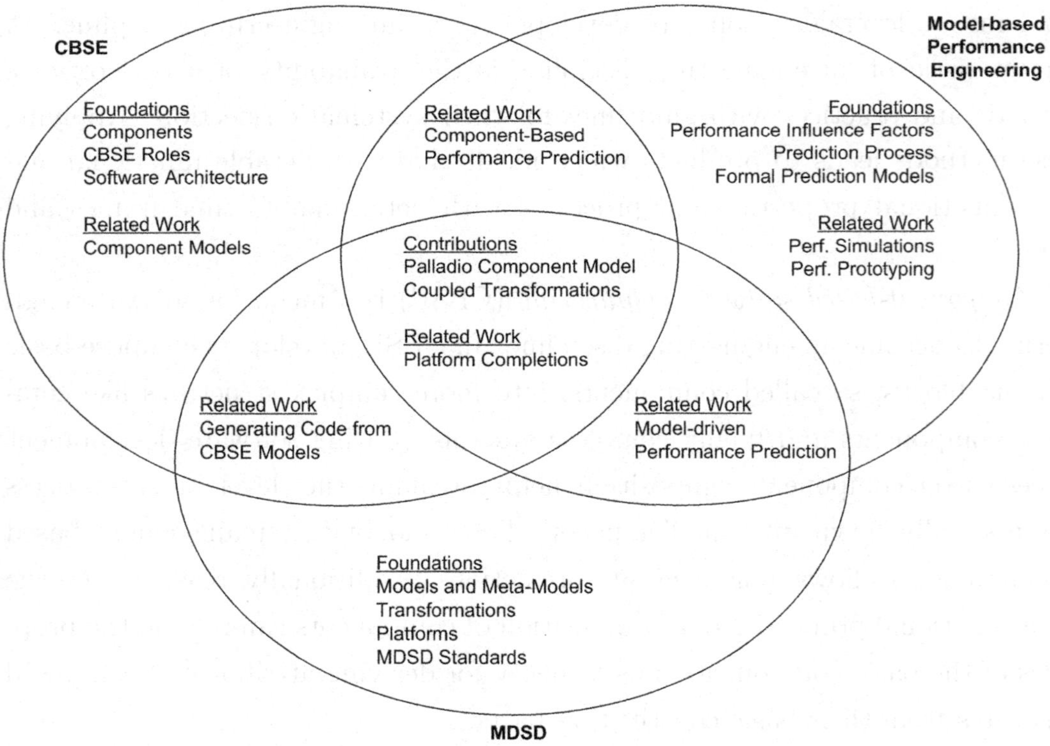

Figure 2.1: Research Areas Involved in this Thesis

This section is structured based on the three areas introduced above and depicted in figure 2.1. First, the sections 2.1.1-2.1.3 introduce the necessary foundations of component-based software development. Based on this, section 2.1.4 surveys existing component models, their analysis methods, and code generation capabilities to highlight differences to the component model introduced in this thesis. Second, sections 2.2.1-2.2.3 introduce the foundations of MDSD necessary to understand the concepts presented in this thesis. Third, sections 2.3.1-2.3.3 introduce the foundations of performance prediction methods based on software design documents. As this thesis uses simulation and prototyping techniques to derive the performance of component compositions, sections 2.3.4 and 2.3.5 briefly give references to other approaches also using the same techniques. Section 2.3.6 gives an overview on other approaches doing performance predictions based on components and their composition while section 2.3.7 focuses on methods using automatic MDSD transformations to derive performance models. Finally, section 2.3.8 discusses approached which use transformations to include implementation platform details into their performance predictions which is closely related to Coupled Transformations.

2.1 Components, Architecture and Component Models

Components are the central build blocks in CBSE. However, the term component is used in computer science in a wide variety of contexts with different meaning. In order to clarify the term, the following section gives a definition, which is used for the remainder of this thesis.

2.1.1 Software Component

The definition used in this thesis is given by Szyperski et al. (2002) in their book on component-based software engineering.

Definition: Software Component (Szyperski et al., 2002) *A software component is a unit of composition with contractually specified interfaces and explicit context dependencies only. A software component can be deployed independently and is subject to composition by third parties.*

The following paragraphs explain the basic parts of the definition of a software component in more detail, i.e., contractually specified interfaces, explicit context dependencies, independent deployment, and third-party composition.

Contractually Specified Interfaces Components solely use interfaces to collaborate with their environment, i.e., any accessible component service has to be part of an interface provided by the component. These interfaces need to be contractually specified which refers to the design-by-contract principle introduced by Meyer (1997). This principle introduces a contractual relationship between some software entity requiring a service offered by some other entity. If the client fulfils a set of preconditions when requesting a service, the server guarantees the service's postconditions. Interface contracts may exist on different levels of abstraction. For example, Beugnard et al. (1999) lists signatures, protocols, synchronization constrains, or Quality of Service requirements as abstraction levels.

Explicit Context Dependencies A component has *explicit context dependencies* only. As a consequence the component has to specify what it expects from the environment in which it is used. Many of the component models (cf. section 2.1.4) use the concept of required interfaces to enable the specification of services required by a component.

Independent Deployment A component has to be deployable independently of other components. Note, that this defines the smallest software entity which can be regarded as a component: A software entity which can not be further divided into smaller entities that are independently deployable is a basic component.

Third-Party Composition Components are subject to third-party composition, i.e., their creator is not necessarily the person who composes them. This characteristic is inspired by an engineering principle of building software applications in a distributed way. On the one hand, there are creators of software components. They are supposed to be experts for the functionality a component offers. Hence, they realise the functionality of components, specify provided and required interfaces, and finally, put them into repositories from which other developers retrieve them for composition.

The person composing two or more components is often called assembler. The assembler is responsible for connecting required with provided interfaces to fulfil the needs of the component. In so doing, the composite structure gets functionality based on its constituting components. A major assumption often made in this process is that the creator of the component and the assembler only communicate using the component's specification. More information on this idea of dividing the development tasks among different developer roles can be found in section 2.1.2.

Discussion Even if the cited definition of a software component is the one which is cited commonly, there are still several issues remaining with this definition which are discussed in the remainder of this section.

Cheesman and Daniels (2000) raised the issue of having no means to differentiate a component's development stage. Hence, they suggest to differentiate component specification, implementation, deployment, and run-time stages. In the specification stage only a component specification is available, e.g., a set of interfaces the component should provide. In the implementation stage, the specification has been implemented using some programming language, i.e., the component's code offers the specified interfaces. When put in an execution environment, such an implemented component becomes a deployed component which finally gets instantiated and executed at run-time. Szyperski et al. (2002) require a component to have no (externally) observable state. In the classification introduced, this puts components on the type or specification level.

Another issue is the usage of the term "component" in many different computer science areas with different semantics. Even Szyperski accepts the fact, that (software) component is a term used with various meanings. He comments on this situation by giving a definition, which only captures the most basic common characteristic of all definitions and can be derived by the origin of the word component: "Components are for composition [...]. Beyond this trivial observation, much is unclear." (Szyperski et al., 2002).

A final issue stems from the lack of precision of the definition which renders it useless to decide whether something is a software component or not. For example, a component has to specify it context explicitly. As context is a term which is unclear without further explanations, it remains unclear which elements should be contained in such a context specification. It is commonly accepted to include the set of services required from other components in the context by the means of required interfaces. However, besides the required interfaces there can be additional dependencies to the context. For example, a specific execution environment (e.g., operating system and its services, middleware platform, virtual machine, etc.) might be needed to execute the component. A context model respecting these additional factors has been proposed by Becker et al. (2006c) and is presented in more detail in section 3.2.2.

2.1.2 CBSE Developer Roles

In CBSE literature, there is a division of the whole development task on several executing roles. However, the roles available and their specific tasks vary depending on the pursued goals of the respective methods. The following gives a short overview on the common understanding of the CBSE roles and briefly highlights some differences between them. The role model used in this thesis is presented in section 3.1.1.

Figure 2.2 shows the common roles involved in CBSE processes and the development artefacts they produce.

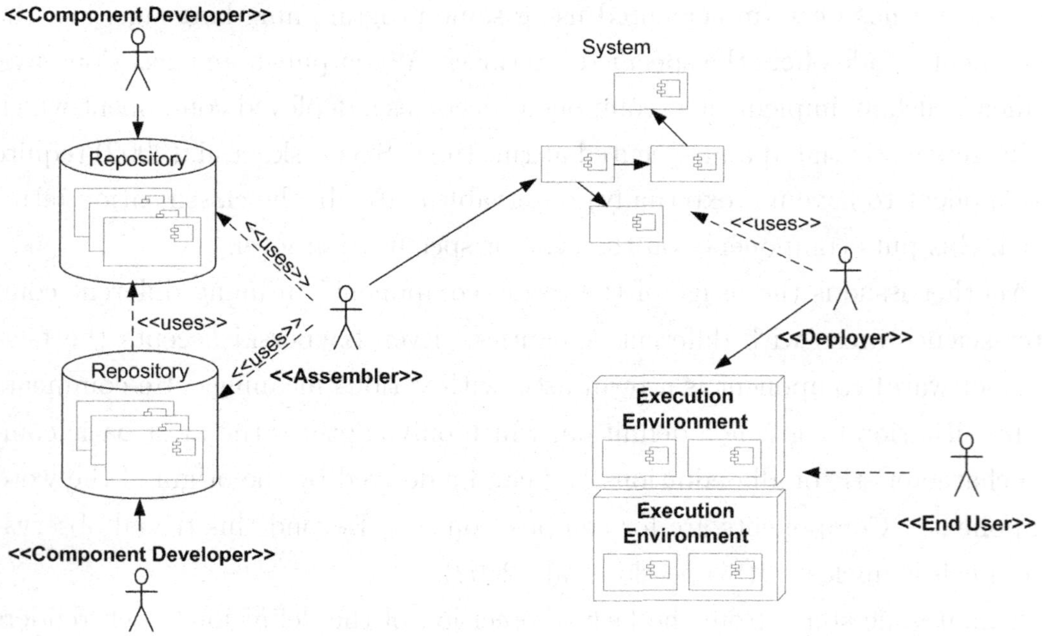

Figure 2.2: CBSE Developer Roles and their Artefacts

Component Developer Component developers create components which they store in so called repositories once they are implemented (cf. for example

Lau and Wang (2005)). The repositories serve as database of the components developed and are assumed to be searchable with the aim of an easy retrieval of components with suited functionality.

Some processes additionally consider the development of composed components, i.e., components whose realisation is based on components itself. For example, (Ritter, 2000, p. 6) introduces composed components as a mean of building new domain specific components from more basic or generic ones. Composed components are produced to be put into the repository when finished.

Assembler Assemblers retrieve components from a set of available repositories and combine them with the aim of creating an application. This is done by composing the components, using the offered functionality to create new functionality. Some processes differentiate this step further into component composition and component configuration. Ritter (2000) mentions in the context of business information system components the possibility of performing so called parameterisations. This often includes using special interfaces of the components introduced for supplying configuration options (Overhage, 2006).

In addition to the introduced tasks, some components utilise frameworks which need to be provided and configured by the assembler. Configuration options usually deal with technical aspects of components and their composition. For example, in Java EE the assembler configures component container providing extra-functional features like authentication or component persistency.

Deployer After composing the application, software architects pass the application's blueprint to so called deployers who are in charge of installing the components in run-time execution environments. The execution environment contains run-time services needed by the components (like frameworks, application servers, etc.), basic layers (like virtual machines, operation systems, etc.), and finally the hardware needed to execute the aforementioned. The deployer is also in charge of setting configuration parameters available at the listed layers. However, this is constrained by the architecture as designed by the assembler.

End-User Finally, the application is started by the deployer and ready to be used by end-users. They use the functionality offered by the application, usually without knowing any of the details on the composition or deployment.

Example: Java EE Roles The Java Platform Enterprise Edition specification V5 (Sun Microsystems Corp., 2006) defines so called Platform Roles. The specification introduces seven roles: Java EE product provider, application component provider, application assembler, deployer, system administrator, tool provider, and system component provider.

The Java EE product provider is responsible for implementing the Java EE run-time environment (i.e., an application server). Application component providers correspond to the introduced component developers. However, in Java EE the term component is used in a wider sense as it can also contain the production of artefacts like HTML pages or document design.

The application assembler corresponds to the introduced assembler. His tasks contain the assembly of the components provided by the application component providers "into a complete Java EE application" (see (Sun Microsystems Corp., 2006, p. 18)). Additionally, he specifies a set of unresolved dependencies which have to be resolved by the deployer. This set includes system external calls or database connections just to name some.

The deployer is responsible for resolving unresolved dependencies and physically installing the binary components on the respective execution environments. In the Java EE role model there is the additional role of the system administrator how is responsible for monitoring and maintaining the running application. This also includes providing and maintaining the hardware infrastructure. In the role model presented in figure 2.2, both roles are combined into the deployer role.

The Java EE specification does not introduce the role of the end-users, however, it contains two additional roles. According to the specification, tool providers are in charge of implementing the tools described in the specification. System component developers enrich the Java EE platform with additional generic components and services usable by assemblers or deployer. This includes database connectors, messaging support services, or authorisation components.

2.1.3 Software Architecture

Software architects compose components into systems by assembling components. Shaw and Garlan (1996) called the resulting system of components and connectors a *software architecture*.

Definition: Software Architecture (Shaw and Garlan, 1996) *Software architecture [is a level of design that] involves the description of elements from which systems are built, interactions among those elements, patterns that guide their composition, and constraints on these patterns.*

Software architectures contain elements from which systems are built. As already stated, most architectures use components as such elements. Connectors commonly specify component interaction. They are mediating entities that determine how messages are exchanged between the components. The patterns and constraints which enforce specific ways of combining components can either be given as architectural design patterns (cf. Buschmann et al. (1996)) or as styles (cf. Clements et al. (2003)).

The SEI's (Software Engineering Institute) website currently favours the following definition of the term software architecture over a large list of alternative definitions, historical and recent ones.

Definition: Software Architecture (Bass et al., 2003) *The software architecture of a program or computing system is the structure or structures of the system, which comprise software elements, the externally visible properties of those elements, and the relationships among them.*

Again, the definition contains the comprising software elements and their relationships of a system. Additionally, the definition takes into account explicitly externally visible properties of these elements. The SEI's website explains externally visible properties as follows: ""Externally visible" properties refers to those assumptions other elements can make of an element, such as its provided services, performance characteristics, fault handling, shared resource usage, and so on." (Carnegie Mellon University, 2007). Hence, this definition takes extra-functional properties explicitly into account.

The SEI website (Carnegie Mellon University, 2007) lists some interesting consequences and interpretations of the definition given. The following gives a selection of them based on relevance for this thesis. First, a software architecture is an *abstraction* of the real system, as it omits the details of the internals of the elements of the architecture. Only externally observable behaviour or properties are part of the architecture. This makes components well-suited elements of a software architecture as components usually only expose externally visible properties. And second, the behaviour of software elements is part of the architecture if it is observable by other elements in the architecture. The elements need this information to be written and connected in a way that allows correct interaction among them.

2.1.4 Component Models

The following section gives a survey on existing component models for later evaluation against the requirements needed for the model introduced in this thesis. Lau (2006) defines the term component model as follows:

Definition: Component Model (Lau, 2006) *"The cornerstone of any CBD methodology is its underlying component model, which defines what components are, how they can be constructed and represented, how they can be composed or assembled, how they can be deployed and how to reason about all these operations on components."*

A component model specifies all the possible information which can be specified *about* a component or a composition of components on different levels of detail. The definition highlights information about the component, its implementation (representation) or compositions of components as essential parts of a component model. Additionally, a component model defines analytical methods using the specified information, e.g., how to combine components to get new functionality or how to reason about extra-functional properties of compositions.

However, the term component model is misleading. As a component model specifies models of components (either in source code form or as plain model entities) it is a meta-model (see also section 2.2.1). However, the term component model is established, hence, this thesis sticks to it. Nevertheless, it is important to keep in mind that component models are meta-models in the context of this thesis even when omitting the meta- prefix.

Several component models exist, each designed with specific design criteria to deal with specific problems. Such a model is a goal-driven abstraction of some entities (see also section 2.2.1). Often, the abstraction is directed towards specific analysis methods. The analyses can be focused on functional or extra-functional properties. The first class deals with the question how to evaluate the functionality of a system built from components in order to compared it to the requirements. The second class is directed at evaluating extra-functional properties like performance, reliability, availability, etc. Besides abstractions for analysis purposes, there are some component models, which serve for communication and/or documentation purposes.

The remainder of this section provides a survey on existing component models classified by the aims they have been designed for. First, this section introduces industrial component models. Developed by industrial companies, these models support the development of hierarchical, distributed, and interoperable systems and industrial software projects commonly apply them when building real-world, executable systems. Documentation oriented-models, like UML, serve as mean to specify component-based architectures. They capture the structure and the behaviour of systems with a focus on functional analysis and management of the construction process. Finally, analysis oriented models combine a specification formalism with methods to analyse certain extra-functional properties based on the specification results. Components used in such models often only exist as model entities without a specification how to transform the defined components into implementation entities.

Industrial Component Models Industrial projects commonly apply industrial component models when building real-world systems. This category usually contains COM (Microsoft Corporation, 2007) and .NET (.NET, 2007) from Microsoft, Java EE based components (like EJB (EJB, 2007) or Spring (Spring, 2006)) and components following the CORBA Component Model (CCM) published by the Object Management Group (OMG) (2006a).

The main concept of these models is to use the existing concept of objects coming from object-oriented programming paradigm and enrich it with additional concepts coming from the definition of a component. For example, EJB or Spring use so called plain old Java objects (POJOs) to represent a component. One notable exception is the COM platform which was introduced in the early 1990ies, when the use of object-oriented languages was not yet widely adopted. However, the concept of having a virtual function table (Ellis and Stroustrup, 1990) to map calls on interfaces to implementation code is the usual way of implementing objects in object-oriented environments. This moves the ideas of COM close to those of the other models. Hence, the following omits a further differentiation of COM from the other industrial models.

These models mainly focus on the static (class based) structure of components by defining concepts like components, provided interfaces and connectors between components. Programmers usually do not define required interfaces explicitly. They simply use other interfaces in their component implementations without explicitly declaring them as required interfaces. For example, COM and .NET use implicit required interfaces. Hence, their infrastructure does not check the availability of required components during deployment. An application fails at run-time if the components try to look up required components which are unavailable in the respective environment. Additionally, more advanced layers of interface models like protocol specifications are usually either omitted at all or only mentioned in the documentation in a human-readable form. Hence, as a result, automated analyses of component compositions are impossible in these component models.

However, other than in some research oriented models, well-defined rules how to implement components exist. They range from (binary) coding standards to protocol definitions for remote inter-component communication. Additionally, these models specify the run-time environment to some extend, for example by the specification of application servers in Java EE or the object request broker (ORB) in CORBA. Opposed to these additional elements, industrial models lack support of the analysis of extra-functional properties as most analysis methods need some behavioural specification.

Besides their limitations from a specification point of view, industrial component models are important in the context of this thesis as target platforms for transformations of the later introduced component model (the Palladio Component Model, see section 3) to implementations.

Documentation-oriented Component Models The component model introduced in the UML2 Superstructure specification (Object Management Group (OMG), 2005c) is the most important one in the category of documentation oriented models due to the wide-spread use of UML. It contains components, their inner structure, and provided and required interfaces. By using assembly connectors, software developers compose components and delegation connectors describe how the control flow is routed to inner components. The following paragraphs detail on these concepts.

A component in UML2 inherits from a UML2 class. As a consequence, it can be seen as a special kind of class having all the capabilities of a class, including the ability to inherit other classes. In addition to the attributes and relations of the UML2 class, a component can have provided and required interfaces and a set of realisations. Each realisation references a single classifier, which contains the realisation. As a realisation can be any classifier it is possible to have classes or other components as realising entities (both cases are depicted in the specification). In case of having a class as realisation, the class is the implementation of the inner part of the component. Opposed to that, components as inner parts of a component introduce another level of hierarchical decomposition. There are several notations to depict a component in a diagram (figure 2.3). The notations offer different degrees of detail on the component.

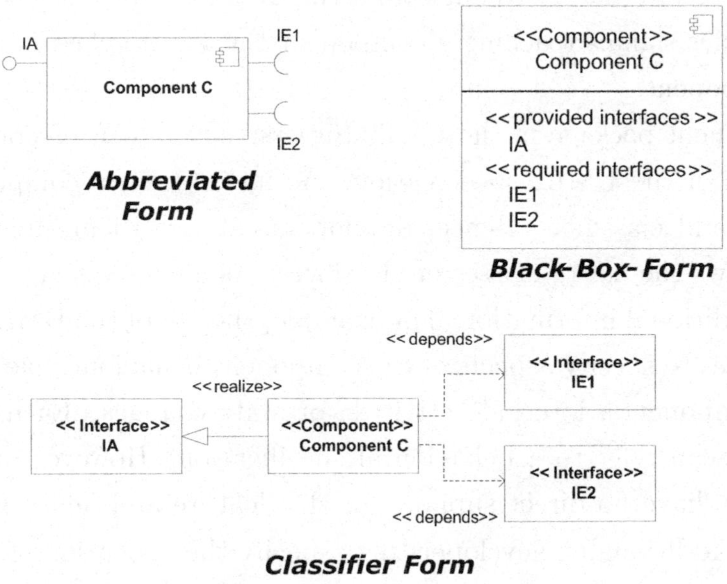

Figure 2.3: UML2 Syntaxtical Notations for a Component and its Interfaces

The component meta-class has two references to the UML2 interface meta-class. One reference contains the set of interfaces provided by a component, the other set contains the interfaces required by a component. However, OCL derived functions determine the sets' contents. The provided interfaces are the union of the interfaces realised by the component, by one of the realising classifiers or by any of the ports of the component. The required interfaces are similarly the union of the required interfaces of the component, of its realising classifiers and of the required interfaces by its ports. This basically maps the provided and required interfaces of a UML2 component to the concepts which are already available to UML2 classes.

For the composition of components, UML2 offers the connector meta-class. This class has an attribute *kind* which can turn the connector either into an assembly connector or into a delegation connector. Assembly connectors link a required interface of one component to the provided interface of another component. The UML2 Superstructure specification defines "[..] that signals travel along an instance of a connector, originating in a required port and delivered to a provided port" (see (Object Management Group (OMG), 2005c, p.151)). The UML standard defines the semantics of delegation connectors similarly. However, they deliver signals from ports or interfaces provided by a component to the realising entities. This results in two types of delegation connectors: one connecting provided ports or interfaces and one connecting required ports or interfaces. The first class handles signals reaching a component the second class handles signals leaving a component.

The component package in the UML2 Superstructure can be combined with other packages of the UML2 specification. As introduced, a component inherits from class and classifier. Hence, developers can use them anywhere where the UML2 allows the use of classes or classifiers. As a consequence, components can contain additional information. For example, the use of the UML2 behaviour packages enables to specify aspects of the component behaviour, like interactions with other components, internal activities, or state changes. Each single component service can refer to a behavioural specification. However, many UML2 modelling tools have no direct support for this feature and hence most models do not use it. Additionally, developers may specify the allocation of components on hard- and software environments in UML2 deployments.

Despite its comprehensive meta-model, the UML2 lacks support for analysing extra-functional properties. However, profiles like the UML-SPT profile (Object Management Group (OMG), 2005b) aim at extending the UML2 for this use case. As many performance prediction methods use UML profiles, the discussion of profiles follows in section 2.3.2.

Architecture Description Languages (ADLs) Research focused on Architecture Description Languages (ADLs) since the 1990s. Their aim was to document and analyse architectures based on formal descriptions of components, connectors, and their composition. Despite the fact, that there have been many different ADLs with different abstractions and aims, research seems to be discontinued in this area.

Medvidovic and Taylor (2000) published the latest available survey on ADLs. This work contained a classification schema to evaluate the different ADLs with respect to their achievements in comparison to the aims of the ADL community. However, all ADLs surveyed in the article failed in several of the requirements listed. As the listed requirements are still important requirements for current software architecture research they are briefly listed in the following. Afterwards, some selected ADLs are presented.

Their classification of ADLs distinguishes requirements for modelling components, requirements for modelling connectors, requirements for modelling their composition, and the tool support available for the ADL. Modelling components deals with modelling the structural and behavioural aspects of components, like interfaces or service descriptions. Modelling connectors deals with the same aspects but for communication entities. The requirements for the compositions deal with aspects of managing component architectures during their life-cycle. Finally, the requirement for tool support refers to support for editing model instances and applying analysis methods.

These requirements have been used by Medvidovic and Taylor (2000) to judge the ADLs available at the time of their writing. The list includes ACME, Aesop, C2, Darwin, MetaH, Rapide, SADL, UniCon, Weaves, and Wright. All ADLs support the specification of components and connectors, seven of them utilise at least partially a graphical syntax. For the specification of the components semantics (behaviour) all surveyed ADLs offer either no support or process algebra based languages like CSP or the π-calculus. Support for non-functional properties is offered by several ADLs. However, many of them only allow the specification of annotations without giving them a semantics. Hence, they are not used in architectural analysis. Only MetaH, Rapide, and UniCon offer analysis support for their non-functional specifications. The focus of their analysis is on real-time and schedulabilty. However, to the best of our knowledge, none of the mentioned ADLs was specifically designed with the aim of design-time prediction of Quality of Service attributes (Balsamo et al., 2004b).

Fractal Fractal is a feature rich component model, including provided interfaces, required interfaces, at run-time reconfigurable connectors, and composite components. It was published by Object Web (2006), an open source middleware provider. However, France Telecom did the initial development. Developers use the "Fractal ADL" to specify architectures, which is an XML-based description of the static composition of components by their connectors.

Fractal components include so called controllers. Controllers configure various aspects involved in a component-based software application. The supported aspects contain, without being complete, support for component life-cycle, connector creation and alteration, component meta-data queries, method call interception, or component instance redeployment/migration.

Mappings exist which map the (descriptive) core standard to implementations in several programming languages. The set of available languages contains Java, .NET, Smalltalk, C, C++, and a special language targeted at the development of distributed and grid-computing based applications. France Telecom applied Fractal in industrial projects which demonstrates a certain degree of maturity. However, Fractal lacks support for extra-functional analyses.

SOFA The SOFA (SOFtware Appliances) component model, described by Plasil and Visnovsky (2002), focuses on checking component interactions. In SOFA, components consist of a frame and an architecture. The frame determines the provided and required interfaces of the component and the external behaviour. The architecture specifies the inner structure of the component, i.e., how a component is composed from other components.

The design goal of SOFA is the analysis of component interactions. This is realised by so-called behaviour protocols, which are specifications of interaction protocols. Interfaces have protocols which specify the sequence of method calls accepted or emitted by a component depending on whether the interface is provided or required. When attached to a frame, the behaviour protocol establishes a link between the services offered by a component and those required. It specifies the emitted calls on any of the required interfaces as reaction to a service call to one of the provided services. SOFA supports asynchronous call behaviour by differentiating between the initiation of a call and returning from a previous call. Developers use a textual syntax to specify behaviour protocols which is similar to regular expressions or process algebra terms.

A transformation exists which transforms SOFA components into an implementations based on the Java version of the Fractal implementation. As a consequence, SOFA component implementations inherit all capabilities of a Fractal component. SOFA has been applied in an industrial case study at France Telecom. However, SOFA lacks support for QoS-annotations.

Embedded Systems Component Models There are several component models designed and applied in embedded systems. These component models often form the foundation for product line approaches. These approaches enable the construction of a whole family of similar but unique products with respect to their hard- and software-configurations in order to serve a larger market.

KOALA Phillips developed the KOALA (C[K]omponent Organizer and Linking Assistent) component model and applied it to support a product line approach for consumer electronics like TV sets. According to van Ommering et al. (2000), the KOALA model uses concepts of the ADL Darwin and Microsoft COM. Its components have explicit provided and required interfaces and are bound independently of their construction, i.e., there is a strict borderline between the roles of component developer and assembler. It utilises repositories to store components and interfaces for Phillips.

The model has explicit support for parameterising the components in certain component assemblies. The components may use special required interfaces to retrieve their configuration from attached configuration components. This allows changing a component's configuration by connecting different configuration components. Furthermore, the model supports component adaptations by the possibility to declare a required interface as being optional. Such an interface may not be connected in an assembly. The component can query the optional interfaces for bound components and behave differently depending on the query's result. Finally, KOALA supports partial evaluation of parts of the code at assembly time to decrease resource demand at run-time.

As KOALA is applied to build the software part of embedded systems, a transformation exists for mapping models to C code skeletons and header files. The transformation uses direct C method calls to reflect component bindings.

KOALA does not support the specification of extra-functional properties.

RoboCop The RoboCop component model (Bondarev et al., 2004) is another component model with focus on embedded systems. In RoboCop, a component consists of a set of related models. These include component interface specifications, documentation, extra-functional models like timing models, reliability, or memory footprint, and the component's source and binary code.

RoboCop also supports a strict distinction of developer roles. Developers in different roles develop and assemble components. The allocation to hardware nodes and the specification of the users behaviour are other tasks necessary for doing analyses with RoboCop.

A complete RoboCop model consists of RoboCop components connected to each other by connectors. Connections support synchronous and asynchronous calls. However, the call's type depends on the call specification in the component behaviour and not on the connector (as in most ADLs). In addition to the components and connectors, developers must specify the hardware units of the embedded system before doing analyses. The behaviour model contains resource demands of the actions specified as constant maximum demand of processing cycles of the executing resource.

Additionally, RoboCop models allow the specification of parameter values used in method calls. In contrast to many other component models, this allows taking parameter influence into account. Before analysing a RoboCop model, analysts must provide constant values for these parameter values (Bondarev et al., 2005).

RoboCop is accompanied by a simulation tool which focuses on properties of embedded real-time systems such as: mutual exclusions, schedulability, deadline misses, and synchronization constraints. In addition, simulation runs yield timing and resource consumption data. Timing data covers response time and waiting times.

Recently, Bondarev et al. (2006) extended RoboCop's analysis methods by a method which automatically generates alternative architectural models, analyses them, and picks the most appropriate with respect to certain properties.

Further Reference To conclude this literature survey on component models, there is a recent comprehensive survey published by Lau and Wang (2005) containing further component models omitted here.

2.2 Model-Driven Software Development

Model-driven Software Development (MDSD) aims at leveraging the role of software models in the software development process. Models become the central artefact of this process. The ultimate aim is to construct models of higher abstraction levels which can be translated fully automatically into models of lower abstraction levels (including source code). In so doing, the development process envisioned replaces code writing by creating model instances of domain, task, or problem specific high-level models.

The following sections introduce several concepts central to MDSD. The first section gives definitions of the basic terms like model, meta-model, etc. and discusses them briefly. The following section summarises model transformation techniques. Generative programming, as a special kind of transformation methodology is included into this discussion as one of generative programming's core contributions, the feature diagrams, plays a central role in later sections. The final section 2.2.3 discusses MDA's platform concept in relation to code generation and model analysis.

2.2.1 Model / Meta-Model / MOF

This section defines the terms model and meta-model and relates them to the MDA approach defined by the OMG.

Model Models play the central role in MDSD. Despite their importance, no established definition in the context of MDSD could be found. A definition, which best fits the understanding of a model in this thesis, has been published on the ModelWare website. This definition is used in the remainder of this thesis.

Definition: Model (ModelWare, 2007) *"A formal representation of entities and relationships in the real world (abstraction) with a certain correspondence (isomorphism) for a certain purpose (pragmatics)."*

Uhl (2007a) gives a similar definition in German in the "Handbuch der Software-Architektur" (Reussner and Hasselbring, 2006). He uses classical characteristics of a model identified by Stachowiak (1973) and transfers these concepts to software models. As these characteristics are similar to the characteristics in the given definition, the following discusses the three characteristics available in ModelWare's definition.

According to this definition, models have three main characteristics: abstraction, isomorphism, and pragmatism. *Abstraction* is the property of a model to remove details of the modelled object. It is a representation of the object which is abstracted with respect to certain attributes. The selection of the model's attributes is guided by the aim of the model (cf. with the pragmatism aspect).

A model can be seen as the result of a projection (in a mathematical sense). The real world object is projected onto its model representative by removing the unconsidered attributes. This projection is an *isomorphism* if the projection of the real world entities on the model entities still allows conclusions to be drawn from the model entity onto the real world entity with respect to the aim of the model. The term refers to the equivalence (iso = equal, morph = shape) between the model and the real world entity.

A projection is *pragmatic* if its definition is done based on a well defined aim. Common aims include easing the understanding of complex structures or deriving properties based on some reasoning theory.

Example To give an example, the following discusses a software model with respect to the given characteristics. An interface protocol model based on finite state machines (FSM) fulfils the characteristics. FSM based interface models allow describing the set of valid call sequences which can be processed by an interface. Transitions represent service calls, states the time between service calls. The set of words accepted by this FSM is equivalent to the call sequences accepted by the interface.

This model is an abstraction of the real world object as it reduces an interface to the set of accepted call sequences. For example, technical details, concurrency aspects, or extra-functional properties are disregarded. It is an isomorphism because the set of call sequences accepted is the same for the model entity as for the real interface. Sometimes, FSM's might not be powerful enough to model the set of valid sequences in a way which can be translated to the real world object (for example, a stack's protocol can not be modelled by a FSM). This would violate the isomorphism characteristic. The FSM protocol model is pragmatic if it is combined with protocol interoperability tests for example. Interoperability checking can be performed using FSMs in an efficient way. Hence, FSMs are a pragmatic model for the task of performing protocol interoperability checks (cf. Becker et al. (2004)).

Meta-Model The website `metamodel.com` (metamodel.com, 2007), defines a meta-model as follows:

Definition: Meta-Model (metamodel.com, 2007) *A metamodel is a precise definition of the constructs and rules needed for creating semantic models.*

Uhl (2007a) defines meta-model as (translated from German):

Definition: Meta-Model (Uhl, 2007a) *A meta-model is a model defining a set of models which are called instances of the meta-model.*

Common understanding of the definitions is that a meta-model somehow characterises a set of models which are instances of the meta-model. In the context of the first definition, an instance would be a model which has been built using the constructs defined in the meta-model and is not violating the rules associated with these concepts.

Conforming to the conceptual models introduced by Völter and Stahl (2006), a meta-model defines at least rules for the concepts depicted in figure 2.4.

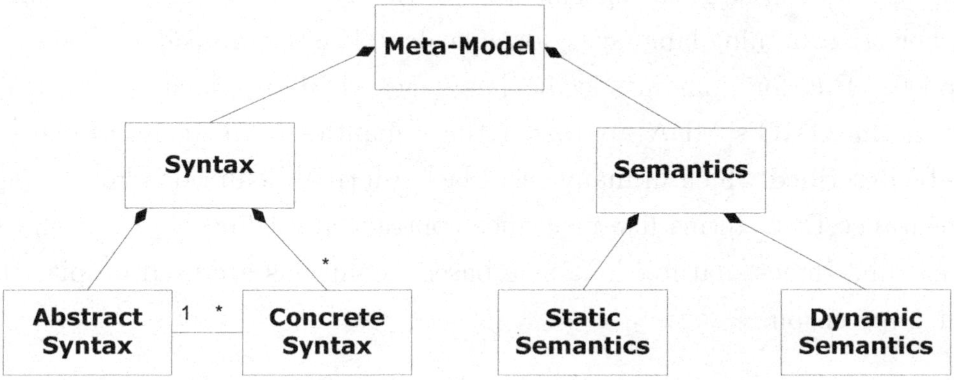

Figure 2.4: The parts of a meta-model

According to figure 2.4, rules describing a meta-model instance are either syntactic or semantic rules. Syntactical rules can be split further into rules on concrete syntaxes and rules for the abstract syntax of the model instance. The abstract syntax of a model represents model instances in the concepts of the meta-model independent of concrete machine or encoding specifics. Consequently, a concrete syntax is a set of rules which specifies the encoding of the abstract concepts. These terms are commonly used in compiler construction: The concrete syntax of programming languages is often defined as text files built according to certain structuring rules given as grammar. The abstract syntax of a programming language is usually represented in abstract syntax trees.

The static and the dynamic semantics form the parts of the semantics of a meta-model. Static semantic is defined as rules which further constraint the set of syntactical valid model instances. For example, if the model syntax allows to have an arbitrary amount of wheels for a car object then a static semantic rule could constrain the amount to five wheels (4 normal and one spare). The static attribute refers to the fact that the constraints can be checked without "executing" the model, i.e., without knowing its intention. Dynamic semantics finally specifies the intention of the model concepts, i.e., how to interpret the model instances in a given context. For programming languages, static semantics contain for example type checks done by the compiler while dynamic semantics define what the program does during its execution.

However, the borderline between the different types of rules is not always strict. Consider again the example with the car and its wheels. It would have been also possible to specify the constraint as part of the syntactical rules by only allowing cars with five wheels for syntactic valid model instances.

Another major issue is the specification of the dynamic semantics of a meta-model. For programming languages, formal calculi like the *lambda*- or *pi*-calculus are applied. But for domain specific languages (DSLs), which are of central interest in the OMG's MDA approach, the semantics of elements of the DSL have to be described which in many cases lack a formal definition. For example, in an insurance DSL, terms like insurance contract are defined by laws and not formal calculi. Hence, natural language based definitions are used despite their inherent imprecision.

Technical Foundation In the MDA approach published by the Object Management Group (OMG) (2006c) a set of technical foundations is defined. Specifications are available for many of the technologies needed to implement a tool chain for specifying meta-models, modelling, and transforming the resulting model instances. The standardisation efforts are directed mainly at allowing interoperability on the model level between tools developed by different vendors. As it is assumed that most of these technologies are applied in a model-driven development process the essential standards are introduced briefly and existing implementations are referenced.

The Meta Object Facility (MOF) The Meta Object Facility (MOF) (Object Management Group (OMG), 2006d) is a meta-meta-model which allows the definition of meta-models and forms the central element in the OMGs MDA approach. Initially, the MOF emerged in the context of the Unified Modelling Language (Object Management Group (OMG), 2005c) in which it has been applied to model the UML. Its core concepts are similar to the concepts available in UML class diagrams, but as they are on different meta-levels the concepts are different. Based on its roots in UML class diagrams, concepts like classes, associations, and multiple inheritance are available. MOF also uses a similar concrete syntax as UML class diagrams, which can sometimes lead to confusion. In order to avoid this kind of confusion, meta-models are explicitly marked in their figure captions in the remainder of this thesis.

The following discusses briefly the difference between EMOF and CMOF introduced in recent MOF versions. This helps to understand the meta-model presented in section 3 which is an EMOF instance. Additionally, the technical concepts used in the context of MOF, which are needed for the prototypical realisation of this thesis' concepts, are introduced, i.e., XMI, JMI, or OCL.

Currently, a new version of the MOF standard is being finalised (MOF 2.0). In MOF 2.0, the MOF is split into two parts: Essential MOF (EMOF) and Complete MOF (CMOF). EMOF is "[..] the subset of MOF that closely corresponds to the facilities found in OOPLs and XML" (see Object Management Group (OMG) (2006d, p. 43)). The idea of EMOF has been introduced in the MOF specification by IBM based on the experience gained in implementing the MOF 1.x standard. In the course of implementing MOF, the developer team in charge realised that implementing the full MOF standard would lead to performance drawbacks. Hence, the team focused on the concepts they considered as required frequently. The resulting implementation is the Eclipse Modelling Framework (EMF) (Eclipse Foundation, 2006) and its meta-model ECORE (see figure 2.5). The subset of MOF found to be "essential" for EMF has been proposed for standardisation as EMOF. As a consequence, the EMF developers announced to deliver a EMOF compatible implementation soon after the final MOF2.0 specification will be available. In contrast, the CMOF contains the a revision of the model elements available in MOF 1.x. A remarkable difference between EMOF and CMOF is the availability of first-class associations which is only true for CMOF.

There are several standards accompanying the MOF standard. In order to exchange models between different tools, a machine readable concrete syntax is needed. For this, the *MOF XML Metadata Interchange (XMI) mapping specifi-*

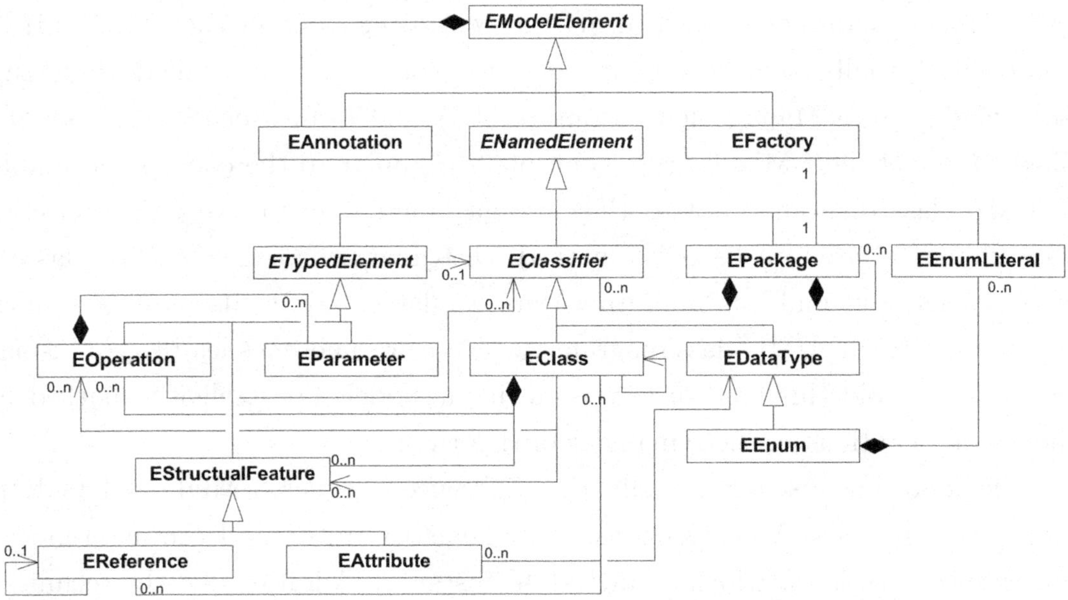

Figure 2.5: The ECORE meta-model

cation Object Management Group (OMG) (2006b) defines a mapping of model instances to a XML serialisation and vice versa.

The *Java Metadata Interface* (JMI) specification contains a mapping of MOF instances to Java interfaces which can be used to create and manipulate model instances of a MOF-based meta-model. MOF-based code-generators generate Java classes based on MOF instances to store model instances as object graphs. The EMF code generator (Eclipse Foundation, 2006) used to implement the meta-model presented in this thesis is an example for a JMI implementation.

The *Object Constraint Language (OCL)* (Object Management Group (OMG), 2006e) serves as a mean to further restrict the set of valid UML as well as MOF model instances. In the later case the available OCL elements include only a subset of the whole OCL specification (the one which is based on the common core between UML and MOF). Designers of meta-models frequently use OCL to define the static semantics of their meta-models. The expressive power of OCL is that of a three-level Kleene logic with equality according to Brucker and Wolff (2002). Support for OCL in tool implementations is still immature. The Eclipse Technology project has developed a plugin (Eclipse Foundation, 2007a) to add OCL support to the Eclipse UML2 plugin. Support for OCL expressions in EMF can be added manually by enhancing EMF's code generator.

2.2.2 Transformations: MDA / Generative Programming

The construction of models helps to understand and analyse complex systems. However, a central idea in model-driven software development is to create models of *software systems* with the final aim of *generating* the respective system. In a model-driven software construction process, transformations or generators translate models into binary code automatically.

This idea is quite old as generative techniques have been applied in compiler construction for a long time (cf. Aho et al. (1986)). Programs written in a programming language are transformed by compilers into executable binary code which is a generative process. However, compiler frontends (i.e., lexer and parser) usually process a fixed set of programming languages and compiler backends generate code for a fixed amount of processors.

In contrast to this, in model-driven techniques users are allowed to define their own meta-models (including their concrete syntax) and user-defined transformations. Hence, only the meta-meta-model and the transformation engines are fixed, but not the meta-model and the transformations. Both can be defined by the end-user for specific purposes.

Note, that the fact that meta-models and transformations *can* be specified, they *need* not be specified. As with any other software artefact, third party software developers can simply reuse them. However, the reuse possibilities depend on how specific a meta-model and its transformations are designed with respect to a certain domain. Very specific meta-models can only be reused in very few other cases, where generic meta-models can be reused in many cases. The same is true for programming languages: general purpose languages like Java can be used for a wide range of problems while domain specific languages are specialised for a specific domain.

The following paragraphs give an overview on exiting generation and transformation techniques. Czarnecki and Eisenecker (2000) have introduced the idea of using generators to raise the level of abstraction in the software development process in their book on Generative Programming already in 2000. However, their work on domain modelling and domain variance analysis using feature diagrams is still applied especially in the area of software product line engineering (Lee et al., 2002).

More recent approaches are based on MOF or EMF as meta-models and utilise specialised transformation engines. They can be classified into Model-2-Model transformations and Model-2-Text transformations.

Finally, the overview concludes with a section on best practices for writing transformations. This is important as the analysis of transformations should concentrate on the most common types of transformations.

Generative Programming Czarnecki and Eisenecker (2000) introduced the concept of Generative Programming. The idea is to use generators to generate program code. An input specification parameterises the generation process. It defines how the generated code should look like. In Generative Programming, a domain analysis identifies all variabilities of a given target domain for which the generator generates code.

The identified variabilities in the target domain are formally captured in so called feature diagrams. A feature represents a certain aspect of the domain which either exists in an instance of the target domain or not. Additionally, features may also carry additional attributes which characterise them in more detail. Relationships among the features capture constrains among them, e.g., features may require other feature as prerequisites or be mutually exclusive with other features. Feature diagrams support a graphical concrete syntax which allows to specify them in an easy understandable way. Figure 2.6 shows an example for a feature diagram.

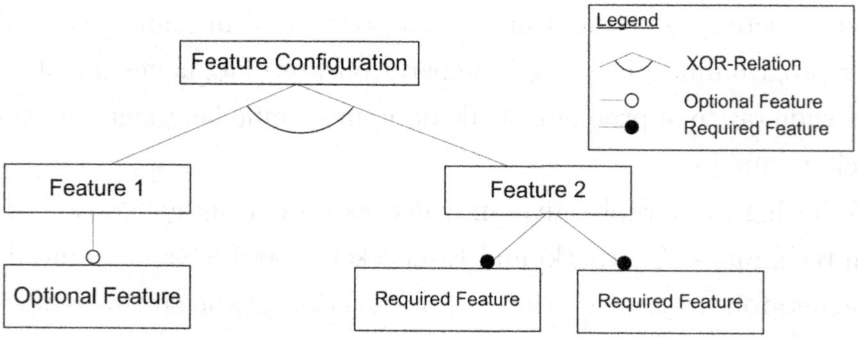

Figure 2.6: Example for a Feature Diagram

An instance of a feature diagram, is called a (feature) configuration. Any configuration of the feature diagram in figure 2.6 either has `Feature1` or `Feature2` selected. If `Feature1` is selected, the optional feature may also be selected. If `Feature2` is selected, both required features also have to be selected.

Feature diagrams and their configurations are specialised to parameterise generators. This thesis uses them to parameterise model transformations as model transformations are special types of generators.

MDSD Transformations Commonly, transformations in the context of MDSD are classified into two types: model-2-model (M2M) and model-2-text (M2T) transformations. The following paragraphs briefly introduce each class.

Model-2-Model Model-2-Model transformations transform an instance of a meta-model A into an instance of a meta-model B. Usually, meta-model A and B are instances of the same meta-meta-model in such a transformation. A and B need not necessarily be different.

The transformation is specified in some special language executable by a specific transformation engine. The transformation language itself can be an instance of the meta-meta-model of A and B, but this is no necessary prerequisite. Figure 2.7 gives an overview on the introduced relationships.

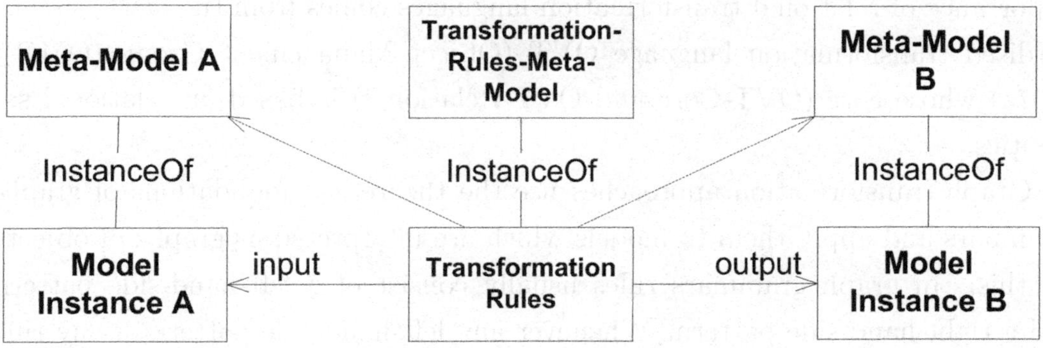

Figure 2.7: Function of a MDSD-Transformation Engine

As shown in figure 2.7, transformation rules use concepts of the source and the target meta-model to specify their effect. Hence, they are specific to the meta-models involved. A rule for a class in meta-model A is matched to instances of this class found in model-instance A. The matching objects are then transformed as specified into objects in model-instance B. These objects are instances of meta-model B.

For example, a model-transformation capable of transforming an instance of UML2 into an instance of a meta-model for Entity-Relationship-Models (ER-Model) may contain the rule to transform any instance of a UML2 class into an entity of the ER-Model. Additionally, any instance of an UML2 association is transformed into a corresponding relationship in the ER-Model. These rules demonstrate how the transformation maps concepts of the UML2-Meta-Model (class, association) to concepts of the ER-Meta-Model.

There is a wide range of available transformation engines and languages summarised and classified in a recent survey by Czarnecki and Helsen (2003). The most important types for model-2-model transformations are direct-manipulations, relational, graph-transformation-based, or hybrid approaches.

Direct-manipulations can be used if equal source and target meta-models are used and the result of the transformation is stored directly in the same model used as input. They are applied frequently to add platform specific (see section 2.2.3) information to a platform independent model.

Relational approaches specify the transformation rules as formal relations. This is done by defining a relationship between a selected set of source and target objects using constraints. The transformation engine takes the set of relations and either tests if the relationships are fulfilled resulting in a boolean value or alters the target model such that none of the relationships is violated. The importance of relational transformation languages comes from the OMG's standardised transformation language QVT (Object Management Group (OMG), 2007a) whose core (QVT-Core and QVT-Relational) is based on relational semantics.

Graph-transformation approaches use the theoretical foundations of graph-grammars and apply them to models which are interpreted as graphs of objects for this. In graph grammars rules usually consist of a left-hand-side pattern and a right-hand-side pattern. Whenever any left-hand-side pattern of any rule matches to an object-sub-graph of the input model that part of the model is replaced by the structure given via the right-hand-side pattern. The process is repeated as long as matching left-hand-side patterns remain.

Finally, hybrid approaches combine the power of several other approaches. The Atlas Transformation Language (ATLAS Group, 2007) developed by INRIA in France is the most important language in this category. It combines declarative (relation based) rules with imperative rules. ATL's importance comes from the fact that ATL is supplemented by one of the most mature tools for EMF based model-2-model transformations.

Czarnecki and Helsen (2003) also mention the use of transformations which are directly based on model instances stored in their concrete syntax as defined by XMI. As XMI is a XML based language, XSLT, a transformation language for transforming XML files, can be used as transformation language. Some of the model-based performance prediction methods described in section 2.3.7 take this approach.

Discussion Current model-2-model transformation engines posses the potential to alter the way MDSD is applied in practice. However, the current state of research, tool development, and industrial case-studies is still immature. Uhl (2007b) lists a bunch of unresolved issues whose solutions he considers a necessary prerequisite for enterprise-scale MDSD use. Research is still directed at defining the right level of abstraction and expressiveness for transformation languages. Additionally, development processes which are tailored for MDSD need to be researched. Available tools are often restricted to research prototypes, industrial quality tools are still under development. QVT which is the designated standard in the OMG's MDA vision is still in the process of finalization and is considered too complex to be fully implemented. Using XSLT as model-2-model transformation language should become obsolete if more mature tools for higher level transformations are available. Also industrial case studies need mature tool support to become feasible.

Compared to model-2-model transformations, model-2-text transformation engines and languages are more mature.

Model-2-Text Model-2-text transformations can be seen as a special class of model-2-model transformations where the target meta-model is simply an arbitrary text file. However, as most non-MDSD tools use a textual concrete syntax (like compiler for programming languages, XML tools, ...) an efficient generation of textual artefacts is important to reuse those tools. Hence, special transformation engines generate textual artefacts from models. According to Czarnecki and Helsen (2003) and Rentschler (2006) visitor and template based approaches are used in current tools.

Visitor based approaches traverse the graph of objects in the source model by using the visitor design pattern (cf. Gamma et al. (1995)). In this pattern, a visitor object traverses a graph of objects and executes at each node which it traverses code specific to the type of the node.

Template based approaches use templates which are text artefacts enriched with small code snippets. The code snippets are executed at transformation time and their result is inserted into the surrounding text artefact. The code execution is used to query information from the source model.

Model-2-text transformations for the proof-of-concept implementation in this thesis have been written using XPand, the template language available in the EMF-based open-source generator framework openArchitectureWare (openArchitectureWare (oAW), 2007). A recent survey on model-2-text engines can be found in a seminar work by Rentschler (2006).

Transformation practices There is a close relationship between design or architecture patterns and MDSD transformations. Patterns are common solutions to reoccurring problems (Gamma et al., 1995). Transformations are used to capture expert knowledge on how to transform instances of models in a repeatable, executable way. Often, patterns are part of the expert knowledge needed in this mapping. This is especially true for model-2-text transformations which usually respect best-practices. Hence, Quality of Service analyses of generated code has to cope with patterns frequently. This is especially important as many patterns alter extra-functional properties.

In particular, patterns are useful if the source model contains concepts of higher abstractions where the abstractions are taken from pattern literature. For example, a communication meta-model for connectors might offer a set of different connectors like call and block, message passing, reliable unicast, etc. (cf. Hohpe and Woolf (2003)). Each connector in this list corresponds to a pattern. The model-2-code transformation generates instances of the pattern during connector transformation.

Additionally, patterns are applied if the generated code should be later mixed with manual written parts. As a separation of generated and manually modified code offers several advantages, patterns like the template method pattern are applied to mix generated and manually written code (Völter and Stahl, 2006).

2.2.3 Platforms and Platform Specific Models

In the OMG's MDA guide (Object Management Group (OMG), 2006c), transformations are used mainly to transform models of higher abstraction levels into models of lower abstraction levels. The MDA guide uses the term platform to express the different layers of abstraction. The guide defines the term as follows.

Definition: Platform (Object Management Group (OMG), 2006c) *"A platform is a set of subsystems and technologies that provide a coherent set of functionality through interfaces and specified usage patterns, which any application supported by that platform can use without concern for the details of how the functionality provided by the platform is implemented."*

The term's origin comes from technological platforms like Java EE or .NET offering supporting services easily accessible by applications. Woodside et al. (2007) state "the term platform refers to technological and engineering details that are irrelevant to the fundamental functionality of the application."

The platform examples given in the MDA guide cover a wide range of different aspects and abstraction levels. The given generic platforms contain object-orient systems, batch-systems, or dataflow systems which is a very high level of abstraction. Technology specific platform examples mentioned are CORBA or Java EE which both can be seen as instances of the generic platform component-based application. The MDA guide even considers vendor specific platforms for a standardized platform like Java EE which is implemented by different vendors.

After selecting a specific platform it is possible to differentiate models into such that contain details of this platforms and those which are free of concepts of this platform. The later are called platform independent models (PIM) and the former platform specific models (PSM).

According to the MDA guide, transformations bridge the semantic gap between a PIM and a PSM. In the generic pattern for this, a transformation takes the PIM and optionally additional information and generates a PSM. The amount of additional information can vary to a large extend from not taking any additional information to sets of models parameterising the transformation process. For a single platform, this process is depicted in figure 2.8 on the left hand side.

The right hand side of figure 2.8 depicts the case in which several transformations are used to modularise the transformation into several steps where each step adds certain aspects of its platform. Consider for example a transformation which generates Java EE code for the Sun Application Server. In this case, the first transformation generates a Java EE model which is independent of a specific application server and the second transformation adds specifics for the Sun Server resulting in a model specific to the combined platform of Java EE applications on a Sun Server.

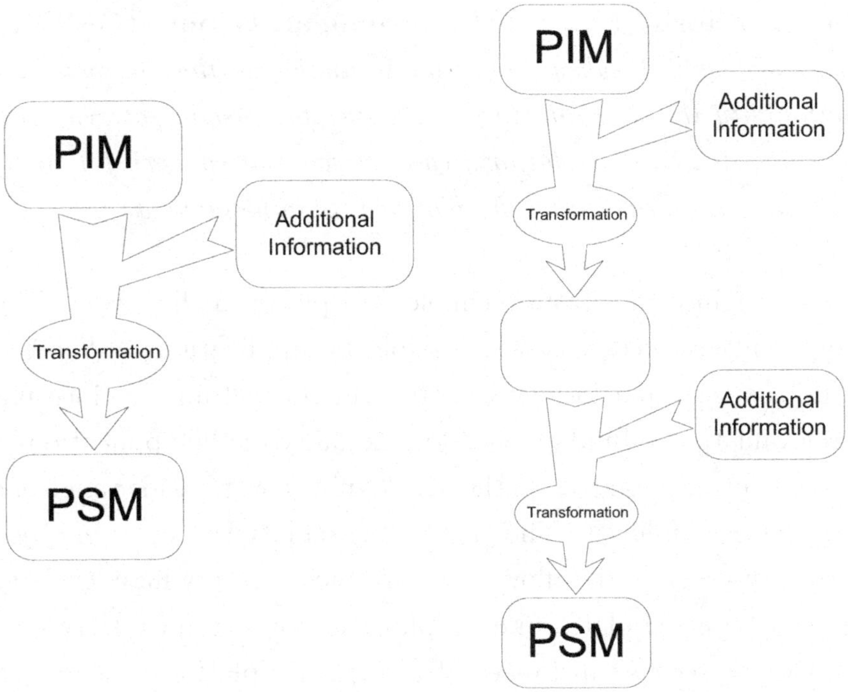

Figure 2.8: PIM to PSM Transformations

Still missing is a discussion on the information which can be supplied additionally. Transformations transforming PIMs into PSMs encapsulate knowledge on how to transform such a PIM into a PSM. A PIM is an abstraction of a PSM generated from it (by abstracting the platform specific information). However, the inverse function of an abstraction is not unique. Consequently, there is usually a set of possible PSMs which can be generated from a single PIM.

Without additional information, a transformation has to choose exactly one of the possible results. This is not preferable, as the possible choices often encapsulate *design decisions* which impact functional and non-functional properties of the resulting system. As design decisions can only be taken in the context of a design problem, the creator of the transformation would need further information to take the right decisions. This results in transformations being inflexible as they are specific for their decision context. To provide the necessary flexibility, the creator of a transformation can foresee possible design decisions and parameterise the transformation. The allows the *user of the transformation* to take the respective design decisions.

The MDA guide contains several suggestions for additional information. The most established one is the use of so called *marks*. In case of marks, the additional information is called a mark model. Marks are specific to concepts of a certain platform. They can be seen as flags which can be attached to objects of the PIM to indicate a specific treatment by the transformation. For example, a transformation of UML components to Java EE components can respect marks for the type of the Java EE component to generate. In case of UML source models, stereotypes can be used as marks for model elements. The Java EE transformation defines for example the stereotypes `<<Statefull>>` and `<<Stateless>>`. When attached to a UML component, the transformation generates statefull or stateless EJBs respectively.

An other option suggested in the MDA guide is the use of pattern information as additional information. In this scenario, a platform is frequently applied together with a set of patterns (as introduced in section 2.2.2). The patterns support common tasks when working with the platform. The selection of patterns for elements of the PIM is controlled through additional models.

Discussion The platform concept of the OMG's MDA approach is often criticised. Völter and Stahl (2006) consider its application impractical, at least not with today's tool support. Their counter proposal called architecture-centric model-driven software development (AC-MDSD) uses only a single transformation which directly transforms a model into code. The lack of a more precise definition of the term platform in the MDA guide is another issue with the concept. To conclude, reports of industrial projects which apply the MDA process with a chain of model-2-model transformations succeeded by a model-2-text transformation are still lacking. Nevertheless, the central idea of having parameterisable transformations which transform artefacts of higher abstraction levels into lower abstraction levels can be applied successfully as for example reported by Völter and Stahl (2006) and demonstrated in this thesis.

2.3 Performance Modelling and Prediction

Performance prediction of software systems is in the focus of research for a long time. Two main reasons exist for this. First, unresolved performance issues in software systems render the system under construction useless in most cases as performance requirements exist for almost any software system. Despite their crucial role for success, they occur frequently (Glass, 1998). The early evaluation and prediction of the performance of a system can safe a lot of time and money for late redesigns (Williams and Smith, 2003). Second, performance evaluation methods are rather simple to validate as taking measurements and comparing them to predictions is not as difficult as with other quality attributes. One reasons for this is, that in contrast to many other extra-functional properties, for performance several established metrics exist. Common metrics include end-to-end response time, resource utilisation, and system throughput.

The importance of performance analysis has lead to several approaches for performance evaluation. The most important formalism is likely queuing networks (Bolch et al., 1998a). However, many others exist like stochastic Petri-nets (Bause and Kritzinger, 2002) or Stochastic Process Algebras (SPAs) (Hermanns et al., 2002). Many of these formalisms rely on a semantics defined as generalised semi Markov chains as used by M. Bravetti (1998a). Depending on the kind of analysis and the assumptions met by the system, analytical, simulation-based, or hybrid solution methods are available.

However, the formalisms referenced above rely on numerous assumptions which often do not hold in complex software system. In addition, they are usually not part of the education of software designers or architects who normally know how to specify a software system using (subsets of) UML. Hence, necessary specifications for performance prediction methods should be done in software design models like the UML. For this, several approaches exist - mostly UML profiles like the UML-SPT or MARTE profile.

The following sections give an overview on the area of model-based performance prediction. First, it gives an overview on the influence factors on the performance of a software component in section 2.3.1. Section 2.3.2 introduces a general process of model-based performance prediction including a brief summary of existing performance input models like UML-SPT. Finally, section 2.3.3 gives an overview on existing general purpose performance prediction methods. Related work to the contents of this thesis come from the area of CBSE-based performance prediction methods (Section 2.3.6) and model-driven performance prediction methods (Section 2.3.7).

2.3.1 Influence Factors on Software Performance

This paragraph discusses the factors influencing the performance of (component-based) software systems before the next section gives an overview on current performance prediction approaches. Figure 2.9 gives an overview initially published by Becker et al. (2006b).

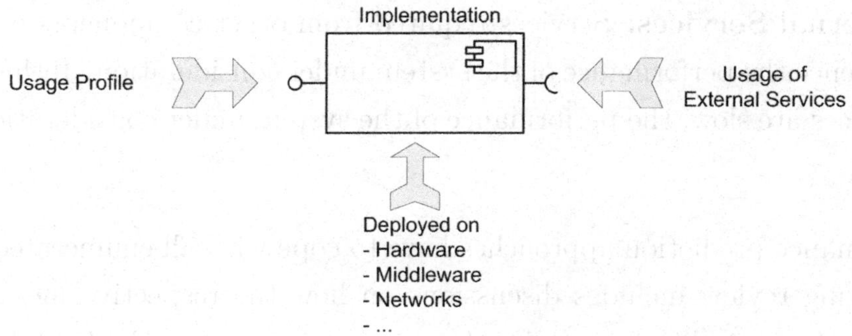

Figure 2.9: Influence Factors on the Performance of Component-Based Software Systems

As depicted in figure 2.9, four factors are important for the performance of a component.

1. **Implementation:** The implementation of a software component has an impact on its performance. The selection of algorithms and data structures has an impact on the processing and memory demand. The Big-O notation is commonly used as an approximation of the demand for processing power as well as for memory consumption.

2. **Deployment:** The hardware on which a software system executes influences the performance. The processing rate of the processor, the transfer rate of the memory bus, etc. correlates to a software system's response time. As a consequence, practitioners use the "kill it with iron" paradigm to solve performance problems in software systems by using faster hardware. However, this is either expensive or infeasible if the amount of hardware needed exceeds a certain limit. On top of the hardware performance impact comes the performance impact of additional software layers like operating systems or middleware software.

3. **Usage Profile:** The interaction of the users with the software system also has an impact on its performance. This includes the sheer amount of users but also their behaviour and the amount and type of data they exchange with the system. The more users access a system concurrently the more load is put on the underlying hardware resources which become

a bottleneck. Analogously, larger chunks of data require more processing power from CPU, harddisk, or network resources.

4. **External Services:** Services required from other components or systems influence the performance of the system under consideration. If the external services are slow, the performance of the system under consideration is also slow.

Performance prediction approaches have to cope with all enumerated factors. The following review includes discussions on how the respective methods deal with the factors. A difference exists for general purpose methods and methods for component-based systems. In general purpose methods it is usually assumed that all factors and respective specifications are known to a single developer. In CBSE the information is spread among the developer roles which adds an additionally level of complexity as discussed further in section 2.4.1.

2.3.2 Performance Prediction Process

Model-based performance prediction methods work according to a common process which is depicted in figure 2.10.

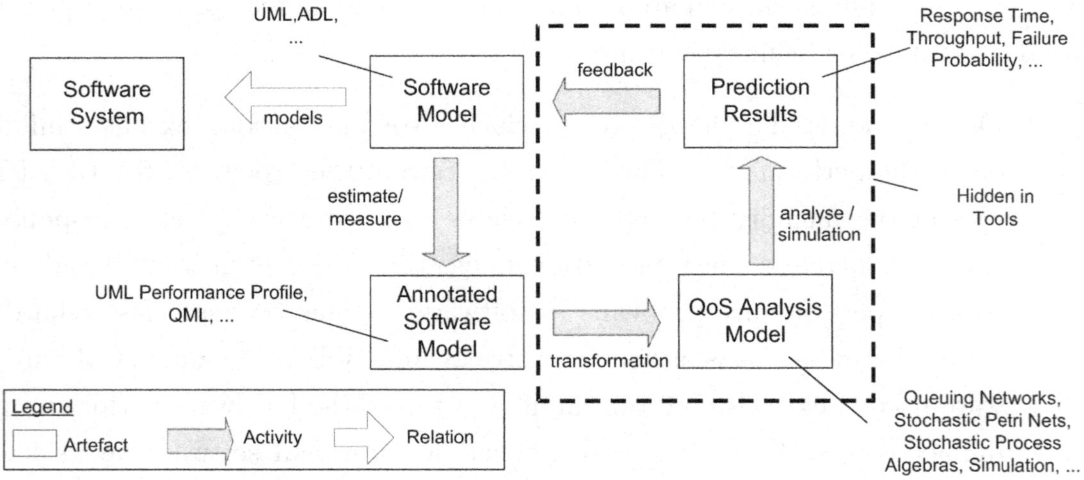

Figure 2.10: Model-based Performance Prediction Process (based on (Object Management Group (OMG), 2005a, p. 9-2))

The process starts with a software system's model. The respective system can be an already existing system, but it needs not necessarily. The system model is expressed in a design-oriented modelling language like the UML. Hence, it is called the *design model*. It is the task of the software designer to create it. Usually, this model exists already as part of the software engineering process without performance engineering.

Performance prediction needs additional information not present in most design languages like UML. In such cases, the first step in the process is to annotate the design model with performance data. For UML models, UML profiles determine the amount of additional data. The annotations cover resource demands, branching probabilities, input parameter characterisations, workload specifications, etc.

The following three process steps should be executed by tools. First, these tools transform the annotated input model into a performance (QoS) analysis model, e.g., a queueing network model. Second, (standardised) tools solve the prediction model instance, resulting in metrics on the elements of the prediction model like overall response time or the queue length of a specific wait queue. The set of available metrics depends on the modelling formalism and its solver's capabilities.

Finally, the prediction tool relates the prediction results back to the originating software model. It stores the results as annotations on elements of the design model. The feedback is supposed to answer the evaluation questions, for example, whether a specific response time maximum can be reached with the given workload and resources. Additionally, in cases in which the results indicate insufficient performance, the feedback should indicate the main sources of these issue.

The final step is crucial for the overall success of the prediction method. However, it is difficult to realise because of the semantic differences between the analysis model and the design model. At least, the whole transformation tool chain needs tracing capabilities to trace back elements of the analysis model into elements of the design model. But even in the context of fully traceable transformations, the source of a performance issue can be ambiguous. Imagine the analysis results in a resource being overloaded. The question remains if it is overloaded because of too many requests arriving or because of the requests being too resource consuming. Even if an answer exists to this question, the questions remains which part of the software must be altered.

Input Models The performance prediction process introduced in this section uses annotated models for the transformation into analysis models. For many prediction methods this means UML models annotated using the UML profile for Schedulability, Performance and Timing (UML-SPT, Object Management Group (OMG) (2005b)) designed for UML 1.4. Other options are the UML Profile for QoS (also designed for UML 1.x, Object Management Group (OMG) (2005a)), and the UML-MARTE profile (designed for UML2, currently under construction, Object Management Group (OMG) (2006f)). Other meta-models explicitly designed for QoS predictions already contain measures to add performance information to the design model, for example KLAPER (Grassi et al., 2005). However, the amount of information is similar.

UML-SPT Profile Because of its widespread use in current performance prediction approaches, the following paragraph briefly introduces the UML-SPT profile. The profile consists of three main parts: modelling of real-time, modelling of schedulability, and modelling of performance. A general resource model is available for use in all three parts. Only the performance and resource model relate to the context of this thesis.

In the performance model, scenarios described as sequence or activity diagrams define performance critical execution paths. Scenarios consist of a sequence of steps. The first step caries annotations specifying the workload of the scenario. Workloads can either be closed or open. In a closed workload, a population of n users execute the scenario concurrently. After finishing a scenario run, they hold for a short delay called think time after which they execute the scenario again. In an open workload, users, which enter the scenario at a specific arrival rate, execute the scenario one time.

Annotations on steps specify performance relevant information like the resource demand of the step in time units, average repetition count, or execution probabilities. Annotations for resources are twofold. The stereotype `PAResource` marks software resources having their own thread of control, resources marked with `PAHost` represent hardware processors. The later, usually denoted as UML2 nodes, carry annotations on their processing rate, scheduling policy, and context switching time. `PAResources` have tagged values for the capacity of the resource, time to acquire and release, and scheduling policy.

In addition to the annotations, SPT supports the use of variables and mathematical expressions in tagged values. In this way, additional expressiveness is available. For example, the specification of resource demands becomes hardware independent if a conversion factor is multiplied with each demand expressed in an independent unit, e.g., a demand of 10 CPU instructions multiplied by 1 ms per instruction results into a demand of 10 ms.

2.3.3 Performance Prediction Methods

In figure 2.10, a transformation transforms the annotated design model into a QoS prediction model. In case of performance predictions, several performance modelling formalisms exist. The following gives a brief overview on the most important ones, i.e., Queuing Networks, Stochastic Process Algebras, and Stochastic Petri-nets.

Queuing Networks The most important formalism for performance prediction is likely queueing network theory. In fact, most recent performance prediction methods as surveyed by Balsamo et al. (2004a) use queueing networks. In queueing networks, queues and their service centres represent processing resources which process workpackages or jobs queuing for service. Jobs travel through a network of service centres using probabilistic routes. The result of a queueing network analysis gives the average response time of the overall system, waiting times for queues, average queue length, and server utilisation. An example queuing network is depicted in figure 2.11. The network has a closed workload. A delay server models the think time of the users (indicated by the clock at the bottom). After a processing step on the CPU, jobs either use a hard-drive with a probability of 30% or a network resource with a probability of 70%.

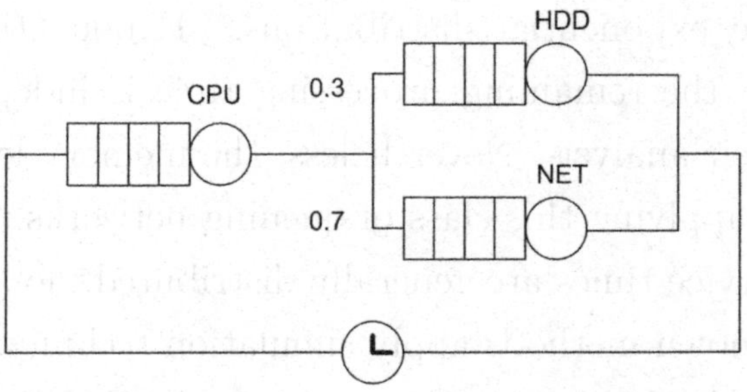

Figure 2.11: An example Queuing Network

For a certain class of queuing networks (namely product form queuing networks) analytical methods exist, which compute the results precisely in very short time. However, this class is rather restrictive and does not reflect real computer systems in many cases because of its strong assumptions. For example, many realistic scheduling disciplines like priority queues cause a queuing network to be not in product form. For this, the class of extended queuing networks exists which can be solved by iterative methods like the Mean-Value-Analysis (MVA) (Bolch et al., 1998a) or by means of simulation (depending on their assumptions).

The complexity of a queuing network depends on the characteristics of the service centres and the assumptions on the jobs. Each service centre has at least a specification on its service time, the number of servers, and the queuing policy. Service times can be deterministic (constant), exponentially distributed or arbitrary distributed. The number of servers is a natural number greater or equal one. The queuing policy determines the order of job processing. Common in computer systems are First-In, First-Out (FIFO) and processor sharing queuing policies. A FIFO queue processes jobs in their order of arrival. A queue with processor sharing processes each job in its queue for a certain amount of time after which it switches to the next job.

For the jobs processed by the network a specification of their arrival rate and job classes is needed. The arrival rate can again be deterministic, exponential or arbitrary distributed. It characterises how many jobs arrive in a given timeframe. Job classes partition the jobs into different types. Each type may specify a different service time demand for the servers in the network. Additionally, jobs can have distinct priorities which allow them to enqueue at a server's queue in front of jobs having a smaller priority.

For some combinations of queues and jobs analytical solutions exist. Many of these classes use exponential distributions. Exponential distributions are "memory-less", i.e., the remaining processing time is independent of the job's state which ease their analysis. Nevertheless, the memory less assumption must be tested for when applying this class of queuing networks. For networks where arrival rates and service times are generally distributed, no analytical solution is known. The only known methods apply simulation techniques.

An important tool using queuing networks is the SPEED tool (see also (Smith and Williams, 1997)) which implements the SPE method as introduced by Smith (1990). It is used in the experimental setting decribed in section 5.2. Therefore, the following briefly introduces it.

In SPEED software designers specify two models: a software execution model using software execution graphs and a hardware model. The software execution model models a performance critical scenario of the system under consideration. It supports control flow constructs like forks, branches, backward jumps, and several call types. Actions in the execution graph can issue demands to the system's resources in hardware independent units. The hardware model gives the processing rate of the resources. The combination of the software and hardware model finally gives hardware dependent execution times by multiplying the demands with the processing rates. The SPEED tool transforms both models into a queuing network automatically. The transformation derives for this routing probabilities, arrival rates, servers, etc. from the input models. Depending on the complexity of the result model, SPEED chooses either an analytical method or a simulation based-approach to get the results. Feedback is given to the software developer by different colours highlighting spots in the scenario which are performance critical.

Several enhancements for queuing networks exist, because of their popularity. Most notably for software modelling is the extension of queuing networks by layers. In layered queuing networks (LQNs) as introduced by Woodside et al. (1995), servers can issue requests to other servers during the processing of a job for their client. In LQNs software entities and hardware entities are nodes in an acyclic graph. This graph represents the dependencies of the nodes during job processing. Arrows going from one node to other nodes indicate that during the processing of a job on the source node, the target nodes are used. Consequently, hardware nodes only have incoming arrows as they process their jobs directly. As for queuing networks, tools exist which solve LQNs either analytical or by means of simulation depending on the underlying assumptions.

Stochastic Process Algebras Based on general process algebras like CCS developed by Milner (1980), extensions for performance prediction exist which introduce stochastic time demands for the actions of the algebra. The advantage of using a process algebra is the possibility to specify the (possibly concurrent) behaviour of the processes in more detail. Compared to queuing networks where the routes of the jobs in the network are usually probabilistic, the processes of a process algebra behave according to the semantics of the algebra. This also allows formal analysis of additional system properties like deadlock freedom.

Early extensions used annotations on the actions of the algebra to denote exponential distributed time demands of the actions. Examples for such algebras are TIPP (Götz et al., 1992), PEPA (Hillston, 1996), or EMPA (Bernardo and Gorrieri, 1998). For an analysis, the process specifications are transformed into Markov chains exploiting the memoryless property of the exponential distribution.

More recent process algebras like MoDeST (Bohnenkamp et al., 2006) or SPADES (Harrison and Strulo, 2000) also deal with general distributed time consumptions. Again, models based on general distributions can not be solved analytically resulting in a need for a simulation based evaluation tool.

Stochastic Petri-Nets Enhancements exist for Petri-nets as introduced by Petri (1962) which enable performance predictions based on Petri-net models. A Petri-net consists of a set of places and transitions, which are traversed by tokens. Transitions remove and add tokens on places whenever they fire. Transitions are active whenever more tokens are on all places affected by the transition as required by the transition's specification. Among all active transitions one is selected to fire resulting in the final change of the Petri-net's state. Petri-nets are well suited to analyse concurrent behaviour and according properties like deadlock freedom.

Stochastic enhancements (Ajmone Marsan et al., 1989) add exponential distributed activation times to transitions which specify a minimum time which has to pass at least for the transition to fire again. Additionally, probabilistic routing of the tokens can be specified. As with stochastic process algebras, stochastic Petri-nets rely on Markov chains offering the already discussed capabilities.

2.3.4 Performance Simulations

Simulation techniques are often used to evaluate performance models such as queueing networks, stochastic Petri nets, stochastic process algebras or specialised models built for a specific purpose. They offer the advantage of having more realistic and hence more complex models. However, their disadvantage is the time it takes for the simulation to come to results which are sufficiently precise.

In the survey on model-based performance predictions techniques by Balsamo et al. (2004a), simulation models by de Miguel et al. (2000) and Arief and Speirs

(2000) are described. In addition, the UML-PSI tool by Marzolla Balsamo and Marzolla (2003) derives an event-driven simulation from UML system models.

In a recent approach, Cortellessa et al. (2007) use UML models annotated using the UML Real-Time (UML-RT) profile and transform them into a specifically designed simulation.

Additionally, commercial approaches exist. Gorilla UML (Gorilla Logic Inc., 2007) is a simulation engine for UML models. HyPerformix (HyPerformix Inc., 2007) is a simulation tool to determine performance bottlenecks. However, due to the lack of publicly available specifications of their engines, a detailed discussion of these tools has to be omitted.

However, none of the reviewed simulations targets specifically component-based software systems.

2.3.5 Prototyping

Prototyping is a method commonly used in engineering disciplines. After initial model building and evaluation, engineers built prototypes which serve for early quality analyses. According to Bardram et al. (2005) architectural prototypes also serve as an early mean to evaluate many quality attributes of software architectures.

Especially for performance evaluation, many aspects left out in the software architecture's model might have a significant impact. Hence, prototyping is often used to predict the performance of the resulting system at early development stages. Compared to model-based approaches, prototyping mostly offers more accurate results. However, the costs for developing and testing a prototype are also much higher as it involves programming, installing and measuring the prototype.

The high costs of the latter tasks arise due to the effort to build prototypes and setting up the measurement environment. For example, external applications which are needed by the prototype have to be installed in a test environment. Workload generators have to be written and distributed which simulated the estimated workload of the system. The executing hardware might be needed twice: one time for the prototype testing and another time to not interfere with still running legacy applications.

2.3.6 CBSE Performance Prediction

Besides having good input models and accurate analysis models, performance prediction for component-based software systems adds an additional level of complexity by the introduction of the development roles (see section 2.1.2). As the developers acting in these roles may be different persons most likely belonging to different organisations, the information needed for conducting a performance evaluation is spread among the developer roles. The component developer knows for example how the component is realised while the software architect knows how the system is assembled of components.

Taking into account the identified influence factors on the performance of a component-based software system (see section 2.3.1), a relationship between the developer roles and the influence factors becomes clear:

- Component developers posses the information on the implementation details
- Software architects know about the system's assembly from which the destination of external service calls can be derived by following the assembly connectors
- Deployers know about the hard- and software platform and how the components are allocated on the platforms
- Domain Experts know about the (planned) use of the system

Hence, prediction models specifically designed for the prediction of component-based software systems have to cope with this distribution of knowledge by using parameterized performance models for components. Becker et al. (2006b) surveyed existing component-based performance prediction methods including a discussion on the support for parameterized component performance models.

The following paragraphs highlight only those methods based on models briefly (labelled MB1-MB7 in the survey paper). The other methods are partially based on measurements. Hence, they can not be used in a plain model-driven application scenario. For details on them, directly consult the survey (Becker et al., 2006b).

RESOLVE-P Sitaraman et al. (2001) take the usage of the components into their predictions by using an extended Big-O Notations to specify the time and memory consumption of software components depending on the input parameters passed to service calls. Additionally, composing services is supported on an abstract level by composing the specified Big-O demands.

PACC Hissam et al. (2002) give a conceptual framework for a so called "Predictable Assembly". Such an assembly consists of certified components whose properties are combined according to a composition theory. The framework takes component properties (implementation knowledge) and their assembly (architects knowledge) into account. However, as it is only a conceptual framework it depends on the actual method used whether further influence factors are respected.

CB-SPE Bertolino and Mirandola (2004) apply the SPE method to component-based systems by separating component performance models and assembly models. In so doing, external service calls and the execution environment become parameterized. However, the software architect has to specify a performance critical scenario in analogy to the SPE method. As he should not posses information on the component internals, this is a drawback of the method. Furthermore, the method does not take input parameters into account.

CBML Wu and Woodside (2004) use LQN models of components to build parameterized component models. For each component an LQN model specifying its provided and required interfaces as well as the control flow and resource usage dependencies. These single component LQN models are combined according to an assembly model into a system LQN model which gets evaluated. Wu and Woodside (2004) also consider inserting components which they call completions (Woodside et al., 2002) for environmental services like middleware services into the system model automatically to increase the prediction accuracy of the environmental influence.

CB-APPEAR Eskenazi et al. (2004) present a method for the performance prediction of existing components which undergo evolution. A parametric performance model is derived for these components by putting them into a testbed which figures the dependencies between method invocations and invocations of environmental services out. Depending on the complexity of the parametric dependency, the resulting model is either analytical or simulation based. However, the approach makes strong assumptions which are necessary to derive the performance models by testing.

ROBOCOP In the prediction method associated to the already introduced ROBOCOP component model, Bondarev et al. (2005) introduce a prediction method for embedded systems designed using ROBOCOP. The method can deal with implementation details specified by the component developer parameterized by external services, the component's hardware environment, and usage. However, due to its focus on embedded systems, the support for parameterisations of the latter is limited. For example, input parameters can only be specified as constants or the component's access to the execution environment is expected to be precisely given in hardware metrics. Support for software layers like operating systems or middleware platforms is outside the scope of this work.

Hamlet Hamlet et al. (2004) execute components and measure how the component usage propagates requests in order to gain accurate performance predictions. However, their component model is limited as in their model components are simple functional transformations having only a single service.

2.3.7 Model-Driven Methods

In the area of software performance engineering, the idea to use model-driven techniques gained some attention recently. Model-driven techniques aim at a fully automated execution of the transformations presented in the process overview in section 2.3.2. However, model-driven performance prediction methods require suitable meta-models due to their automated execution. These meta-models formalise the syntax and semantics of the source and target model to a degree necessary for automatic processing. The following first reviews three performance meta-models. Based on a survey by Di Marco and Mirandola (2006), it then introduces a selection of model-driven performance prediction approaches.

Performance Meta-Models Cortellessa (2005) compares three different *performance meta-models*: The performance domain model of the UML-SPT profile (Object Management Group (OMG), 2005b), the Core Scenario Model by Woodside et al. (2005), and the Software Performance Engineering (SPE) meta-model by Smith and Williams (2002).

All meta-models may serve as annotated software models in the model-based performance prediction process (cf. figure 2.10). Cortellessa (2005) classifies their concepts into three classes: software behaviour, resources, and workload. The software behaviour aims at describing the software execution at run-time. A common concept among the meta-models is the description of this behaviour as scenarios which contain a set of linked steps. Each step can interact with the hardware resources it is deployed on. All meta-models contain concepts to specify the (probabilistic) control flow during system execution. However, their support for data flow specifications is very limited.

In the resource area all meta-models differentiate between active resources which actively process demands and passive resources which represent locks. Other characteristics of resources deal with describing the resources themselves, e.g., their scheduling discipline.

In the workload area all meta-models support open and closed workloads. Both types can have different attributes to characterise them, e.g., arrival rate or think time.

As all meta-models target at the description of monolithic systems, none contains explicit support for modelling component-based software systems. However, their common concepts briefly introduced above serve as starting point to create a CBSE-aware performance meta-model.

UML-to-LQN Petriu and Wang (2000) present an conceptual approach to convert UML collaborations automatically into LQN models using graph transformations. The approach supports a limited set of architectural patterns, namely pipe-and-filter, broker and client-server. However, for each pattern several variants are discussed. Petriu and Shen (2002) give an implementation of these concepts as an early model-driven approach to performance evaluation of UML 1.x models annotated using the UML-SPT profile. Due to the immaturity of the technological foundation of model-driven approaches in 2002, the transformation uses the serialised XMI format of the UML model instance. It takes collaborations, deployment diagrams, and activity diagrams into account.

To become practical the approach restricts the full power of UML and adds additional semantic constraints, which are specified informally. The activity diagrams have to correspond to the architectural patterns described as collaborations. Furthermore, they have to be specified in a way which allows a transformation into a AST-like syntax tree for every object taking part in a collaboration. One constraint opposed on transformable activity diagrams is that they have to be partitioned among the communication partners by the use of UML swim-lanes.

KLAPER An approach to deal with the problem of having many possible design notations (like UML, OWL, etc.) which all need to be transformed into several possible performance models (like Queuing networks, Petri-nets, etc.) is the Kernel Language for Performance and Reliability analysis (KLAPER). It is a meta-model designed to serve as intermediate model for model-transformations. Instead of having a transformation from every design model into every analysis model, transformations use KLAPER as intermediate model. As such, transformations are needed from any design model into KLAPER and from KLAPER into any analysis model, significantly reducing the overall amount of transformations.

KLAPER's core concepts base also on the concept of components which offer services and which are connected via connectors. A set of connected actions (similar to activity diagrams) specify the behaviour of the component's services. Annotations exist directly in the meta-model to specify resource consumptions and failure rates. As KLAPER is an intermediate language, KLAPER models are supposed to be complete and not parameterised by the influence factors given in section 2.3.1.

SAP Di Marco and Inveradi (2004) present a model-driven, component-based performance prediction approach called Software Architecture Performance (SAP). The approach uses SPT-annotated UML2 instances as input models. It takes UML Use Cases as workload specifications, UML Component diagrams for the static structure, and UML sequence charts for component interactions. It transforms these models into a multi-chain queuing network, i.e., a queuing network in which classes of jobs exist which each may have individual routes through the network. The mapping maps components to service centres in the queuing network and use cases to job classes.

The transformation works in a compositional way. It combines the behaviours of different components into a large system behaviour by using the structure of the component's composition. While this allows a parameterisation over external service calls, the components have to specify their resource demands in time units as the transformation disregards component deployment and usage.

2.3.8 Platform Completions

Woodside et al. (2002) coined the term "completions" for aspects of a software system which are left out from system models due to reasons of abstracting from the real complexity but which have a significant impact on the performance of the system. To give an example, consider an architectural system model showing simple connections between components which model the fact, that the components exchange messages to communicate. In the real system, this communication is causing several activities usually performed by a middleware: Marshalling and demarshalling of service names and parameters, performing broker lookups, building up TCP frames, transmitting them, etc. Depending on the performance scenario, these activities might be responsible for performance bottlenecks. The enrichment of a design model with specifications relevant for performance analysis is called (model) completion by the authors.

The OMG's MDA idea of having a PIM and a PSM conforms to some extend to the idea of performance completions. A software model without completions can be seen as a PIM, it does not contain specific performance information of underlying software layers. Hence, a model containing completions can be seen as PSM. It contains the information needed to do a performance prediction.

Some authors have aimed at providing automated model-transformations to include such completions into design models in order to reach a higher prediction accuracy.

Verdickt et al. (2005) present a transformation which includes the performance impact of a CORBA based middleware into UML models. The UML model's structure has to be similar to the one used by Petriu and Shen (2002). UML collaborations specify the possible communication patterns which the transformation expands. The transformation takes the timing information of the middleware's services as parameters according to an ad-hoc XML schema.

Grassi et al. (2006) present an approach which uses a QVT-Relations transformation to include the performance overhead caused by communication links into KLAPER models. For this, the transformation selects links in the model and replaces them by the actions performed by the middleware which are part of the transformation. Due to the lack of working QVT engines, the approach has been validated by executing the transformation manually.

Wu and Woodside (2004) envision the use of components as platform completions as already mentioned in section 2.3.6 on CBSE prediction methods. They planned a library of components for example database, middleware, or file system components. Based on a set of rules, these completions should be added into the models. They also point out, that this should be done automatically. However, they seemed to have discontinued this work.

2.4 Discussion of the Existing Approaches

The following sections list requirements for component-based architecture design and prediction resulting from the introduced foundations. Section 2.4.1 gives an overview on them classified by the involved research areas (cf. figure 2.1 in the motivation to this chapter). Section 2.4.2 uses the literature surveys presented at the end of each related research area section as basis to judge the state-of-the-art. Based on this and the requirements presented in section 2.4.1, section 2.4.2 presents the resulting deficiencies targeted in this thesis.

2.4.1 Requirements for Model-Driven, CBSE Predictability

Each introduced area of research offers advantages for a software development process. Hence, combining these areas is desirable. In detail, three main requirements result from supporting each of the areas involved:

- Firstly, a CBSE development process should be supported. The CBSE method offers advantages due to better component specifications and shared workload among the developer roles.

- Secondly, the envisioned software development process in this thesis should be based on the inclusion of models and model-transformations in order to benefit from the advantages of MDSD (cf. section 2.2). Especially, it is an aim to use the close relationship between a model and the code generated from it to increase performance prediction accuracy.

- Thirdly, model-driven performance predictions of the specified architectures should be supported to enable architectures whose design decisions are based on predicted quality attributes. The following paragraphs investigate each requirement in more detail.

In detail, from the CBSE requirement result the following sub-requirements:

1. Support for the CBSE development roles (cf. section 2.1.2) requires distributed modelling activities: Each role has specify those parts of a complete system model it possesses information about. This effectively splits the complete system model into sub-models specific to each of the roles.

2. Support for a Parameterised Component Model: A model of a software component has to be parameterised by the identified influence factors (see section 2.3.1). Such parameterisations allow using the *same* model of a component in different reuse scenarios. It is part of the responsibilities of the component developer to specify his components in such a parameterised way. By specifying their sub-models, other roles finally fix the parameters resulting in a complete model. However, when designing each role's DSL, it is important to keep the models as small as possible, i.e., information derivable from other information is determined automatically.

3. Gray-Box Components: The black-box component principle should be preserved for reasons of information hiding and encapsulation (cf. section 2.1). However, performance prediction requires at least abstract models of internal component activities to estimate their resource demands. Hence, a refined black-box view on components is favoured: tools gain access to the internals of components, but the developer still only gets the information on component interfaces. In practice, this is the way components are distributed today if the bytecode is taken as the specification of the internal behaviour of the component. The bytecode is only accessed by tools like virtual machines and not by the developer.

4. Third Party Deployment: In order to support the CBSE development process as presented in section 2.1, not only component models but also component implementations must support varying external influence factors after the implementation phase. However, existing target middleware platforms still have limited build-in support for a strict distinction of the CBSE roles. As a consequence it is required to overcome such limitations by appropriate measures encoded in transformations. Often, existing design or

architectural patterns solve these problems. Whenever they exist, they should be applied.

Model-driven software development aims at increasing the effectiveness of software development activities by automating the transitions from more abstract models of the system to more concrete ones. Hence, the requirements aim at saving time and money to effectively automate as much as possible of this process:

1. Meta-Model Foundation: In order to use standard transformation engines, a meta-model is needed based on a standard meta-meta-model. The required meta-model should have a clearly defined syntax and its semantics should be as precise as possible. Model elements should be accessible by standard compliant transformation engines. A counter-example to this is the tagged-value annotations used in SPT as they need upfront parsing. Instead of such strings, all relevant information should be accessible via meta-model classes.

2. Meta-Model Applicability: When designing a meta-model all parts of it (abstract and concrete syntax, static and dynamic semantics) deserve attention. Especially the concrete syntax is crucial for the applicability of the meta-model. Without a well-designed concrete syntax, the meta-model is not applicable. Case studies or experiments with common software developers offer a measure to evaluate whether the meta-model is suited.

3. Transformations Bridge Abstraction Levels: In MDSD automated transformations are used to bridge the gap between an abstract model and more concrete models or code. The transformations should execute automatically and may be parameterised by mark models to reflect mapping alternatives.

4. Standard Compliance: As much of the technology as possible should be founded on standards or de-facto standards. The resulting ability to reuse standard compliance tools leads to a higher efficiency compared to self-developed tools and transformations. One reason for this is that it allows to use powerful transformation engines which allow complex operations. Such operations, like matching complex object structures, need sophisticated knowledge and hence, are hard and error-prone to implement. Additionally,

it eases the exchange of tools and models which enables to use specific tools for specific tasks.

Detailed requirements resulting from the main requirement to have performance predictions included in the envisioned software development process are:

1. Integrated Validation: As in other engineering disciplines, the software development process favoured in this thesis should support model validation and refinement steps after initial evaluations. They base on measurements performed with prototypes and (parts of) the final system.

2. Prediction Result Expressiveness: Performance predictions should result in enough information to make the right design decisions. Sometimes mean response times or average queue load is sufficient for this. But in many scenarios it is not as trade-offs are involved. For example, speeding up one class of requests might slow down another making it hard to state which alternative offers the better performance. In order to deal with the problem, this thesis favours distribution functions of stochastic results over characteristic values like mean or standard deviation. The predictions have to deal with that.

3. Annotation Inputs: It can be hard to adjust performance annotations like arrival rate estimates to predefined distribution types. This is even more true in a distributed development environment where the final prediction model input is calculated from several specifications done by different developer roles. Hence, support for arbitrary distribution functions for stochastic input values is needed.

Requirements which result from the combination of CBSE and MDSD are:

1. Support For Distributed Model Transformations: Model transformations can only take place when the model information needed for a specific transformation is complete. Some transformations have to be executable by roles independent from others. For example, a transformation deriving code skeletons for component implementations from component models has to be executable by the component developer independent from other development roles. Additionally, transformations which derive prediction models have to produce partial prediction models which are combined in a finalising step.

Requirements which result from the combination of the model-driven approach and performance prediction are:

1. Model-Driven Predictions: Performance predictions have to be based on models. Models offer a cost effective way of doing early analyses and what-if scenario evaluations.
2. (Semi-)Automatic Prediction Model Generation: In a model-driven context, model transformations translate design models into prediction models. To guide the transformation, developers can add manual additions like performance annotations or *completion* specifications to the transformation as parameter.
3. Exploit the Generative Nature of the Implementation Generation: Code is generated by transformations guided by input models. However, transformations add additional information to intermediate models or final code fragments. This can be done either fully automated or semi-automated guided by parameters specified by the user as mark model.

2.4.2 Resulting Deficiencies

Judging existing approaches for each of the three foundation areas against the requirements given in section 2.4.1 results in a list of deficiencies in existing approaches.

Component Models Component models offer support for the CBSE processes and compositional reasoning. The industrial component models even offer support for implementing components on middleware implementations. However, they still have limited (if any) support for advanced concepts like composed components or explicit required interfaces and do not support performance analyses.

Fractal offers advanced component concepts like composed components and run-time reconfiguration which is also supported in Fractal platform implementations. However, it misses quality evaluation methods.

Documentation-oriented models like the component model of UML2 suffer from imprecision and ambiguities. Additionally, support for performance annotations is only available as meta-model extension via profiles. However, due to its MOF based meta-model, UML2 itself has a well-defined abstract syntax which would allow model transformations using standard transformation engines. However, many UML tools still do not support exporting standard compliant XMI files which decreases tool interoperability.

Architecture Description Languages have been designed with the aim of analysing software architectures. However, from the surveyed literature only few ADLs support quality annotations and analyses namely MetaH, Rapide, and UniCon (cf. section 2.1.4). Their focus is on real-time and schedulability analysis, which is unsuited for early design phase performance evaluation. Additionally, they have not been designed for standardised model transformations as their meta-model is commonly not expressed using a standard meta-meta-model.

SOFA possesses an explicit meta-model and also supports advanced component concepts like composed components. However, analyses focus on protocol and implementation conformance checks via model-checking. Performance analysis is not supported.

Embedded component models offer some support for early quality analysis. Especially the RoboCop component model is related to the component model used in this thesis as it supports the partitioning of models to describe components and thus could also be used in a software development process with several involved developer roles. The extensions introduced by Bondarev et al. (2005) allow the specification of resource consumptions, behavioural specifications and constant input parameter dependencies. However, given the focus on embedded systems many models used in their work only support a limited scope adding several strong assumptions on the system to be modelled. For example, it is assumed that the time needed to process a job can be derived exactly, which might be valid for an embedded controller but which is not valid for a business information system running on several software layers without real-time guarantees.

CBSE Performance Prediction Methods The CBSE prediction methods survey in section 2.3.6 all aim at supporting performance prediction for component-based software systems. However, as the original survey by Becker et al. (2006b) showed, only few of them support all of the CBSE developer roles involved.

The most comprehensive support has ROBOCOP. It supports all developer roles including the impact of different input parameter usages in the usage context. However, it targets at embedded systems and thus, can make several simplifying assumptions like exactly available hardware demands or constant input parameters only. Based on these assumptions, ROBOCOP supports worst-case and schedulability analyses important in the embedded domain. In this thesis, focus is on probabilistic, average case analyses more important for business information systems which do not need hard deadlines.

Additionally, non of the CBSE prediction methods supports model-driven *code generation* from their model instances. However, the close relationship of generated code and its performance at run-time is in the focus of the Coupled Transformations method presented in section 4.1. To demonstrate this, this thesis presents a Java EE mapping of PCM instances in section 4.6 and elaborates on the resulting performance impact.

Model-Driven Performance Prediction In order to do model-driven component-based performance predictions a meta-model is needed to specify the component-based architecture and the performance of single components. In the meta-models surveyed by Cortellessa (2005), i.e., UML1.x with SPT annotations, the SPEED meta-model, and CSM, many concepts needed for performance predictions like modelling the control flow, the workload, the hardware environment, or performance annotations exist. However, as Cortellessa (2005) concludes, non of them has explicit support for component-based software development.

The SAP approach by Di Marco and Inveradi (2004) explicitly bases it performance predictions on component-based development. It already includes compositional reasoning on the performance of component-based architectures by combining single characteristics of single component into a system's prediction model. The used transformation can also handle different kinds of workloads by mapping them on different routes in the used queuing network. However, it also has some drawbacks. First, it misses support for a parameterised component deployment as each component has to specify its resource demand in hardware-dependent times. Second, due to its foundation in the UML, it inherits the issues with UML's imprecise component model (see section 2.1.4). Third, it is unclear how the authors apply the SPT profile which is designed for UML1.x to UML2 model in which the semantics of the profiling mechanism changed significantly. However, they have to rely on UML2 as they use its improved component and collaboration models.

Petriu and Wang (2000) transform SPT annotated UML1.x models into LQNs. However, it is not targeting component-based developments due to its focus on UML collaborations. Additionally, the same issues with the UML meta-model apply as discussed for SAP.

KLAPER from Grassi et al. (2005) also claims to support component-based software systems. However, KLAPER is not aligned with the CBSE developer roles and uses a very broad component term which includes software- and hardware components. Its aim is to provide an intermediate model for transformations into performance predictions models. For this, it is based on EMOF instead of using the UML. However, the few available analysis transformations also make strong assumptions on the KLAPER instance like exponential distributed workloads so that KLAPER is disregarded in this thesis.

This thesis does not use the UML as input model to avoid several issues (Becker et al., 2008b). The most important are the missing support for creating partial models (to support the CBSE roles), the unavailability of performance annotation profiles for UML2 (UML2 is needed because of the enhanced component model over UML1.x), the complexity of the meta-model which would require introducing many restrictions to reflect the component concept favoured in this thesis (like disallowing inheritance for components), and the issues with tool interoperability with the XMI produced by different UML modelling tools (cf. the paragraph on UML in section 2.1.4). Instead, this thesis defines a EMOF based meta-model which has explicit support for CBSE developer roles (see section 3.1) and the required parameterisation by the different influence factors on performance (cf. section 2.3.1). Using an EMOF based meta-model also eases to use of standard model transformation engines.

Platform Completions The introduced platform completions (see section 2.3.8) all aim at integrating platform specific details into performance prediction models. The methods by Verdickt et al. (2005) and Grassi et al. (2006) successfully include details on component connectors into the prediction models. However, they do so in an all-or-nothing approach, i.e., they replace all connectors with *the same* details. They do not use information on the transformation of the design model into its realisation which allows a more flexible control which completions to add in which cases (cf. section 4.1).

The approach by Wu and Woodside (2004) envisions the use of completion components to model platform aspects like different software layers (middleware, databases, filesystems, etc.) or networking. The authors plan to use a library of completion component to include them into the prediction model based on a set of rules not explained further. While the central idea of these completion components gives means to add platform details into prediction models, Wu and Woodside (2004) did not follow up on the idea in future work. In this thesis, their ideas are reused and extended. Instead of using CBML, this thesis uses the PCM which offers further advantages over CBML (cf. previous paragraphs). In this thesis, the rules Wu and Woodside (2004) planned to use for the inclusion of different completions are derived from the code transformation.

Chapter 3

The Palladio Component Model

The Palladio Component Model deals with many of the introduced requirements (cf. section 2.4.1) like explicit support for CBSE roles, an explicit model for component contexts, and CBSE performance predictions based on arbitrary distributed random variables. A brief history of the model and its evolution shows how the requirements have been included over time.

The model builds on parametric contracts introduced by Reussner (2001). They describe the intra-component relationship between the provided and the required interfaces of components by specifying the invoked required services during the execution of a provided service. Early versions focused on the execution order of required services which has been used for automated component protocol adaptations (Reussner, 2001). Parametric contracts use so-called service effect specifications (SEFFs) to specify the inner behaviour of a component. Reussner (2001) uses finite state machines (FSMs) where states represent component states and transitions represent calls to required services. Becker et al. (2003) introduce a first attempt to a meta-model formalisation of the SEFF concept based on an EBNF grammar.

Reussner et al. (2003) extend the concept of parametric contracts to analyse software reliability by annotating SEFF transitions with failure probabilities. Reussner et al. (2004) further enhance the SEFF to enable performance predictions. In this work, states of the SEFF's FSM represent component internal computations while transitions still represent calls to required services. Random variables attached to states are used to specify time spans. They specify for how long a component remains in the respective state before issuing the following external call. By this, the model considers already the influence of component external service calls (cf. section 2.3.1).

The SEFF used for performance prediction has been embedded into a more complex meta-model, which explicitly introduced components, interfaces, and connectors as model concepts. However, the corresponding implementation to create, serialise, and analyse instances of the model was based on ad-hoc, manual-written code. Editor support for the concrete graphical syntax of the model was initially implemented by Uflacker (2005) and later on extended by a student project group (Krogmann and Becker, 2007).

The master thesis by Krogmann (2006) introduced an ECORE instance of the PCM's meta-model enabling the use of standardised, model-driven techniques. Additionally, he extended the model by an explicit component context concept as described by Becker et al. (2006c) and further types of components. The explicit context allows additional parameterisations, namely execution environment and usage.

Becker et al. (2007) enhance the model further by introducing a new SEFF concept called Resource Demanding SEFF (RD-SEFF) reflecting parametric dependencies to input parameters (as developed by Koziolek et al. (2006)) and the execution environment. For this, an extension to the PCM's meta-model introduced so called stochastic expressions. Component developers can use them for example to specify resource demands depending on characterisations of input parameters. The stochastic expressions replaced the former FSM state annotations.

Additionally, the model has been split to reflect the CBSE developer roles. For each role a subset of the whole meta-model's concepts has been defined. Thus, a domain specific language (DSL) for each developer role is introduced. Furthermore, Becker et al. (2007) introduce a model-based simulation tool for predictions.

Based on this, Koziolek et al. (2007) have added additional concepts to specify return value abstractions for external calls and component configuration parameters. Additionally, the authors introduce a model-driven approach to derive an analytical performance prediction model using model-2-model transformations.

Three additional transformations for PCM instances have been developed and are described in section 4. They are an essential part of this thesis' contribution. The first replaces the model-based simulation by a model-driven simulation framework which uses a model-2-code transformation to generate the simulation's code. The second generates a prototype and the last code skeletons.

The complexity of the PCM's meta-model makes it difficult to discuss all concepts in detail here. A technical report of the University Karlsruhe contains the detailed specification (Reussner et al., 2007). Here, the current state of the PCM is briefly introduced to understand the transformations and validations presented in section 4 and section 5.

The usage and data-flow dependent parts of the PCM have been developed by Koziolek (2008). To allow a distinction, section A.1 gives an overview on the PCM's packages and their respective creators. It also contains a comprehensive overview on all transformations in the context of the PCM including their creators (see figure 3.1 and A.2).

3.1 Palladio Development Process

This section first introduces the component-based development process underlying the PCM as published by Koziolek and Happe (2006). Afterwards, it refines this process to reflect the requirements resulting from the integration of MDSD.

3.1.1 PCM Development Process

Overview The PCM distinguishes five developer roles: the component developer, the software architect, the system deployer, the domain expert, and the QoS analyst. Figure 3.1 shows all roles including the model artefacts they create.

The roles (depicted on the left hand side) correspond to the roles introduced in section 2.1.2. In the PCM, each of the roles is responsible for a certain submodel of a system specification. Component developers model interfaces, components, and data types. Software architects take components and their specifications as provided by component developers and assemble the components into systems. System deployers capture hard- and software execution environments in so-called resource environment models, e.g., physical servers and their operating systems. When given a system model, i.e., an assembly of components from the software architect, they allocate the components on respective hard- and software resources. Finally, domain experts model user behaviour. For this, they specify the user's arrival process, their system interaction and performance relevant characteristics of the input parameters.

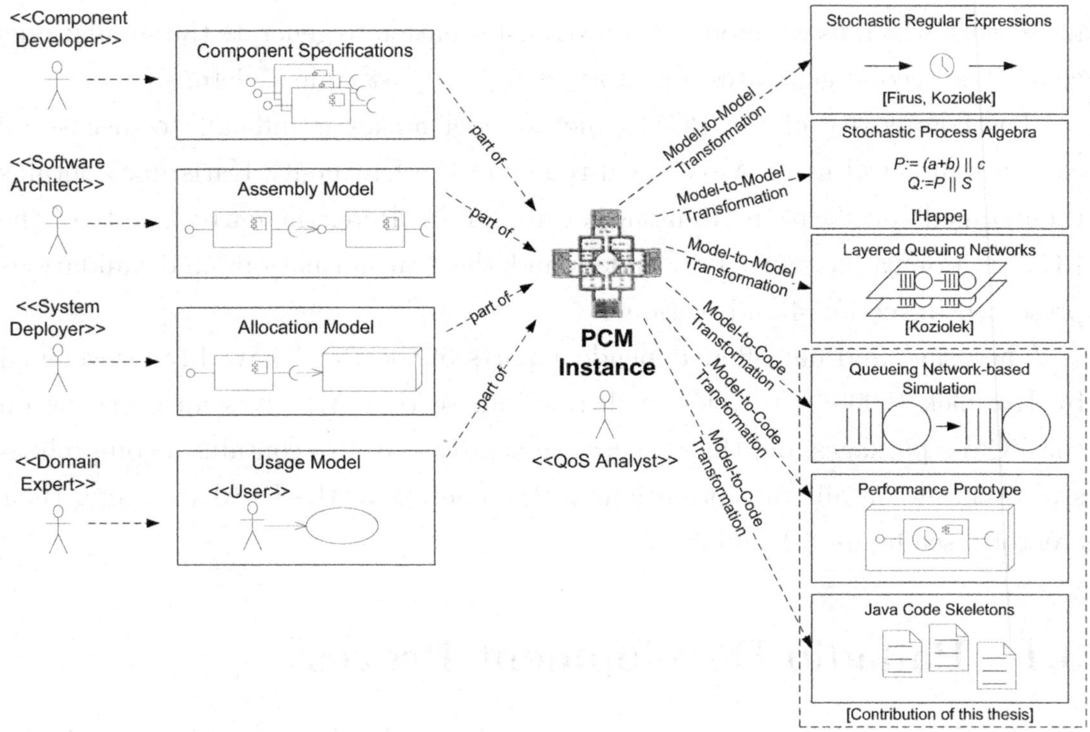

Figure 3.1: The PCM Developer Roles and the Transformation Artefacts

On the right hand side of figure 3.1, the output of existing model transformations is depicted. At the time of writing, six transformations exist. However, the transformation into a stochastic process algebra called Capra is still under development by Happe (2008). The first working transformation maps PCM instances into stochastic regular expressions. Firus et al. (2005) initially developed it and Koziolek (2008) extended and implemented it in his thesis. It allows only the analysis of single user workloads. The second transformation maps PCM instances into instances of the Layered Queueing Networks (LQNs) performance prediction model and is also presented by Koziolek (2008). However, LQNs support only certain types of random variable distributions and produce only mean values of the resulting metrics.

One of the contributions of this thesis are the following three transformations. The first of them derives a simulation in Java based directly on the PCM's constructs (see section 4.4). It is not subject to the restrictions of the afore described transformations. The second transformation uses simulation concepts and combines them with final application code into a prototype implementation which can be used for performance testing on the final execution environment (see section 4.7). The last transformation derives code skeletons for Java EE, which bridge semantic gaps between the PCM's concepts and Java EE's concepts (see section 4.6).

Process Model Koziolek and Happe (2006) describe how the existing CBSE development process by Cheesman and Daniels (2000) can be enhanced to include QoS analyses. For this, the developer role's tasks have been identified and the flow of artefacts has been described in detail. In this thesis, the process is further enriched with tasks in which model transformations for prototyping and implementation are executed (see section 3.1.2). Figure 3.2 shows an overview of the process.

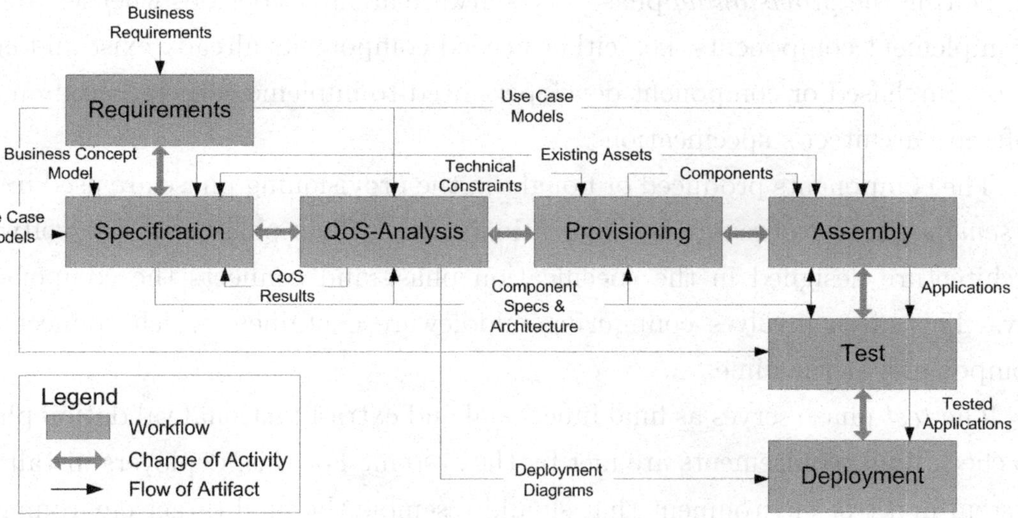

Figure 3.2: Process Model of the PCM (Koziolek and Happe, 2006)

The process consists of seven workflow steps: requirements, specification, QoS analysis, provisioning, assembly, test, and deployment. The following briefly describes them.

The *requirements* phase captures the business requirements for the system under construction. This contains the system's business domain and business context, the functionality it should provide, and the extra-functional requirements it should fulfil. The result of the requirements phase is a conceptual domain model forming a domain vocabulary and a set of system use cases. The creation of these models is the task of the domain expert.

In the *specification* phase, software architects use the domain model and the use cases and design a component-based software architecture realising the requirements. They decide how to decompose the system into components resulting in specifications of needed components and their composition. In later iterations of this phase, decisions on the components are influenced by identified QoS issues from the QoS analysis phase and the availability of pre-existing components acquired in the provisioning phase.

In the *QoS analysis* phase, the QoS analyst uses the specification of the components, their composition, and the target soft- and hardware environment to derive performance metrics. Based on these metrics, the QoS analyst can judge whether the software architecture fulfils its extra-functional requirements. If the architecture fails to fulfil its requirements, the QoS analyst may suggest design alternatives to improve the architecture.

During the *provisioning* phase, the software architect decides whether to buy or implement components, i.e., either needed components already exist and need to be purchased or component developers need to implement them based on the software architect's specifications.

The components produced or bought in the provisioning phase are used in the *assembly* phase to create the application's code. This phase uses the software architecture designed in the specification phase and connects the components qly. This often involves configuring middleware containers which connect the components at run-time.

The *test* phase serves as final functional and extra-functional validation phase to check if all requirements are met by the system. For this, deployers install the system in a test environment that should resemble the final target environment.

Finally, the deployer installs the system at the customer's side, in the *deployment* phase. After this step, the system is ready to be used by its end-users.

The following section elaborates on how to refine some of these steps when using MDSD techniques in a CBSE context. It also provides a more detailed discussion of the specification and QoS analysis phase.

3.1.2 Introducing MDSD into the Palladio Development Process

Motivation As introduced in the previous section, the PCM supports a role-based software development process. In contrast to this, MDSD usually assumes the existence of fully specified models. Transformations map such complete models to code. Hence, support for distributed modelling is weak. For example, when using UML input models the problem arises that most UML tools do not support creating partial models which reference each other. Additionally, in literature there is still a lack of information on how to create models when developing in teams where the developers act in different roles. Völter and Stahl (2006) present initial ideas on this issue. However, these ideas target at creating a single model in a team. The PCM has explicit support for developer roles which are usually assumed to be different persons spread among different geographical locations and organisations. The transformations presented in this thesis deal with this requirement as there is not a single transformation but a transformation for each of the developer roles. There is a transformation for component developers, one for software architects, one for deployers, and one for domain experts as explained in the following.

A second requirement needs to be included in the process. As introduced in section 2.2.3, when mapping abstract high level models to lower level realisations, often mark models add additional information to the transformation to determine how the abstract model elements are mapped to a specific target model. These mapping decisions have an impact on the generated artefacts and their performance (cf. section 4.1). Hence, these mark model artefacts have to be included in the data flow in the presented process model.

The following paragraphs give an overview on the transformations, their artefacts and their integration in the development process as presented in section 3.1.1.

Specification and Provisioning The specification and provisioning phases require two refinements. First, the software architect additionally needs to encode decisions taken on the technical realisation of the architecture by creating mark models. Second, component developers additionally use code transformations when implementing components. Figure 3.3 shows details of these steps. Refinements in comparison to the initial publication by Koziolek and Happe (2006) are presented using an italic font.

The changes for the software architect only involve specifying mapping options for the technical realisations (depicted as output of the specification phase). For example, consider the system should be implemented as Java EE application. Then the software architect can additionally specify the configuration of the EJB component container, e.g., authentication requirements, the marshalling protocol to use, etc. (for the Java EE mapping in this thesis these options are

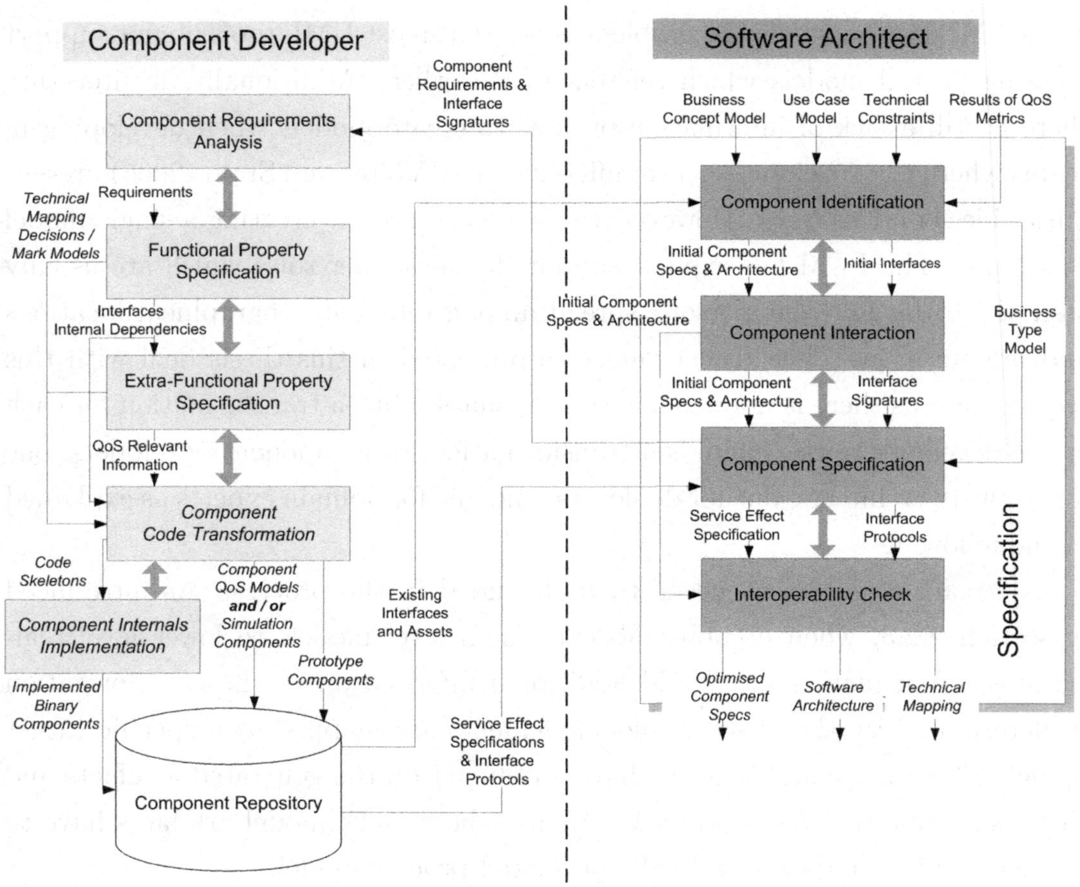

Figure 3.3: MDSD-Refined Specification Workflow

presented in section 4.6.3). The information specified for the technical mapping is used in the QoS analysis phase to refine the predictions and in the assembly phase to create respective middleware configuration files.

The workflow of component developers changes by the use of transformations as they may use transformations to generate code for component implementations (the last two steps on the left hand side of figure 3.3). Based on the component specifications in the PCM, code is generated which reflects the model. As the PCM's behavioural specification is too abstract to fully generate the component's implementation, the generated artefacts are code skeletons which have to be completed in a subsequent step. As for the software architects in the previous paragraph, it is possible to add mark models to specify mapping options (for the Java EE mapping in this thesis these options are presented in section 4.6.1).

In contrast to the originally published process, the modified process additionally supports executing the transformations which transform the component

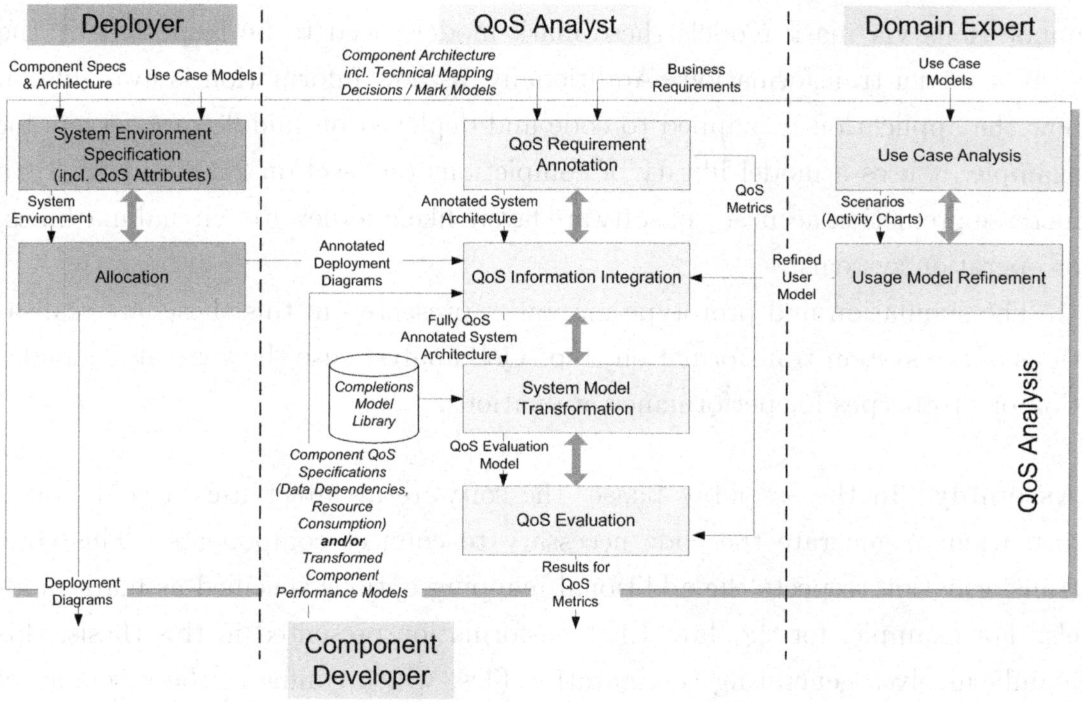

Figure 3.4: MDSD-Refined QoS Analysis Workflow

specifications into their corresponding performance models. In the context of this thesis this means a representation of the component specification as simulation component for SimuCom (see section 4.4) or as performance prototype component for ProtoCom (see section 4.7). This option was added to the workflow to support use cases in which component developers may resist to share their component specifications to preserve their business secrets. In this situation they can distribute the binary code of their components together with the binary code of the simulation and prototype components. However, whether this protection is sufficient can be doubted as the binary code of the prototype or simulation components may be reverse-engineered, but this also applies to the component's binary code itself and is illegal in many countries.

QoS analysis The QoS analysis phase has only been modified slightly as it already included model-transformations in the original version (see figure 3.4, modifications in italics font).

The introduced refinements include additional information on the code mapping, i.e., the mark model instances, of the PCM elements into the prediction process. As component developers and software architects can add mapping annotations via mark models these mark models need to be respected by the system model transformation. Additionally, as now information is available on how the application is mapped to code and deployed on middleware servers for example, it uses a model library of completions (cf. section 2.3.8 and 4.5.3) to increase prediction accuracy of software layers like middleware, virtual machines, or operation systems.

The simulation and prototype mappings presented in this thesis are realisations of the system transformation step. QoS analysts use the generated simulation or prototypes for performance evaluations.

Assembly In the assembly phase, the software architect uses a code transformation to generate the code necessary to connect components. This code transformation respects the additional mapping options specified as mark models. For example, for the Java EE transformation presented in this thesis, this mainly involves generating configuration files, which configure the assembly of the components according the the software architecture and mark model.

Test and Deployment In the test and deployment phases, a transformation for the deployer creates additional helper artefacts like build scripts which pack and deploy the components as specified in the allocation model. A transformation for the domain expert derives functional unit tests and extra-functional load drivers from the usage model.

Implications of the Division of Roles

Matching Artefacts: Transformations executed at different locations by different roles need to make assumptions on the identifiers of the generated artefacts. For example, when mapping PCM components to Java, the name attribute of the component and its repository may be used to generate a full qualified name (FQN) for the component's implementing Java class. However, subsequent transformations have to *know* this mapping rule, i.e., the ID to generate correct references to the components.

The following briefly discusses alternatives to the ID matching problem which do not rely on matching FQNs. Design patterns may serve as source for solutions to the mentioned problem. First, creation patterns of Gamma et al. (1995) and Buschmann et al. (1996) help decoupling the components from their instantiation and implementation. Especially the Broker pattern can help in this setting by providing a central registry for mapping component IDs to component instances. Per repository a Broker could be generated which contains a mapping of the PCM's globally unique component IDs (GUIDs) to instances of the component. The Broker can use a Prototype factory pattern to create the respective implementations based on the ID given. By this, the FQNs of the implementations can be hidden completely inside the repository's implementation as implementation detail. For legacy components, a manual implementation of the Broker is needed which then maps their component IDs on legacy implementations. This solves at least the naming issue by the use of PCM GUIDs, but it still relies on the (common) knowledge that the components have to be retrieved from the Broker. This kind of common knowledge is always needed for distributed automated transformations.

Dependencies: Each transformation has to result in a stand alone artefact, like a JAR file in Java. These files follow the same dependency rules which also hold for the model artefacts in the PCM. Repository models of component developers depend on the repositories containing components and interfaces reused for creating the new components. Accordingly, the code artefact generated by the component developer's transformation depends on the code artefacts generated from the referenced models. The system model depends on an arbitrary number of repositories from with the components are referenced. Accordingly, the generated artefacts for the system implementation depend on the availability of the code artefacts of the component developers. For other artefacts according rules apply.

3.2 PCM Core Concepts

After introducing the PCM's development process, the following sections introduce the PCM's meta-model. The discussion starts with PCM Core meta-classes used multiple times in the PCM. They are entities carrying a globally unique ID (GUIDs), an abstract model for entities which provide and require interfaces, an abstract model to describe entities composed from other entities, a model, called stochastic expressions, to specify random variables, and an explicit model for the context of components.

Globally unique identifier are used to identify components possibly developed independently by component developers in different organizations at different geographical locations. The PCM's technical report provides (further details in Reussner et al. (2007)). Interface providing and requiring interfaces are part of the PCM's role concept described in section 3.4.1. Section 3.4.4 introduces composed structures in the context of composite components.

The following subsections deal with the remaining two core concepts, stochastic expressions and the explicit component context model. Both concepts are important for the understanding the simulation transformation (see section 4.4).

3.2.1 Random Variables and Stochastic Expressions

In the PCM, all developer roles use *random variables* to specify performance properties. Random variables allow them to characterise situations under uncertainty. Highly affected by uncertainty is the domain expert who has to estimate future behaviour of users. The domain expert uses random variables to explicitly capture the uncertainty of the specifications.

In the PCM, random variables allow specifications of either stochastic processes or dependencies between sub-models by using them as variable in one sub-model which gets assigned in a different sub-model. Examples where developers may use random variables are:

- Characterisations of Input Parameters: Describes the performance relevant characteristics of parameters of component services.
- Inter-Arrival Time: Describes how much time passes between the arrival of two subsequent users (in open workload scenarios as introduced in section 3.8.1).
- Think Time: Describes how much time passes between the execution of a user scenario and the start of the next execution of this scenario (in closed workload scenarios as introduced in section 3.8.1).
- Loop Iteration Count: Describes the number of repetitions of a loop.
- Guarded Branch Transitions: Used to determine whether to conditionally execute a certain behaviour.

Mathematically, a random variable is defined as a measurable function X from a probability space to a measurable space. More detailed, a random variable is a function $X : \Omega \rightarrow \mathbb{R}$ with Ω being the set of observable events and $\mathbb{R}$ being the set associated to the measurable space (Trivedi, 2001). Examples for observable events in the context of software models specified in the PCM have been given in the enumeration in the previous paragraph.

A random variable X is usually characterised by stochastical means. Often statistical characterisations, like mean or standard deviation, model a certain system aspect with sufficient accuracy. However, they exist only if the measurable space is of numeric type (like $\mathbb{R}$) and if they exist, they still might not model the reality with sufficient accuracy for decision making. For example, to evaluate service level agreements, often the 90%-percentile of a distribution function is of interest. However, it is only available if more detailed information is available than mean values or standard deviations.

A more detailed description is the probability distribution. A probability distribution yields the probability of X taking a value in a set of possible values. For discrete random variables, it can be specified by a probability mass function (PMF), giving the probabilities for X taking the value t ($P(X = t)$), and for continuous random variables, it can be specified as probability density functions. The event spaces Ω supported by the PCM include integer values $\mathbb{N}$, real values $\mathbb{R}$, boolean values and enumeration types (like "sorted" and "unsorted") for PMFs and real values for PDFs.

PDFs introduce an additional challenge, as probabilities for X to take a certain value are only meaningfully available for ranges of X ($P(X \in [a; b])$). Hence, PDFs either rely on a closed form, which gives a formula for ($P(X \in [a; b])$), or a discretisised approximation. Such an approximation gives the probabilities for a certain selected set of intervals $[a; b]$ without giving details of the distribution of subranges $[d; e] \in [a; b]$. The PCM uses such discretisised approximations and assumes a uniform distribution for the ranges given.

In addition to specifying single random variables, it is often necessary to build new random variables using other *random variables* and *mathematical expressions*. For example, to denote that the response time is 5 times slower, developers would like to simply multiply a random variable for a response time by 5 and assign the result to a new random variable. For this reason, the Stochastic Expressions language supports some basic arithmetic operations (∗,−,+,/,...) for numeric domains as well as logical operations for boolean expressions (==,>,<,`AND`,`OR`,...).

In contrast to related meta-models like UML-SPT, random variables in the PCM are based on an explicit ECORE meta-model for so called Stochastic Expressions. The meta-model has been derived from an EBNF grammar using the Interpreter design pattern (Gamma et al., 1995, p.243). A parser is supplied which accepts words compliant to the EBNF grammar and derives an ECORE model instance compliant to the ECORE meta-model. Stochastic Expressions are available to model transformations in a standardised way. Details of the grammar and the meta-model can be found in the PCM's technical report. Section 4.4.2 gives details on how the presented simulation interprets Stochastic Expressions.

3.2.2 Context Model

The PCM heavily relies on the idea of having an explicit component context model. The context model of a component captures all information relevant for doing functional and extra-functional reasoning on a component which becomes available *after* the component's implementation phase (Becker et al., 2006c). By this, the component context separates component implementation done by the component developer from component assembly, allocation, and usage. Note that the following uses the term context in a narrow sense. For example, it excludes the business context of the component resulting from its requirements. The context as used here focuses on functional and extra-functional analyses of component compositions.

Different deployments of the same component results in different context information. For example, the component can be connected differently or allocated on different execution environments. Having an explicit meta-model for the component context allows a separation of the CBSE developer roles as follows. The component developer creates implementation specifications of components which are parameterised by aspects depending on the component context, e.g., the binding to other components or the allocation to hardware resources. Afterwards, the remaining developer roles contribute their context-dependent information. This information determines the value of the parameters in the component developer's implementation specification finally resulting in a complete specification of the component *in its context*. Hence, all model transformations based on the PCM have to deal with the context model and combine the parameterised component specification and its context into a *context-specific* component specification.

Currently, the PCM's context model uses two dimensions to distinguish context information. The first separates the information according to the developer role that is able to specify the information. The second differentiates context information which has to be specified manually by a developer and context information which analysis methods can derive automatically. The PCM's meta-model contains *only* meta-classes for context information that has to be specified manually. An explicit model for the computed context information is not part of the PCM as it may depend on the analysis method. Koziolek (2008) gives a meta-model for the computed context used in his transformations. The simulation in this thesis uses no explicit derived context model but encodes it directly in the simulation's state (see section 4.4.8 for details).

To give an overview on the context model of a component, table 3.1 lists the sub-contexts and their classification. The upper row of table 3.1 highlights the parts of the component context which need manual specification, the lower row gives those properties which can be derived from the specified information.

The following discusses the entries of table 3.1 in detail. As the context idea is a general principle, it does not depend on an actual realisation. The way it is currently implemented in the PCM's meta-model is only one alternative which will be extended in future work. However, to ease understanding, references are given which point to the PCM's meta-model realisation where available.

Assembly Context The upper left field shows attributes of the specified *assembly context.* A component's position in an assembly of components is determined by (a) its parents composite structure it is part of, e.g., a system or a composite component, and (b) the connectors attached to its required interfaces (for the implementation of the assembly context in the PCM's meta-model see section 3.4.4). As an example for different connectors, figure 3.5 shows two instances of the component `SyncCache` each of them using a different component to provide their service.

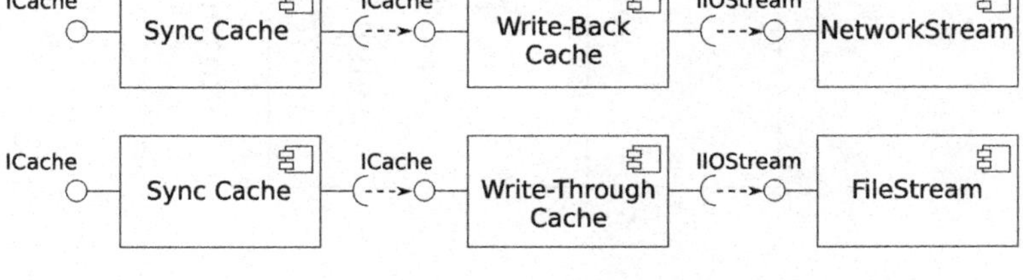

Figure 3.5: The same Component in different Assembly Contexts (Becker et al., 2006c)

	Assembly Context	**Allocation Context**	**Usage Context**
Manual specification necessary	Connection, Containment	Allocation, Environment config: - Concurrency, security, ... - Container properties - Component configuration	System usage: - Call probability - Call parameter - Workload
Automatic computation possible	*Functional* Parametric Contracts	*Extra-Functional* Allocation dependent QoS-Characteristics	Inner Usages

Table 3.1: The PCM's Context Model (based on Becker et al. (2006c))

Based on the specified assembly context, Parametric Contracts introduced by Reussner (2001) allow to derive which services of the provided interfaces of a component are available depending on the connected required interfaces.

In the context of this thesis, connectors available in the assembly contexts are transformed into technical realisations like RPC calls. They realise calls to required component services at run-time. Generated components have to provide means to establish such connections after their implementation phase as specified in the assembly context by the software architect.

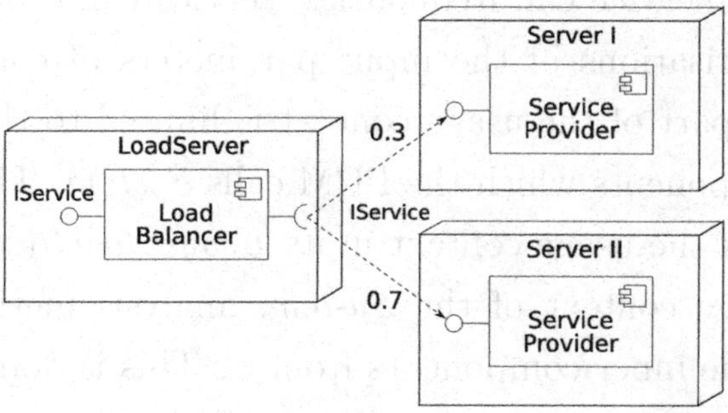

Figure 3.6: The same Component in different Allocation Contexts (Becker et al., 2006c)

Allocation Context The specified allocation context (upper row, center column of table 3.1) contains information on the allocation of a component onto a soft- and hardware environment (see section 3.7.2 for the realisation of the allocation context in the PCM). The software environment may contain all layers of software hosting a component, like middleware servers, virtual machines, or operating systems. Additionally, it may contain the configuration options of these layers. Support for software layers is still very limited in the PCM. Future work can use the allocation context to store information on software layers hosting a component.

In addition to the executing software layers, the allocation context stores a reference to the hardware environment which executes a component. The hardware environment contains information on the physical hardware like CPU, harddisks, memory, etc. Figure 3.6 depicts a component in different (hardware) allocation context.

Using the information given in the allocation context, analysis methods can derive execution-environment dependent quality attributes from their respective independent specifications. For example, the simulation presented in this thesis uses the allocation context to determine which simulated resource processes a demand issued by a component and how long it takes on the given hardware platform to process the demand. Additionally, it uses the information in the hardware environment to configure its queuing network's service centres.

Usage Context The usage context of a component (right column of table 3.1) gives information on how a component is used via its provided interfaces. The information contain service call frequencies, service call order and probabilities, as well as characterisations of the input parameters of component calls. The manually specified part of the usage context is limited to the outermost part of an assembly of components which the PCM calls *System*. The PCM implements the specified part of the usage context in its *UsageModel* (see section 3.8).

Having the usage context of the *System*, analysis methods can derive the usage contexts of the inner components from it. This is done by evaluating how components transform their own usage context into usage contexts of components connected to their required interfaces.

To give an example for a different usage context, consider figure 3.6 again. Let the numbers 0.3 and 0.7 attached to the assembly connectors denote the probability of routing a call to the component in server 1 or in server 2 respectively. Then the usage context of the component allocated on server 2 contains a higher call frequency to its services than the component allocated on server 1.

In this thesis, transformations use the specified usage context to generate workload drivers from it. They simulate the behaviour of users, the request frequency caused by them, or characterisations of the data they pass to the system.

Section 4.4.8 gives details on the different types of contexts in the simulation based analysis method SimuCom introduced in this thesis.

3.3 Interfaces and Datatypes

Interfaces are the means which components use to offer services and on the other hand require services from other components. As such, they serve as software contracts for the components stating what can be expected from an interface implementer or what is needed by an entity requiring a certain interface. Common categories for information available in interfaces are technical and syntactical information (like the supported technology platform and signature lists), protocol information and semantic information (pre- and post-conditions, informal/descriptive semantics). The PCM currently covers the syntactic information of the signature lists and can be extended to also support protocols which is disregarded in this thesis. Interfaces also play a central role in code transformations as they form the technological basis for component interaction. As such, they are often explicitly required by middleware platforms to deploy components.

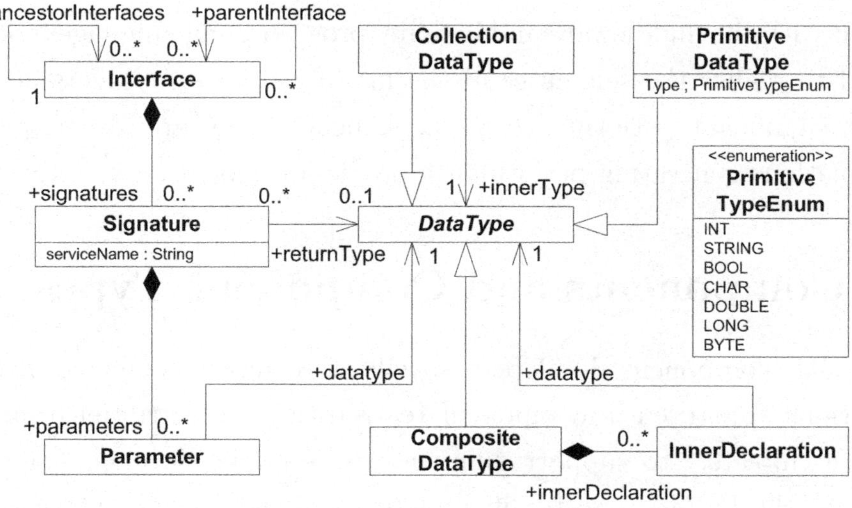

Figure 3.7: *Interfaces* and *DataTypes*

In order to specify *Interfaces*, the PCM also introduces *Datatypes* (see figure 3.7). *Datatypes* are used to express the data needed by services. The PCM supports different types of *Datatypes*: *PrimitiveDatatypes*, *CollectionDatatypes*, and *CompositeDatatypes*. *PrimitiveTypes* cover the basic types available in most programming languages like integer, string, real, byte, etc. *CollectionDatatypes* represent collections like arrays, sets, lists, etc. They specify the type of the collection's elements as inner type. *CompositeDatatypes* represent types which consist of a set of other elements. They are defined as value datatypes, i.e., by default their content is copied in case of using the type in a method call and the copy is used in the called service. Types which support inner methods like classes and reference datatypes are not yet supported as they significantly increase the complexity when doing performance predictions. Code transformations use the datatype specifications to generate programming language interfaces, database schemas, or persistency configurations for object-relational mappers.

Interfaces in the PCM describe the syntactical details of their services by the means of *Signatures*. A *Signature* consists of a return type, a service name, an ordered list of *Parameters* and an unordered list of *Exceptions*. Each *Parameter* carries a modifier which states whether the modifications done to the values of the passed variable are visible when the call returns. Based on IDL, the available modifiers are IN, OUT, and INOUT. If no explicit modifier is set, IN is used as default. Interfaces, parameters and modifier deserve special interest in code transformations. Interfaces often need to follow certain standards in order to be compliant with the middleware and in many programming languages special code is needed to realise the semantics of the modifiers. The modifiers additionally can have significant performance impacts, hence, they are also important for transformations generating performance prediction models.

3.4 Components and Component Types

In the PCM, component developers specify and implement components. The specifications are stored in component repositories and retrieved from there by software architects. To support different stages in the development cycle of a component, the PCM supports different types of components which have to be treated differently in model transformations.

The types are based on the semantics of provided and required roles in the PCM. Hence, a brief overview introduces the roles and their semantics in order to introduce the component types afterwards. The PCM's technical report (Reussner et al., 2007) contains additional details on the component types.

3.4.1 Provided and Required Roles

According to the definition of a component (cf. section 2.1), its functionality and its communication with its environment is specified by the means of its provided and required interfaces. As interfaces exist independently of components in the PCM (Reussner et al., 2007), their relationship to components is given by the concept of roles. Roles associate interfaces to components and exist in two types: provided roles and required roles. A provided role specifies that a component offers a certain interface, a required role specifies that a component requests a certain (implementation of an) interface from its environment.

A provided role in the PCM indicates that the component is potentially able to offer all services defined in the interface referenced by the role. This corresponds to the common understanding of an implemented interface in object-oriented programming languages like Java. However, for the component to actually offer all its services, it is necessary that all required roles are bound to other components. A weaker definition of provided roles is given by Reussner's parametric contracts (Reussner, 2001) which is potentially supported by the PCM but outside the scope of this thesis.

In the PCM, a required role indicates that during the execution of a provided component service, the component eventually may issue a call to a service listed in the interface referenced by the required role. Transformations have to map required roles such that they can be initialised after the component's implementation phase depending on the *AssemblyContext* specified by the software architect. Whether a component is restricted to only use the set of services available in its required roles depends on the component type as introduced in the next section.

3.4.2 PCM Component Types

The PCM uses different component types to characterise components in different stages of their design (see figure 3.8).

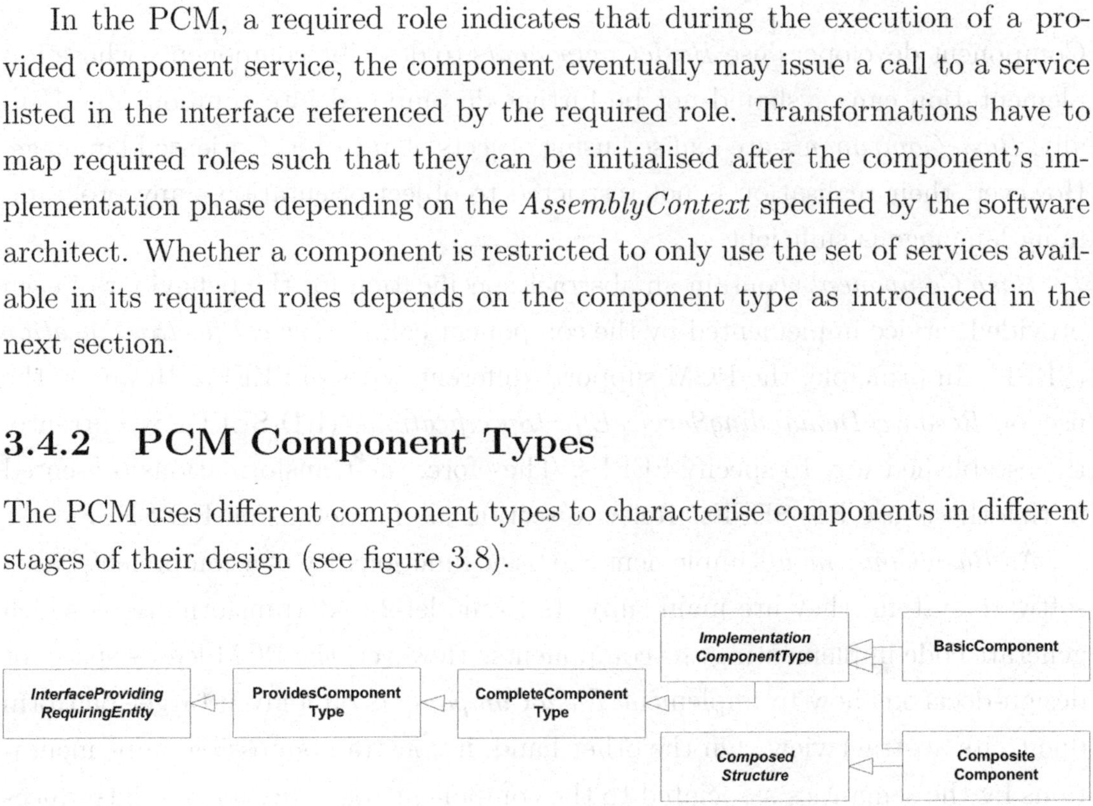

Figure 3.8: Component Types in the PCM (Reussner et al., 2007)

Depending on the semantics of the required roles, two types are differentiated. *ProvidesComponentTypes* may use the specified required roles and additionally introduce further required roles, i.e., for *ProvidedComponentTypes* required roles are not mandatory. As such, they serve as early specification of the services expected from a component. Software architects can use them to specify the functionality which component developers need to implement.

After refining *ProvidedComponentTypes* in the development process, the set of required roles becomes mandatory eventually, i.e., the component must not use services not declared in any of its required roles. Such a component is called a *CompleteComponentType*.

ImplementationComponentTypes finally add an abstract specification of the component's implementation. *ImplementationComponentTypes* exist in two variants: *BasicComponents* and *CompositeComponents*. Both types are detailed in the following sections.

3.4.3 Basic Components

Component developers use *BasicComponents* to describe components whose implementation can or should not be further decomposed into components. Usually, *BasicComponents* are realised using objects of any object-oriented language. However, their realisation is not restricted to object-orientation - any programming language is sufficient.

BasicComponents contain an abstract specification for the behaviour of each provided service implemented by the component called *ServiceEffectSpecification* (SEFF). In principle, the PCM supports different types of SEFFs. However, the use of *ResourceDemandingServiceEffectSpecifications* (RD-SEFF) is currently the established way to specify SEFFs. Therefore, the transformations presented in this thesis use RD-SEFFs. Refer to section 3.5 for details on RD-SEFFs.

As *BasicComponents* implement the basic functionality of a component-based software system, they are main subjects to model-2-text transformations which generate code implementing the components. However, the PCM leaves space for design-decisions how to implement *BasicComponents* on a given target platform due to its abstract view. On the other hand, it constraints possible implementations by the semantics associated to the component roles. Section 4.6 introduces a mapping to Java EE which makes the involved design decisions explicit.

3.4.4 Composite Components

CompositeComponents are the second type of *ImplementationComponentType*. A *CompositeComponent* combines the functionality of other components (its *inner* or *child components*) to offer its own functionality. As such, its implementation is solely done by composing existing components.

CompositeComponents are specialisations of the more general concept of a *ComposedStructure* which describes an entity built by composing components abstractly (see figure 3.9). A *ComposedStructure* consists of connectors and

AssemblyContexts. The latter correspond to the specified assembly context introduced in section 3.2.2. *AssemblyContexts* uniquely specify the use of a component in an assembly of components, i.e., its connections to other components and its parent *ComposedStructure*. The link *encapsulatedComponent* points to the component used in the *AssemblyContext*.

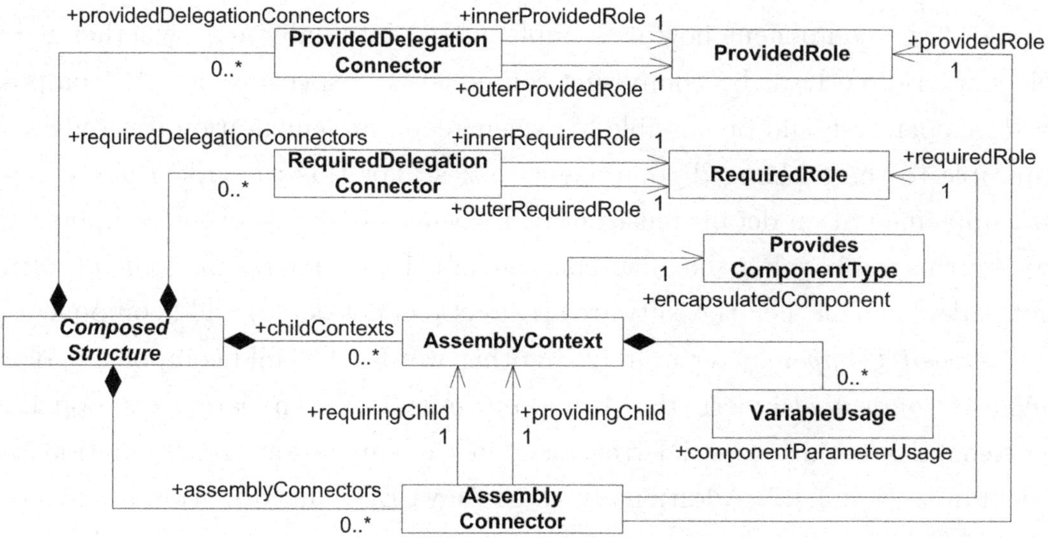

Figure 3.9: The meta-model of a ComposedStructure

There are three different types of connectors in a *ComposedStructure*: *ProvidedDelegationConnectors*, *RequiredDelegationConnectors*, and *AssemblyConnectors*. *ProvidedDelegationConnectors* connect the roles of the *ComposedStructure* itself to roles of child components. Any request for service to the role of the *ComposedStructure* is routed to the inner component which actually serves the request. As a consequence, *ComposedStructures* are only logical containers for other components. They do not provide additional functionality on their own. *RequiredDelegationConnectors* delegate calls to a required role of an inner component to a required role of the *ComposedStructure*.

Finally, *AssemblyConnectors* connect the child components allowing interaction among them. For this, a required role is connected to a compatible provided role, i.e., the interface of the provided role has to be a sub-type of the required interface. Whenever the requiring component issues an external call, the call is delivered to the providing component connected to the *AssemblyConnector*.

The preceding description of the connectors omitted the role of the *AssemblyContext*. As there can be multiple uses of the *same* component in different

AssemblyContexts, connectors also need to specify the *AssemblyContext* of the components they connect. As they connect the roles of the components, connectors are said to connect *roles in contexts.*

Coming back to *CompositeComponents*, an additional constraint compared to arbitrary *ComposedStructures* exists. A *CompositeComponent* serves as alternative to implementing a *BasicComponent.* However, it should be hidden from the user of the component how it is implemented internally, e.g., whether it is implemented directly or by composing components. Especially, for the component developer it should be possible to exchange an implementation if it remains compatible to the exchanged component's roles. For this to work, the component's implementation details must not be relevant for the use of the component. However, this implies that the inner components of a *CompositeComponent* form a unit of deployment, i.e., the software architect can not deploy child components of a *CompositeComponent* separately. In other words, the child components of a *CompositeComponent* inherit the *AllocationContext* of their parent component. This semantics requires special treatment in the simulation transformation as detailed in section 4.4.7. Additionally, in the Java EE transformation it leads to several issues discussed in section 4.6.1.

3.5 Resource Demanding SEFF

As already introduced in section 3.4.3, the *ResourceDemandingSEFF* (RD-SEFF) is currently used to model the inner behaviour of component services of *BasicComponents* (see figure 3.10). For this, RD-SEFFs follow abstraction rules.

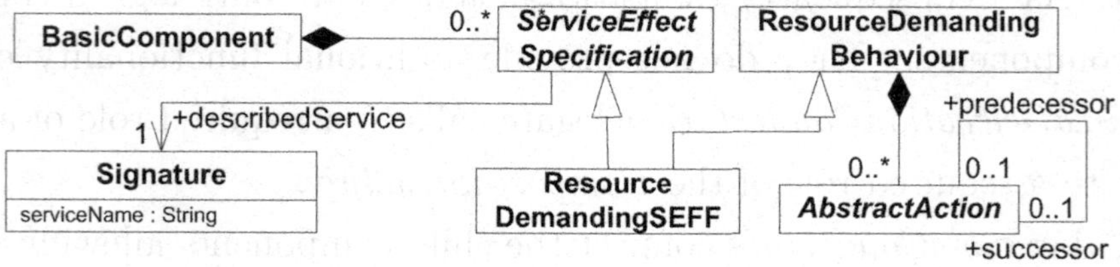

Figure 3.10: The RD-SEFF and its Relationship to *BasicComponents* (Becker et al., 2007)

First, they reduce the behaviour of a component to its interaction with its context. The context consists of external components connected to *RequiredRoles* and the component's run-time environment which executes the component's internal computations and provides basic services like middleware or operating system services. The latter interaction is specified using *InternalActions* in the PCM (cf. section 3.5.5). Additionally, the component's control flow constructs are part of the behavioural model if they have an impact on the component's context interaction.

Second, the data flow and its impact on the control flow is captured using abstractions of service parameters as introduced by Koziolek et al. (2006). Parameters are characterised using performance relevant abstractions of their values or, if no such abstraction exists, by dividing the possible parameter values into partitions resulting in similar performance and giving a probability for each partition. The abstraction of parameters is limited to those passed to a component in interactions with its context, e.g., input parameter of a component service or results of external service calls (there are some exceptions to this basic rule introduced later). Further details including examples of variable characterisations are given in section 3.5.1.

The following sections introduce the concepts of the RD-SEFF. Sections 3.5.1 to 3.5.3 describe external calls and the handling of input and output parameters. Section 3.5.4 highlights the special role of characterisations of inner elements of *CollectionDatatypes*. Section 3.5.5 introduces *InternalActions* used to model component internal computations. *ParametricResourceDemands* specify the resource demands caused by these computations as introduced in section 3.5.6. Section 3.5.7 provides means to model software locks. Finally, section 3.5.8 introduces the control flow elements available in the PCM.

3.5.1 External Calls

Interaction among components is specified using *ExternalCallActions*. An *ExternalCallAction* models a synchronous, blocking call to a service in the interface of the specified required role. Note, that the component developer only specifies the *RequiredRole* and not the component, which should be called. This ensures that the software architect can specify the bound component later.

To model the data flow, i.e., the data passed to an *ExternalCall* and returned from it, the PCM uses parameter characterisations as described in the next section.

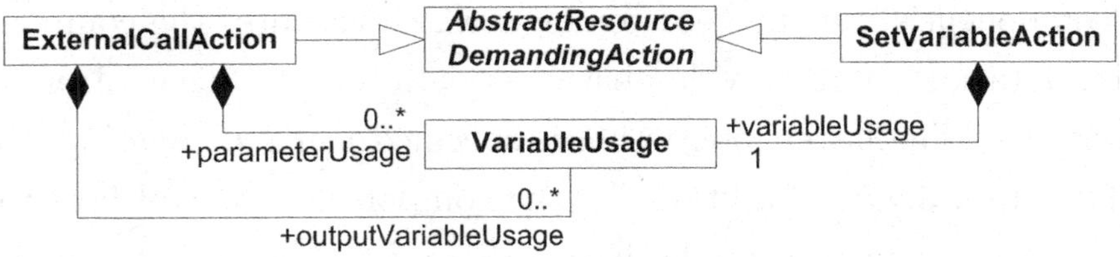

Figure 3.11: *ExternalCallAction* and passing of Parameter Characterisations (Becker et al., 2007)

3.5.2 Service Parameters

A service's parameters may have significant impact on its resource demand. For example, the resource demand of a sorting service offered by a component depends on the size of the collection to sort. Thus, parameters have an impact on *ParametricResourceDemands* (cf. section 3.5.6). Additionally, the control flow of a service may depend on parameters as introduced in section 3.5.8.

As introduced in section 3.3, a service signature has n input parameters and m output parameters. To capture their performance impact, component developers can attach specification on these parameters. For this, they use so called *VariableUsages* in *ExternalCallActions*. The PCM's meta-model supports a set of input *VariableUsages* and a set of output *VariableUsages* for *ExternalCalls*. The parameter characterisations introduced in the following are part of the usage context (cf. section 3.2.2) and have been introduced by Koziolek et al. (2006) for UML-SPT and included into the PCM's meta-model by Becker et al. (2007).

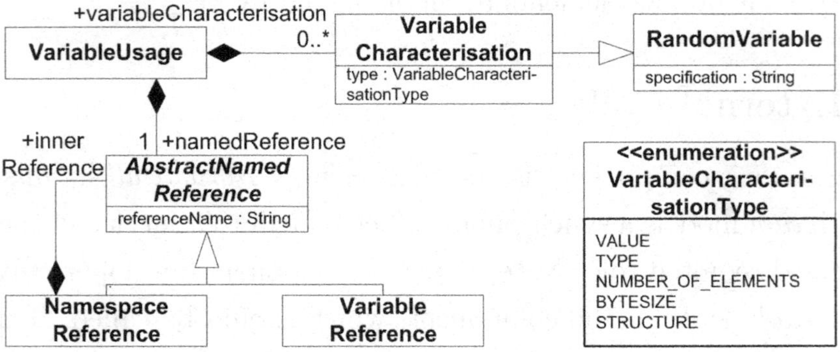

Figure 3.12: *VariableUsages* and Characterisations (Becker et al., 2007)

For accurate predictions all concrete values of all parameters should be available ideally. However, it is often infeasible to fully specify them - for specification as well as for analysis reasons. The resulting state space is simply to large to analyse. Additionally, it is often unnecessary for performance predicitions. In the sorting example, it is sufficient to know how many array elements should be sorted - the value of each element to sort does not matter performance-wise.

To deal with this, Koziolek et al. (2006) introduced five abstractions of parameters which allow to specify the performance critical information of parameters (see figure 3.12). All of them are represented by random variables in the PCM:

1. **VALUE**: This random variable contains the actual value of the parameter and should be used only in cases where no other characterisation is sufficient to capture the performance relevant aspect of the parameter. The type of the random variable is the same as the parameter's type. As a consequence, this characterisation is only available for primitive data type, like integer, string, etc.

2. **STRUCTURE**: STRUCTURE random variables specify a certain characteristic of the data's format. For example, for arrays an important information could be whether the array is sorted or unsorted, for a tree it might be whether the tree is balanced or not. Whether a certain structure of a parameter has an impact on the performance of a component service highly depends on the algorithms used to implement the service. Taking the sorting example again, for Quicksort it makes a difference whether the array is already sorted or not while for Heapsort it makes little difference. The type of the STRUCTURE random variable is an enumeration defined by the component developer.

3. **TYPE**: The TYPE random variable specifies information about a parameter in cases where the parameter can be used in a polymorphic manner and where the performance depends on its *actual* type. The type of the TYPE random variable is an enumeration containing all possible subtypes of the parameter's type.

4. **BYTESIZE**: The BYTESIZE random variable is used to describe the memory footprint of a parameter. It can be used whenever the amount of data processed makes a difference performance-wise. For example, analysis tools based on the PCM should use available BYTESIZE characterisations to determine network loads (see section 4.6.3 for the realisation in the simulation presented in this thesis). The type of the BYTESIZE random variable is Integer.

5. **NUMBER_OF_ELEMENTS**: The NUMBER_OF_ELEMENTS random variable is only applicable to parameters whose type is a *CollectionDataType*. For those parameters, it describes the element count of the elements in the collection. This type of characterisation is useful whenever a service iterates over a given set of elements and the performance depends on the iteration count. The type of the NUMBER_OF_ELEMENTS random variable is Integer.

Using these parameter abstractions, it is possible to characterise service parameters in the PCM using input *VariableUsages*. For example, to characterise the number of elements in a collection passed to a sorting service, the following can be specified

$$\texttt{fieldToSort.NUMBER\_OF\_ELEMENTS} = \texttt{IntPMF}[(10; 0.5)(20; 0.5)]$$

In this case `fieldToSort` must be the name of the formal parameter in the sorting service's signature used to pass the collection to the service. The actual number is specified as random variable (using the stochastic expressions language). In the example, it has the value 10 in 50% of all cases and 20 in all other cases. Any input parameter having an `IN` or `INOUT` modifier can be characterised in this way.

Output parameters (having modifiers OUT or INOUT) and the return value of a service can be characterised using output *VariableUsages*. An output variable usage takes the result values or performance relevant characterisations of them and maps them to random variables in the calling SEFF. For this, the output *VariableUsages* create new local random variables and assign those variables the returned values. In case of mapping return or OUT parameter abstractions, the output *VariableUsages* introduce new random variables which have to be disjoint from those already existing in the calling SEFF. In case of parameters having `INOUT` modifiers the output mapping is restricted to characterisations of the variable actually passed to the call as INOUT parameter. For example, when calling a service with the signature `void m(INOUT a)` binding `a` in the calling statement to `b`, i.e, `m(b)`, the output mapping can only characterise abstractions of `b`. If the respective abstraction of `b` already exist, they are overwritten. Due to this restriction, the output mappings for INOUT parameters result automatically from the model. Analysis transformations should derive the respective mappings automatically, thus, lowering the specification effort.

For example, if the `fieldToSort` in the previous sorting example is an `INOUT` parameter, the following output *VariableUsage* specification is derived automatically:

$$\texttt{field.STRUCTURE} = \texttt{fieldToSort.STRUCTURE}$$

where the sorting service guarantees that `fieldToSort.STRUCTURE = "Sorted"` to specify that it returns the field sorted. The next section explains how result characterisations and output parameter characterisations are bound to values in the called service.

3.5.3 SetVariableAction

The RD-SEFF supports returning characterisations of the output parameters to the calling RD-SEFF. For this, performance characterisations of return, INOUT and OUT parameters can be set in coresponding RD-SEFF. In order to specify the characterisations returned to the calling RD-SEFF, the PCM contains the so called *SetVariableAction*. This action assigns the results of stochastic expressions to random variables representing the return, INOUT and OUT parameters. Note, in analogy to the policy for input parameters, only characterisations relevant for the performance should be set.

However, the random variables characterising the output parameters are not available in subsequent actions of the SEFF in which the *SetVariableAction* appears. They can solely be used in output *VariableUsages* of *ExternalCallActions* calling the service in which the *SetVariableAction* is used. This is a restriction which reduces the possible complexity of the resulting performance prediction model. Nevertheless, a characterisation may be set multiple times in different *SetVariableActions* in a RDSEFF. In this case, the last *SetVariableAction* determines the returned value.

For example, the sorting service used as example in the previous sections, contains a *SetVariableAction* which assigns the value `"Sorted"` to the `fieldToSort.STRUCTURE` random variable.

3.5.4 Inner Elements of Collections

For parameters having a collection data type the special keyword `INNER` exists, which allows to characterise the inner elements of collections. For example,

$$\texttt{fieldToSort.INNER.BYTESIZE} = \texttt{UniInt}(1000, 2000)$$

specifies the memory footprint in bytes of each element in the collection to be uniformly distributed in a range between 1000 and 2000 bytes.

`INNER` characterisations *do not describe specific single elements* of a collection, i.e., it is not possible to specify the first element, then the second, and so forth. Additionally, it is assumed that every time when the characterisation of a collection's inner element is used, it refers to a *different* inner element. In the simulation mapping this means that a different sample of the random variable is returned every time the variable is accessed (for details see 4.4.2). Mathematically this means, each use of an `INNER` characterisation has to be stochastically independent of its former uses. This may lead to specifications which do not reflect reality correctly. For example, for a service which processes a specific element of a collection and returns the processed element the characterisations would not be independent in reality and the assumption would be violated. For special cases, like processing collections in a loop, special constructs are available in the PCM to get more realistic specifications (see section 3.5.8 for details). However, the amount of states of the resulting Markov chain underlying the simulation model grows when using a dependent specification in contrast to an independent model (cf. section 4.4).

For further details on the semantics and the realisation of `INNER` characterisations in SimuCom see section 4.4.2.

3.5.5 InternalActions

InternalActions abstract from computations done by a component internally, i.e., without interacting with other components. However, during a computation a component utilises hardware resources. An example for a calculation, whose execution time depends on the input parameters, is the afore mentioned sorting algorithm. Depending on the chosen algorithm and the number of collection elements, the component needs different CPU processing power from the hardware environment on which the component is allocated.

An *InternalAction* uses *ParametricResourceDemands* to specify resource demands to hardware resources (see figure 3.13). The list of *ParametricResourceDemands* is ordered, the specified demands are issued sequentially to their respective hardware resource types (see section 3.5.6 for details).

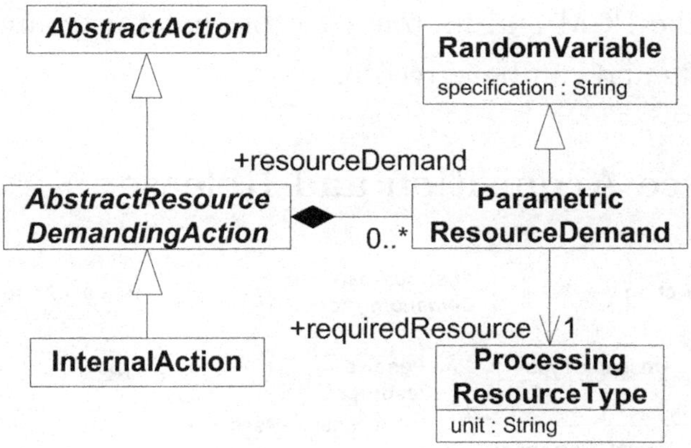

Figure 3.13: *InternalActions* and their *ParametricResourceDemand*

3.5.6 Parametric Resource Demands

Component developers specify the resources on which the *ParametricResourceDemand* should be executed in an abstract way. They use a common repository, the *ResourceTypeRepository*, which contains so called *ProcessingResourceTypes*. *ProcessingResourceTypes* include resources which process jobs actively until the job is fully processed. Examples for these are CPUs, disks, etc. The component developer only specifies that a CPU resource type is needed, however, he does not specify which CPU will be used finally. The indirection of the *ProcessingResourceType* separates the hardware model from the behaviour specification of the software model resulting in a software model parameterised for different execution environments.

Additionally, for each *ParametricResourceDemand* the component developer specifies the actual demand as a stochastic expression. This expression is the defining formulae of the resource demand's random variable. It may depend on other random variables like characterisations of the input parameters (cf. section 3.5.1). For example, a component developer uses the specification `fieldToSort.NUMBER_OF_ELEMENTS ^ 2` to characterise the CPU demand of a sorting algorithm of complexity class $O(n^2)$.

However, the component developer has to ensure that the resulting demand's unit is compatible with the resource types' specification. This is crucial to ensure interoperability between the component developer and the deployer. For example, if the component developer and the deployer agree on specifying CPUs demands in CPU instructions, both have to stick to this type or provide at least a conversion function from their unit to the commonly agreed on unit. It remains an assumption of the PCM and its role concept that this common unit for the resource types exists and can be agreed on.

3.5.7 Resource Acquisition and Release

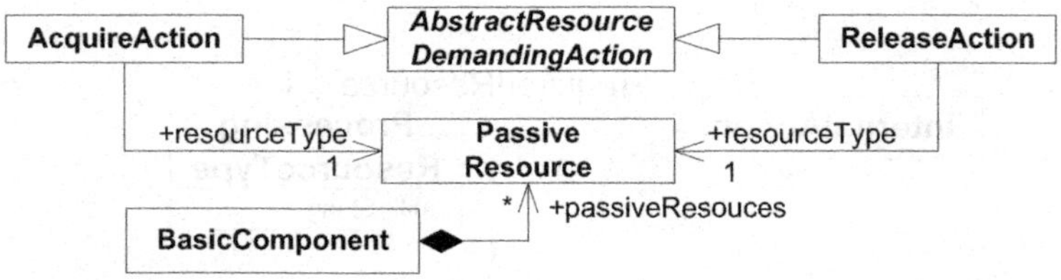

Figure 3.14: Resource Acquisition and Release (Becker et al., 2007)

Another type of actions dealing with resources are those which model the acquisition and release of software locks (see figure 3.14). A software lock in the PCM models a semaphore (Tanenbaum, 2001) as it is commonly used in operation system construction. A semaphore is used to protect a certain resource which exists in a limited number $n = N_{MAX}$. Any time a resource is acquired, n is reduced by one, every time a resource is released again, it is incremented by one. By this, n reflects the amount of resources left. If n drops below zero, any process or thread trying to acquire the resource is blocked until the resource becomes available again. The order in which a released resource is distributed among waiting processes is assumed to be FIFO in the current PCM version.

The PCM has *AcquireActions* and *ReleaseActions* to reflect resource acquisition and release respectively. Both action refer to a so called *PassiveResource* which specifies the type of the limited resource, i.e., threads in a thread pool, database connections, etc. *BasicComponents* declare all *PassiveResources* they use (see figure 3.14). *Aquire-* and *ReleaseActions* can only use *PassiveResources* of the *BasicComponent* they belong to.

3.5.8 Control Flow

The RD-SEFF contains concepts to model the control flow of the service's execution. However, these constructs should only be used *if they have an impact on the interaction of the component and its context*. This is the same requirement already introduced in the discussion of parameter characterisations. If it has no impact on the interaction with the context, the control flow is hidden in the implementation of the component's service and abstracted by *InternalActions*.

The design of the control flow constructs is intentionally different from those in UML activity charts even if the basic ideas are comparable. However, in contrast to UML activity charts, the RD-SEFFs control flow constructs use a similar representation as the abstract syntax trees of structured programming languages like Java. For example, a loop is not modelled by a control flow reference pointing at an action already executed earlier. It is modelled by a loop action which explicitly contains a sequence of actions representing the loop body. After repeating the inner behaviour n-times, the course of actions continues at the successor of the loop action. The same is true for branch actions, forks, etc.

The rationale behind this kind of modelling is the avoidance of ambiguities which can arise when analysing models with control flows models based on arbitrary graphs like UML activity diagrams. Additionally, making nested behaviours explicit eases the handling of model instances in both types of model transformations - transformation into analysis models as well as transformations into implementations. The reason for this is that there is no need for the transformations to figure out the start and end of inner behaviours. Additionally, performance annotations like iteration counts can annotate directly the corresponding control flow actions. As a consequence of the explicit modelling of nested behaviours, each behaviour is a chain of actions going directly from the (only) start action to the (only) stop action.

An overview of the available control flow concepts is given in figure 3.15.

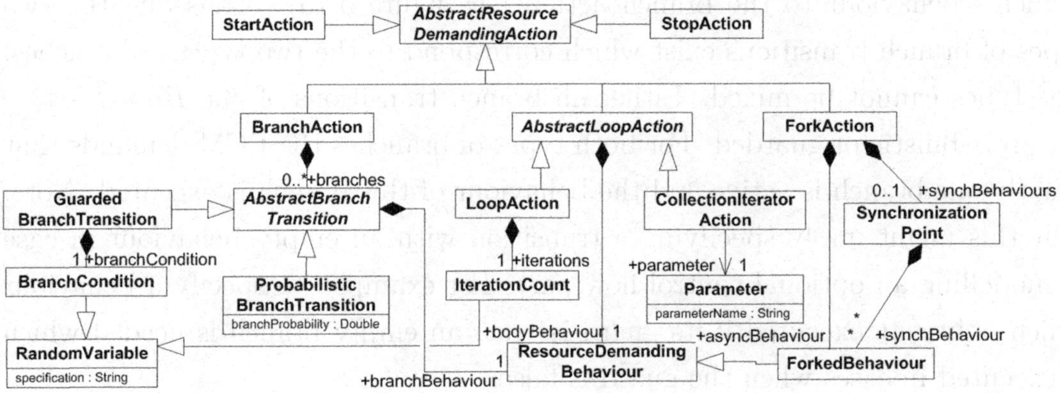

Figure 3.15: Control Flow concepts in the PCM (Becker et al., 2007)

Loops The PCM supports two types of loop actions: *LoopActions* and *CollectionIteratorActions*. *LoopActions* as introduced by Koziolek and Firus (2006) repeat their loop body for the given amount of loop iterations. The number of iterations is determined by a stochastic expression of type Integer. As a requirement, the PCM assumes all loops to be bounded. Hence, modelling infinite loops is unsupported. To model the number of loop repetitions, a stochastic expression defines the iteration count as random variable. Component developers specify a probability for each iteration count up to a maximum count N, e.g., mathematically $P(\texttt{iteration\_count} = n) = p_i$ with $P(\texttt{iteration\_count} = n) = 0$ for all $n > N$.

CollectionIteratorActions repeat their inner behaviour for every element of a parameter of *CollectionDatatype*. As a consequence, *CollectionIteratorActions* execute the loop body for each element in the collection, i.e., `NUMBER_OF_ELEMENTS` times. Additionally, all *INNER* characterisations of the iterated parameter stay constant during the evaluation of all actions of the loop body. This allows the specification of stochastical dependent actions. For example, a component compresses a set of files and stores the result in a database. As the size of each stored file depends on the size of the uncompressed file, a *CollectionIteratorAction* keeps this size constant, i.e., it does not re-evaluate the corresponding `INNER` characterisation on every access.

Alternatives The PCM offers two types of branch actions to specify alternatives in the control flow of a component's service: *ProbabilisticBranch*es and *GuardedBranch*es. The PCM uses so called *BranchTransitions* to associate the branch's behaviour to the branch action (see figure 3.15). Consequently, two types of branch transitions exist which correspond to the two types of branches. The types cannot be mixed. Either all branch transitions of one *BranchAction* are probabilistic or guarded. For both types of branches the PCM demands that exactly one branch is active and the behaviour of this branch is executed. Note, that this might imply specifying a transition with an empty behaviour in case of modelling an optional control flow part. For example, to specify a behaviour which only gets executed if its guard is true, an empty branch is needed which is executed in cases when the guard is false.

ProbabilisticBranchTransitions model behaviour which is random in its nature or which cannot be specified more precisely by capturing its data dependencies. For each *ProbabilisticBranchTransition* a probability is given for executing the behaviour of that transition. The probabilities of all branch transitions have to sum up to 1 as a result of the requirement that exactly one transition has to be taken.

GuardedBranchTransitions use random variables of boolean type to specify which transition executes. Each transition contains a random variable called its guard condition. However, the guard condition can dependent on other random variables from whose its own distribution can be derived. In order to ensure that exactly one branch condition evaluates to `true`, all branch conditions are evaluated using the same values for the involved random variables, i.e., the conditions are evaluated stochastically dependent. From this requirement, it follows that it is disallowed to use INNER characterisations in branch conditions as they are always evaluated independently.

For guarded branch transitions an additional constraint results for the analysis of their inner behaviour. As the guard condition has evaluated to true, it is known that the condition is true while evaluating its inner behaviour. Hence, the analysis of the inner behaviour is done under the stochastic condition that the random variable of the branch's guard condition is true. For example, the guard condition

$$\texttt{files.BYTESIZE} > 200$$

defines a restriction on the `files.BYTESIZE` random variable. Hence, in the inner behaviour of the corresponding branch transition, all random variables depending on `files.BYTESIZE` have to be evaluated conditionally with the condition $\texttt{files.BYTESIZE} > 200$:

$$P(f(\texttt{files.BYTESIZE}) = X | \texttt{files.BYTESIZE} > 200)$$

with $f(\texttt{files.BYTESIZE})$ being the definition formulae of a random variable depending on the random variable `files.BYTESIZE`. Bayes' law applies (Sachs, 1997, p. 78) for evaluating the resulting formulae. However, in simulation runs, it is much easier to ensure the respective semantics (see section 4.4 for details on the simulation's semantics).

Forks In the PCM *ForkActions* are used to split the control flow into sub control flows. Each control flow then executes its inner behaviour independent of the other forked behaviours. However, if they use the same resources while processing their behaviour, concurrent resource usage leads to resource conflicts which might have significant performance impacts. Each behaviour starts with a copy of the forking behaviour's variable characterisations. The *ForkAction*, which started the *ForkedBehaviours*, waits for the subset of synchronous *ForkBehaviours* to finish their execution before it continuous its own control. Synchronous fork behaviours are attached to the *ForkAction*'s *SyncronizationPoint*. Asynchronous fork behaviours which are not attached to the *SynchronizationPoint* execute until they reach their own stop action - independent of the *ForkAction* which initiated their execution.

For *ForkedBehaviours* attached to the *SynchronizationPoint*, it will be possible to return results of their computations to the initiating *ForkAction* in future versions of the PCM. Happe (2008) currently defines the necessary meta-model changes.

3.5.9 Concluding remarks

Using the introduced concepts, RD-SEFFs allows to specify the behaviour of a component service in an abstract way. The abstraction is directed towards the interaction of the component with its context. It allows using a component in different contexts while still being able to predict the performance properties of the component. The parameterisation on the context respects the assembly, allocation and usage context (cf. section 3.2.2).

3.6 Systems

The system model is the domain specific language of software architects in the PCM. In a *System*, components are composed into a fully functional application, ready to be deployed and used. The system model corresponds to the classical view of a software architecture as described by the components and connectors viewpoint introduced by Clements et al. (2003). Like *CompositeComponents*, *Systems* inherit from *ComposedStructure* in the PCM (cf. section 3.4.4). As such, they can contain inner components embedded in assembly contexts and may have provided or required roles.

Systems contain a set of *AssemblyContexts* for inner components, a set of provided and required delegation connectors each and a set of assembly connectors connecting its inner components. Additionally, they may have *ProvidedRoles* (sometimes called SystemProvidedRoles) and *RequiredRoles* (sometimes called SystemRequiredRoles). As these concepts have been discussed already when introducing *ComposedStructures* in section 3.4.4, they are omitted here.

Discussion In contrast to other component models, in the PCM, a *System* is not a special *CompositeComponent*. However, *Systems* and *CompositeComponents* share the common concept of a *ComposedStructure*. The rationale behind this design decision is that the composition of systems is usually done in a different ways than the composition of components, e.g., by using service-oriented technologies.

Additionally, in the PCM there is the afore mentioned visibility difference between a *System* and a *CompositeComponent*. Deployers only have access to the inner structure of a *System*, but are not allowed to access the inner structure of *CompositeComponents* used in this *System*. The inner structure of *CompositeComponents* is only available to the component developer who actually created the *CompositeComponent*. For everybody else, there is no difference between a *BasicComponent* and a *CompositeComponent*.

The following sections deal with additional concepts specific for *Systems*: System QoS annotations and component parameters.

3.6.1 System QoS Annotations

Software architects have to provide performance annotations for system *RequiredRoles* as they cannot be derived from other information. Additionally, inner components of a *System* may contain *Complete-* or *ProvidesComponentTypes*. In order to perform performance predictions, the software architect also has to add performance annotations to these entities. For this task, *QoSAnnotations* exist which associate stochastic expressions to system *RequiredRoles* and inner *Provides-* and *CompleteComponentTypes* adding the missing information. For system *RequiredRoles* a random variable for the time needed for the external system call depending on the service's parameters can be specified. Additionally, the return value's characterisations may be specified.

For *ProvidedRoles* of *ProvidesComponentTypes* or *CompleteComponentTypes* in their respective *AssemblyContexts* the same basically holds. The software architect or the QoS analyst may attach a random variable to such roles to allow performance predictions already in early stages of the development phases of components. However, these annotations have been used rarely. Hence, their support in transformations is limited and subject to future work.

3.6.2 Component Parameters

The performance relevant behaviour of components can depend on the internal state of these components, e.g., the response time of a database depends on the amount of data stored in it. However, including a full specification of the component state and the way it changes over time into the PCM's meta-model might confront creators of analysis methods with a state space problem. In order to avoid such issues on the one hand but offer the flexibility of parametrisation, the PCM contains the concept of component parameters which characterise the state of components in an abstract and static way.

To model component parameters, component developers can attach a set of *VariableUsages* including default values to *ImplementationComponentTypes*. For example, a component developer of a database component can declare that the component supports a characterisation of the number of entries in the database (`data.NUMBER_OF_ELEMENTS`). The component developer can use this parameter in the database component's RD-SEFFs to specify state dependent behaviour, e.g., a larger resource demand for query operations if more data is stored in the database. Software architects can attach *VariableUsages* to *AssemblyContexts*, in which they put the components, having the same variable name as the *VariableUsages* provided by the component developers. If they provide such a *VariableUsage*, the provided value overrides the component developer's default value. Additionally, domain experts may also provide *UserData* annotations in their *UsageModels* which also refer to an *AssemblyContext* and override any value specified there. For example, in the database example above, the domain expert would use a *UserData* to specify the number of entries in the database for a specific usage scenario.

However, component parameters still remain restricted to specifying the internal state of components as they cannot be changed. They hold the same value during a performance analysis, i.e., they do not allow to specify performance relevant dynamic component state changes. This limitation remains to keep analysis models solvable.

3.7 Allocation

After a *System* has been modelled by the software architect, the deployer allocates the system's inner components to hardware units and middleware entities. For this, the deployer models the hardware environment in a so called *ResourceEnvironment*. Using the created *ResourceEnvironment* model, the deployer creates an *Allocation* which establishes the link between the system's *AssemblyContexts* containing the system's inner components and the *ResourceEnvironment*. The respective information is stored in so called *AllocationContexts*.

The following sections briefly introduce the *ResourceEnvironment* and *Allocation* models.

3.7.1 Resource Environment

The PCM uses the *ResourceEnvironment* model to specify the hardware environment on which the component-based software system runs. This information is crucial for performance predictions. The simulation presented in section 4.4 uses it to simulate job processing.

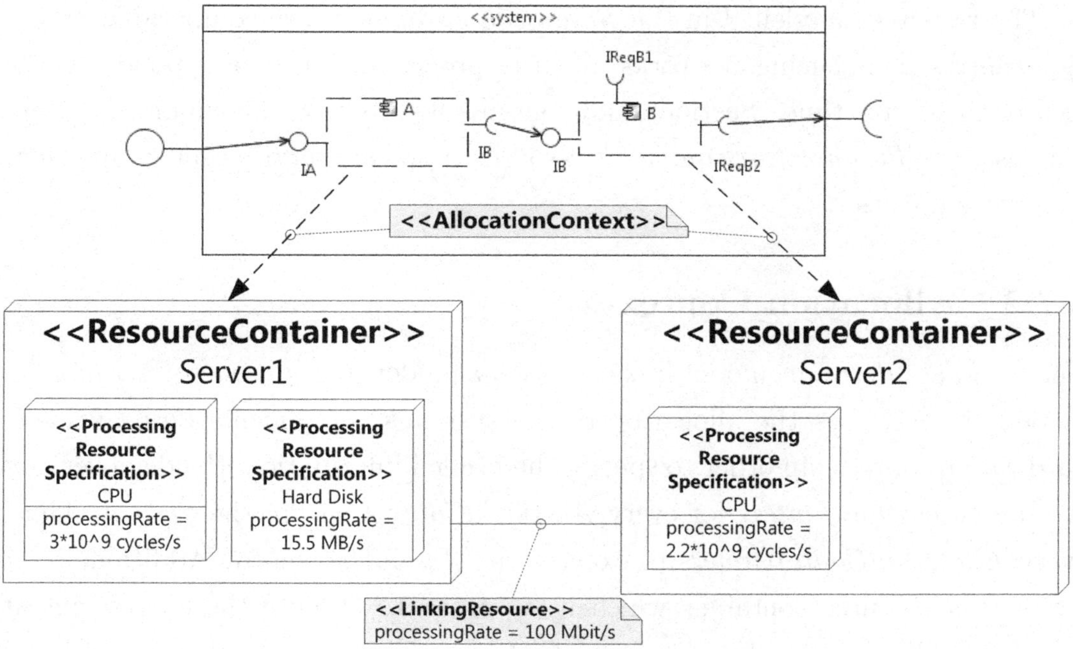

Figure 3.16: The PCM's *ResourceEnvironment* (Becker et al., 2007)

A *ResourceEnvironment* (see figure 3.16) basically contains two types of elements:

1. *ResourceContainer*: Resource container correspond to physical machines like server or PCs. They contain an arbitrary number of *ProcessingResources*. *ProcessingResources* model resources which actively process jobs

like CPUs, harddisks, etc. Each *ProcessingResource* conforms to one of the *ProcessingResourceTypes* introduced in section 3.5.6. Each *ProcessingResource* is described using a so called *ProcessingResourceSpecification* which specifies the rate in which the resource processes resource demands. For this, an abstract unit is used and it is specified how many abstract units the resource can process per second, i.e., CPU cycles per second or bytes read per second.

2. *LinkingResource*: Linking resources connect *ResourceContainer* allowing components to communicate which are not located on the same *ResourceContainer*. As such, *LinkingResources* abstract from networking infrastructures like LAN or WANs. For *LinkingResources* the PCM uses a throughput (bytes per second) and a latency specifications to characterise its performance.

The resources modelled in the *ResourceEnvironment* are comparable to service centres in queueing networks and the processing rate corresponds to the reciprocal service time. Section 4.4.3 contains details how the simulation mapping uses the *ResourceEnvironment*'s resources to create service centres and their respective queues.

3.7.2 Allocation Contexts

The PCM's *Allocation* model links a *System* model to a *ResourceEnvironment* model. It describes the allocation of the system's components onto available hardware resources. In order to specify the needed information, the deployer creates an *AllocationContext* for every *AssemblyContext* within the *System*. Thus, every *AllocationContext* refers to exactly one *AssemblyContext*. Additionally, it refers to a resource container which is supposed to execute the component at run-time. The deployer has to ensure that all resource types (cf. section 3.5.6) needed in any of the SEFF's *InternalActions* of all components deployed on a container are available in the container.

The PCM's technical report contains further examples and more sophisticated use cases of the *Allocation* model (Reussner et al., 2007, p. 60ff).

3.8 Usage

As introduced in the section on the PCM's roles (see section 2.1.2), the domain expert is responsible to model the behaviour of the system's users. This includes the course of the user's interaction with the system as well as the data the users exchange with it. The PCM uses the so called *UsageModel* for this task, which is described in the following subsections. The usage package has been added to the PCM by Koziolek (2008). Hence, a detailed discussion of this extension is given by Koziolek (2008). The following gives a brief summary of the usage package.

3.8.1 Usage Model and Usage Scenarios

A *UsageModel* serves as container for all interactions with the system. As such it contains a set of *UsageScenarios*. A *UsageScenario* is a typical interaction with the system performed by a particular group of users. The semantics of the *UsageModel* defines that the system's performance is evaluated under all the scenarios running concurrently. For example, in a web shop, one group of users are customers browsing for and buying products. Another group contains administrative users which maintain product prices, generate reports, order supply on low stocks, etc. Administrators access the system not as frequent as customers do. Hence, the amount of users and thus the frequency of jobs generated by users depends on the usage scenario.

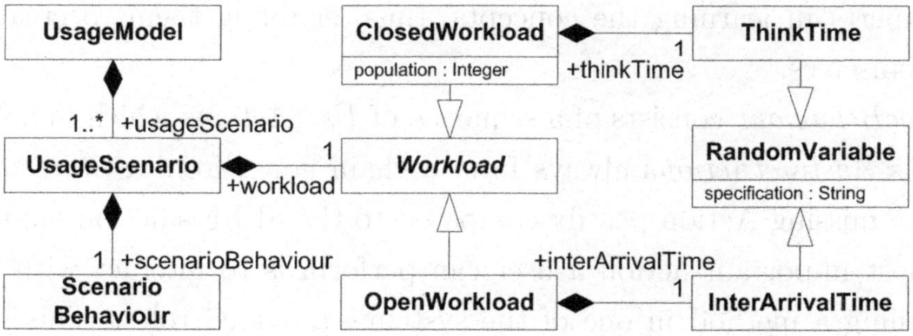

Figure 3.17: *UsageModel*, *UsageScenario* and Workloads (Becker et al., 2007)

To specify the interaction frequency, each *UsageScenario* contains a *WorkloadSpecification* (see figure 3.17). There are two types of *WorkloadSpecifications*: *OpenWorkloads* and *ClosedWorkloads*. Both workload types have their origins in queueing network theory. However, there are PCM specific adjustments.

OpenWorkloads describe a job arrival process in which users arrive at the system, execute their usage scenario and leave again. The frequency of their arrival is given by the time that passes between two users arriving at the system. This time span is described as random variable in the PCM characterised by an arbitrary stochastic expression. This allows for classical *InterArrivalTime* distributions like the Poisson distribution as well as arbitrary distribution functions. Note, that *OpenWorkloads* allow to specify infeasible arrival rates, e.g., arrival rates larger than the resulting departure rate.

ClosedWorkloads use a constant number of users which execute usage scenarios, delay their execution to think in order to prepare their next steps and start again. The think time is a random variable described by a stochastic expression which again allows classical distributions as well as arbitrary ones.

Contained in each *UsageScenario* there is a *UsageBehaviour* described in the next section.

3.8.2 UsageBehaviour

A *UsageBehaviour* models the steps executed by a single user in a *UsageScenario*. Its structure is similar to the SEFF's structure. However, compared to the SEFF is offers a reduced set of modelling concepts, i.e., it disallows parameter dependencies in control flow annotations, has no resource demands, no forks, and no acquire or release actions. The reduced complexity is expected to help domain experts in learning the concepts, thus, enabling them to create usage models themselves.

A *UsageBehaviour* consists of a sequence of *UserActions* which in analogy to the SEFF's *AbstractActions* always form a chain going from a *Start* to a *Stop* (notice, the missing Action postfix compared to the SEFF's action names).

The most important action a user can perform is to interact with the system by calling a method in one of the system's provided roles. This so called *SystemEntryLevelCall* is the equivalent of an *ExternalCallAction* in the SEFF indicating a user's request for service. As in the SEFF the call is blocking until a it returns with a result.

SystemEntryLevelCalls can have input *VariableUsages* having the same meaning as in *ExternalCallActions*. However, the random variables characterising the input parameters like `NUMBER_OF_ELEMENTS` can not depend on other

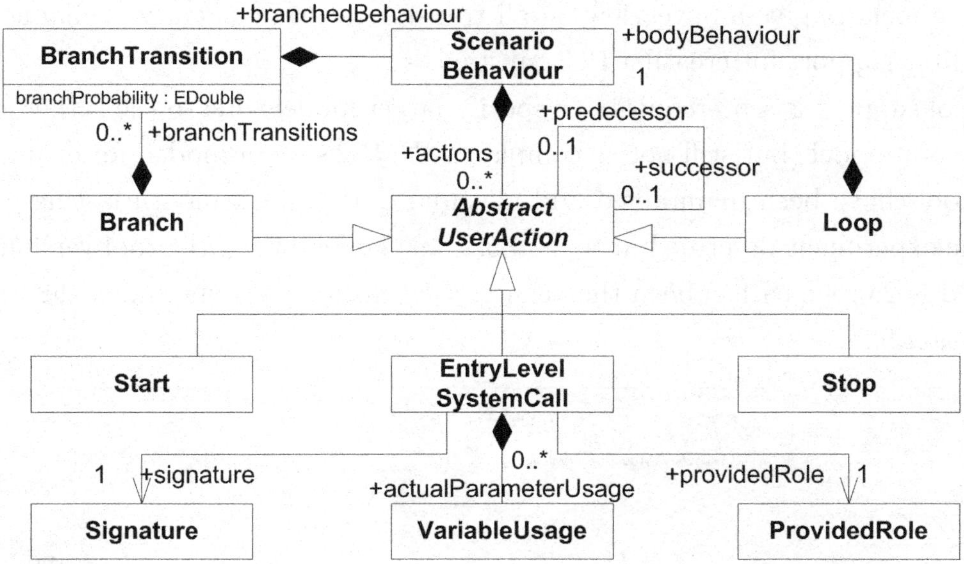

Figure 3.18: Different *UserActions* (Becker et al., 2007)

variables in the usage model. They have to be composed from literals only including literals describing random variables having a certain fixed distribution.

Besides *SystemLevelEntryCalls*, *UserBehaviours* can contain control flow constructs. Supported are probabilistic branches in *Branch* actions and *Loops* with a random amount of loop iterations. As there are no random variables depending on other variables in the usage model, there are no equivalent actions to *GuardedBranchTransitions* or *CollectionIteratorActions*.

3.8.3 Usage Context

Using the information available in the *UsageModel* the usage context of the system calls can be derived. Based on this information, the usage context of the system's inner components is determined. An analytical approach to this is presented in the PhD thesis by Koziolek (2008).

3.9 Tool support

The PCM has mature tool support. Figures 3.19 and 3.20 give screenshots of the version used in the experiment described in section 5.2, figure 3.1 at the beginning of this section gives an overview on the analysis methods, and figures A.2 and A.3

in the appendix give an overview on all transformations currently available and the editor support for creating PCM instances.

Tool support is a prerequisite to specify larger models due to the rather complex meta-model (but still not as complex as UML2's meta-model, for example). The tools have been maintained and matured during a six month lasting effort for the experiment described in section 5.2. In the following, the tool version described is 2.0, which has been the version used during the experiment described in section 5.2.

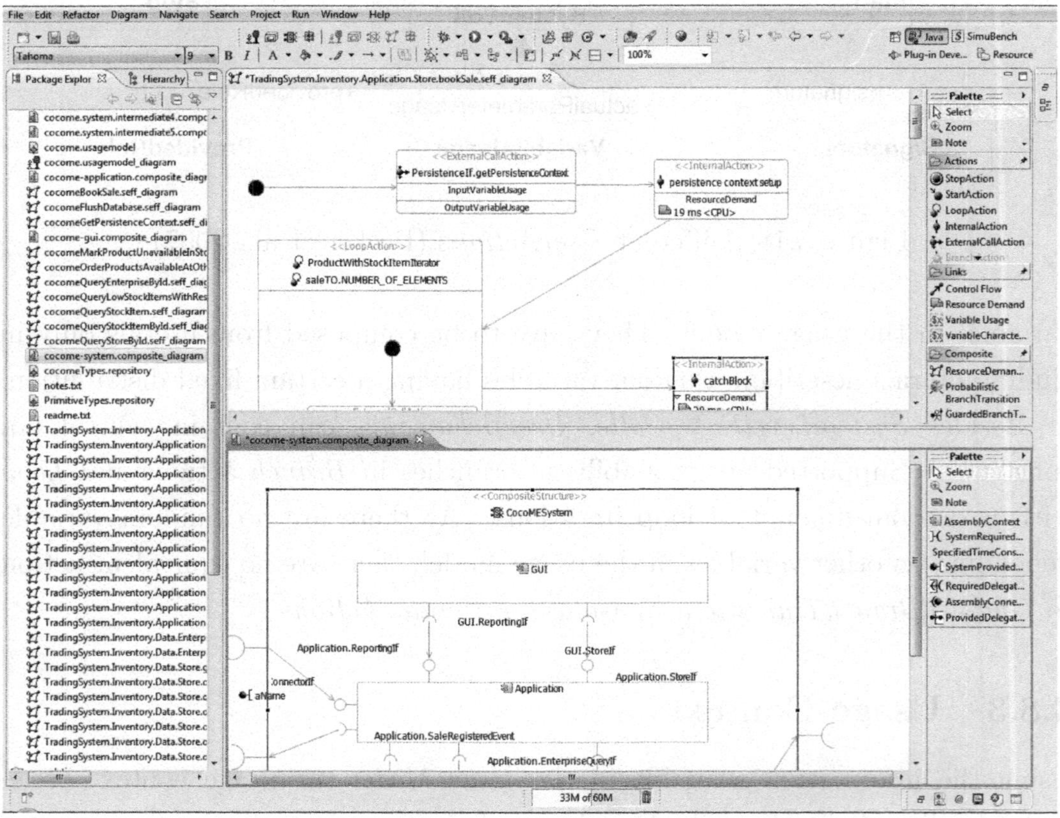

Figure 3.19: Screenshots of Version 2.0 of the PCM's Eclipse Tools - Modelling Perspective

The tools build upon the Eclipse Modelling Framework (version 2.3, Budinsky et al. (2003)). The PCM uses EMF's ECORE as meta-meta-model. For the concrete syntax of the PCM, graphical editors exist generated to a large extend using the Graphical Modelling Framework (GMF, version 2.0, Eclipse Foundation (2007c)) which itself uses the Graphical Editing Framework (GEF, version 3.3, Eclipse Foundation (2007b)).

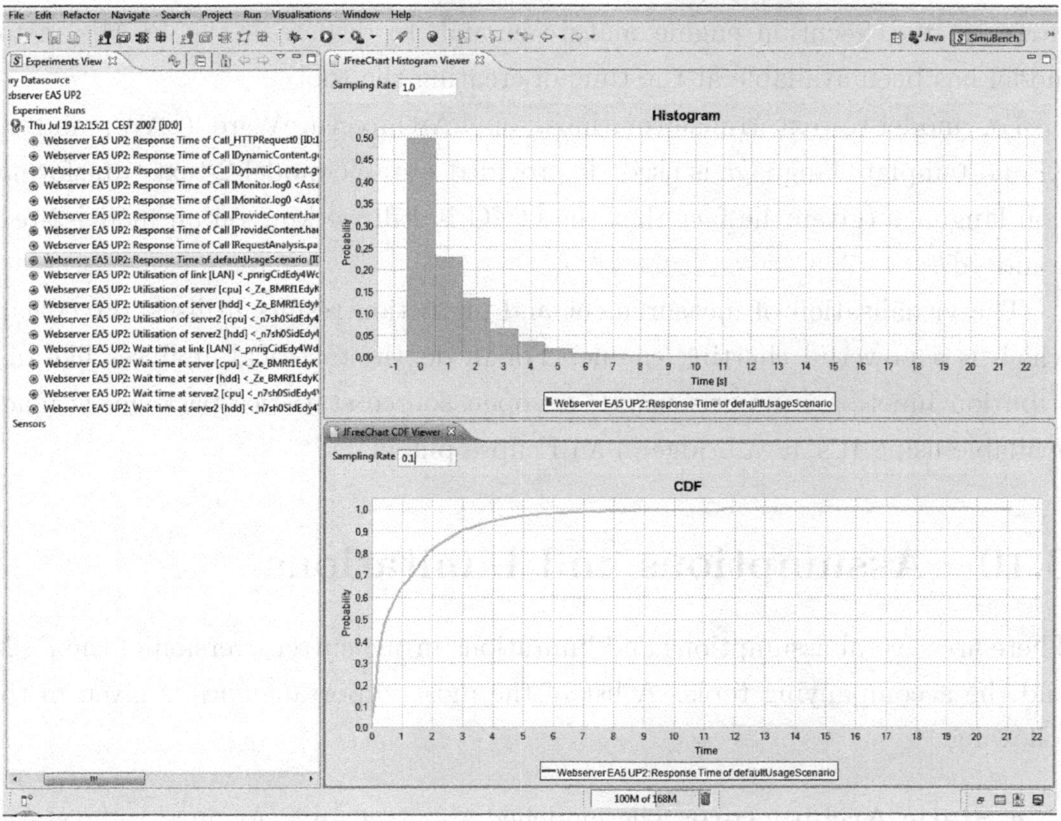

Figure 3.20: Screenshots of Version 2.0 of the PCM's Eclipse Tools - Analysis Perspecitve

The static semantics of the model is implemented using OCL constraints in the meta-model which are checkable at modelling time. For performance annotations custom editors have been developed which support syntax highlighting and context sensitive code completions for specifying stochastic expressions. The editing support is based on an EBNF based grammar for the concrete syntax. The abstract syntax is again realised as EMF meta-model making it available for model transformations. A type system implemented for the stochastic expressions checks the entered expressions for correctness of their static semantics. This is an advantage over the UML profile based modelling languages like UML-SPT where unsupported editing of strings has to be done.

For model-to-model transformations mainly Java is used. The reason for not using standard transformation languages and transformation engines is rooted in the immaturity of the current implementations of these tools. However, as the tools mature, most transformations should be expressible using OMG's QVT.

However, no execution engine mature enough to deal with the PCM's meta-model has been available at the time of creating the tools.

For model-to-text transformations, openArchitectureWare (oAW) and its XPand template language is used. It provided a stable model-2-text transformation language (given the fact that the OMG is still working on an model-2-text standard).

The visualisation of measurement and prediction results utilises JFreeChart which is a powerful charting engine. For in depth statistical analyses like distribution function comparisons, R, an open source statistics package, is made available using R's Java bridge in an Eclipse plugin.

3.10 Assumptions and Limitations

There are several assumptions and limitations in the current version of the PCM and the accompanying tools. A list of the most important ones is given in the following.

- **Static Architecture**: The modelled architecture is assumed to be static. This means that neither the connectors change nor that the components can move like agents to different hardware resources.
- **Abstraction from State**: It is assumed that the behaviour of the system is determined by the parameters of the service calls only. No internal state of components or the run-time environment is regarded. The PCM does not consider components at run-time, which may adapt their behaviour to change their QoS properties dynamically. These QoS-aware components are beyond the current scope of the PCM.
- **No Memory Allocation Effects**: Components might allocate and free memory during request processing. In multi-user cases, components may additionally struggle to get access to the memory bus which is often granted mutually exclusive. Both effects can have a significant impact on the resulting performance (for measurements, see Happe et al. (2006)). However, the PCM still disregards them.
- **No Support for Streamed Data**: The PCM's support for datatypes is limited to primitive types, collections and records. For larger amounts of

data, streaming is used. Streaming causes a continuous load on the CPU and the network. This type of data handling is currently not supported.

- **No Support for Exceptions**: The PCM's model concepts do not yet contain concepts for modelling exceptional conditions and aborts resulting from them. It is assumed that no exceptions occur in the analysed usage scenario. Related to the missing exceptions are concepts like timeouts, retries, etc.

- **Limited Support for Event-Based Systems**: The PCM's initial design assumed synchronous, blocking calls. Hence, the PCM does not support event-based systems which usually rely on asynchronous message passing.

- **Information Availability**: It is assumed that the necessary model information like service effect specifications and parametric dependencies are available and have been specified by the component developer, software architect, system deployer and domain expert. The PCM also assumes that different component developers are able to agree on common parameter abstractions. Future work is directed to retrieve as much information as possible from the automated analysis of component code.

- **Limited Support for Concurrency**: Quality properties of concurrent systems are still hard to predict. Especially on multi-core processor systems several effects like the CPU caches and scheduling strategies lead to differences between the observed system timing behaviour and corresponding predictions. Existing prediction methods like SPE or LQNs also neglect these effects. This is an area of open research in the performance prediction community.

- **Limited Support for Modelling the Execution Environment**: The PCM's resource model assumes that processing resources can be described by a processing rate only. But often more than a single influence factor is important. For example, to characterize modern CPUs solely by the clock frequency is often not sufficient any more. The CPU architecture, pipelining strategy, or the cache sizes as well as the run-time and middleware platform and their configurations can have a significant influence on the execution time (Liu et al., 2005). The performance prototype (see section 4.7) is a countermeasure against this limitation as the need to have a precise resource environment model available is dropped by using the real one.

- **Mathematical Assumptions**: Mathematical assumptions and limitations reduce the models' complexity. For example, for the simulation they reduce simulation run length and memory consumption. Current versions of the PCM assume for example stochastical independent resource demands. The only exception to this is the `CollectionIteratorAction` which allows a dependency on parameter characterisations of the current iteration element.

Chapter 4

Transformations

The following sections describe the transformations of PCM instances into different artefacts based on different platforms. This embeds the PCM into a MDSD process and integrates model-driven software development, component-based software development, and performance predictions.

The available targets are

1. SimuCom (Simulation for Component-Based Systems): A simulation environment which allows to predict performance metrics of component-based systems modelled in the PCM. It simulates resources based on the modelled *ResourceEnvironment*. The simulation is based on queuing network theory.

2. ProtoCom (Prototype for Component-Based Systems): A prototype which mimics the modelled resource demands of the system using different resource consumption strategies. These strategies replace the abstracted code of internal actions, i.e., it does not contain the application logic but code which is performance-equivalent to the missing logic. The prototype is executed on the actual target execution environment. The prototype's implementation is directly compileable, in the sense that it is fully generated and can be run without additional code. While running, ProtoCom measures execution times from which it computes performance metrics. This allows the evaluation of the system's performance under more realistic conditions.

3. POJO or EJB Code: This target generates code skeletons to be completed by the developers to implement the application for JAVA or Java EE platforms. The code is incomplete for *InternalActions* and hence for data

processing. As a consequence, manual coding is needed to finish the implementation. However, as much information as possible is preserved from the PCM instance.

This thesis investigates model transformations having close relationships to each other. For this reason, the results of the transformations share a common part while other parts are different (see section 4.2 for details). As a consequence, the transformations have similar results based on the transformation of PCM concepts into Java. A different approach, by Koziolek (2008) and Happe (2008) presented in their PhD theses, is a transformation of the PCM into a stochastic process algebra. However, compared to the code transformation, there is a larger semantic gap when transforming into the process algebras.

This section is structured as follows. First, the Coupled Transformations method is introduced in section 4.1. It is applied in this thesis' application context of model-driven, component-based software engineering. After some basic techniques in section 4.2, which are used in all transformations, the transformations are described in sections 4.3 to 4.7. Section 4.4 elaborates on the transformation into SimuCom. Section 4.5 describes basic methods for the realisation of Coupled Transformations in this thesis. Section 4.6 gives mappings of some of the PCM's concepts to Java EE code. Existing design alternatives are captured in feature diagrams and a parameterisation of SimuCom, which reflects the impact of decisions made, is discussed. Section 4.7 finally shows how SimuCom's and the code mapping can be used to quickly build ProtoCom protoypes.

4.1 Coupled Transformations Method

In this section, the Coupled Transformations method is first introduced informally. Afterwards, a formalisation is given in section 4.1.2.

4.1.1 Motivation

When doing model-based or model-driven performance prediction with current methods (Balsamo et al., 2004a), the method relies on the information available in the source model, e.g., UML models annotated with the UML-SPT profile. However, the performance of a software system is a run-time property, i.e., a property of the deployed and executed implementation of the system. Hence, one problem is to ensure that the implementation corresponds to the model.

However, if the model has been used as blue print by a team of developers to implement the corresponding system manually, it often can not be ensured that the code corresponds to the model. Implementation rules used by the developer team help to reduce the variability, but even with strict rules and code reviews, trying to ensure compliance between the model and the code, there are design decisions involved in implementing abstract model concepts which may lead to different implementations of the same concept by different developers as in the following example.

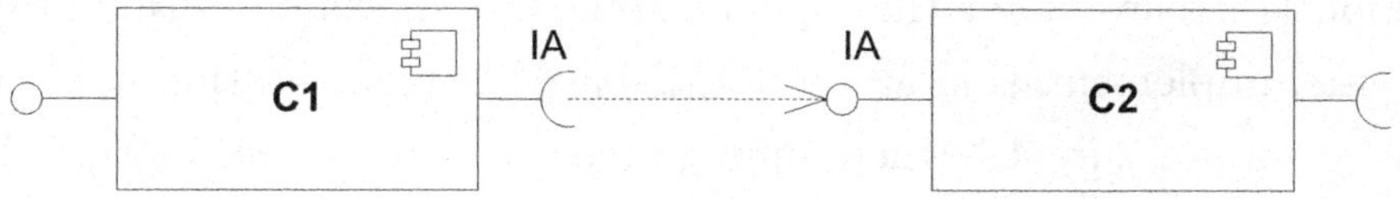

Figure 4.1: Motivating Example for Coupled Transformations

As a running example, consider the structural view of an simple architectural model in figure 4.1. It shows two components `C1` and `C2` communicating using a connector. Now, consider two teams of developers which have to implement a corresponding system using a middleware platform like Java EE. The first team uses remote method invocations (RMI) to realise the connection, the other team uses SOAP. Both teams' implementation is valid as it is consistent with the given model (assuming no additional information or implementation rules existed). However, being functional equivalent, the performance impact of both implementations is different because of the larger protocol overhead caused by SOAP. Hence, model-driven performance predictions have to rely on correct implementation assumptions on the connector for their predictions to become accurate.

A solution to the presented consistency problem between model and code is provided by a model-driven development process. Using deterministic transformations to transform a model into an implementation eliminates the non-determinism assumed for manual implementation, i.e., the result of a transformation solely depends on the input model. In addition, transformations restrict the degree of freedom for mapping model instances to implementations to the degree of freedom available in the model as the mapping to implementations is fixed in the transformations and cannot be changed. However, in cases with multiple mapping options, this raises the question which option to use in the transformation. Considering the example again, the question would be whether to generate a RMI or a SOAP based implementation in the transformation.

One approach could be to include the design alternatives in the source model, i.e., by introducing different types of connectors in the model. However, this idea undermines the abstraction property of a model as defined by Stachowiak (1973). Due to the goal-driven abstraction of a model, unimportant details of the modelled objects are omitted. As a consequence, there can be different objects having an equal model. Looking at figure 4.2, this is depicted on the left hand side. There, three different objects have the same model as they only differ in attributes abstracted away by the model's abstraction rule. The omitted information is irrelevant for the model's aim. In our example, this means that a RMI based implementation and a SOAP-based implementation have the same model as given in figure 4.1 when aiming at presenting the conceptual structure of the system by removing its realisation details. Abstracting from the concrete connector implementation keeps the model comprehensible and does not overload it with information. Additionally, it may even be infeasible to add all possible types of connector implementations that exist to the model's constructs as it would imply to include all connector types of all existing and also all future implementations. As a way out, the OMG introduced PIM and PSM models (c.f. section 2.2.3) to separate implementation (platform) dependent aspects from implementation (platform) independent ones.

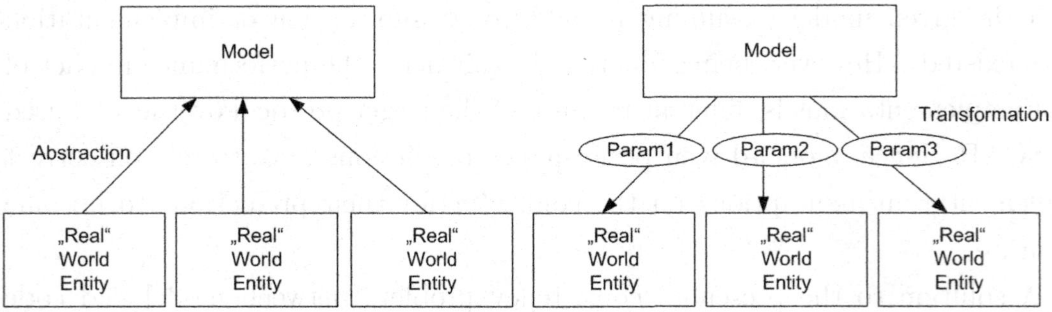

Figure 4.2: Model Abstraction and Model Refinement

If the additional information can not be part of the source model as argued above, two options remain. Either it is part of a transformation parameter (mark model) or is encoded as fixed design decision in the transformation. Consider again the three modelled objects on the left hand side in figure 4.2. As they have the same model, either a parameterised transformation or three different transformations are needed, if the original modelled objects shall be generated as shown on the right hand side of figure 4.2. In the connector example, either a RMI and a SOAP based transformation is needed to generate both alternatives or a transformation which makes this decision explicit as a transformation parameter.

Taking these considerations of model-to-code transformation into account, the aim is to improve the prediction model. Performance predictions deal with the performance of the *implemented and deployed* system, i.e., the system which contains all information added by transformations and their mark models. However, current performance prediction methods only use the information available in the design model omitting the information added by transforming the model into an implementation. Hence, the solution presented here is to *automatically* include the information available in implementation transformations into the prediction transformation (see figure 4.3).

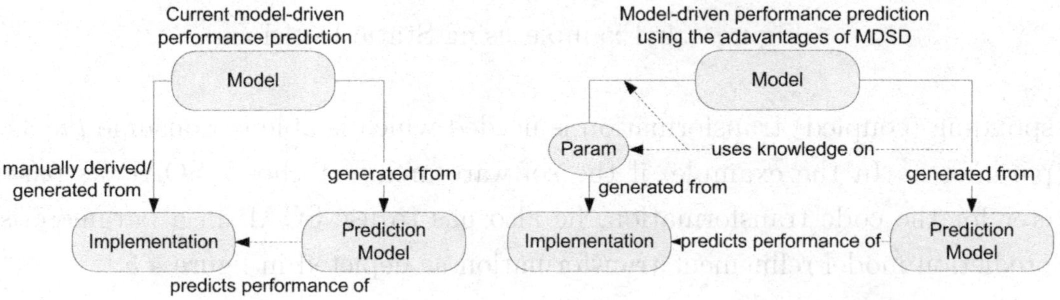

Figure 4.3: Using Transformation Knowledge in Coupled Transformations

For transformations without a mark model (see figure 4.4), then their result is solely determined by their input model. In this case, the transformation's creator has encoded his implementation or platform dependent decisions into the transformation. In the connector example, this would mean choosing from two transformations: one for RMI and one for SOAP. Assume the software architect choses the RMI transformation as indicated by the black dot in figure 4.4, then a transformation has to be used to automatically enrich the performance prediction model with RMI specifics like the RMI specific protocol overhead. As this transformation is related to its respective code transformation, it is called *coupled* transformation, given the whole approach its name: Coupled Transformations method. Analogously, if the SOAP based transformation was used, a transformation for enriching the prediction model with SOAP specifics (like SOAP's protocol overhead) would be used.

If instead a parameterised transformation is used (see figure 4.5), i.e., one that offers the choice between RMI and SOAP as a parameter, then also a corre-

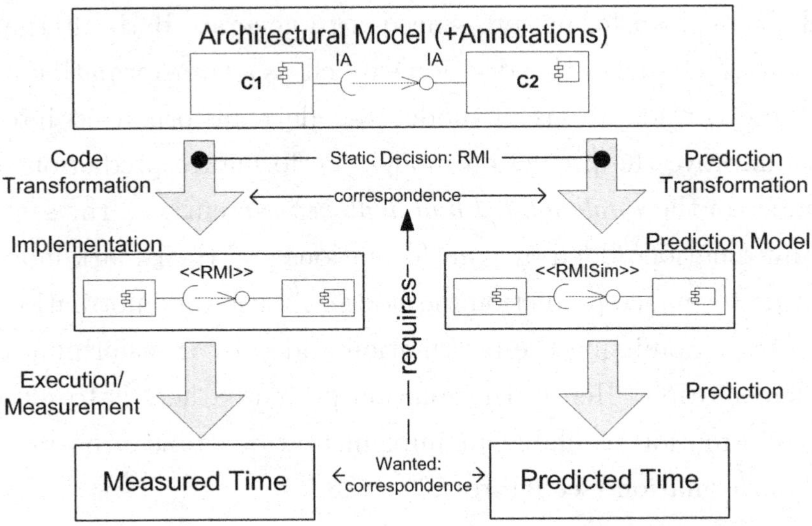

Figure 4.4: Example using Static Decisions

sponding (coupled) transformation is needed which is able to consume *the same* parameter. In the example, if the software architect choses SOAP as parameter for the code transformation, he also has to use SOAP in a parameterised prediction model refinement transformation as depicted in figure 4.5.

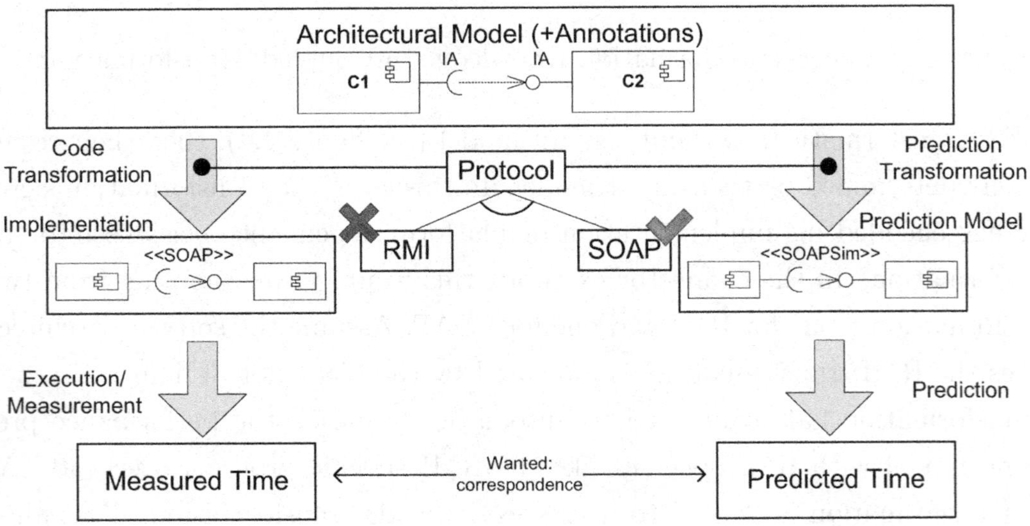

Figure 4.5: Example using Parametric Decisions

Discussion The following discusses the application of the presented idea to other parts of this thesis and alternative approaches which might work to include the implementation decisions into the prediction model.

Captured Performance Influence Factor: Based on the influence factors on the performance of a component in section 2.3.1, i.e., external services, execution environment, usage profile, and implementation, the factor which can be captured more accurately by including knowledge on the transformations into the prediction process is the implementation. It is possible to capture the *design and implementation decisions* encoded *into the transformations* in more detail.

Application in this Thesis: In section 4.6 a transformation of PCM instances into Java EE code skeletons is given. In order to include the performance impact of the design alternatives available in this mapping, Coupled Transformations are used. For example, choosing a protocol when mapping connectors as used in this motivation is picked up again in section 4.6.3. The presented transformations encode design alternatives in transformation parameters as presented in the example in figure 4.5. For each mapping, the respective coupled transformation, which automatically enriches the prediction model making it more accurate, is described.

Reverse Engineering as Alternative: An alternative approach to Coupled Transformations is conceivable: Generate the prediction model directly based on the code and ignore the design model completely. However, this implies reverse engineering the code into a performance prediction model which, in general, is a difficult task. The difficulty lies in the fact that the code usually does not contain all information available in abstract models any more. For example, performance annotations are not part of the code, this kind of information can not be reverse engineered and hence is lost. In particular, recovering the behaviour of *InternalActions* to derive their resource demands parameterised by their dependencies on contextual influence factors is a challenging task. One approach working towards (semi-automatic) recovery of performance models for components by analysing their implementation is followed by Krogmann (2007).

4.1.2 Formalisation of Coupled Transformations

This section captures the idea of Coupled Transformations formally. First, it defines model transformations and chains of transformations. Based on this, it introduces a formalisation of Coupled Transformations. Finally, it elaborates on the use of Coupled Transformations in the context of the PCM.

Models and Meta-Models Let MM denote a meta-model expressed as instance of some meta-meta-model MMM, e.g., the PCM is an EMOF instance as introduced in section 3. Then the set of all valid model instances of the meta-model MM is defined as

$$inst(MM) = \{M | M \text{ is a valid instance of } MM\} \tag{4.1}$$

Note, that an instance is valid only if it conforms to MM's abstract syntax and (static and dynamic) semantics where MMM defines the semantics of the term conformance. For example, using EMOF as meta-meta-model, i.e., $MMM = EMOF$, then the MOF specification's semi-formal definition of conformance applies (Object Management Group (OMG), 2006d, p.53 cont.). Using the introduced notation, the following holds for example: $inst(PCM)$ is the set of all valid component-based system-models expressible in the PCM. $PCM \in inst(EMOF)$ expresses the fact that EMOF is the meta-model used to define the PCM. $EMOF \in inst(EMOF)$ formalises the fact that EMOF is an instance of itself (cf. section 2.2.1). As already introduced in section 2.2.1, $inst()$ is analogue to the set of words accepted by a language where the language definition, e.g., as EBNF grammar, replaces the meta-model.

Transformations This paragraph introduces transformations. Let t be a computable function which maps an instance of a source meta-model MM_{src} and an instance of a mark meta-model MM_{mark} to an instance of a target meta-model MM_{dest}:

$$t : inst(MM_{src}) \times inst(MM_{mark}) \rightarrow inst(MM_{dest}) \tag{4.2}$$

The function t represents a parameterised transformation. For example, consider a transformation:

$$t_{\text{PCM}\times\text{EJBMARK}\rightarrow\text{EJB}} : inst(PCM) \times inst(EJBMARK) \rightarrow inst(EJB)$$

mapping instances of the PCM ($inst(PCM)$) to instances of a meta-model to define EJB based applications. The latter serve as basis for the generation of an EJB based implementation. The transformation takes EJB specific parameters, e.g., which kind of Java EE communication the connectors use, as instances of an EJB mark meta-model ($inst(EJBMARK)$). Another transformation mapping PCM instances to Fractal (cf. section 2.1.4) implementations has the following definition

$$t_{\text{PCM}\times\text{FRACTMARK}\rightarrow\text{FRACT}} :$$
$$inst(PCM) \times inst(FRACTMARK) \rightarrow inst(FRACT)$$

where $FRACT$ is a meta-model to describe instances of the Fractal component model and $FRACTMARK$ a mark model used to define Fractal specific implementation details. Notice, the role of the mark models in the two examples given as parameter set specific to the destination meta-model.

The previous discussion did not cover the case in which a transformation has no mark model, i.e., takes no parameters other than the input model instance. For this, let $EMPTY$ denote the *emtpy* meta-model, for which $inst(EMPTY) = \epsilon$ holds. This is analogue to the empty word used in grammar definitions. A parameterless transformation t is then

$$t : inst(MM_{src}) \times inst(EMPTY) \rightarrow inst(MM_{dest}) \tag{4.3}$$

In this case, t takes the empty set as second parameter $t(m, \epsilon)$ with $m \in inst(MM_{src})$.

Chains of Transformations Next, this paragraph introduces composed transformations, which represent an ordered *chain* of transformations as introduced in section 2.2.2. Let $T = \{t_i | i \in [1 \ldots N-1]\}$ be an ordered set of transformations t_i which are executed sequentially with t_1 being the first transformation and t_{N-1} being the last one. Each transformation t_i maps instances of meta-model MM_i and instances of mark model MM_{mark_i} to instances of meta-model MM_{i+1}:

$$t_i : inst(MM_i) \times inst(MM_{mark_i}) \rightarrow inst(MM_{i+1}) \tag{4.4}$$

The following shows that a chain of transformations is itself a transformation t_{comp} fitting the definition in equation 4.2, that transforms instances of MM_1 directly into instances of MM_N using mark model $MM_{mark_{comp}}$, where $MM_{mark_{comp}}$ is a meta-model which is derived by combining the meta-models $MM_{mark_1} \ldots MM_{mark_{N-1}}$. More precise

$$MM_{mark_{comp}} = MM_{mark_1} \times MM_{mark_2} \cdots \times MM_{mark_{N-1}} \tag{4.5}$$

$$inst(MM_{mark_{comp}}) = \{(ma_1, ma_2, \ldots, ma_{N-1}) | ma_i \in inst(MM_{mark_i})\} \tag{4.6}$$

An element $\vec{ma}_{comp} = (ma_1, ma_2, \ldots, ma_{N-1})$ of $inst(MM_{mark_{comp}})$ characterises a full set of parameters or mark model instances of all transformations t_i contained in a transformation chain, i.e., ma_i is a valid parameter for transformation t_i.

A transformation $t_{comp} : inst(MM_1) \times inst(MM_{mark_{comp}}) \rightarrow inst(MM_N)$ is the composed transformation of a chain of transformations t_i if

$$t(m_1, \vec{ma}_{comp}) = t_N(t_{N-1}(\ldots t_1(m_1, ma_{comp1}) \ldots), ma_{compN-2}, ma_{compN-1}) = m_N \tag{4.7}$$

where $m_1 \in inst(MM_1)$, $m_N \in inst(MM_N)$, and $\vec{ma}_{comp} \in inst(MM_{mark_{comp}})$.

Writing $m_i \xrightarrow{t_i(ma_i)} m_{i+1}$ as abbreviation if $m_{i+1} = t_i(m_i, ma_i)$ holds, a chain of transformations $t_1 \ldots t_N$ can be written as follows

$$m_1 \underbrace{\xrightarrow{t_1(ma_1)} m_2 \xrightarrow{t_2(ma_2)} \ldots \xrightarrow{t_{N-1}(ma_{N-1})}} m_N$$

$$\Leftrightarrow \quad m_1 \xrightarrow{t_{comp}((ma_1, ma_2, \ldots, ma_{N-1}))} m_N$$

The following extends the previous PCM to EJB example into a chained transformation by appending a second transformation. This transformation adds details specific for the Sun Application Server, i.e., special configuration setting only available in this server. If both transformations are executed in a chain, a transformation results, which transforms PCM instances into EJB applications for the Sun Application Server.

Let the additional transformation be:

$$t_{\text{EJB}\times\text{SUNAPPMARK}\rightarrow\text{EJBSUN}} : \\ inst(EJB) \times inst(EJBSUNMARK) \rightarrow inst(EJBSUN)$$

where $SUNAPPMARK$ denotes a mark model defining parameters specific the Sun's application server and $EJBSUN$ denotes an extended EJB meta-model containing Sun Application Server specific settings. Then, the transformation chain is

$$m_{PCM} \xrightarrow{t_{\text{PCM}\times\text{EJBMARK}\rightarrow\text{EJB}}(ma_{EJBMARK})} m_{EJB} \\ \xrightarrow{t_{\text{EJB}\times\text{SUNMARK}\rightarrow\text{EJBSUN}}(ma_{SUNAPPMARK})} m_{EJBSUN}$$

The equivalent composed transformation is then

$$m_{PCM} \xrightarrow{t_{comp}(ma_{EJBMARK}, ma_{SUNAPPMARK})} m_{EJBSUN}$$

The example shows how transformation chains can separate several aspects of a transformation into separate transformation steps.

Coupled Transformations The following uses the introduced chained transformations to formalise Coupled Transformations as introduced in section 4.1.1. For this, consider a chained transformation t_c with $t_{c1} \dots t_{cN-1}$ as sub-transformations. Note, that this includes the special case of a single transformation if $N = 2$. t_c maps a high level input model $m_{c1} \in inst(MM_{c1})$ into a low level output model $m_{cN} \in inst(MM_{cN})$ (e.g., the left transformation depicted in figure 4.5). For the following, it is assumed that $t_{c_{N-1}}$ is a model-2-text transformation and m_cN is an implementation (code representation) of m_{c1}. The transformation uses the mark model instances $ma_{c1} \dots ma_{cN-1}$.

Additionally, consider a transformation t_q which derives an analysis model $m_{qN} \in inst(MM_{qN})$ for some quality property q of an input model $m_{q1} \in inst(MM_{q1})$. The aim of Coupled Transformations is to reuse the information added by t_c in t_q. Hence, the first step is to use the same input model for t_q

$$m_{q1} = m_{c1} = m_1 \text{ and } MM_{c1} = MM_{q1} = MM_1 \tag{4.8}$$

For example, if t_{perf} is a transformation which derives a performance analysis model ($q = perf$) from a PCM instance, the same input model is used to derive the performance model as the one which was used to derive the implementation.

Second, in order to include the information added by t_c, t_q is structured in a way that it reflects t_c. For this, let t_q be a chained transformation with $t_{q1}, t_{q2}, \dots t_{qN-1}$ where N is the same N as in t_c. Now, every t_{qi} adds information relevant for analysing the quality property q to the analysis model which corresponds to the information added by t_{ci}.

As such, t_{qi} depends on its respective t_{ci}. t_{qi} includes the information relevant to property q into the analysis model. For example, for performance as quality property, resource demands caused by behaviour added by t_{ci} to the model are included by t_{qi}. To continue the example, if t_{ci} maps PCM's assembly connectors to SOAP calls, t_{qi} adds resource demands for marshalling using SOAP, transmitting a SOAP message, and unmarshalling the SOAP call. Note, in the case where t_{ci} always maps the assembly connectors to SOAP calls, no mark model exists, i.e., t_{ci} takes ϵ as second parameter. However, even in this case, t_{qi} depends on t_{ci}: it also always considers the SOAP's resource demand in its analysis transformation.

Formally, the transformation t_{qi} depends on the transformation t_{ci}, i.e., it can be derived by some functional dependency from t_{ci}. The dependency itself is influenced by the quality property p. For example, if the quality property is performance, the resource demands generated by the output of t_{ci} are important. If the quality property is reliability, the failure probability of the output of t_{ci} is important.

As the output of t_{ci} depends on the parameter or mark model ma_{ci}, the same parameter has to be considered as well in t_{qi}. Hence

$$ma_{qi} = ma_{ci} = ma_i \tag{4.9}$$

For example, consider the mapping of PCM assembly connectors to Java EE communication protocols again. If the transformation developer changes transformation t_{ci} responsible for generating the communication aspect in a way which allows the transformation's user to choose between SOAP or RMI as communication protocols using a mark model instance, the transformation output uses RMI or SOAP accordingly offering different quality. For example, SOAP causes a higher resource demand as it marshals the data to transmit more verbose by using XML than RMI which uses a binary data representation. As a consequence, t_{qi} needs to know whether the RMI or the SOAP option has been chosen in t_{ci}. For this reason, it is necessary to pass the same mark model instance to t_{qi} as it has been passed to t_{ci} before.

To give the full picture, consider a transformation chain t_c which derives the application's implementation and its parameters $ma_1, \ldots ma_{N-1}$:

$$\underbrace{m_1 \xrightarrow{t_{c1}(ma_1)} m_2 \xrightarrow{t_{c2}(ma_2)} \ldots \xrightarrow{t_{cN-1}(ma_{N-1})} m_{cN}}$$

$$\Leftrightarrow \quad m_1 \xrightarrow{t_c((ma_1, ma_2, \ldots, ma_{N-1}))} m_{cN}$$

The resulting transformation chain t_q which derives an analysis model for quality property q depends on the same set of parameters $ma_1, \ldots ma_N$ and transforms the same input model m_1:

$$\underbrace{m_1 \xrightarrow{t_{q1}(ma_1)} m_{q2} \xrightarrow{t_{q2}(ma_2)} \ldots \xrightarrow{t_{qN-1}(ma_{N-1})} m_{qN}}$$

$$\Leftrightarrow \quad m_1 \xrightarrow{t_q((ma_1, ma_2, \ldots, ma_{N-1}))} m_{qN}$$

To summarise, t_q is a transformation, which not only includes the information available in the source model m_1 but also the information encoded in the transformations t_{ci} which refine the source model into the application's realisation.

Application in this Thesis After introducing the general idea, the following discuses the application of Coupled Transformations in the remaining parts of this thesis.

1. **Focus on Performance Properties:** The quality property is restricted to the domain of performance analysis, i.e., $q = p$. However, this is only to narrow the focus of this work. The idea can be applied to other quality properties as well.

2. **Code Output:** For the transformation t_c it is assumed that the meta-model MM_{cN} is an appropriate model for source code like the abstract syntax generated from a EBNF grammar. With this, $t_c(m_1, \vec{ma})$ is the application's source code. It is usually generated by t_{cN-1} which is a model-2-text transformation in practice.

3. **No Manual Interactions:** In cases where the source code transformation t_c is incomplete, i.e., results in code skeletons, the final code completion is done manually by developers. However, this is non-formal process, whose outcome usually highly depends on the developer. It is even very likely that the same code skeletons will be completed differently by the same developer, if it is done repeatedly with some time in between. For these reasons, manual transformations are disregarded in t_q. Hence,the following only reasons on automated and computed transformations.

4. **Chained Analysis Model Transformation:** The current practice is to derive an analysis model without taking implementation refinement transformations t_{ci} into account, i.e., $m_{qN} = t_q(m_1, \epsilon)$ with $N = 2$. That is, the analysis model m_{qN} is derived directly from the design model m_1. As elaborated in the foundations on performance annotations (see section 2.3.2) sometimes m_1 is not used directly but rather m_1' with m_1' being the design model annotated manually with performance annotations. For example, for prediction methods based on UML and UML-SPT annotations, m_1 would be the design model without annotations and m_1' the annotated SPT model. In such cases it is assumed that m_1 denotes the initial model for *both* transformations, i.e., for modelling languages which need annotations, it is the annotated model.

5. **Availability of the Analysis Transformations:** To put this theoretical model into practice, it is necessary to have t_{qi} which reflect the impact of

the output of t_{ci} on the quality property q. It is the burden of an expert for quality attribute q to analyse t_{ci} and to derive the transformation t_{qi}. Additionally, t_{qi} depends on the life- and maintenance cycle of t_{ci} and has to be adapted whenever t_{ci} is changed. However, as transformations can be reused the extra-effort pays off in cases where the transformation is used frequently because both transformations have to be written once but can be used multiple times.

6. **Feature Models as Mark Models:** The transformations in this thesis are based on feature models as mark models. The meta-model MM_{mark_i} of the i-th mark model is a meta-model describing all configurations of the i-th feature model. However, this does not cause a limit in general applicability of the method for other common types of mark models like stereotypes and tagged values or arbitrary complex MOF decorator models because basically they all add parameters to the transformation. However, the different types of mark models offer different degrees of freedom on the parameterisation (see section 4.5.2).

In the following, a transformation of the PCM into code and into a simulation-based prediction model is introduced, which uses the idea of Coupled Transformations. The transformations require a mark model based on feature diagrams, allowing limited parameterisations. This applies Coupled Transformations to this thesis' application scenario which aims at an integrated model-driven process for component-based, predictable software development. However, this is due to the focus of this thesis on component-based software development. The idea of Coupled Transformations can be applied to any model-driven software development approach if some preconditions are met:

- Depending models: A model depending on the implementation model is needed in order to couple the transformations. For example, for the prediction of performance or other QoS attributes, the prediction model depends on the implementation model.

- Generation of code: The implementation is partially or fully generated by transformations resulting in deterministic code blocks.

- Availability of QoS annotations: QoS annotations attached to the source are often necessary to cover parts of the system not handled by code transformations. However, for transformations which generate the complete code, they might not be needed.

4.2 Modular Transformations

Before presenting the actual transformations, this sections introduces some basic ideas used to realise the transformations which support the following requirements (introduced in section 2.4.1). First, transformations for the PCM need to be split among the developer roles. How to accomplish this has already been introduced in section 3.1.2. Second, structuring the transformations in a special way eases support of Coupled Transformations and allows reuse among common transformation parts. In order to support the special structuring, the Template Method design pattern (Gamma et al., 1995, p.325) is ported to the used template engine. The following gives details on this.

The transformations developed in this thesis are model-2-text transformations mapping PCM instances to code. The decision to favour model-2-text transformations over model-2-model transformations is grounded on the unavailability of working model-2-model transformation engines, e.g., a QVT engine, at the time of writing. Nevertheless, most of the time this thesis describes the transformations on a conceptual level. It only presents model-2-text transformation templates occasionally to illustrate special issues.

Conceptually, a migration to model-2-model transformations when mature model-2-model transformation engines become available should be no problem. These engines can be used to shift parts of the transformation logic on the model level removing it from the model-2-text transformations.

There are at least two possible options to realize transformations where one transformation depends on the other as it is the case for Coupled Transformations. One option which is always available is to implement the code and prediction transformations independently from scratch. To link both transformations, the transformations read the same parameter set (mark model). This offers the advantage to focus on the target platform of the respective transformation both in its implementation and in its generated output. For example, the simulation transformation could use all features of the underlying simulation framework, producing a highly optimized simulation code. However, when looking at the generated output, the difference between a specialized simulation implementation and a specialized code skeleton implementation is potentially high, making it difficult to include the same parameterisations in both transformations in order to validate the Coupled Transformations ideas.

Hence, a different approach is used in this thesis. The idea originates from the Template Method design pattern Gamma et al. (1995) used in object-oriented languages. The pattern is applied in cases where a base algorithm exists which forms a common skeleton for a whole set of algorithms. Each instance of the algorithm only changes the behaviour at certain predefined spots in the total algorithm. The base algorithm is the template which contains the so called template methods, which defer their actual implementation to implementations in subclasses.

Some transformation languages support inheritance which is needed to use the Template Method pattern (e.g., in the upcoming OMG Model-2-Text standard (Object Management Group (OMG), 2007b)). However, these engines are still immature. Because of this, the transformations presented in this thesis use the template-based model-2-text engine of openArchitectureWare, version 4.2 (oAW) (openArchitectureWare (oAW), 2007). The idea is to use oAW to simulate the Template Method pattern. OpenArchitectureWare offers a template override facility which can be used to simulate inheritance, the exact technical details are omitted here as they are highly dependent on the actual transformation engine and subject to change as the transformation engines - including oAW - further mature.

However, conceptually, the Template Method pattern allows to define transformations which share a common part, based on common templates. However, certain parts of the transformation output change based on the selected set of template methods (see figure 4.6). The transformations presented in sections 4.4-4.7 utilize the template method based approach. Depending on the actual target (SimuCom, ProtoCom, or code skeletons) certain parts of the output change while others remain constant. This allows the transformations to support multiple targets which share a common transformation core. This common core also eases the inclusion of the same mark model in all transformations which is needed for Coupled Transformations.

Consider the following example to understand transformations based on template methods. To generate code from a RDSEFF, a transformation has to visit all *AbstractActions* in a behaviour sequentially from the *StartAction* to the *StopAction* and generate code for each type of action visited. Now consider a *LoopAction* in this chain of actions for which code should be generated. Having

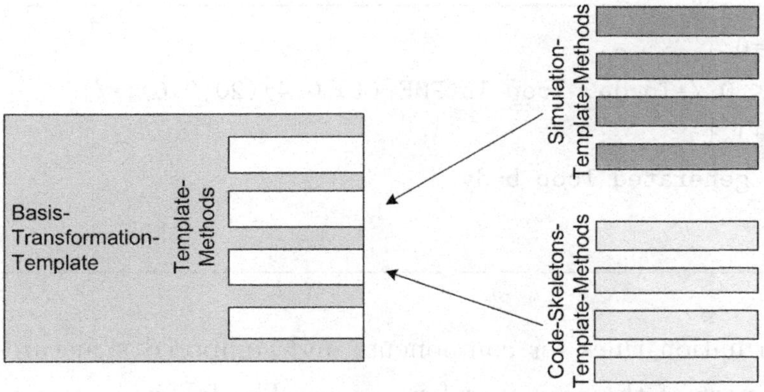

Figure 4.6: Template Methods used to Implement Coupled Transformations

SimuCom as target, the code has to determine the value of the random variable describing the number of loop iterations and then iterate over the loop body for this amount of times (see listing 4.1). The transformation generating a code skeleton generates a loop control flow statement like `for`, but in contrast to the simulation transformation, the loop iteration count is not known. Hence, a comment is generated from the loop iteration count specification (see listing 4.2). This information informs the programmer about the assumptions in the model from which the code has been generated. This allows him to give feedback in case the assumptions prove wrong during implementation. In such a case, the model can be adjusted accordingly.

Listing 4.1 Simulation Loop

```
int max_count = evaluate("IntPMF[(10;0.4)(20;0.6)]");
for (int i=0; i < max_count; i++) {
        // generated loop body
}
```

In this example, common behaviour in both transformations is to iterate on the actions of a RDSEFF. The different code fragments generated for the *LoopAction* is specialized behaviour in a template method.

For the SimuCom transformation all PCM concepts related to random variables are part of special template methods like the loop action shown in the example. This especially includes the interaction with simulated hardware resources loaded with resource demands in *InternalActions*. On the other hand,

Listing 4.2 Code Skeleton Loop

```
for (int i=0;
        i < 0 /*To do, loop IntPMF[(10;0.4)(20;0.6)]*/;
        i++) {
        // generated loop body
}
```

the transformation rules for components and composed structures is common and hence, part of the core transformation. The following sections give more details.

The template method based transformations also enable to easily create the ProtoCom mapping, which uses a mixture of the template methods for the simulation mapping and the code-skeleton mapping. For this, missing behaviour in the PCM model instance is replaced with simulated behaviour. Only a small amount of the template methods is specifically dedicated to the prototype mapping while all others are simply reused. Simulating resource demands on real hardware resources is the only part specific for ProtoCom. It replaces SimuCom's resource demand processing based on simulated hardware resources.

4.3 Mapping Overview

Before presenting SimuCom, ProtoCom, and the Java EE mapping in detail, this section gives an overview on the different mappings and how the deal with the various concepts available in the PCM (see table 4.1).

All transformations map elements of the PCM's *Repository* to Java interfaces, data types and classes. They represent component implementations and are the result of the component developer's transformation. Important to notice is that data types are not supported in SimuCom and ProtoCom as they only use parameter characterisations. In all mappings, a component is always reflected by a least one Java class. All transformations map *CompositeComponents* by generating façades for its provided interfaces which then delegate the calls to instances of the inner components.

All mappings generate code that *instantiates* for each *AssemblyContext* in the PCM an object of the class (or the classes) associated to the component

PCM Concept	SimuCom	ProtoCom	JavaEE / EJB
Interfaces	Java Interface	Java Interface	Java Interface
Data types	N/A	N/A	Java Data types
Provided Roles	Port Classes	Port Classes	Port Classes
Required Roles	Feature Dep.	Feature Dep.	Feature Dep.
Provides-, CompleteComponentTypes	Classes w/ fixed Delays	N/A	N/A
BasicComponents	Classes w/ simulated SEFF	Classes w/ simulated SEFF	Classes with Code Skeletons
CompositeComponents	Facade Class	Facade Class	Facade Class
ComletionComponent	Facade Class	N/A	N/A
AssemblyContext	Instance of Comp. Class	Instance of Comp. Class	Instance of Comp. Class
AssemblyConnector	ConnectorCompletion	Feature Dep. RPC Call	Feature Dep. RPC Call
AllocationContext	Mapping to Sim. Resources	Deployment Script	Deployment Script
Resources	Simulated Resources	N/A	N/A
UsageModel	Workload Driver	Workload Driver	Load Tests

Table 4.1: Overview on the Mappings

contained in that particular context. The *AllocationContexts* and the resources are important only for SimuCom which uses them to simulate resource demands.

The *UsageModel* is used in all mappings to generate code which simulates the behaviour of users. For each *UsageScenario* the generated code contains a workload driver which spawns threads that simulate single users with the frequency given in the respective workload description. SimuCom and ProtoCom use these workload drivers to take measurements of the overall response times while the Java EE mapping uses it as load test driver.

Notice that some mappings depend on feature configurations (*RequiredRoles*, *AssemblyConnectors*). They are subject to closer investigation and their impact is modelled using Coupled Transformations. Section 4.6 gives details on the mapping options and how their different performance impact is reflected.

The following discusses all mappings in detail.

4.4 Simulation Mapping

The PCM is a meta-model designed to describe component-based software architectures in order to analyse performance properties. The design is specifically targeted at model-driven analysis, i.e., automated model transformations map instances of the PCM into analysis models.

In this thesis, SimuCom is introduced. SimuCom is a simulation model and corresponding tool for PCM instances, whose concepts are closely bound to the PCM's concepts to ease its realisation. Implementing a simulation for the PCM offers several advantages and disadvantes, which the following paragraphs discuss.

Arguments for using a simulation instead of analytical methods to analyse PCM instances are

1. **Model Capabilities and Complexity**: Due to its requirement to deal with arbitrary distributed random variables – especially for resource demands – a queuing network for PCM instances would have G/G/1 or G/G/m service centres, i.e., service centres that have an arbitrary distributed service time and arrival rate. It is common in literature to solve this class of queuing networks using simulation engines, e.g. in (Kounev, 2006; Kounev and Buchmann, 2006). Nevertheless, for special instances and result metrics of these networks there are also analytical solutions

available (Bolch et al., 1998a). However, as the PCM aims at general applicability, following the simulation based approach is a reasonable choice. Furthermore, using simulation allows to generalise the produced simulation result to the *distribution* of the system's response time in contrast to the mean-value based analysis done by most analytical methods. Additionally, a simulation-based approach allows to analyse complex service centres with complex scheduling strategies under concurrent load in order to reflect complex hardware resources and real operating system scheduling behaviour.

2. **Meta-Model Evolution**: The PCM's meta-model is continuously evolving to reflect the upcoming requirements when modelling real systems or validating the prediction accuracy. The simulation can be adjusted to deal with a lot of these requirements more easily than defining a mapping into a formal analytical model. Because of this, it is much easier to evolve the meta-model in a trial-and-error process by testing new features in the simulation. Only for features, which demonstrated their usefulness, more complex, possibly analytical transformation should be derived.

3. **Availability of Computation Power**: The recent trend in hardware design is to include multiple cores into one CPU. Simulation based methods gain an special advantage from this trend as not only more complex and realistic simulation become executable but also the concurrent execution of the same simulation model with different initial parameters. This results in multiple models simulating at the same time making simulation-based "what-if" scenarios being more feasible.

Disadvantages of using a simulation-based analysis method are

1. **Time and Memory Consumption**: Simulation takes a significant amount of run-time to get accurate results comparable to analytical predictions and usually consumes large amounts of memory to record the required data.

2. **Case-Based Analysis**: A single simulation run always reflects a single outcome of a random experiment. As a consequence, for example questions asking for amount of users necessary to cause a resource overflow require several simulation runs to approximate this number. Analytical

models often provide such information directly. Only iterative methods need repetitions, but usually much less than simulation-based methods.

3. **Unlikely Situations Hard to Find**: Situations whose occurrence is very unlikely but whose impact on the analysis result is rather large are hard to analyse in simulation-based methods. For example, in a component-based architecture exists a control flow path whose occurrence probability is very low but whose response time is a magnitude of all other control flow paths. In such a case, the simulation run might miss this case, resulting in a misleading result.

4. **Long Control Flow Paths**: A problem specific to simulating the behaviour of software is the existence of loops with large iteration counts (infinite loop iterations are forbidden in the PCM). As each iteration has to be simulated in a precise simulation run, simulation run-time becomes a significant factor. However, heuristic approaches might help to cut down the run-time in case of large iteration numbers, e.g., by replacing them with normal distributed approximations.

Especially the easy support for meta-model evolution which allows fast testing of meta-model changes makes the simulation-based approach the first choice for getting feedback on the meta-model and its concepts which has been important during the PCM's design.

4.4.1 SimuCom Overview

This section gives a brief overview on SimuCom's transformation structure and the simulation parts. SimuCom is based on a model-2-text transformation which transforms instances of the PCM into Java code (see figure 4.7). The generated code uses the so called SimuCom platform which provides a framework or platform for the simulation. It executes the generated code and the generated code uses functions offered by the platform. This separation between generated code and platform code is based on the architecture centric MDSD development process introduced by Völter and Stahl (2006). The platform itself is based on the Java discrete-event simulation framework Desmo-J (DESMO-J, 2007). The descriptions in the following section explain how the transformation maps the elements of the PCM's meta-model to simulation code. Occasionally, it present fragments of the used code generation templates to ease understanding (cf. figure 4.7).

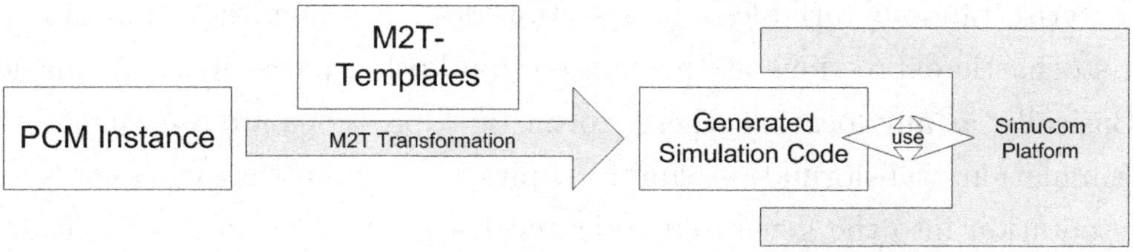

Figure 4.7: Overview on SimuCom's Transformation Structure

This paragraph gives an overview on the parts of the simulation before subsequent sections discuss details of each part.

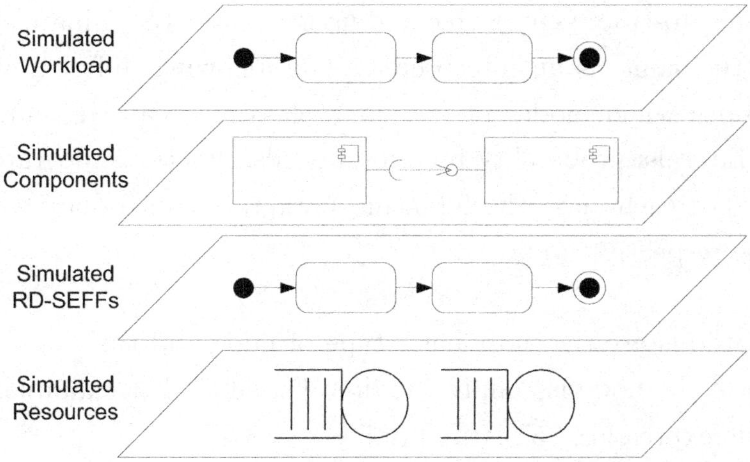

Figure 4.8: Overview on SimuCom's Parts

The simulation is based on a simulation of resources (see figure 4.8). For this, SimuCom simulates G/G/1 queues as described in section 4.4.3. Load for the simulated resources is generated by a simulated workload (see section 4.4.4). For each user a thread is started which traverses the (simulated) system. The thread passes through simulated components (see section 4.4.5) and their (simulated) RD-SEFFs (see section 4.4.6). While passing RD-SEFFs, the simulation threads evaluate the contained stochastic expressions (see section 4.4.2) and generate respective resource demands or pass on to external components. The following gives the details on each of the elements.

4.4.2 Evaluating Stochastic Expressions

As introduced in section 3.2.1, the PCM uses so called stochastic expressions to characterise random variables. This section describes how the simulation deals with stochastic expressions as this is used in all other parts of the simulation.

Basically, at any location where stochastic expressions are used in the PCM, the simulation transformation simply copies the stochastic expression's string representation into the generated code and leaves it to SimuCom's platform to parse and evaluate the expressions. As an enhancement, the simulation's transformation can be improved in future work to generate code which represents the stochastic expressions semantics directly and hence, makes the additional parsing superfluous. However, the basic concepts stay the same.

In the current implementation, the SimuCom platform generates the stochastic expression's abstract syntax tree and uses a visitor to evaluate the expression thus acting the same as an interpreter. The following differentiates five basic classes of nodes where nodes of the same class are realised similar. The five classes are: Literals, probability function literals, functions, operators, and variable nodes. For each class the following paragraphs introduce how the visitor evaluates the respective nodes.

Literals Literals are the most basic type of node and their evaluation is easy as the value of the node is simply the literal's value. For example, the value of the stochastic expression "5" is simply 5.

Probability Function Literals Probability function literals are used to characterise random variables, i.e., their value is determined by drawing samples in the simulation. The simulation uses the so called inversion method to evaluate probability function literals (Law and Kelton, 2000). The basic idea of this method is to derive the inverse function of the cumulative distribution function of the probability function literal $F^{-1}(p) : [0..1] \rightarrow D$ which maps probabilities to values of the sample space D. D depends on the type of the random variable, e.g., `BYTESIZE` characterisations yield Integers while `STRUCTURE` characterisations yield enumeration types. A uniform distributed random variable is generated by a pseudo-random number generator $u \sim U(0,1)$ and $X = min\{x|F(x) \geq u\}$ is returned as result. It can be shown, that X's distribution follows the given probability function literal (Law and Kelton, 2000).

The evaluation differentiates two cases: Discrete and continuous probability function literals. For discrete random variables, F^{-1} is a stepwise function which can be computed efficiently by comparing the drawn uniform value u to the upper limits of the steps.

For BoxedPDFs, which approximate continuous random variables in the PCM, F^{-1} is defined in intervals, where each interval represents a box. As the PCM assumes a uniform distribution inside each box, the inverse of each section is a linear function. This allows efficient calculation of random samples of BoxedPDFs.

For example, consider a probability function literal `DoublePDF[(4;0.3)(8;0.7)]`. This specification defines a continuous random variable whose values fall in the interval [0..4) with probability 0.3 and in the interval [4..8) with probability 0.7. The cumulative distribution function is $F(x) = x * 0.3/4$ for $x \in [0, 4)$ and $F(x) = 0.3 + (x - 4) * 0.7/4$ for $x \in [4, 8)$. The inverse cumulative distribution function $F^{-1}(y)$ is $F^{-1}(y) = y * 4/0.3$ for $y \in [0, 0.3)$ and $F^{-1}(y) = (y - 0.3) * 4/0.7 + 4$ for $y \in [0.3, 1)$.

Functions The SimuCom platform is able to deal with a set of standard functions developers can use in stochastic expressions. Currently, the SimuCom platform supports two types of functions; mathematical functions and random number generators for standard distributions. A visitor evaluates mathematical functions, like **Truncate** or **Round**, by applying the respective Java methods to the function's parameters. For random number generators, like `Norm` for normal distributed samples or `Exp` for exponential distributed samples it uses the SSJ Java library (L'Ecuyer and Buist, 2005). The result of visiting the stochastic expression's AST nodes corresponds to the result of the respective SSJ function (see (L'Ecuyer and Buist, 2005) for details).

Operators For operators, such as `+,-,*,/,<,>,==`, etc., the visitor again uses the standard operators provided by Java. Their precedence order is respected when constructing the stochastic expression's AST. As random variable evaluation is always based on drawing samples of the random variable, the results of visiting stochastic expression AST nodes are always primitive values, which can be used in operations directly.

Variables In stochastic expressions, variables are used to express parameterisations of random variables. They allow to characterise the usage profile in a parametric way (cf. section 3.5.1). From the viewpoint of simulating PCM instances, variables normally (i.e., besides INNER variables) contain a *sample* of a random variable because when the variable is first used, the stochastic expression defining the variable is evaluated and the resulting sample is stored in the variable. The case-based analysis performed in the simulation leads to the use of samples for all random variables.

The simulation uses a process oriented view for users, i.e., users and their requests are simulated using threads. This lets a simulation run look similar to the execution of the real application (however, based on abstract models instead of real application logic). Because of this, an adjusted variant of the concept how variables are organised in real programs can be used to realise variables in SimuCom.

When a compiler generates code for a program, it uses stack frames to implement variable scopes in the program (Muchnick, 1997). A scope is a range in the program in which a certain variable can be accessed. For example, a method is a scope for method local variables, a loop declaration forms a scope for the loop's body, etc. Whenever a scope is entered by the control flow, a new stack frame is put on the stack. Such a stack frame can optionally have a parent frame depending on whether variables of the surrounding scope should be visible. The semantics of a stack frame when looking for the value of a variable is to first look in the topmost stack frame. If the variable is contained in this frame its value is returned. If not, the parent frame is searched for the variable and so on.

The SimuCom platform uses this concept for managing variables in stochastic expressions. Each simulated thread representing a simulated user or one of its requests has a simulated stack on which stack frames can be pushed or popped. When pushing a new stack frame to the stack, the simulated thread additionally has to specify whether the stack frame currently on the top of the stack becomes a parent stack frame or not. When looking for a variable, the semantics as described above is applied: If the variable is in the topmost frame its value is returned, if not, the parent stack frame is queried, and so on. If none of the searched stack frames contains the variable, an exception is raised. By this, the parent relationship defines the scope of the search for variables. It is important for different types of scopes: When executing a call to another component a new stack frame is pushed on the stack *without* a parent frame. This prevents the access to variables defined in the stack frame of the calling service.

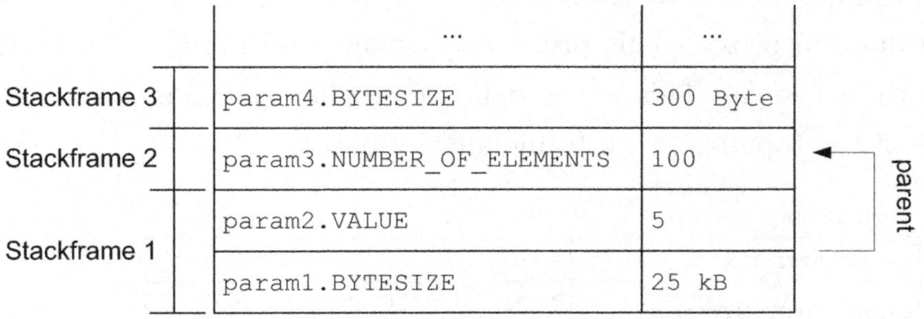

Figure 4.9: An example for a Simulated Stack

For example, consider the simulated stack in figure 4.9 (Notice, that the stacks in this section grow downwards as usual in compiler construction literature). The stack's topmost frame is stack frame 1. It contains two variables, `param1.BYTESIZE` and `param2.VALUE`. Its parent stack frame is stack frame 2 which contains `param3.NUMBER_OF_ELEMENTS` and has no parent frame. On top of stack frame 2 is stack frame 3 which contains the variable `param4.BYTESIZE`. However, this stack frame is currently unavailable. It becomes available again if stack frame 1 and stack frame 2 get popped from the stack.

In this context, the stochastic expression "`param1.BYTESIZE`" evaluates to 25 kilobyte. The expression "`param3.NUMBER_OF_ELEMENTS`" is also allowed as it is contained in the parent stackframe and results in 100. The expression "`param4.BYTESIZE`" is not allowed in this context and would lead to an exception if evaluated against this simulated stack as it can not be reached when following the parent stack frame relationship. Finally, to give an example of a more complex stochastic expression "`param1.BYTESIZE * param3.NUMBER_OF_ELEMENTS`" evaluates to 2500 kilobytes. The latter expression could be an example for a random variable specifying a parametric resource demand for an *InternalAction*.

Late Evaluation Some variables need a so called late evaluation. This means, their value is not determined when they are initially added to their stack frame but later because the evaluation of these variables may result in different samples of their underlying random variable on every access to their value. An example of such a variable is the `INNER` characterisation of collections (cf. section 3.5.4). This characterisation describes the elements contained in a collection. For them, it is assumed that every time when they are used, a different element of the collection is used (cf. Koziolek (2008)). Consequently, the value of the variable is re-evaluated on every access.

For variables with late evaluation, the simulated stack frame contains a so called evaluation proxy. This proxy encapsulates all information needed to re-evaluate the variable. This is the defining stochastic expression and a copy of the state of the topmost stack frame and its parents.

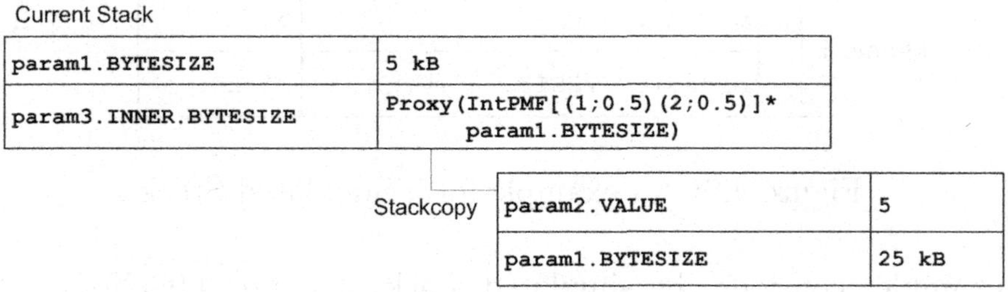

Figure 4.10: Stackframe with Proxy for Late Evaluation

Consider the (artificial) example given in figure 4.10. In this example, the current stack frame contains the variables `param3.INNER.BYTESIZE` and `param1.BYTESIZE` where `param3.INNER.BYTESIZE` is a late evaluating variable. According to the introduced semantics, the stochastic expression "`param3.INNER.BYTESIZE`" evaluates to 25 kByte with a probability of 0.5 and to 50 kByte with a probability of 0.5. Notice, that every evaluation of this stochastic expression can result in a new result with the given probability distribution.

The sections on mapping user (section 4.4.4) and component behaviour (section 4.4.6) contain the initialisation and use of the simulated stack and its stack frames. Before presenting them, simulated resources are introduced as foundation of the SimuCom platform.

4.4.3 Simulated Resources

The simulation is based on simulated resources which simulate the behaviour of instances of the PCM's resource environment. Simulated resources build the foundation of the simulation.

A PCM's resource environment defines two types of resources which are both important for the simulation: *ProcessingResources* and *CommunicationLinkResources*. Basically, both types of resources act the same: Jobs arrive - possibly concurrently - at the resource and demand for their processing. If the resource is already busy with processing another job, the jobs are put in a waiting queue, in which they remain until the resource becomes available. This behaviour is best reflected by queues as defined in queuing network theory (Bolch et al., 1998a). Hence, the simulation uses queues and their service centres to reflect simulated resources.

However, the queues needed for simulating PCM instances have to deal with the following requirements. Some of them make it difficult to reuse existing tools.

1. **Generally Distributed Service Times**: As the resource demands in the PCM are characterised by random variables which can have arbitrary distributions, e.g. BoxedPDFs as introduced in section 3.2.1, service centres have to deal with arbitrary distributed service times.

2. **Generally Distributed Arrival Times**: The arrival time of a job at a queue depends on how the control flow runs through a component-based architecture as this influences when an *InternalAction* in a RD-SEFF is reached. Additionally, it also depends on the previous resource demand processed - if there is one. As the previous demand is generally distributed, its departure rate which is the arrival rate of the following demand is also generally distributed. Hence, in general the arrival rate at a PCM resource is arbitrary distributed.

3. **No Replication**: In the current PCM version, replication of *ProcessingResources* is impossible as the modelling of scheduling of multiple resources, e.g., multicore CPUs, is still subject to research. Together with the previous requirements, this makes PCM queues currently $G/G/1$ queues using the common queuing network classification scheme for queues.

4. **Multiple Job Classes**: As each resource demand is characterised by a possibly different random variable, each demand coming from a specific *InternalAction* falls into a job class specific for this action, i.e., a job class exists for each *InternalAction* which uses a specific *ProcessingResource*.

5. **Support for Different Scheduling Policies**: The current PCM version supports three types of (common) scheduling strategies for *ProcessingResources*: processor sharing, FCFS (First-Come, First-Serve), and delay. They represent a set of common scheduling strategies in queuing network theory (Bolch et al., 1998a). Each service centre in SimuCom has to support these scheduling strategies.

6. **Support for Response-Time Distributions**: For each queue, at least the distribution of the overall processing time and waiting time for the jobs as well as its service centre's utilisation has to be recordable in order to give feedback on the simulation results to the software architect. In queuing network tools, frequently only the average times are available, e.g., (Bertoli et al., 2007; Bolch and Kirschnick, 1993).

As a consequence of the given requirements, a special resource implementation, which encapsulates a queue and the job processing, has been implemented in the SimuCom platform without the use of external libraries. The following describes details of the resource's realisation.

A simulated resource offers a method to its client called `process`. It takes a simulated thread and a demand as arguments. The demand is a double value which is a sample of the random variable characterising an hardware-independent resource demand. This demand is divided by the processing rate of the resource to make it hardware-dependent. The processing rate is set during the resource's initialisation. The resulting value is the resource demand of the resource in standard time units (seconds), i.e., the time the resource would need to process the demand if no concurrency and hence no waiting time existed. For example, an *InternalAction*'s demand evaluates to 100 CPU instructions. If this demand has to be processed by a simulated CPU resource having a processing rate of 10^9 CPU instructions per second, the time demand added to the resource's queue is $100/10^9 = 10^{-7}$ seconds. For simulated network links, the hardware-dependent demand is the bytes to transmit divided by the network's throughput plus the network's latency.

The following formalises a resource queue's behaviour as time passes. SimuCom uses this for its event processing described afterwards. Each queue has a state which contains a list of demands currently processed and the point in time of the last event processed. Disregard the latter for the moment as it is only important for event processing.

Queue State and Time Passing Let *Demand* be the set $UUID \times \mathbb{R}_0^+$. An element $d \in Demand$ describes a demand as a tuple with an unique identifier and its remaining processing time at the resource currently processing it. In the following, $time(d)$ is a shorthand notation for the remaining time part of the vector, i.e., for a vector $d = (id, d_r)$, $time(d) = d_r$. To explicitly refer to the ID of a demand, the following uses $id(d) = id$.

Let

$$\vec{d_n} = (d_1, \ldots, d_n) \in D_n = Demand^n$$

be a vector describing the state of a queue. Each element d_i of a vector $\vec{d}$ describes the remaining processing time for this demand at the resource to which the queue belongs to. The vector is ordered, i.e., for all $i < j$ d_i arrived before d_j at the resource. The set of all possible vectors of demands is

$$D = \bigcup_{i \in \mathbb{N}_0} D_i$$

with $D_0 = Demand^0$ denoting an empty vector, i.e., the vector (). As a consequence, any vector of demands of an arbitrary length i is in D. Hence, the state of a queue $\vec{d}$ is an element of D. The following uses $\vec{d} \in D$ to denote a queue state of arbitrary length. If length is important, $\vec{d_n} \in D_N$ is used. Initially, the state of all queues is (), i.e., the queue is empty.

Let the function $process : D \times \mathbb{R}_0^+ \rightarrow D$ characterises the change of the state of a queue when time passes. The formula $process(\vec{d}, t_\triangle) = \vec{d}'$ holds if the queue's state is $\vec{d}'$ after a timespan of $t_\triangle$ given the initial queue state was $\vec{d}$ and no new demands arrived in the timespan $t_\triangle$. The definition of *process* depends on the queue's scheduling policy. For SimuCom's scheduling disciplines, *process* is given in a succeeding paragraph.

Assuming *process* is given, let the function $nextDone : D \rightarrow \mathbb{R}$ be

$$nextDone(\vec{d}) = max\{t_\triangle | t_\triangle \in \mathbb{R}_0^+ \wedge process(\vec{d}, t_\triangle) = \vec{d}\}$$

That is, *nextDone* gives the time which has to pass since the initial queue's state until finishing the next demand in the queue under the condition that the queue's state is not changed by newly arriving demands.

Note, it is only necessary to define *process* explicitly for $t_\triangle \in [0..nextDone(\vec{d})]$. The remaining values can be determined inductively. $process(\vec{d}, t_\triangle)$ is equal to

$$process(process(\vec{d}, nextDone(\vec{d})), t_\triangle - nextDone(\vec{d}))$$

if

$$nextDone(\vec{d}) < t_\triangle$$

holds.

Simulation Event Processing The behaviour of simulation queues depends on `process` and `nextDone` but also on simulation events. SimuCom simulates queues based on events occurring at specific points in simulation time. Two types of events are involved in simulating a queue depicted as arrows in figure 4.11 (Note, that figure 4.11 only shows the changing queue elements and omits the last event time t_l). The `JobArrival` event occurs in the simulation when adding a new demand to a queue. The `JobDone` event occurs whenever the processing of a job in a queue finishes. Each simulation event contains the current simulation time t_e. As already indicated, in SimuCom the state of a queue is a tuple $(\vec{d}, t_l) \in D \times \mathbb{R}_0^+$ with $\vec{d}$ being the queue's state as introduced and t_l being the last point in simulation time at which the queue has changed its state. The initial state for all queues is $((), 0)$, i.e., their queue is empty and the last state change happened at simulation start.

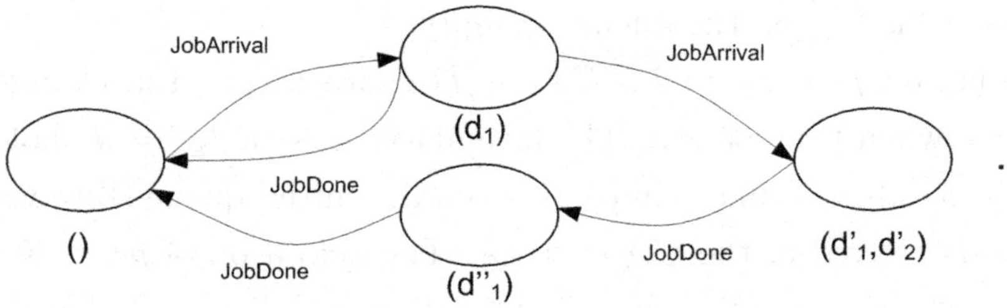

Figure 4.11: Queue Events and Corresponding Queue State Changes as Stochastic Timed Automata

Arrival of a new demand is indicated by a raising `JobArrival` event in the respective simulated resource, which notifies the queue about the new job. SimuCom suspends the issuing thread until processing is done. The queue reacts to the `JobArrival` according to its scheduling strategy. For this, each queue has to provide a formulae for the *process* function which reflects its scheduling policy.

When a `JobArrival` event is processed at event time t_e by a resource, first it updates its state to reflect the current time using the last event time t_l from $(\vec{d}, t_l)$ to

$$(process(\vec{d}, t_e - t_l), t_e)$$

Then it adds the new demand d_{n+1} to the process queue by changing its state from $(\vec{d_n}, t_e) = ((d_1, \ldots, d_n), t_e)$ to $(\vec{d}'_{n+1}, t_e) = ((d_1', \ldots, d_n', d_{n+1}'), t_e)$.

Then it computes

$$t_{next} = nextDone(\vec{d}')$$

Now, SimuCom deletes all JobDone events which might exist for the resource. The simulation schedules a new JobDone event at simulation time $t_e + t_{next}$.

If a JobDone event, which signals the end of processing a job in a resource's queue, is processed at simulation time t_e the following state changes occur. First, the state is updated from $(\vec{d}, t_l)$ to

$$(\vec{d}', t_e) = (process(\vec{d}, t_e - t_l), t_e)$$

to reflect the current time. Then, for all i with $time(d_i) = 0$, the corresponding demand d_i is removed from the queue, hence, the queue's state changes from $((d_1, \ldots, d_n), t_l)$ to $((d_1, \ldots, d_{i-1}, d_{i+1}, \ldots, d_n), t_l)$. As a consequence, all threads waiting for their demand d_i to be processed by the queue resume their control flow. Finally, the next JobDone event is scheduled as specified in the JobArrival event.

Finally, let $rt : ProcessingResource \times Demand \rightarrow \mathbb{R}_0^+$ be a function characterising the total time (response time, rt) spent in the queue of a *ProcessingResource* to process a given demand, i.e., rt is the processing time plus the time spent waiting in the queue. Let rt^d_{start} be the simulation's event time for the JobArrival event of the given demand d (uniquely identified by its ID) at processing resource pr and rt^d_{end} be the simulation's event time for the JobDone event for demand d, then $rt(pr, d) = rt^d_{end} - rt^d_{start}$. Note, rt^d_{end} depends on the simulation's random progress making the result of rt also random. It depends on the initial, random state of the queue and all random JobArrival events occurring during the processing of the demand associated to rt_{end}'s JobDone event. Section 4.6 uses rt to describe the performance impact of the presented code mapping decisions.

Scheduling Strategies The behaviour of the scheduling is controlled by the *process* function which is introduced for the three scheduling algorithms supported by the PCM in the following. As introduced above, it is sufficient to specify *process* for $nextDone(\vec{d}) \leq t_\triangle$, which is assumed to hold in the following paragraphs.

Processor Sharing Processor sharing is an idealised approximation of the Round Robin scheduling strategy (Lazowska et al., 1984). The processor sharing scheduling strategy assumes that switching from one job to the next does not consume any time. Additionally, the time quantum diverted to each job is assumed to be arbitrary close to zero. This makes the resource look as if it processes the demands simultaneously.

For this type of scheduling, the function *process* is defined as

$$process((d_1, \ldots, d_n), t_\triangle) = (d_1^{'}, \ldots, d_n^{'})$$
$$\text{with } id(d_i^{'}) = id(d_i) \wedge time(d_i^{'}) = time(d_i) - \tfrac{t_\triangle}{n}$$

For example, for three demands (denoted without their IDs) $\vec{d_3} = (5, 10, 20)$ seconds and a passed time of $t_\triangle = 15$ seconds, subtract $15/3 = 5$ from each demand $process((5, 10, 20), 15) = (0, 5, 15)$, i.e., the first job in the queue has been fully processed. This triggers a `JobDone` event which changes the state of the resource to $((5, 15), t_l + 15)$ by removing the finished job. The processing of the demand 5 seconds took $rt(pr, 5) = 15$ seconds.

FCFS First-Come, First-Serve scheduling first fully processes the first arrived job, than the second, and so on. The function *process* for FCFS scheduling is

$$process((d_1, \ldots, d_n), t_\triangle) = (d_1^{'}, \ldots, d_n^{'})$$

with

$$id(d_i^{'}) = id(d_i) \wedge time(d_i^{'}) = \begin{cases} time(d_1) - t_\triangle & i = 1 \\ time(d_i) & i \neq 1 \end{cases}$$

Delay Delay scheduling is a scheduling strategy in which the processing of the jobs is independent of the amount of jobs at a resource, i.e., the resource exists in an unlimited number. The *process* function is

$$process((d_1, \ldots, d_n), t_\triangle) = (d_1^{'}, \ldots, d_n^{'})$$
$$\text{with } id(d_i^{'}) = id(d_i) \wedge time(d_i^{'}) = time(d_i) - t_\triangle$$

After explaining how the SimuCom platform implements simulated active resources using queues, the following introduces the transformation which maps PCM *ActiveResources* and *LinkingResources* to simulated resources.

For each *ResourceContainer*, a simulated resource container is created which maps demands issued by components on simulated queues according to the requested *ResourceType*. A simulated resource container is a simple container object containing all simulated active resources. The transformation instantiates a simulated resource in the simulated resource container's constructor for each *ActiveResource* in the corresponding PCM instance's *ResourceContainer* (see figure 4.12).

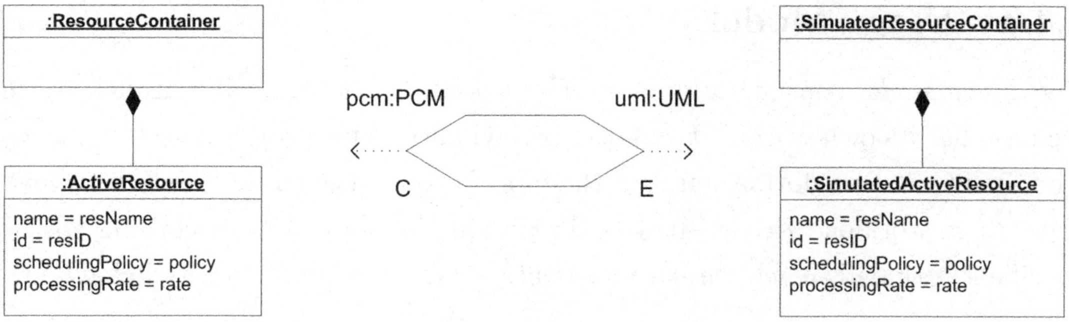

Figure 4.12: Mapping of ActiveResources

The *LinkingResources* require minor changes in their treatment by the transformation. They have an additional specification for their latency, but they don't have a scheduling policy specification as the PCM currently always assumes FIFO processing for them. In the SimuCom platform, there exists a class SimulatedLinkResource which shares a common abstract class with SimulatedActiveResource. The current realisation of this class always uses a FCFS scheduling strategy as demanded by the PCM's specification. The FCFS scheduling discipline is an initial approximation to the behaviour of a network which usually can transmit only one package at a given point in time. The latency is added to the time demand of the transmission in the current implementation. This demand is derived by multiplying the amount of data to be transmitted with the specified throughput of the network. As the mapping of *LinkingResources* is as straight forward as the mapping of *ProcessingResources* it is omitted here.

In SimuCom, demands to *LinkingResources* are derived automatically in a so called performance completion. As for an explanation of this idea several additional concepts are needed, its explanation is deferred until section 4.6.3.

The behavioural model for network resources is a strong abstraction of the real behaviour of a network neglecting issues like collisions, the used protocol, or the network's routing mechanisms. However, to make it more realistic, the example requires more sophisticated models like network simulations as used by Verdickt et al. (2007), which is out of the scope of this thesis.

The next section discusses the mapping of the usage model into a workload driver for the simulation.

4.4.4 Usage Model

The *UsageModel* consists of a set of *UsageScenarios* running in parallel. Each scenario has its own workload and user behaviour specification (cf. section 3.8.1). The SimuCom transformation uses the models to transform them into workload drivers. A workload driver spawns threads in the simulation according to the specified workload - each thread represents a simulated user and its behaviour.

Closed Workload Driver In the generated simulation, a closed workload driver is instantiated and started for each *UsageScenario* having a *ClosedWorkload* specification This closed workload driver evaluates the population specification, which is copied from the PCM instance. Then, it instantiates a number of so called closed workload user objects equal to the population. The closed workload user class is defined in the SimuCom platform and contains the common behaviour loop of a closed workload user: execute scenario, draw a sample of the think time random variable, wait for the evaluated time, and, finally, restart the whole process (see figure 4.13).

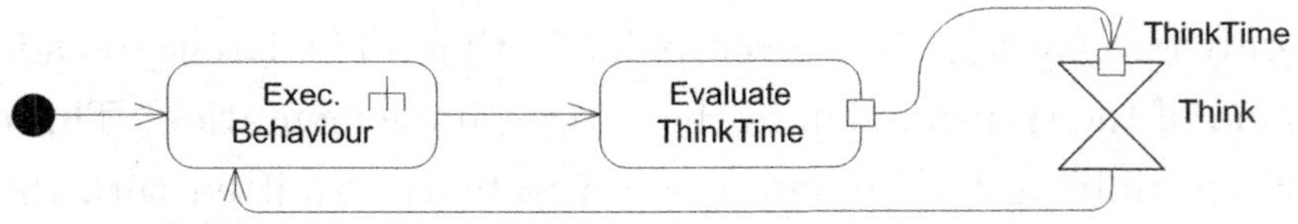

Figure 4.13: Activity diagram showing the generic closed user behaviour

The executed behaviour (as indicated by the opaque behaviour action in figure 4.13) is generated from the *UserBehaviour* as explained after the open workload driver below.

Open Workload Driver For *OpenWorkloads*, the transformation instantiates an open workload driver, also part of the SimuCom platform. The open workload driver is used to generate an open workload in the simulation. In an open workload, users arrive at the system, execute their behaviour, and leave again. To simulate this, the open workload driver spawns a thread when a user arrives, which starts executing its behaviour. Afterwards, the workload driver draws a sample of the inter-arrival time random variable, waits for this time span, and restarts again (see figure 4.14).

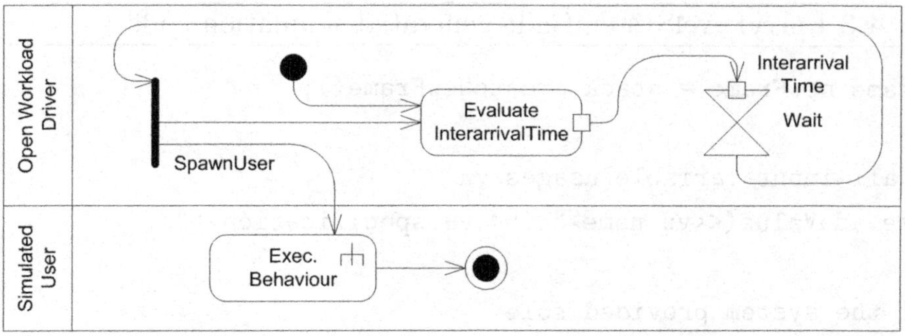

Figure 4.14: Activity diagram showing the behaviour of the open workload driver

User Behaviour The opaque behaviour actions in figures 4.13 and 4.14 represent the user's behaviour as specified in the *UserBehaviour* part of a *UsageScenario*. In order to generate code which behaves as specified in the model, a visitor-based approach is used in the generator templates. A visitor begins at the *Start* action of the *UserBehaviour* and traverses the behaviour following the successor reference until it reaches a *Stop* action. For each action it executes a different transformation depending on the type of the action visited. The following presents the different code templates for the different action types.

Start The generated code for the start node initialises a new simulated stack (cf. section 4.4.2). Additionally, a sensor is initialised which records the total time demand for executing the *UserBehaviour*.

Stop The generated code for the stop action stops the time sensor and records the result. It additionally removes the simulated stack.

Loop Code generated for a loop evaluates the stochastic expression for the loop iteration count and loops the inner behaviour the evaluated times.

Branch The code generated for a branch draws a uniform distributed random number in the interval [0,1]. With this number it applies the inverse cumulative distribution function method (see section 4.4.2) with the probabilities for the respective branch transitions as discrete probability distribution. The result is the number of the branch transition to execute.

EntryLevelSystemCall The most complex code is generated for entry level system calls. The logic is given in pseudo-code in the following. The `<<..>>` expressions in the listing indicate that this is replaced by the respective PCM instance's data. As shown in listing 4.3, first a new stack frame is created and put on the stack. This will be the stack frame for the called service's execution. Then, for all input variables *VariableUsages*, which are the input parameter

Listing 4.3 EntryLevelSystemCall: generated simulation code

```
Stackframe newFrame = stack.createNewFrame();

// for all input variable usages vu
newFrame.addValue(<<vu.name>>, "<<vu.specification>>");

// call the system provided role
system.getRole<<calledRole>>().<<calledService>>(stack);
stack.pop();
```

characterisations, their value is evaluated and stored using their name in the new stack frame. Finally, the called system role is retrieved from the system variable which is initialised in the constructor of the usage scenario with the global instance of the system created at simulation start. Using this role, the call is executed passing the prepared stack. After the call, the stack frame is removed from the top of the stack.

4.4.5 Composite Structures

The *EntryLevelSystemCalls* issued in the code of the workload drivers are directed to a *System*. A *System* is a special *CompositeStructure* to which also *CompositeComponents* belong. As there are only small semantic differences between these structures, in the following they are treated uniformly.

SimuCom's transformation uses the same mapping that is used for mapping PCM instances to POJOs. As this is a complex mapping, its presentation needs additional space. Hence, the discussion of the exact mapping is deferred until section 4.6.2. For the following, it is sufficient to get an informal idea of the basic concepts important to the simulation.

The *CompositeStructure*'s mapping creates an instance of the Java classes generated for each *ImplementationComponentType* for each component in an inner *AssemblyContext* (for *CompositeStructures* a façade class is created which creates the *CompositeComponents* inner structure, cf. section 4.6.2). Afterwards, each POJO instance is connected to its required POJOs as specified in the *AssemblyConnectors* of the *CompositeStructure*. For the details of how the connection is established see again section 4.6.2.

More important in particular to the SimuCom transformation are *component parameters* (cf. section 3.6.2). Component parameters specify performance relevant component configurations, which can be described by a random variable, *but*, which can not be changed at component run-time. Component developers declare component parameters in their specifications and suply a default value for them. Software architects may override the default with their own values. Domain experts may finally override the specification again, however, the values set by the domain experts and the software architect should be disjoint.

The POJOs generated by the mapping of PCM components to code support call interception in the ports generated for their provided roles. For details, see section 4.6.1. Call interception allows to add additional behaviour before or after executing the component's behaviour. SimuCom's transformation uses this interception mechanism to implement component parameters. The mapping idea is based on features provided by the simulated stack frames. When a service call is executed by a component, the interceptor first intercepts the call and adds three new stack frames to the stack.

First, it adds a stack frame containing the component parameters as defined by the component developer having the topmost stack frame as parent frame. On top of this frame, it adds a stack frame containing the component parameter overrides specified by the software architect in their *AssemblyContext*. This stack frame has the component developer's frame as parent frame. Afterwards, a frame containing the usage parameter values taken from the *UserData* specified by the domain expert is added having the software architect's frame as parent.

Due to the semantics of the stack frames, the variable specification of the domain expert and the software architect override those of the the component developer. However, for all variables which are not specified by the domain expert or the software architect, the semantics of the parent relation for stack frames guarantees that the specification provided by the component developer is used.

To illustrate the mapping of component parameters to simulated stack frames, consider the example given in figure 4.15. In this example, two components called Client and Server communicate. The component developer has specified three component parameters for all instances of the Server component: `a.VALUE`, `b.BYTESIZE`, and `log.VALUE`. For each of the parameters, default specifications exist. The software architect has overruled the `log.VALUE` and set its value to true which, in this example, turns on the Server component's logging mecha-

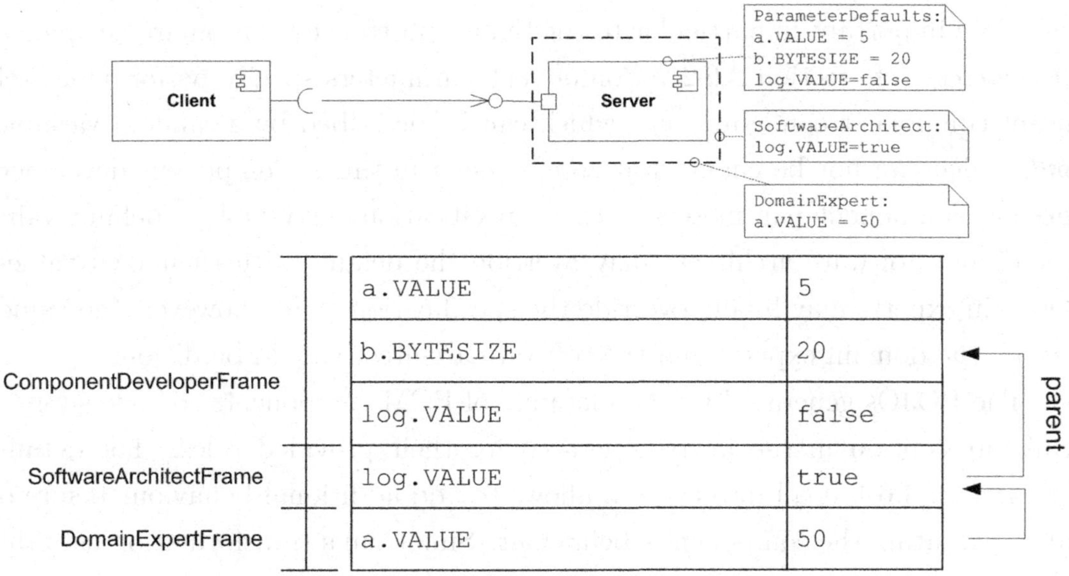

Figure 4.15: Example for Component Paramter Stack Frames

nisms. The domain expert has overridden the parameter `a.VALUE` setting it to a larger value. Note, that `b.BYTESIZE` remains unchanged, i.e., when accessing it in a stochastic expression its value is 20 as indicated by the component developer.

To complete the description of the realisation of component parameters in SimuCom, it remains to be said that the generated interceptor code removes the added stack frames when the call is done.

4.4.6 Resource Demanding SEFFs

The mapping of RD-SEFFs is similar to the mapping of *UserBehaviour*. The RD-SEFF consists of a sequence of AbstractActions which start with a *StartAction* and end with a *StopAction*. There is only a single chain of actions going from the *StartAction* to the *StopAction* as defined by the successor relation of *AbstractActions*. In analogy to the mapping of *UserBehaviours*, SimuCom's transformation iterates over the actions and for each action type an action specific code-generator template is used to generate the code.

The following gives for each action type an informal mapping description and pseudo code for the transformation as appropriate for better illustration.

StartAction The code generated for a *StartAction* of a RD-SEFF creates a stack frame for the return parameter characterisations of the simulated service call. This frame is not put on the stack, but used in *SetVariableActions* and returned when the service's execution terminates. For other types of *ResourceDemandingBehaviours* like inner behaviours of loops or branches no code is generated for their *StartActions*.

StopAction For *StopActions* of RD-SEFFs a return statement is generated which returns the result stack frame created in the *StartAction* to the calling SEFF. For other types of *StopActions* no code is generated.

InternalAction *InternalActions* abstract from computations done inside in a component without interaction with other components. The PCM's abstraction for *InternalActions* uses a set of resource demands specified by random variables instead of the actual code of the internal computations. The resource demands consume their resources in the order in which they are attached to the *InternalAction.*

In order to issue the demand to the targeted simulated processing resource (cf. section 4.4.3) the generated code has to retrieve this resource. For this to work, the POJO representing the current component contains its *AssemblyContext* ID, which is set on initialisation. Using this ID, the code generated for an *InternalAction* looks up the needed simulated active resource via a hashmap generated from the allocation model (cf. section 4.4.7). Notice, that the reference to the respective resource is not hard-coded into the component's code. This enables the component developer's code transformation to be executed independent from other transformations like transformations for the *System* or *Allocation.*

The generated code performs two actions for each *ParametricResourceDemand.* First, the simulated active resource is retrieved as described in the previous paragraph. After retrieving the respective resource, the generated code evaluates the resource demand's stochastic expression as described in section 4.4.2 and asks the resource to process this demand. The actual processing which finally consumes simulation time, has already been described in section 4.4.3.

A template in pseudo code, used to generate the described code, is given in listing 4.4.

ExternalCallAction For *ExternalCallActions* code is generated which performs the call in three steps. First, the stack frame for the called service is prepared. For this, the generated code contains an evaluation of the input *Vari-*

Listing 4.4 InternalAction: code generation template

```
<<FOREACH parametricResourceDemand AS demand>>
        SimulatedResource res = context.getResource(myAssemblyID,
                "<<demand.activeResource.id>>");
        double demand = evaluate("demand.specification");
        res.load(demand);
<<ENDFOREACH>>
```

ableUsage for every input parameter characterisation. This is analogue to the template in listing 4.3 for *SystemLevelEntryCalls*. In the second step, the generated code retrieves the required role of the call and a reference to the component bound to this role via an assembly connector as introduced in section 3.4.4. A generated call passes the prepared stack containing the prepared method's stack frame to the called service. The result stack frame returned by the service call is stored temporary. In the third step, the generated code evaluates the output *VariableUsages* against the returned stack frame stored in the previous step. The variables declared in the output *VariablesUsages* and their evaluated values are stored in the calling method's current stack frame. In so doing, they become available to all actions following the *ExternalCallAction*.

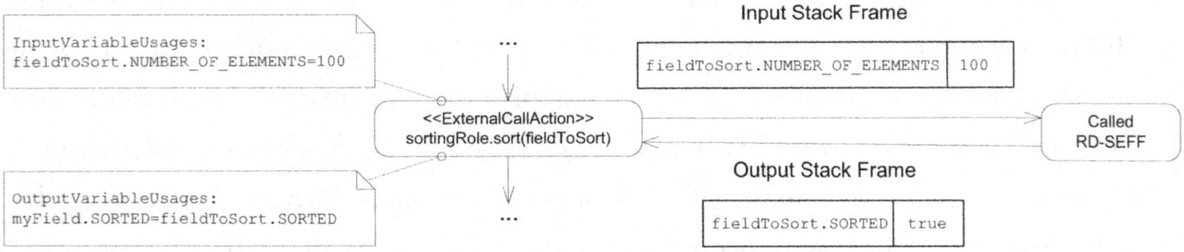

Figure 4.16: Example for an ExternalCallAction and its Stack Frames

To illustrate the mapping, consider the example given in figure 4.16. This example is similar to the one introduced in section 3.5.1 where input and output *VariableUsages* have been explained. A component is called to sort an array. As the sorting's resource demand depends on the number of elements in the field to sort, this information is passed to the called service. An respective input stack frame is created and passed to the called service as indicated by the stack frame over the arrow going to the called service in figure 4.16. The called sorting service returns the field which is now sorted as indicated by the output stack frame on the return arrow going from the called service back to the *ExternalCallAction* in figure 4.16. The output *VariableUsage* maps the random variable `myField.SORTED` to the value of the random variable `fieldToSort.SORTED` which has been set to `true` by the sorting service.

SetVariableAction The PCM uses *SetVariableActions* to specify the result of the computations of a service called on a component. The semantics is that the values set by this action are only available in output *VariableUsages* of the *ExternalCallAction* which initiated the execution of the current service. Note, this implies that the values are also unavailable in the current RD-SEFF. Additionally, the last executed *SetVariableAction* on a specific random variable determines the returned value.

As already introduced in the *Start-* and *StopAction* mapping, the SimuCom mapping uses a dedicated result stack frame to realise this semantic. The result stack frame is unavailable when evaluating stochastic expressions of the current RD-SEFF. Additionally, the stack frame also supports the semantics that store actions on already existing random variables overwrite the previous values. Because of this, the mapping of *SetVariableActions* simply inserts the evaluated specified *VariableUsages* of the *SetVariableAction* into the result stack frame.

Special attention has to be paid if the random variable to set is an `INNER` characterisation. In this case, a late evaluating random variable has to be stored with the current stack frame as evaluation context (cf. section 4.4.2).

The template for generating the respective code is given in listing 4.5.

Listing 4.5 SetVariableAction: code generation template

```
<<FOREACH setVariableUsage AS vu>>
   <<IF vu.isInnerCharacterisation()>>
      resultFrame.add("<<vu.name>>",evaluate("<<vu.specification>>"));
   <<ELSE>>
      resultFrame.addProxy("<<vu.name>>","<<vu.specification>>",
          currentFrame);
   <<ENDIF>>
<<ENDFOREACH>>
```

LoopAction For *LoopActions* the generated code evaluates the iteration count random variable using the current method stack frame. The resulting integer value serves as upper bound for a loop statement iterating for the evaluated amount of times. The inner behaviour's code of the loop results from applying the templates described here recursively. As *LoopActions* execute their body behaviour stochastically independent, no new stack frame is needed for the loop's scope in the code.

CollectionIteratorAction *CollectionIteratorActions* form a special case of a loop action where the loop iterates over the elements of a parameter having a *CollectionDataType*. The special semantics for *CollectionIteratorActions* is that their loop body is executed with a specific element of the collection which impacts `INNER` characterisations of the parameter.

To illustrate the difference between the semantics of a *LoopAction* and a *CollectionIteratorAction*, consider the following example. A loop has two *InternalActions* in a sequence and its surrounding service has a parameter `col` of *CollectionDataType*. The elements of the parameter `col` have a characterisation

$$\texttt{col.INNER.BYTESIZE} = \texttt{IntPMF}[(\texttt{10}; \texttt{0.5})(\texttt{1000}; \texttt{0.5})]$$

Both *InternalActions* have a resource demand of `col.INNER.BYTESIZE`. For a *LoopAction* the independence assumption during the execution of the loop body implies that the first `col.INNER.BYTESIZE` can evaluate to 10 while the second may evaluate to 1000. However, this case will never happen in the real program as either the current element is small, i.e., its size is 10, or it is large, i.e., its size is 1000. Regardless of its actual size, the size stays the same in all *InternalActions*, hence, the options for the total resource demand of the loop are either $2*10 = 20$ or $2*1000 = 2000$ if evaluated in a *CollectionIteratorAction*.

The SimuCom code transformation maps the semantics of the *CollectionIteratorAction* to stack frames. First, the generated code evaluates the `NUMBER_OF_ELEMENTS` characterisation of the parameter which is iterated in the loop. Then it loops as often as the result of this evaluation. However, at the start of the loop body it creates a new stack frame using the current topmost stack frame of the stack as parent. This frame is pushed to the stack to form a new topmost element. To fill this stack frame it collects all available `INNER` characterisations of the parameter being iterated over in the loop. For each characterisation found, it draws a sample of the random variable associated to this characterisation. The result is stored in the created loop body stack frame. Then code for the inner loop behaviour is generated recursively. After this code block has been executed, an additionally generated call removes the loop stack frame from the stack.

Branches The mapping of *BranchActions* to simulation code distinguishes two cases depending on the branch transition type. If all transitions are *ProbabilisticBranchTransitions* then a probability for executing each branch's behaviour is given and all probabilities have to sum up to 1. This is analogue to the *Branch* in a user behaviour and its mapping has been explained already in section 4.4.4. Hence, it is omitted here.

Only available in RD-SEFFs, there is a second type of branch transitions called *GuardedBranchTransition.* Each *GuardedBranchTransition* contains a boolean random variable which represents the condition for executing the transition's behaviour.

GuardedBranchTransitions have semantical implications on the evaluation of their transition's behaviours. First, the conditions of the branches form random variables whose value is fixed after a transitions has been chosen. The chosen condition has to be `true` and all others have to be `false`. Hence, the evaluation of the behaviour has to be done stochastically dependent. Second, when evaluating the guard conditions, a variable which occurs in at least two conditions should evaluate to the same value in both cases. The following paragraphs discuss both cases in more detail.

To explain the first case, consider a branch having two branch transitions and additionally a boolean random variable A. The first branch transition has the guard $A = \texttt{true}$, the second has the inverse guard of the first one which is $A = \texttt{false}$. When executing the behaviour of the first branch transition, it is already known that A is `true`. Hence, all actions in the behaviour of this branch have to be evaluated under the stochastic condition that random variable $A = \texttt{true}$. The same holds for the second transition, only that in this transition the condition is $A = \texttt{false}$. In general, the semantics of evaluating the inner behaviour of a *GuardedBranchTransition* is defined as the evaluation under the stochastical condition that the random variable defining the transition's guard is `true` (cf. section 3.5.8).

In the simulation this semantics is obeyed without any further actions *if* the condition only refers to variables whose values in the current stack frame are not variables with late evaluation. In this case, the evaluation of the condition is *deterministic* and not stochastic any more as it depends on constant samples stored in the actual stack frame. Hence, it is always the same and because of this it is always an stochastical dependent evaluation. For example, a stack frame for the previous example could contain A with value `true`. Then every evaluation of A results in *true*, hence, the value cannot change and this results in a dependent evaluation. The other case in which conditions uses variables with late binding is more complex and discussed after discussing the second case as this case already introduces restriction which ease the following discussion.

The second case is about fulfilling the user's expectations that all conditions are evaluated with the *same* value for the variables in the conditions. This differs from the normal independent evaluation of random variables in the PCM. Consider the above example again where the branch's conditions have been A = `true` and A = `false`. If A is a stochastic variable, for example $A = \texttt{BoolPMF}[(\texttt{true}; 0.3)(\texttt{false}; 0.7)]$, then it makes a difference if a sample of A is drawn once and used to evaluate *both* conditions or whether a sample of A is drawn on every occurrence of A. In the latter case, there is a probability of both branch conditions to become `false` and also one for both branch conditions to become `true`. This is unwanted as it makes it impossible for the component developer to ensure that exactly one branch evaluates to `true`. Hence, the PCM defines to evaluate the conditions stochastical dependent for all variables in guard conditions.

However, this causes a problem with `INNER` random variables, as their evaluation is independent by definition, because potentially two different elements of the collection could be meant. As it is unclear for `INNER` variables in branch conditions if different or if the same collection element is meant by the component developer, the current PCM version forbids the use of `INNER` characterisations in branch conditions.

In the simulation the dependent evaluation of conditions is again unproblematic if only variables are used in the conditions which have basic values in the current stack frame. Then, as argued above, the required semantics is already realised because of the stack frame. As the PCM forbids `INNER` characterisations, the only random variables left which can be used in conditions and which use late evaluation, are the usage component parameters (cf. section 3.6.2) stored in *UserDatas*. However, constructing a stack frame, which contains evaluated usage component parameters (i.e., by resolving the late evaluation), and pushing it on the stack before evaluating the conditions of the branches, solves the problem.

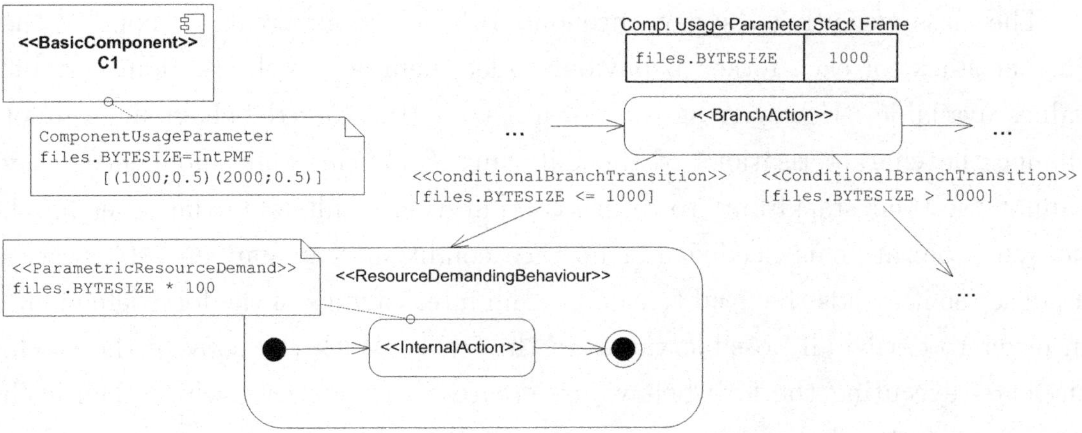

Figure 4.17: Example for Conditional Branch Transitions

To illustrate the introduced concepts consider the example in figure 4.17. In this example, there is a *BasicComponent* $C1$ which has been annotated by the domain expert with a component usage parameter describing for example the size of files managed by the component in its usage context. Additionally, figure 4.17 depicts a part of a RD-SEFF of any of $C1$'s services which contains a *BranchAction* with *GuardedBranchTranstions*. The guards check whether the filesize is below or above 1000, for example because small files use a different caching strategy. For the case that the filesize is less or equal to 1000, the branch's behaviour is shown. In the behaviour, there is an *InternalAction* with a *ParametricResourceDemand* of `files.BYTESIZE * 100`. The conditional evaluation ensures that this demand is never larger than $1000 * 100 = 10^5$. In the given example, it is always $1000 * 100 = 10^5$ as the only filesize which is less or equal 1000 in the set of possible filesizes is 1000. A stack frame which is pushed on the stack before evaluating the branch is shown above the branch action. In this case the current sample for the random variable `files.BYTESIZE` is 1000.

ForkAction For the *ForkAction*, the generated simulation code uses Java threads to simulate the concurrent behaviours. For this, it generates an inner class containing the code for each forked behaviour - regardless of whether the behaviour should be executed synchronously or asynchronously. Two classes of the SimuCom platform then each execute an instance of these inner classes. One class executes all synchronous behaviours and the other one all asynchronous behaviours.

The class executing the asynchronous fork behaviour creates a copy of the current stack for each forked behaviour to let them access the random variable values available. However, as they own a copy, the forked behaviours cannot change the characterisations of the initiating *ForkBehaviour* and hence, they cannot use their stackframe to return computation results. On the other hand, no synchronisation is needed and no race conditions can happen. This eases analyses as it avoids the need to calculate all interleavings of the fork behaviours in order to derive all possible values in the stack. With the copy of the stack, the class executing the fork behaviours creates a new thread, which then each executes a forked behaviour. Afterwards, it returns as it does not not need to wait for the threads to terminate.

The class executing synchronous fork behaviours is similar to the asynchronous. However, after starting the behaviours it uses the Barrier pattern (Douglass, 2002) to wait for all threads to terminate before returning.

Figure 4.18 depicts both types of behaviours.

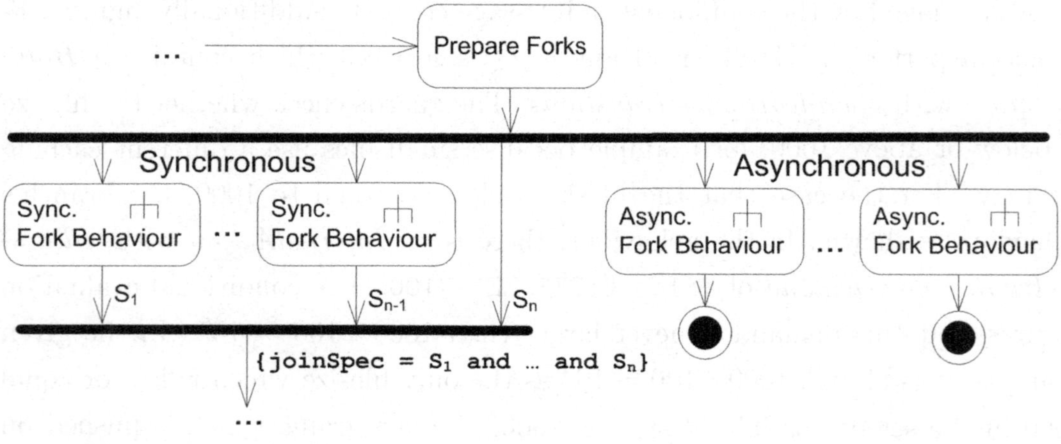

Figure 4.18: Activity Diagram for the Generated Fork Simulation Code

Acquire- and ReleaseAction Resource acquire and release actions model the handling of resources of a limited number. As long as resources are available acquire retrieves them and execution continues. If all resources are occupied, further acquire calls are blocked until the resource becomes available again. The SimuCom framework contains simulated passive resources, manually realising the described semantics based on Desmo-J queues. The reason for manual realisation of the semaphores is simply the instrumentation with sensors which measure the waiting time needed to acquire the resource.

Simulated passive resources are instantiated in the constructor of the POJOs representing the components, i.e., each *AssemblyContext* uses its own passive resource. They offer `acquire()` methods decreasing the amount of available resource instances and `release()` methods increasing the amount of available resource instances. The mapping of *Acquire-* and *ReleaseActions* is therefore straight-forward by calling the respective method on the simulated passive resource matching the one specified in the PCM actions.

4.4.7 Allocation

The PCM's *Allocation* model contains a set of *AllocationContexts*. Each *AllocationContext* links an *AssemblyContext* part of a *System* to a *ResourceContainer*. This link indicates that the component embedded in the *AssemblyContext* is deployed on the referenced *ResourceContainer* (cf. section 3.7). The simulation requires this information to determine the simulated resource which is responsible for processing demands issued by the component embedded in the *AssemblyContext*.

In SimuCom, each simulated component instance stores its *AssemblyContext* ID which is passed to it when it is initialised by its parent *CompositeStructure* (cf. section 4.4.5). It uses this ID to retrieve its simulated resource container whenever it evaluates the resource demands of *InternalActions* in any of its RD-SEFFs.

To allow an efficient retrieval of the resource container, the code generated by SimuCom instantiates a hashmap before the simulation starts and fills it with the allocation information. The hashmap is initialised by code generated from the *Allocation* model in the PCM instance. For each *AllocationContext* in this *Allocation* the generated code adds an entry to the hashmap which links the ID of the *AssemblyContext* referenced by the current *AllocationContext* to the corresponding instance of a simulated resource container retrieved from the simulated resource environment by the ID of the *ResourceContainer* referenced by the current *AllocationContext* (see figure 4.19 for an example).

Special care has to be taken for the inner components of *CompositeComponents* as only *AssemblyContexts* inside a *System* have their own *AllocationContexts*, while *AssemblyContexts* nested inside *CompositeComponents* inherit the *AllocationContext* of their parent component. The code generated by SimuCom realises this behaviour by using the parent's *AssemblyContext* ID whenever components nested inside a *CompositeComponent* need to retrieve their *AllocationContext*.

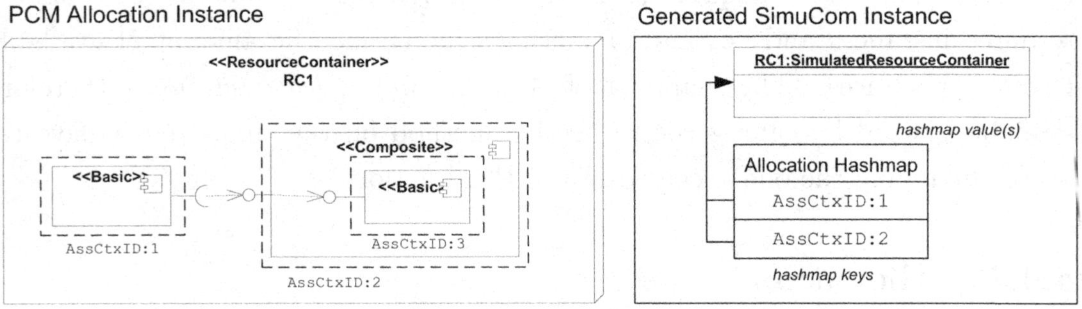

Figure 4.19: An Example for an Allocation Mapping

For example, consider the *Allocation* in figure 4.19. There is an allocation of a *BasicComponent* and a *CompositeComponent* in their respective *AssemblyContexts*. Inside the *CompositeComponent* there is another *BasicComponent*. For all *AssemblyContexts* their ID is given. On the right hand side in figure 4.19, the generated hashmap instance is shown. As described above, the *BasicComponent* inside the *CompositeComponent* uses the *AssemblyContext* ID of its parent to retrieve its resource container. As this ID is 2, it gets the resource container its parent is allocated on.

4.4.8 Component Context in SimuCom

As introduced in section 3.2.2, components in the PCM have a component context which is either specified or computed in analysis tools. Furthermore, the context is split among the developer roles into the assembly context, the allocation context, and the usage context. The following illustrates how SimuCom delas with each of the contexts.

AssemblyContext The manually specified assembly context holds the information on a component's parent *ComposedStructure* and the bindings of its required interfaces. This information is used in SimuCom's mapping to instantiate simulated components as described in section 4.4.5. As the computed assembly context is only of interest for functional analyses, SimuCom disregards it.

AllocationContext The manually specified allocation context stores the information on the allocation of components to resource containers. As described in section 4.4.7, SimuCom uses this information to retrieve the simulated resources which have to process resource demands of simulated components. The computed part of the allocation context contains the hardware-dependent resource demands. SimuCom calculates them on the fly by dividing hardware-independent demands by the resource's processing rate before putting the demand into the resource's queue (see section 4.4.3).

UsageContext The manually specified usage context is reflected by the *UsageModel* in the PCM. SimuCom uses this model to derive its workload drivers from it (see section 4.4.4). Additionally, the *UsageModel* contains the initial values of input parameter characterisations which are used in SimuCom to initialise the stack frame used in *EntryLevelSystemCall*s. The computed usage context is part of the simulations state. Each thread stores a sample of the current parameter characterisations in its simulated stack frame and changes the state of this stack while it traverses the simulated system (see section 4.4.2). The arrival rate of jobs at each component, which is also part of the computed usage context, results implicitly from the ongoing simulation time. As the threads traverse the system, they arrive at components with an arrival rate which reflects the system's control and data flow.

4.4.9 Semantics of the Simulation

The simulation semantics is given by the introduced semantics of SimuCom's queues and their realisation in Java, i.e., SimuCom's execution environment, and the given transformation of PCM instances into Java code which uses the queues. The handling of parameter characterisations is realised by the semantics given for the simulated stack frame.

A specification of PCM semantics to which the simulation sticks using coloured Petri-Nets is given by Koziolek (2008).

4.4.10 Assumptions and Limitations

Three basic types of assumptions and limitations exist: those already present in the PCM, those being of conceptual character for SimuCom, and those which are current implementation limitations. The first type has already been discussed in section 3.10. Hence, the following discusses briefly the other two types.

A general limitation of a simulation based approach is its case-based analysis (see section 4.4). There is no way to ensure that all relevant cases for a design decision will be reached at least once, i.e., a complete coverage of the state space of the analysis model cannot be guaranteed. However, it can be argued that for early performance estimations it is sufficient to have a sufficiently large coverage of the state space. Nevertheless, for other quality attributes such as reliability, which focuses on very unlikely failure events, the simulation based approach might not be applicable.

A limitation of the current implementation is the missing support to specify which parts of the code should be instrumented with sensors. The current realisation generates a response time sensor for each service offered by a component. However, it might be useful to instrument different sequences in the control flow to analyse a particular design decision.

The use of a single model-2-text transformation to translate PCM model instances into the simulation code is cumbersome as the abstraction gap bridged by the transformation is high. A model-2-model transformation should be used to generate an intermediate simulation model, which forms the basis of the simulation code generation. Especially for model manipulations as needed in Coupled Transformations this would ease the task. However, for this, tool support for model-2-model transformation languages and engines have to mature further.

4.4.11 Simulation Time Estimation

The following derives an estimate of the time complexity of a simulation run. It identifies the factors which influence the length of simulation runs. An important aspect in this context is the accuracy needed by the software architect. As the PCM's aim is to support selecting between competing design alternatives, the software architect needs a prediction sufficiently accurate for this.

How long it takes to reach a sufficient accuracy, depends on several factors. First, the differences in the results for the respective design alternatives are important. If the alternatives show large differences in their performance, this is usually visible in simulation results after short simulation times. Second, the complexity of the input model is important. More components having more SEFFs or workloads with larger numbers of users extend the state space of the simulation model significantly. Third, the simulation's stop condition makes a difference. If stop conditions based on confidence intervals and point estimators are used, it may take a long time to reach that confidence level. Opposed to that, using an upper simulation time limit or a predefined number of samples of the resulting distribution function, may yield faster results which are not as accurate. Fourth, the complexity of the result distribution function has an impact. The larger the range of this function is, the longer it takes to simulate a given single case at least once. The following elaborates on the second and third factor as they are under the control of the software architect.

For SimuCom the most expensive basic operations are to draw samples for random variables and to generate and process events in the underlying event-based simulation framework. The number of random variables to draw depends on the upper bound of the number of probability function literals n_{pfl} in all stochastic expressions and the number of probabilistic branches n_{pb} for a single *UsageScenario*. The complexity class for the number of random variables rv needed in a single simulated control flow thread when neglecting the time needed for the scheduling algorithm in the simulated resources is $O_{rv}(n_{pfl} + n_{pb})$.

Note, that n_{pfl} and n_{pb} may depend on other structures, especially loops or external service calls in loops. As loops are simulated, the amount of iterations in the simulation is equal to the amount of iterations specified in the input model. As a consequence, the amount of probability function literals to evaluate or probabilistic branches needs to be multiplied by the loop iteration count for all occurrences of these objects in loop bodies. However, due to the PCM's abstraction many loops in the software are not part of the RD-SEFF as loops which are part of the modelled component become a single *InternalAction* in the RD-SEFF. For example, a bubble sort algorithm which usually consists of two loops can be replaced by an *InternalAction* having a resource demand which reflects bubble sort's complexity of approx. $\frac{n^2}{2}$. However, the precondition for this is that there is no external service call in the modelled loop body. Nevertheless, in general, arbitrary control flow structures can be modelled using the RD-SEFF. Potentially, any number of loops can be nested in a PCM instance, leading to large polynomes for the number of random variables to draw.

For every *ParametricResourceDemand* in every control flow thread two events are generated (cf. section 4.4.3): one for rescheduling the next finished job and one if the job has been processed finally. Let n_{prd} be the upper bound of *ParametricResourceDemand*s caused by executing a single *UsageScenario* and u be an upper bound on the number of concurrent users in the simulated system. Again, n_{prd} also depends on the loop structure of the model as explained in the previous paragraph. Then the number of events needed for this scenario falls in the complexity class $O_{ev}(n_{prd} * u)$. Taking the number of users into account the complexity class for the number of random variables rv to draw is $O_{rv}((n_{pfl} + n_{pb} + n_{prd}) * u)$.

Finally, the number of repetitions for the stochastic experiment where each user executes his scenario once is determined by the simulation stop condition. Let m be the number of repetitions, then the overall simulation run time is of complexity class

$$O(m * (u * (n_{pfl} + n_{pb} + n_{prd})))$$

The stop condition is in many simulations the factor which can be modified easily. SimuCom currently contains two stop conditions: a basic condition which is independent from the input model and which stops the simulation as soon as a given maximum simulation time is reached by the simulation and second a more advanced condition which stops depending on the confidence interval of the mean value estimator of the overall passage time sensor. Additional stop conditions, for example those given by Page and Kreutzer (2005), may be supported in future implementations.

The experiences gained in modelling and simulating the examples given in section 5 showed that the simulation time is not a major issue for small to medium sized system models. They take approx. 5 minutes with up to 200 simulated users on a recent computer to get a distribution function which does not change any more significantly, i.e., sufficient for choosing a design alternative, compared to running the simulation for a longer time. Even a larger model like the PCM model of CoCoME (Krogmann and Reussner, 2008) returns a result in 5-10 minutes which is sufficient for early design time analyses. However, a case study with larger industry style models is still missing (cf. section 6.3).

4.5 Coupled Transformations

The previous section 4.4 introduced the mapping of PCM instances to the SimuCom platform. However, the presented mapping corresponds to the approach of conventional prediction methods, as it transforms the source model *without* taking the code transformation into account. According to the Coupled Transformations method introduced in section 4.1, the knowledge about the code transformation has to be included into the prediction transformation.

For this, model-2-model transformations are added to the transformation chain which generates the prediction model, i.e., the SimuCom instance. Note, that in this case model-2-model transformations are applied despite the technical issues involved due to their immatureness (cf. Uhl (2007b)). However, they have been realised as ad-hoc transformations in Java instead of using a standard transformation engine.

As the Coupled Transformations method is applicable to arbitrary types of platform transformations with arbitrary meta-models for their mark models, the following focuses them to the context of this thesis. It only investigates transformations of the PCM as meta-model for component-based software development. In this setting, several types of platform transformations and different types of mark meta-models can be considered. In the following they are discussed in detail.

4.5.1 CBSE Platform Transformations

As introduced in section 2.1.4, several component models exist that may serve as target platform for realising components and architectures in an MDA sense. Especially, component models with a supporting implementation framework (Java EE, COM, ...) or frameworks built for industry projects (Fractal) are well suited as platform for realising a PCM model in code. Note, that for the code transformation mainly the structural elements and behaviour specifications (*ImplementationComponentTypes*, *Systems*, and RD-SEFFs) are of interest as they can be used as source models for code generation. Especially the hardware model (i.e., *ResourceEnvironment*) is not of interest in code transformations.

When using transformations to realise technology-indifferent components like those available in the PCM on a technological platform, three aspects are of main interest (see table 4.2).

	PCM	J2EE/EJB
Structure	BasicComponents, CompositeComponents	Annotated Java Classes
Behaviour	RD-SEFFs	Method Implementations
Life-Cycle	N/A	Container Services

Table 4.2: Overview on Mapping Aspects For Mapping PCM Instances to EJB

The first aspect is how to map components *structurally*. This means using the platform's concept of a component to realise the component, its inner structure (for composite components), its provided and required interfaces, the data types used, etc. For example, when using EJB3, classes with special annotations realise components structurally and annotated Java interfaces serve as component interfaces as shown in listing 4.6 (Java uses the "@" character to mark annotations). This example declares a stateless EJB with a remote interface called `IMyComponent`.

Listing 4.6 Example EJB Code

```
@Remote public interface IMyComponent {...}

@Stateless public class MyComponent implements IMyComponent {...}
```

Second, mapping component *behaviour* defines how the component acts at run-time. In case of the PCM, this means mapping RD-SEFFs into adequate source code. Due to the PCM's abstraction in the RD-SEFF, this mapping is either incomplete and the resulting code needs additional manual adjustment, or the mark model of the transformation has to specify additional information on the components internal behaviour, e.g., by using UML Action Semantics to specify the behaviour of internal actions (Völter and Stahl, 2006).

Third, the transformation has to respect the component's *life-cycle and run-time services* provided by the platform. For example, in Java EE/EJB the application server uses so-called containers which host components and offer services like component instantiation, service call interception, dependency injection, communication services, security (authentication and authorisation), etc. Many of these services can be configured either via source code or via configuration files.

In the mapping presented in section 4.6 the main focus is on the first and the third aspect. The second is neglected because of the high abstraction of the PCM's RD-SEFFs, which only allows to generate initial code skeletons but not a complete implementation.

The reason for introducing the classification of these implementation aspects is that for different classes different methods to include the performance impact into the prediction model work best. However, before introducing the methods in section 4.5.3, the following section investigates the mark model options.

4.5.2 Mark Meta-Models

As already mentioned, for mapping abstract models into more concrete models at least two alternatives exist. Either, by using constant default values for alternatives in the mapping or by making them explicit in mark models. The use of mark models offers additionally flexibility for the transformation's user and makes the transformation more reusable in several application scenarios. The following discusses UML profiles, configuration models, and full-featured models as candidates for mark meta-models.

- **UML Profiles:** If a transformation uses UML models as input, often a UML profile is used to mark model elements with stereotypes and tagged values (cf. section 2.2.3). The transformation interprets the stereotypes and tagged values and transforms the model elements accordingly. For example, AndroMDA (AndroMDA.org, 2007) uses stereotypes to parametrise the transformation's output, i.e., which classes should be transformed to what type of EJB, e.g., stateful or stateless session bean, or entities. A drawback of profiles is their unavailability for non-UML models like the PCM.

- **Configuration Models:** Configuration models are generalisations of configuration files. Their elements refer to specific model elements in the model they configure (e.g., using MOF references) and contribute additional attributes in a structured way to these elements. Examples for configuration models are configuration files or feature diagrams (cf. section 2.2.2). MDSD transformations use them as so called decorator models where a configuration information has a reference to the element it contains details for. For example, a feature configuration referencing an *AssemblyConnector* can contain details on the technical realisation of this connector, e.g., by specifying that the connector should be implemented using SOAP.

  Configuration models are well suited to describe transformation options because of their clear structure. Developers understand them quickly due to their usually limited set of options. Additionally, they often support expressing constraints which ensures correctness and consistency. However, they are not suited in situations where the set of options is rather large.

- **Full-featured Models:** Full-featured models refer to arbitrary models following for example a MOF meta-model. In contrast to configuration models, which usually only represent a small number of options, full-featured model may be arbitrarily complex. Usually they are also attached to model elements as decorator models. They offer the most flexibility which can make them difficult to understand.

For the transformations presented in this thesis, feature diagrams were chosen because of the mentioned advantages. Especially the rather small set of options eases the creation of transformations which include the selected options into the prediction model. Full-featured models might require complex transformations to reflect all options in the prediction model, however, theoretically, they can be used as well.

For reasons of convenience the transformation supports two types of feature configurations. First, a global configuration for all model elements of a specific type which defines the default settings for transforming the respective elements. Second, configurations can be attached to model elements as decorator models to override the global defaults with element specific values.

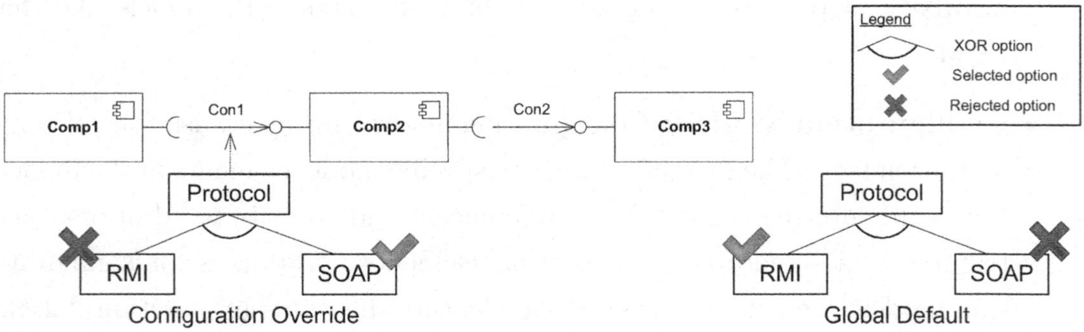

Figure 4.20: An Example for General and Decorator-based Feature Mark Models

Consider the example in figure 4.20, where a transformation offers two options for the communication protocol in the mapping of *AssemblyConnectors*. The user of the transformation has specified that *AssemblyConnectors* should be mapped on a RMI based communication in general. As the depicted connector named `Con2` connecting component `Comp2` and `Comp3` is not referenced by a decoration, the transformation generates an RMI-based implementation for it. For `Con1` the transformation's user attached a decoration which overrides the general chosen option and parametrises the transformation to realise the connector using SOAP.

4.5.3 Methods to Parametrise Analysis Transformations

The following presents two methods to reflect feature-based decisions (as introduced in section 4.5.2) for typical CBSE platform decisions (as introduced in section 4.5.1) in prediction models. The first method handles structure changing design decisions while the second method deals with including middleware/container services decisions.

Structural Changes Modular transformations (as introduced in section 4.2) allow to reflect design decisions encoded in mark model options that affect the structure of the generated code in the prediction model. Remember that this thesis uses modular transformations to generate the implementation's code as well as the simulation-based prediction model. If a feature affects the generated code's structure, e.g., by introducing additional classes, both the implementation and the simulation code is affected. The execution of code inside such an additional class depends on this class' existence. Hence, only if the class exists in the generated implementation code, its corresponding simulation class exists in the simulation.

To clarify this, consider mapping components to classes. A first design alternative maps a single component to a single class. Furthermore it maps component services to public methods of this class. As modular transformations use this design alternative in both the code and the simulation transformation for both output types the generated code has the same structure. However, the modular transformation generates different implementations for the code and for the simulation output (cf. section 4.2). The simulated loop consumes simulation time while the code loop is part of the applications logic.

As a second design alternative consider a mapping which creates specific classes called ports for each provided interface similar to the Façade pattern (this mapping option is discussed in detail in section 4.6.1). Then these ports delegate calls to the actual component implementation. The modular transformation generates ports for both output types, the code as well as the simulation. This allows adding an additional simulated time consumption to capture the performance impact of the call delegation in the simulation model.

Figure 4.21 depicts an example. Next to the transformation arrows the chosen feature configuration for the transformation is shown. Depending on this selection a different structure of classes and interfaces is generated. However, this does not depend on the actual platform (simulation or code) but only on

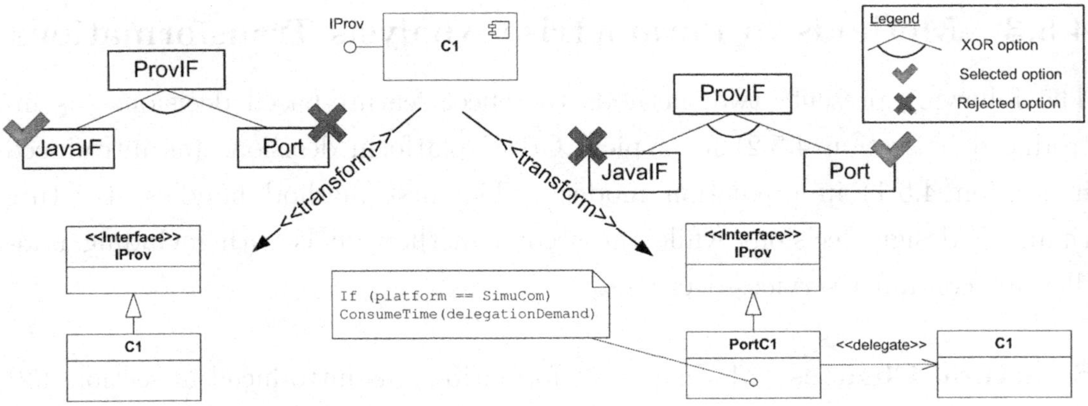

Figure 4.21: Example for Structure Changing Options

the selected features. The only change which depends on the selected platform is indicated in figure 4.21 by an UML note. The code in this node is part of the transformation rule generating the port class. It generates an additional time consumption if the transformation's target is simulation. This is done as described in section 4.2 by using template methods.

Discussion Further examples for structure changing transformation options can be found in section 4.6.1, especially in the context of mapping required roles. In general, if transformation options are derived from design patterns (as in the example above by using the façade design pattern) the design pattern's structural description can be used to derive the structural options. The performance impact of the different structural alternatives need to be analysed by performance experts.

Additionally, note that using modular transformations is not always an option. It fits in this case, as the generated simulation's code is very similar to the generated code skeletons. However, if a specification language for the performance prediction model like stochastic process algebras is used, then the structure of the generated code is not reflected any longer in this language. Hence, it can not be used directly.

Completions For the performance of a software system, middleware services or run-time container services are often an important factor. Hence, having detailed information on the use and configuration of these services can increase the accuracy of a performance prediction significantly. An example has already been given in figure 4.20. There, the choice between SOAP or RMI for the communication protocol for mapping an *AssemblyConnector* has an impact on the performance (as SOAP has a larger protocol overhead it makes its processing more resource demanding, thus, slowing it down).

When looking at a middleware or a component run-time-container, one might consider it to be a (potentially large) composite component, which offers services to its clients, i.e., the components deployed on it. However, if they were modelled as components then there would be two types of components: application components that realise the business logic of the application and framework components which offer additional run-time services to the application components. The PCM itself only targets composing application components in its *Assembly* model.

In the PCM, assembly refers to composing application components to create the business logic while allocation refers to deploying components in run-time environments. As a consequence, allocation deals with putting components in their software run-time environments which are framework components using the afore introduced classification. The allocation relationship between application components and framework components is usually described in a separate deployment viewpoint.

However, for more accurate performance predictions, the allocation on framework components needs to be taken into account because of its performance impact. Coupled Transformations offers a possibility to do this in a parameterised way for those components which can be influenced by generated artefacts like code or configuration files. Additionally, it can be used to include platform details that are not influenced by mark model options but only by the knowledge about the platform the code transformation generates for. For example, when generating for Java EE, the prediction transformation adds Java EE specific resource demands to the prediction model.

Section 2.3.3 describes completions introduced by Woodside et al. (2002) which serve for the purpose of enriching a prediction model by details of vertical application layers in order to improve prediction accuracy. In the context of this thesis, the idea of completions is applied. However, as the PCM is a component model, in contrast to Woodside et al. (2002) the introduced transformations use *special, generated components* as completions. In addition, they *generate* the specification of these completion components. The transformations utilise the advantages of component composition to generate and compose them in a flexible way based on a feature configuration model. Furthermore, they customize the generated completion component depending on the feature configuration of the respective code generation transformation. The following gives details on each of these capabilities.

Completion Components The following requirements lead to the idea of using components as completions.

- **Reuse Existing PCM Model Concepts:** Modelling software parts of lower abstraction layers as components allows to reuse the existing modelling elements of the PCM, including components and their composition theory, interfaces, parameter dependencies, and the RD-SEFF abstraction. All these concepts prove useful in modelling middleware platforms.

- **Compositionality:** The middleware layer uses other layers such as the virtual machine or operating system layer to fulfil its work. By using composite components, the hierarchy of layers can be mapped to a hierarchy of components.

- **Reuse Existing PCM Transformations:** Using components as completions allows reusing of existing transformations. In this case, especially the reuse of SimuCom's simulation code transformation is interesting to get middleware aware performance predictions with little adjustments to the existing method.

- **Exchangeable Middleware Implementation:** Middleware implementations often implement a specific set of standardised interfaces like those defined in the Java EE standard in order to keep them exchangeable by customers. Having a mechanism to keep the middleware implementation exchangeable allows analysing the performance of the application under different middleware implementation models and hence, determining the performance-wise best suited implementation.

- **Revision of PCM Concepts:** Using completion components for modelling the middleware interaction may give additional insights about missing requirements to the PCM for modelling real-world systems and hence, highlights further research directions for the meta-model.

In order to differentiate completion components from components of the application architecture layer the decision was made to extend the PCM's meta-model to introduce them. In order to have flexible completion components, they inherit from *ImplementationComponentType*, which allows to use them everywhere where other implemented components can be used, from *ComposedStructure*, which allows to construct their implementation by composing components, and from *InterfaceProvidingRequiringEntity*, which allows them to offer services and to require other services to fulfil their own. The resulting meta-model is depicted in figure 4.22, where the stereotype `<<pcm>>` marks PCM meta-classes.

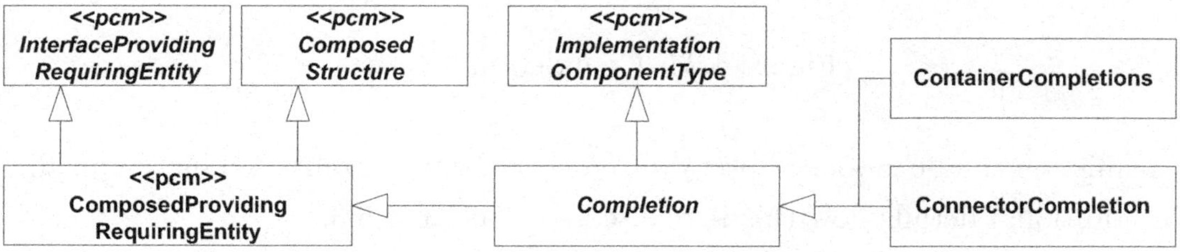

Figure 4.22: Completions Meta-Model

The resulting meta-model is called extended PCM (ePCM) in the following. Note, that the extended PCM is only available to model transformations and not to developers, who specify PCM instances. Also note, that *Completion* is an abstract class and that there are two concrete classes sub-classes of it in figure 4.22: one for connector completions which is used to model communication aspects and one for container completions used to model the impact of the component's runtime container. Note, that it might be necessary for future transformations to extend the list of heirs depending on the aspects to be included into the performance prediction model. Currently, the two completion types given reflect the mapping design decisions given at the beginning of section 4.5.1.

In figure 4.23 both types of completions introduced here are depicted. *ConnectorCompletions* replace *AssemblyConnectors*. Their inner components model the performance impact of communicating components, e.g., for remote communication the demand of networking resources needed to transmit the service call and its parameter values. *ContainerCompletions* wrap components and by adding decorator components (Gamma et al., 1995, p.175) can be used to model the impact of container services like transaction management, security, or component pooling.

Completions inherit the advantages of components, e.g., the capability to compose them with other components. Hence, they allow to apply the completion idea recursively by using *Completions* inside completions. For example, for *ConnectorCompletions* the stack of message filters processing the message for

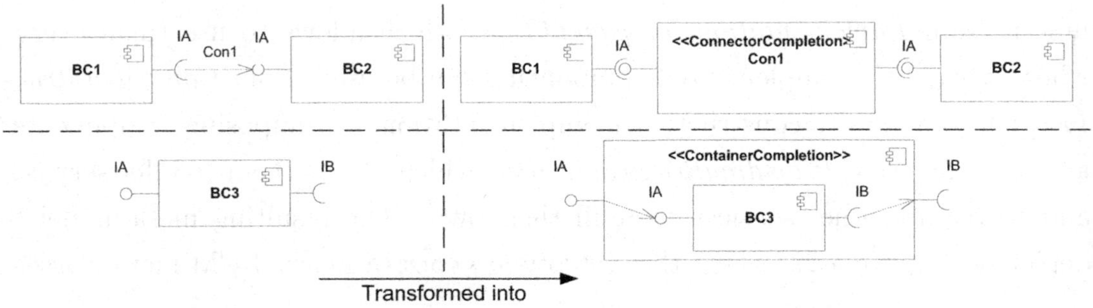

Figure 4.23: Completion Types

transmission can be modelled by *ConnectorCompletions* composed hierarchically. For additional details how this is realised see section 4.6.3.

Discussion The preceding paragraphs introduced the idea to use special types of components to realise completions. In order to combine completions with Coupled Transformations all that remains to be done is to let the feature configuration control the selection and parametrisation of transformations which generate the completions. For example, if the feature configuration specifies that the realisation of an *AssemblyConnector* should use encryption then a transformation is added to the chain of transformations which adds a completion for the encryption. If the feature configuration specifies not to use encryption, this transformation is omitted from the chain of transformations. For other configuration options, for example the number of component replicas in a component pool, the transformation copies the parameter and uses it in the generated completion components.

4.6 Technological Java EE Mapping

Mapping PCM instances to an implementation in an industrial component model like EJB, CCM, or COM (cf. section 2.1.4) aims at preserving as many information in an PCM instance as possible for the implementation phase. Hence, transformations take PCM instances and generate conforming implementations. This helps embedding the PCM in a development process.

Mapping abstract design models to code always requires expert knowledge on the source and target model. The use of transformations allows transformation users to reuse this knowledge - ideally without the need to gain it themselves.

Additionally, as the target model usually is on a lower abstraction level the transformation contains strategies to represent abstract concepts of the source model by single or multiple concepts in the target model. For example, when mapping PCM instances to Java EE implementations, Java EE representations of concepts such as component *RequiredRoles*, INOUT or OUT parameters, *AssemblyConnectors*, or composite components are needed. In many cases, design patterns exist, which already solve the mapping problems. Regardless whether the mapping is based on patterns or not, the elements introduced by the transformation into the target model may cause a performance overhead which has not been part of the abstract system model.

However, as the transformation generates a *deterministic* output solely depending on the input and mark model instances, the performance impact of the mapping can be foreseen and hence used to increase the prediction accuracy of performance predictions. To illustrate how this can be done, this thesis presents such a transformation of PCM instances to POJOs or Java EE code. It uses this transformation to demonstrate how the additional mapping knowledge can be used to improve performance prediction accuracy using Coupled Transformations . The transformation has been implemented prototypically as oAW model-2-text transformation (discussed in detail in sections 4.6.1-4.6.4). It is based on an initial mapping researched in a master thesis by Schaudel (2007).

As target platform, Plain Old Java Objects (POJOs) and Java EE/EJB3 have been chosen. In this selection, EJB3 is a representative of an industrial component model used in many projects. It uses classes to realise components. As such, it is a representative for COM or CCM, which also base on classes. Supporting two output types, POJOs and EJB3, is simple as EJB3 heavily relies on POJOs as realisation entities. However, for the plain POJO mapping several services offered by an EJB container like component creation, dependency injection, and communication infrastructure support, had to be added to the transformation. Where component creation and dependency injection can be easily added to the generated code based on plain Java constructs, the communication infrastructure relies on external libraries like Axis (Apache Software Foundation, 2008) for webservice/SOAP support. Nevertheless, as measuring application response times and debugging the generated code is often much easier without the need for the complex application server and its configuration, experiences showed that the POJO mapping paid off its extra effort. Additionally, the POJO mapping is used in SimuCom to generate the architecture of the simulated system.

When designing a transformation that maps PCM instances to an industrial component model, several requirements affect the design. The following list discusses the most important.

- **Bridge Missing Concepts in the Target Platform**: The PCM has been designed without targeting a specific industrial component model. Hence, it is independent from EJB, CCM, or COM. As a result of this independence, not all concepts available in the PCM have *exact counterparts* in a particular industrial platform. For example, EJB has no support for OUT parameter mappings (see section 3.3). In cases of missing support for PCM concepts, the transformation is responsible for generating code which emulates the missing concept. For example, an OUT parameter can be emulated in EJB by using the TransferObject design pattern (Marinescu, 2002) which encapsulates the return and OUT parameter in an object that is then returned by the service call.

- **Preserve Semantics**: The PCM's concepts have associated semantics as described in section 3 and further detailed in Reussner et al. (2007). Even if the semantics are not defined formally but in natural language, the transformation has to generate code which complies to the PCM's semantics. Otherwise, the transformation's output might not fit the model designer's expectations. For example, when mapping IN parameters, it has to be ensured that the passed parameter is not modified by the called method. As EJB uses call-by-reference for complex data types in local calls, mapping IN parameters of *Composite-* or *CollectionDataType* requires to pass a copy to the called method. As an alternative, the transformation could ignore the semantics. In the example, this would mean to pass the original object instead of a copy and rely on the called method not to change the passed object. For practical reasons, the second alternative is often used in practice. Nevertheless, in this thesis this is considered to be incorrect as the developer gets an implementation which might not correspond to his or her expectations.

  As a consequence, a detailed analysis of the semantics of the platform concepts is needed in order to get a full list of semantic mismatches between PCM concepts and existing platform concepts. For each of the mismatches, a concept is needed to bridge the differences. As with the missing concepts, existing design- or architectural patterns deal with some of these problems.

- **Missing Information in the Source Model**: The PCM's central aim is to allow the creation of architectural models for QoS analysis. To reach this aim, the PCM uses abstractions of middleware specific architectures. Especially, the technical realisation of an architecture is omitted intentionally from PCM model instances. For example, the PCM only contains the information *that* two components communicate but not which communication technology is used to realise it, e.g., SOAP or RMI. In the sense of the OMG's MDA standard, this kind of information is *platform*-dependent and hence, has to be added by the respective platform transformation. For this transformation, platform-specific mapping options may exist which configure how to map elements in the source model. Either the transformations contains a set of hard-coded options or the software architect can specify them using mark models. In the communication technology example, a mark model could specify which protocol to use on each of the *AssemblyConnector*s. Depending on the selection of options different extra-functional properties emerge, which will be included into the analysis model by the Coupled Transformations method.

The actual impact of all items in the list depends on the particular transformation's target platform. For example, a missing concept in EJB like OUT parameters is available in the CCM. Because of this, one can argue that dealing with mismatches is only needed in cases where the platform is not an exact match to the model's abstraction and taking a different platform which supports all concepts would be the solution. As this is true in general, it is impractical as it implies writing a complete platform, which is cost intensive. Reusing existing platforms and bridging semantic gaps in transformations is preferable.

The following sections present the concepts of the prototypical implementation of a mapping of PCM concepts to POJOs and EJBs. Special focus is given to concepts which fall into one of the classes listed before and how the problem is dealt with. For each mismatch, the impact of the problem's solution on the performance is discussed. Finally, it is shown how to include the solution's performance impact into the simulation.

4.6.1 Components

In the mapping presented here, component implementations use Java classes for their realisations (cf. section 4.3). In case of Java EE, the classes use additional annotations to declare their EJB specific metadata. Mapping components requires to map *RequiredRoles*, *ProvidedRoles*, and the internal realisation of components. The following sub-sections discuss these aspects in details. However, a discussion on how to map RD-SEFFs, which model the internal realisation of *BasicComponents*, is deferred until section 4.6.4. This is due to the fact, that the transformation only generates code skeletons for RD-SEFFs which have to be finalised by component developers. Hence, they cannot be analysed for their performance impact in advance.

4.6.1.1 Required Roles

This paragraph focuses on required roles as they often cause problems in class-based component technologies as classes usually do not have explicit required interfaces. Instead, classes often use implicit required interfaces whose binding is unchangeable without changing the class' source code. They instantiate an object of the required type in their constructor and offer no possibility to change this behaviour. In contrast, in the PCM, component developers create *ImplementationComponentTypes*, i.e, *BasicComponents* or *CompositeComponents*. Software architects retrieve the components and assemble them into systems. For this role-based task sharing to work, components need a mechanism that decouples their required interfaces from the component implementation so that they can be connected to other components by the software architect. In component models based on classes, this causes problems because of the missing support for *explicit* required interfaces in object-oriented programming. Because of this, some class-based component platforms do not support explicit required interfaces. In such platforms, components requiring services of other components contain code to retrieve the required reference themselves. As it is usually impossible for the software architect to change the source code of components, fixed encoded component references makes it impossible to alter the component bindings after the component's implementation.

However, EJB has a mechanism to decouple required interfaces and their binding based on dependency injection. Dependency injection is a pattern described in several variants by Fowler (2004). It is based on the Inversion of Control (IoC) principle, which is also known as Holywood principle: "Do not call us, we call you". This principle demands - in our context - the main control flow to run from the middleware to the components and not from the components to the middleware. As a consequence, the middleware which has the initial control flow thread gets control on the component creation allowing it to create and configure components before they actually are used.

The following describes how the prototypical transformation implemented for this thesis maps components to POJOs or EJBs. To illustrate how the model-2-text transformation generates code without showing generator templates, the following uses UML diagrams to give the structure of the generated code. As transformation language, QVT relations are used (Object Management Group (OMG), 2007a) which show the relationship between the PCM instance and the generated code as represented by UML diagrams. Notice, this only serves illustration purposes, the implementation does not use the QVT model-2-model transformations shown but generates the code directly. Furthermore, the depicted relations use the concrete syntax of both the PCM and the UML to ease understanding. The relationships have to be interpreted in a way that such that the target pattern on the left hand side is matched as many times as possible. For every match, the target pattern is emitted by the transformation. The names in the figures represent place holders. The place holder are set according to the matched values in the source pattern and can be used in the target pattern. For more details see the QVT standard (Object Management Group (OMG), 2007a).

Figure 4.24 depicts such a QVT relation for transforming the required roles of any PCM component type into a class-based realisation. It shows a class generated from the component on the left hand side having the same name as the component. The generated class uses the dependency injection pattern to resolve the required role `IRequired`. In the shown variant of this pattern, the class has a public method `setIRequired` which is used by a manager class (in case of EJB this is part of the middleware implementation) to set the dependencies. The manager class is responsible for creating and initialising the component and its required roles as indicated by the `setup` method's implementation given in the UML note.

If dependency injection is used to resolve required roles in a middleware offering dependency injection, the middleware sets the bindings of the component's required roles. It is done whenever a new instance of the component is created. For this, the middleware needs a specification of the required roles of a component created by the component developer. In case of EJB this information is delivered in XML configuration files called deployment descriptors or, in recent EJB versions, as Java annotations, which are part of the class' metadata.

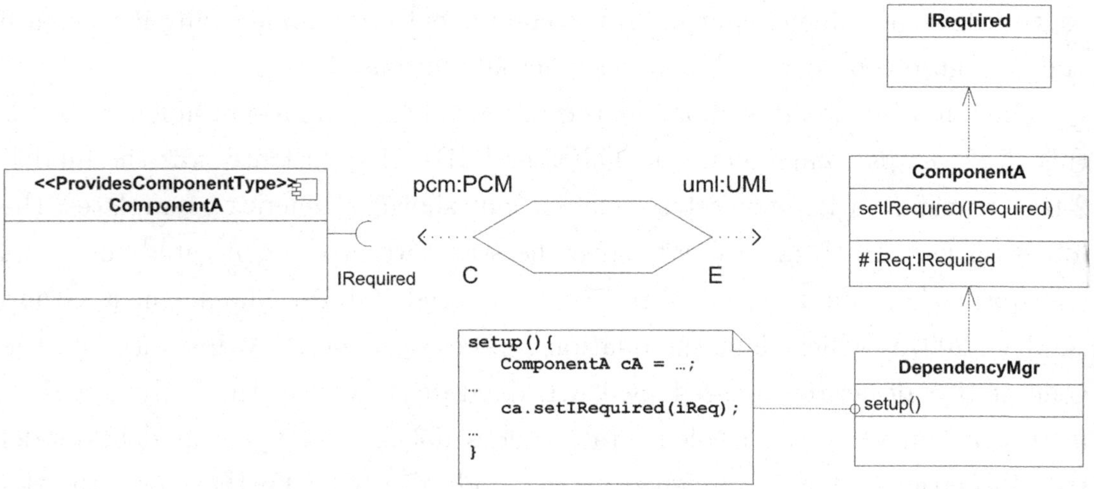

Figure 4.24: Simplified QVT Transformation of a Component using Dependency Injection

For a transformation based on POJOs without middleware support, there is no such mechanism. The POJO transformation introduced here generates code that realises component creation and dependency injection as part of the code generated for composed structures (for details see section 4.6.2).

To further decouple a component and its required services, the component context pattern introduced by Völter and Stahl (2006) can be applied. This pattern decouples a component's implementation from resolving its dependencies (see figure 4.25). This offers increased flexibility and maintainability. For this, the component uses an extra class, in which it holds all required interfaces. The strategy to get references to the components providing the respective interfaces is encapsulated in the component context class and can be exchanged easily. The POJO transformation now uses a different strategy to get the references than the EJB transformation.

For EJB, the dependency injection service offered by the middleware is applied. The transformation generates a deployment descriptor that first injects the references to the needed interfaces into the fields in the context object. Afterwards, it injects the context object into the component it belongs to. In the POJO based transformation, the context class offers a constructor which takes instances of references to all interfaces and sets them accordingly. The constructor is used in the surrounding *ComposedStructure* to create the contexts of all inner components, which is then injected into them (cf. section 4.6.2). Thus, the

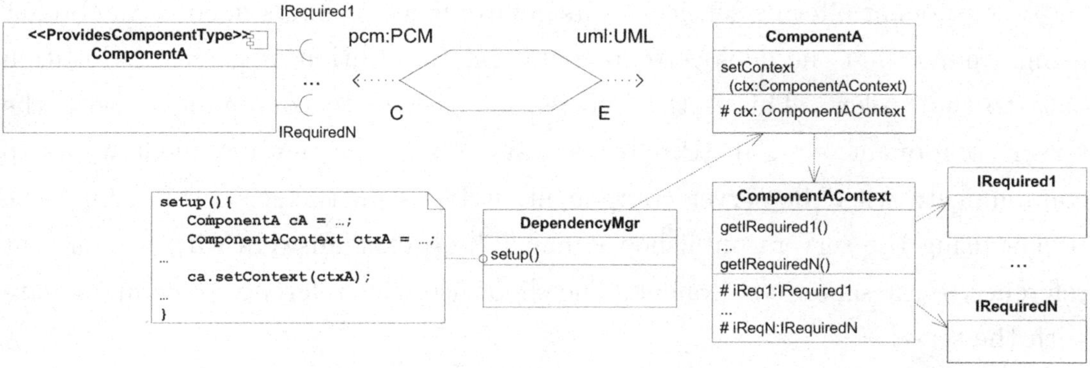

Figure 4.25: Component Transformation using Dependency Injection and the Context Pattern

dependencies can be passed to the component from the outside as instantiated context object.

Applying dependency injection either with or without the context pattern is a common solution to decouple component implementation and usage. However, other common alternatives exist. One such option, is the Broker pattern as introduced by Buschmann et al. (1996). Besides decoupling a client from its server, the pattern additionally introduces location transparency. Location transparency (Coulouris et al., 2000) allows a component to change its physical location, i.e., its hosting environment, without the need for the client to be aware of the location change. Figure 4.26 shows the Broker pattern's basic interaction idea.

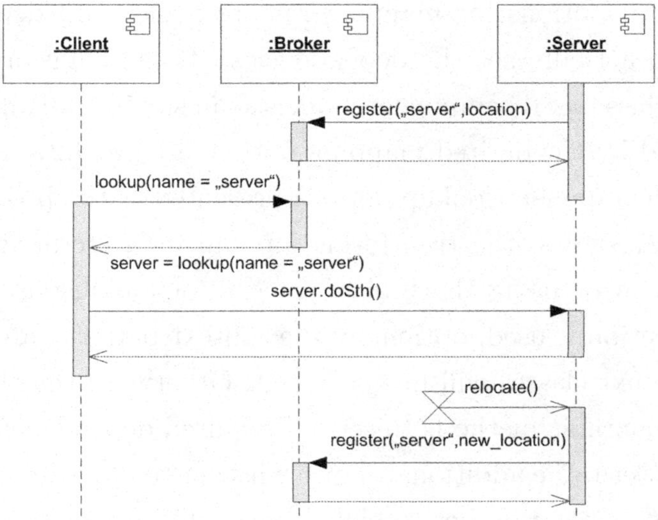

Figure 4.26: Sequence Diagram for the Interaction in the Broker Pattern

A component offering services to its environment registers itself at the broker using a name that the deployer can configure. In addition, it passes its location data to the broker. This is the information needed to communicate with the server component, e.g., an IP address and a port. Whenever a client wants to communicate with the server component, it looks up the server by asking the broker using the servers published name. The broker answers with the current reference to the server component. The client uses this reference to communicate with the server.

To demonstrate how the broker pattern realises the location transparency, in figure 4.26 the server gets a request to relocate itself, indicated by the timed relocate signal. After its physical relocation, the server registers itself again at the broker passing its new location details. The clients can follow two strategies in this context. Either they look up the server once, reusing the reference as long as they can reach the server under the given location. If they fail to contact the server, they re-request a server reference from the broker assuming a server relocation. Another option is to always look up the server before communication.

Using a broker to map required roles is easy in combination with the context pattern. As the context class encapsulates the lookup of required interfaces, the client's server lookup can be done in the context class resulting in the same structural mapping as in figure 4.25. Only the behaviour in the context class changes depending on the two options for the client's strategy.

Feature Model for Required Role Mapping The previous paragraph has introduced several options for mapping required roles and depending on this, methods how to actually set the dependencies. If the transformation of PCM components to class based component models shall support all alternatives, it can be parameterised by the desired mapping option. Figure 4.27 shows the feature diagram for the component lookup options presented in the previous paragraph.

As figure 4.27 shows, the transformation can map required roles using dependency injection or using the broker pattern for looking up components. If dependency injection is used, optionally the context pattern can be used as well. If it is used, context classes will be generated. Otherwise, the class representing the component contains methods to set it's required dependencies itself. In case of the broker pattern, the additional choice whether to use a component reference until a failure occurs or whether to always query for a reference is available.

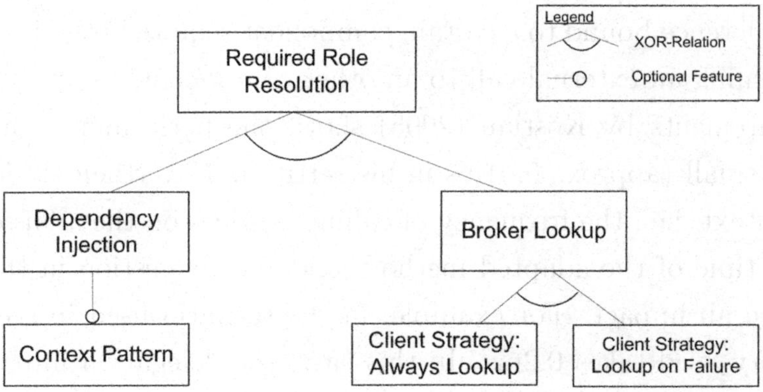

Figure 4.27: Feature Diagram for Required Role Resolution

Reflect again the close relationship between the design patterns and the alternatives available in figure 4.27. It is the aim of different patterns in object-oriented languages to solve the problem of making the dependencies of software components technically explicit and configurable. While checking the available patterns, variants, and combinations of the patterns with other patters showed up as possible solutions to the problem at hand. The pattern's description is often a source for these variants and combination possibilities. A feature diagram has been created making the alternatives explicit. Finally, a parametrisable transformation offers the possible options to the transformation user.

Performance Impact of the Required Role Resolution Features Figure 4.27 offers four possible solutions to map required roles. They all solve the functional requirement of decoupling the artefacts produced by the component developer and software architect by enabling to set the required roles after the component's implementation phase.

However, as they offer different extra-functional properties, the following focuses on the different performance impacts. Making the alternatives explicit using the feature diagram allows to include their performance impact into transformations deriving the performance model. First, the following describes the reasons for the different alternative's performance impacts informally.

Using dependency injection without the context pattern has the lowest performance impact as it increases the costs when creating a component instance for doing the injection, but afterwards has no additional impact. When adding the context class of the component context pattern, an additional call for retrieving the current reference bound to a certain component required role, is needed every time when issuing an external call to an other component.

As measurements by Kostian (2005) show, the performance impact of the delegation is small (approx. 0.01ms in his setting). Nevertheless, depending on the usage context, i.e., the frequency of calling services on the adapted interface, the response time of the adapted method, and the congestion in the system, it still may have an impact. For example, in the scenario used in section 5.1.2 a database query used takes 0.2ms. In this case, the delegation impact would be already 5%.

For the broker based solution, issuing an external call needs a call to the context object which itself queries the broker - depending on the client strategy. Depending on the broker's allocation, each lookup might involve network communication (if the broker is located on a different machine than the client). And even if no network communication is involved, usually inter-process communication is needed to look up the server as brokers commonly execute in different processes. Additionally, a large number of queries can turn the broker's hosting environment into the system's bottleneck further reducing the performance. Hence, the performance impact of retrieving a component reference is further increased compared to the dependency injection based solutions.

It is arguable, that only dependency injection without a context object is a valid choice as all other options are more expensive. This is true performance-wise, but as the other options increase other extra-functional properties, developer possibly choose them. The flexibility is increased in the broker-based solution as there is a central point in the architecture controlling the component's bindings. The context pattern also introduces more flexibility as it encapsulates the required role's resolution strategy. Due to difficulties in finding good metrics for the flexibility and maintainability, the trade-off analysis is out of the scope of this work.

The choice whether to use dependency injection or the Broker pattern also selects the type of method to use for including the performance impact of that choice into the SimuCom simulation. If dependency injection is used, this can be realised using a structural change (cf. section 4.5.3) which is performed in both the generated code skeletons as well as in the generated simulation code. If the use of the Context pattern is not selected, no performance impact has to be modelled and the dependencies become injected directly into the class generated for the component.

If it is selected, a context class is generated in the simulation code and the generated code skeletons. In the simulation case, a template method in the modular transformation inserts the resource demand for retrieving the interface reference from the context class. For this, the transformation adds an *InternalAction* before the code actually retrieving and calling the bound component's service. This internal action contains a CPU demand which corresponds to the one of bytecode for calling an internal method and returning a reference.

When using the Broker pattern for looking up the remote reference, the transformation uses a structural change to add an *ExternalCallAction* to a broker middleware component. This includes the resource demand resulting from this lookup into the SimuCom simulation.

The two options for the Broker lookup can be realised by generating different RD-SEFFs. The option of always looking up the communication partner can be included using a RD-SEFF which unconditionally includes the performance impact by always executing the Broker *ExternalCallAction*. The other option of looking the client up only in case of failure, can be realised by a *ProbabilisticBranchAction*.

Resulting Performance Model Impact Adding an *InternalAction* for the delegation in cases of the Context pattern option causes an additional CPU demand to be processed by the hardware resource on which the respective component is allocated. Let CPU denote the simulated CPU resource used for this, i.e., the simulated resource on which the component is allocated. Additionally, let $d_{delegate} \in Demand$ denote the demand caused by the call delegation (see section 4.4.3 for the description of *Demand*), i.e., $time(d_{delegate})$ is a sample of the random variable which describes the demand caused by call delegation in (simulated) hardware dependent units, i.e., it is the hardware independent demand divided by the CPU's processing rate or a measured value. Using the introduced function $rt : ProcessingResource \times Demand \rightarrow \mathbb{R}_0^+$, which describes the time needed including waiting times to process a demand on a simulated resource (see section 4.4.3), the resulting additional time is simply $rt(CPU, d_{delegate})$.

The broker interaction is a bit more complicated. First, a model-2-model transformation adds an additional required role to each component which has at least one required role using broker lookups. The additional introduced role is connected to a broker component which is assumed to already exist in the architecture. If the software architect forgets to add it to the architecture, the transformation fails with an error message. Figure 4.28 depicts this transformation rule.

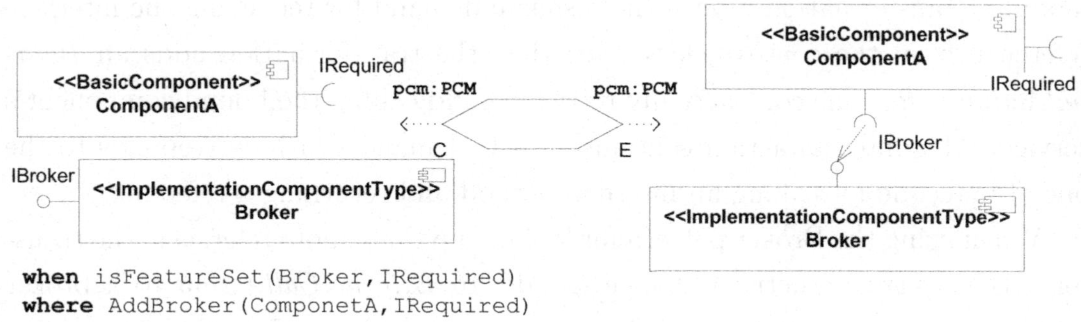

Figure 4.28: Structural Change to add a Broker

The additional relation called `AddBroker` in figure 4.28 adds an additional call for the broker interaction in front of each *ExternalCallAction* using the given *RequiredRole*. It is given in the appendix (see figure A.5 in section A.3). Figure 4.29 shows an example for the transformation.

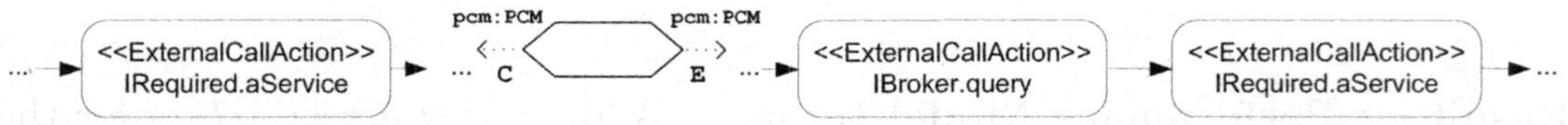

Figure 4.29: Example for Adding the Broker Lookup

The performance impact of the additional *ExternalCallAction* depends on the allocation of the broker component. Two alternatives exist. First, the broker is allocated on a different server than the component using it (see figure 4.30, left hand side). Second, the broker is allocated on the same server than the component using it (see figure 4.30, right hand side)

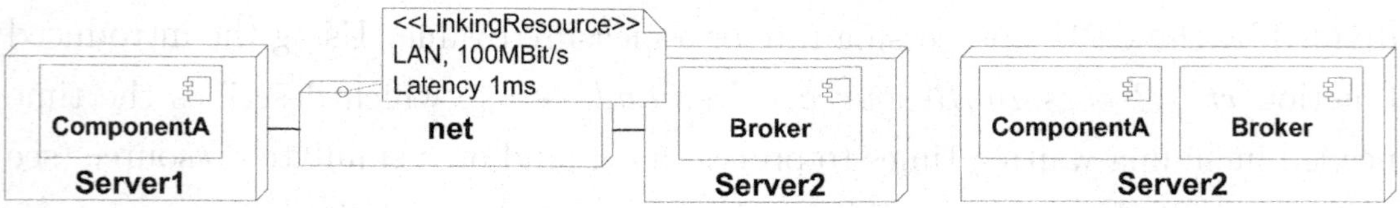

Figure 4.30: Broker Allocation Alternatives

Using $d_{query} \in Demand$, $time(d_{query})$ is a sample of the random variable which describes the hardware-dependent CPU demand of the broker's lookup service. The additional time demand caused by the inclusion of the broker into the prediction model is then the communication time plus the broker's response time. The communication time depends on the allocation alternative and the technical realisation of the *AssemblyConnector* (cf. section 4.6.3). For the sake of simplicity, the following assumes communication only causes resource demands on the network. Thus, it neglects the impact of marshalling, encryption, etc. However, the latter can be included using the more sophisticated model presented in section 4.6.3.

Let $query.BS$ denote the size in bytes of a broker lookup request. Additionally, the variable $query.RESULT.BS$ denotes the response's size in bytes. Both variables depend on the used middleware and have to be measured and afterwards encoded into the transformation. Also, let l_{net} denote the latency and tp_{net} the throughput of the network in the distributed case as specified in the PCM's linking resource. Finally, let S_{CPU} denote the CPU of the server on which the broker is allocated.

Additionally, as the time needed to process demands depends on the simulated resource's queue state in SimuCom and the resource's scheduling discipline, the order in which they occur is important. To indicate this, the operator $\oplus$ is used in the following to sum up times. It is not commutative, i.e., the demands added with $\oplus$ have to occur in order from left to right.

Then, the additional time demand in the distributed allocation given on the left hand side of figure 4.30 is

$$rt(net, query.BS/tp_{net} + l_{net}) \oplus rt(S_{CPU}, d_{query}) \oplus$$
$$rt(net, query.RETURN.BS/tp_{net} + l_{net})$$

The demand consists of the demand for transmitting the lookup request, the time to process the lookup, and the time needed to transmit the answer. Note, as the function rt is used in all cases the time also *includes* the waiting time at the respective simulated resources.

For the non-distributed case depicted on the right hand side in figure 4.30, let $copy : R_0^+ \rightarrow R_0^+$ describe the CPU demand to copy the given amount of bytes to another process space. Also let M_{CPU} denote the CPU resource of the shared physical machine M. With this, the additional time demand for the broker lookup including hardware contention is

$$rt(M_{CPU}, copy(query.BS)) \oplus rt(M_{CPU}, d'_{query}) \oplus$$
$$rt(M_{CPU}, copy(query.RETURN.BS))$$

4.6.1.2 Provided Roles

Provided roles define interfaces offered by a component. In the PCM, interfaces define a list of signatures based on CORBA IDL (cf. section 3.3). In EJB, object-oriented interfaces implemented by the classes which represent components, serve as component interfaces. Often, component interfaces need special markings in these languages, e.g., EJB and COM with .NET use annotations to mark component interfaces.

When focusing on Java POJOs or EJB, two problems arise when mapping PCM interfaces to Java interfaces. First, Java interfaces do not support parameter modifiers and second, there is a problem with having the same signature in different interfaces (c.f. Schaudel (2007)).

The PCM's parameter modifiers define how to pass parameters when making a service call. IN parameters can be read and modified in the called service, however, this does not affect the original contents of the variable passed in the call. INOUT parameter can be read and modified by the called service, the effect of any modifications is also available in the calling service after the call. OUT parameters have to be set by the called service and become available in the calling service as INOUT parameter do (cf. section 3.3).

Basically, mapping parameters with different modifiers is not a PCM specific problem. It is common when mapping CORBA IDL to Java. The Java IDL mapping deals with the problem (Object Management Group (OMG), 2002). The solution is to appropriately copy the contents of the different types as required by the semantics of the respective modifier. Java itself has a call-by-value semantics, i.e., passing a copy, for Java primitive types. For classes, it uses call-by-reference. This means, mapping *PrimitiveTypes* with a corresponding primitive Java type is no problem for IN parameters. For INOUT and OUT, wrapper classes are needed that encapsulate the value making it modifiable. This is also known as boxing. For *Collection-* and *CompositeDatatypes*, which have to be mapped to Java classes, INOUT and OUT need no special treatment, but for IN parameters a copy of the datastructure is needed first. However, it has no impact on the Java signature as does the wrapper in case of primitive types. Performance-wise, only the code generated for actually calling the services has an impact as the interface itself is only a static declaration.

The second issue is based on the possibility to have the same signature, i.e., the same name, parameter list, and return value in different provided roles. The naive approach of mapping the interfaces to Java interfaces does not work any more, because the Java class representing the component can only contain a single implementation of a given method signature. However, in the PCM, the behaviour of a service depends on the role and the signature, i.e., there may exist several equal signatures in different roles having a different behaviour.

One option to deal with this issue is to use *port classes.* The idea of a port class stems from UML where ports can be used to model a communication channel associated to interfaces. However, UML allows multiple required and provided interfaces per port while in this mapping for each provided interface a separate port class exists. Every communication has to pass this port before it triggers a behaviour in the component. Port classes accept the communication, check it, and forward it, if it is valid.

Each PCM provided role uses a single port class for every provided role (see figure 4.31). This class realizes the Proxy pattern (Gamma et al., 1995, p.207). It directly implements the interface of the role. For every signature in the interface, it delegates to an implementation that is part of the main component class. However, the name of the method to which the port delegates is made unique by prefixing it with the port's name (cf. figure 4.31).

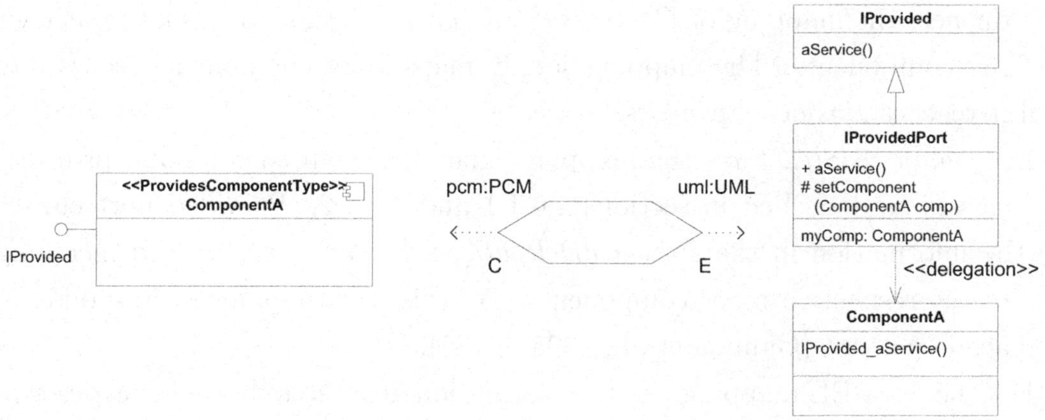

Figure 4.31: Mapping of Provided Roles to Ports

Using this mapping, it is possible to have multiple services with equal signatures in different roles. Each service can have its own implementation according to its RD-SEFF. Besides solving the equal signature problem of Java, ports introduce additional advantages. First, they ensure that a client only uses the role it is actually bound to, as casting the port to any other interface besides to one it implements is impossible. Furthermore, as it also is a proxy in the sense of the

Proxy pattern, it can be used to implement user access control, fail over mechanisms, session control, etc. Because of this, it is preferable to always generate a component port even if no signature naming problem exists.

Performance Impact of the Provided Port Mapping The performance impact of the port based mapping for provided interfaces is on the one hand for creating and initializing the port class which adds to the costs of initialising the component. During run-time the port adds the cost for delegating an incoming call to the component's implementation class. The performance simulation can incorporate the performance impact of the port class as a structural change. In analogy to the required role's context class, where also an additional *InternalAction* is needed, a template method for the simulation transformation can add the *InternalAction* for the additional resource demand caused by the delegation.

4.6.2 ComposedStructures

In the current version of the POJO or Java EE transformation, *ComposedStructures*, i.e., *Systems* and *CompositeComponents*, are being regarded as logical entities only because both do not support hierarchical component structures. As a consequence, the mapping of *ComposedStructures* contains no special treatment for inner components. The mapping simply maps inner components recursively until it reaches *BasicComponents*.

For *ComposedStructures* the mapping generates required roles and provided port classes as described in sections 4.6.1.1 and 4.6.1.2. Provided port classes use the information in the *ProvidedDelegationConnectors* to forward incoming calls to the respective inner components. By this, the mapping corresponds to the Facade pattern (Gamma et al., 1995, p.185).

For the Java EE mapping the transformation generates deployment descriptors which connect the inner components of the *ComposedStructure* according to its *AssemblyConnectors*. It uses the IDs of the *AssemblyContexts* of the inner components to generate unique IDs to identify the components in the deployment descriptors.

For the POJO mapping, the *ComposedStructure*'s constructor instantiates for each contained *AssemblyContext* an object of the embedded component's class. After instantiating all components, it retrieves the provided port classes of the components and injects them in the requiring components by calling their dependency injection methods or registers them in a broker - depending on the selected required role mapping.

If the POJO mapping is used in SimuCom, it additionally passes the *AssemblyContext* ID to the instances of the (simulated) component classes. These components store this ID to retrieve the simulated resources which they use to simulate their resource demands (cf. section 4.4.5).

Discussion The mapping presented here for *ComposedStructures* is insufficient to reflect the semantics of *CompositeComponents* as it does not enforce the constraint that inner components of a *CompositeComponent* are only visible for other inner components of the *CompositeComponent*. Every other component can retrieve a reference to such an inner component registered in the middleware and call its services. However, some options beyond the currently implemented mapping rule exist to protect the components. For example, the inner component's ports can be used to enforce an authorisation protocol. For any component willing to call the service of such a component a login call is needed first. This call checks the credentials and allows subsequent calls if and only if the credentials match. The only remaining thing needed is to add a login call to all required service calls of the inner components of a *CompositeComponent*, in which the correct credentials are added. However, this solution requires the ports to be stateful in order to remember the login state.

An idea for a stateless solution is to use a wrapper on the provided port which provides all methods in the port but requires an additional parameter for the credentials. Its semantics is to check the credentials and if they are correct, then delegate the call to the implementation otherwise reject the call. Only this wrapper is made visible in the middleware. This disallows calling services of the component when not knowing the credentials. For every required role requiring such an adapted provided role via an *AssemblyConnector*, a second wrapper is generated, which adds the correct credentials to every call transparently.

Performance Impact of Mapping *ComposedStructures* Currently, only the performance impacts of the delegation in the provided port class and the required role resolution are included into the prediction model as discussed before (see sections 4.6.1.1 and 4.6.1.2). For the discussed improved mapping options for *CompositeComponents* the following only outlines their performance impact. For the stateful port based solution, the simulation transformation could include the performance impact by using a structural change template method in the transformation. This template method adds an additional *ExternalCallAction* and its demand for the discussed login call. For the second choice of wrapping the ports and automatically provide credentials on the required side and checking them on the provided side, a *ConnectorCompletion* can be used which models the resource demands for adding, checking, and removing the credentials. However, as it is future work to implement the additional options in the transformations, this paragraph only demonstrates that a more complex mapping would have a performance impact which could be captured by Coupled Transformations.

4.6.3 Assembly Connectors

Class-based component models commonly realise connectors using direct object-oriented method calls. The following actions are needed for connectors. First, a call to an external service needs to retrieve a reference to the provided interface of the required component. This includes resolving the port as described in the context of mapping required roles in section 4.6.1. Using the reference, the component initiating the communication hands a message over to its middleware for transmission. The middleware is the Java EE application server in the Java EE mapping or additional libraries like the RMI-package or Axis in the POJO mapping. The middleware processes the message in a chain of actions. For remote calls, the called method's ID and the parameters have to be marshalled on the client's side. The resulting byte stream may be processed by additional processors for encryption, compression, etc. Finally, the message is handed over to the operating system, which uses the available networking hardware for the final transmission. On the server's side, the byte stream is processed in reverse order, e.g., it is uncompressed and decrypted, and the service's ID and parameter values are extracted again. With them, the server's middleware initiates the execution of the requested service. When the initiated service has performed its calculations, the middleware sends the resulting values back to the waiting caller. For the resulting values the same process applies as for the service call. The server's middleware marshals, encrypts, compresses, etc. them and transmits the result to the client. The client's middleware retrieves the results and passes them to the waiting caller.

For the transmission aspect of the technological mapping, middleware systems offer different marshalling protocols and different processing filters. Many of them can be configured via configuration files, which can be generated. However, which options are available depends on the particular middleware and its configuration options. In addition, it also depends on the particular code transformation and the options supported by it. An exemplary feature diagram for a connector mapping is given in figure 4.32.

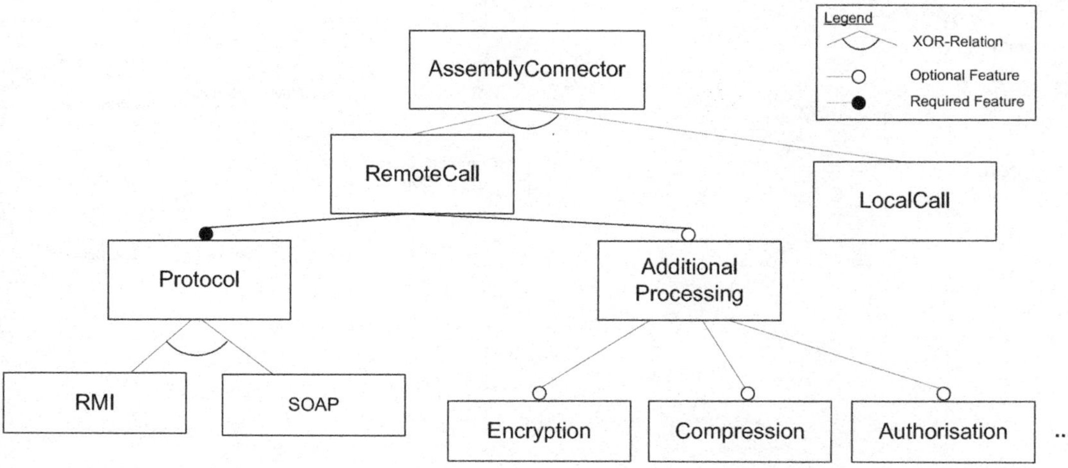

Figure 4.32: Exemplary Feature Diagram for *AssemblyConnectors*

Modelling the Performance Impact of *AssemblyConnector* Realisations To include the performance impact caused by the middleware aspects of the component's communication, a model based on *ConnectorCompletions* suits well. As introduced in the previous paragraphs, components communicate by sending a message from one component to the other. This causes resource demands on the sender's side for message processing, a demand on the networking resource for transmitting the message, and a demand on the receiver's side for extracting the message and initiating the service call. The same demands occur in reverse order for returning the computed result to the caller.

Hence, the aim is to model the process for sending a service request and receiving the response using *ConnectorCompletions*. A transformation generates and inserts these completions into a PCM model instance. Additionally, this transformation has to respect the feature configuration used in the code transformation of a feature diagram like the one given in figure 4.32. Note, that even for transformations not having a mark model, the knowledge on the code transformation and hence, the coupling of the transformations, is important. Knowing that the generated code is based on Java EE allows to analyse and include Java EE specifics on how Java EE does its communication. To include the performance impact of connectors, first the *AssemblyConnector* is replaced with a *ConnectorCompletion* as visualised in figure 4.33. The completion includes the performance relevant middleware aspects of the interaction.

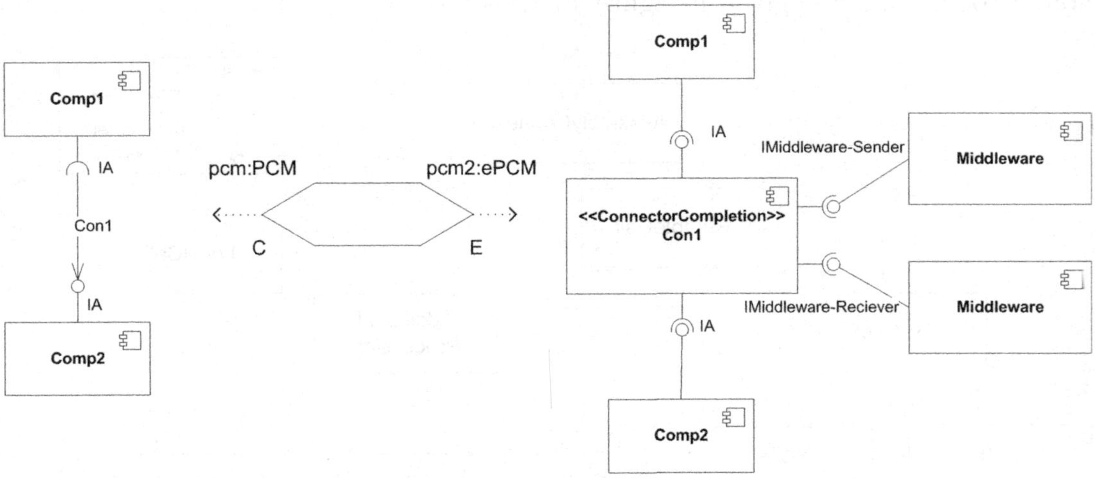

Figure 4.33: Replacing a Connector with a ConnectorCompletion

Figure 4.33 depicts a QVT relation (again using the simplified form in concrete syntax), which shows an in-place transformation of a PCM instance into an extended PCM instance. The transformation adds a *ConnectorCompletion* that replaces the *AssemblyConnector* of the source model. In order to fit into the architecture the *ConnectorCompletion* needs to have roles complying to those used in the *AssemblyConnector* (the roles having the interface name `IA` in the example in figure 4.33). Additionally, it uses two components called `Middleware` to which it forwards all actions needed to process the message. For example, `IMiddleware` offers services to marshal and demarshal a given set of parameters, to encrypt/decrypt a byte stream, etc. Note, that with this kind of modelling all resource demands are located inside the middleware component. By exchanging the middleware component in the model, the software architect can analyse the performance impact of different middleware implementations.

There are two required roles for middleware services to support distributed communication in which the participating middleware components are allocated on different machines. In case of local communication both roles can be bound to the same component. For an existing middleware, a PCM component modelling its performance impact is needed. Models which rely on measurements of the middleware's services parameterised by their input parameter characterisations can be derived for example by applying methods developed by Krogmann (2007).

The inner structure of the *ConnectorCompletion* is generated by a chain of transformations which corresponds to the middleware services that should be considered. As a first example for such a service, consider marshalling, which is needed for all remote communication. Figure 4.34 shows the inner components of a *ConnectorCompletion* for the inclusion of the marshaller's performance impact.

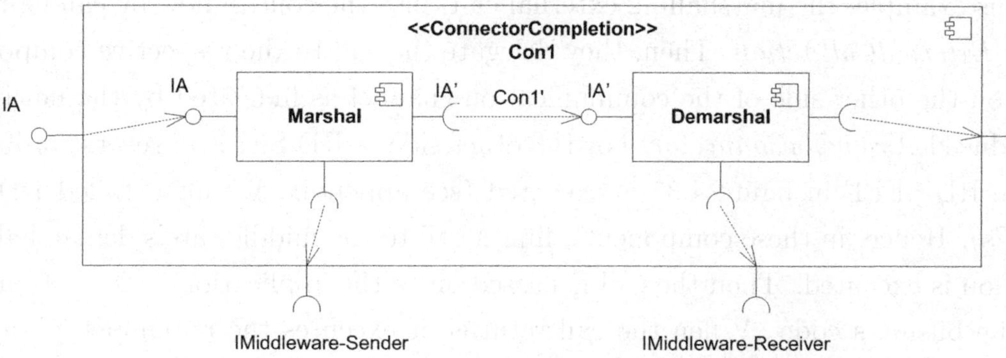

Figure 4.34: Inner Structure of the Generated *ConnectorCompletion*

The generated *ConnectorCompletion* contains two inner components. The first component (`Marshal`) is responsible for modelling actions performed by the middleware on the calling component's side. The second component (`Demarshal`) is responsible for actions of the receiving component's middleware. Note that regardless of the component's name both components contain marshal and demarshal external calls for sending the return values. The names are given from the viewpoint of the service request by the client.

Depending on whether the components act in behalf of the client or the server, the components use the respective required roles for accessing middleware services. Note, that the components within the connector completion do not contain *InternalActions* for the middleware's resource demand. Instead, they only call the middleware services using their required roles.

In order to fulfil the necessary provided role, RD-SEFFs need to be generated for each method in the provided interface of the added components. The generated RD-SEFFs for the `Marshal` component are all identical besides the called service which changes according to the provided service which the RD-SEFF represents (see figure 4.35 for the SEFF without data flow annotations, see appendix A.2 for detailed RD-SEFFs).

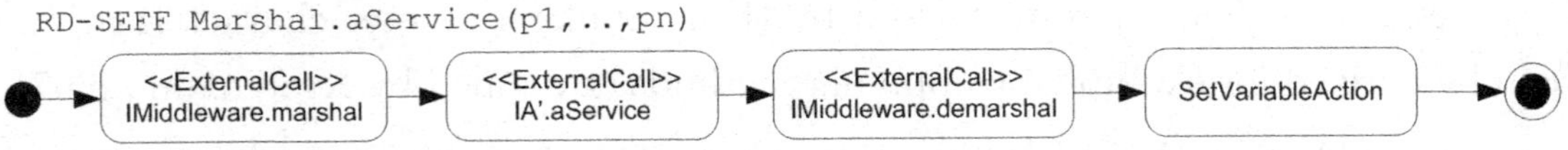

Figure 4.35: Example for a Generated RD-SEFF on the Client's Side

All RD-SEFFs generated for inner components of connector completions follow the same idea. First, they insert a call to the middleware pre-processing chain (in this example, the marshalling external call) into the control flow by calling it in an *ExternalCallAction*. Then, they delegate the call to the respective component on the other side of the communication channel as indicated by the newly introduced *AssemblyConnector*. For the other side, a RD-SEFF in reverse order of the RD-SEFF in figure 4.35 is executed (see appendix A.2 for detailed RD-SEFFs). Hence, in these components, first a call to the middleware's demarshall function is executed. Then the call is passed on to the application logic containing the business code. When the call returns, it executes the remainder of the generated RD-SEFFs, i.e., the result is marshalled on the server's side, passed on, and demarshalled on the client's side. The additional *SetVariableAction* in figure 4.35 is needed to transfer the characterisations of the result and OUT parameters to the caller (see also the next paragraph on parameter dependencies). Note, that for all these calls only their performance impact is considered and not their real functionality as the aim is to only enhance the performance prediction model here.

Parameter Dependencies A remaining problem is how to deal with the parameter and return value characterisations which can be part of a call. They need to be transmitted to the called service and returned to the calling service. However, as introduced, connector completions represent a component from a lower level of abstraction in the architecture. This means, that in a strict modelling approach (i.e., one that follows strictly the implementation) connector completions should not know about interfaces of the application level layer, e.g., `IA` in figure 4.34. Hence, the completions should not use characterisations carrying semantic knowledge like `TYPE` characterisations. However, they have access to `BYTESIZE` and `NUMBER_OF_ELEMENTS` which is needed to estimate the amount of bytes which are transmitted over the network.

In the here presented *ConnectorCompletions*, the marshalling step models the performance relevant aspect of the conversion of the service's parameters into a stream of bytes. These aspects are the processing time needed for the conversion and the size of the resulting stream of bytes. As the size of the resulting bytestream is needed in any of the following processing steps (e.g., encryption or network transmission), the following assumes that marshalling is always the *first step* in the chain of actions needed for communication. With this assumption, all subsequent SEFFs can solely rely on characterisations of the bytestream. However, to use characterisations on the bytestream in the PCM, it has to be part of the parameters in the formal signature of a service (cf. section 3.5.2). Hence, the following uses a workaround to allow characterisations on the bytestream. It introduces the bytestream as additional parameter to all formal signatures of the interfaces used inside the *ConnectorCompletion*.

For this, the transformation derives an extended interface `IA'` from the original interface `IA` and uses it inside the completion (see figure 4.34). Note, `IA'` is only available during the transformation into the performance prediction model and not to component developers or software architects. The signatures of `IA'` are equal to the signatures of the interface `IA` of the connector's required role plus the needed additional parameter *bytestream* required to pass a characterisation of the processed bytestream's length and they way it is changed by processing actions. For example, a signature `void m(int a)` in `IA` is transformed into `void m(int a, INOUT byte[] bytestream)` in `IA'`. This allows the use of *bytestream.BYTESIZE* characterisations in RD-SEFFs of inner components which provide `IA'`. The parameter is `INOUT` which allows to use it also to characterise the bytestream for the service's response. For detailed examples, see the set of generated RD-SEFFs given in appendix A.2. To summarize, it is important to understand, that the marshalling component derives an initial characterisation of the size of the bytestream resulting from marshalling the service's parameters (details follow) and that subsequent processing steps use these bytestream characterisations to derive their own processing demands and the size of the bytestream after their completion.

To give an example, consider a service call having an array of integers as input and result parameters. A client component calls this service with an array of 10 integers. First, the marshalling component derives the initial size of the bytestream. Using RMI, each integer is encoded in 4 bytes resulting in a bytestream of 40 bytes plus some RMI overhead. Assume additionally encryption takes places, causing the bytestream to grow in average 1.5-times. The bytestream characterisation changes from 40 bytes to 60 bytes. These 60 bytes cause an corresponding network demand. On the server's side the bytestream is decrypted again, hence, it size becomes again 40 bytes. Finally, it is demarshalled and the bytestream characterisation is removed. After executing the call, the same processing is performed for the resulting array of integers. The following describes how the marshalling component derives the initial bytesize.

A marshalling service's signature reflecting the middleware implementation would be to take a set of objects and a marshalling strategy and return the objects in a marshalled format, i.e., `byte[] marshal(Strategy s, object[] param)`. The marshal service uses polymorphism on the elements of the `param` collection to serialise the collection's elements according to the given strategy, e.g., use 4 bytes for an integer and 8 bytes for a double value in a binary serialisation protocol like RMI. This polymorphism makes it hard to describe this behaviour with the current PCM's parameter characterisation. Given the fact, that only performance aspects of this service are relevant, a better model is to use arrays of the PCM's *PrimitiveDatatypes* as parameters, e.g., `byte[] marshal(Strategy s, int[] ints, double[] doubles, String[] strings, ...)`. With such a signature, the `NUMBER_OF_ELEMENTS` characterisation for the single parameters can be used to specify how much integers, doubles, strings, etc. have to be marshalled. The transformation can automatically derive stochastic expressions for the actual number from the current service's formal signature. Table 4.3 gives examples for this (in table 4.3, `NoE` is used as abbreviation for `NUMBER_OF_ELEMENTS` and `BS` for `BYTESIZE`).

Formal signature	Resulting characterisations
`m(int a, int b)`	`ints.NoE = 2`
`m(int[] a, double b)`	`ints.NoE = a.NoE, doubles.NoE = 1`
`m(String s)`	`strings.NoE = 1, strings.INNER.BS = s.BS`

Table 4.3: Examples for Calculating the Type and Amount of Data to be Marshalled

The general algorithm to derive stochastic expressions for the number of *PrimitiveDatatypes* is given in the following. Assume the *Signature* currently investigated is stored in the OCL variable *sig*. Then, two sets are derived p_{in} and p_{out} characterising the set of datatypes which need serialisation when calling the service (*in*) and when returning the result (*out*). They are defined by the OCL expressions given in fragment 4.1.

OCL Fragment 4.1 Deriving the Parameter Sets

```
p_in = sig.parameters->select(p|p.modifier=ParameterModifier.IN or
       p.modifier=ParameterModifier.NONE
          or p.modifier=ParameterModifier.INOUT)
p_out = sig.parameters->select(p|p.modifier=ParameterModifier.OUT or
       p.modifier=ParameterModifier.INOUT)
```

A polymorphic overloaded OCL helper function `count` derives partial stochastic expressions for the three different *DataTypes*, i.e., *PrimitiveDataTypes*, *CollectionDataTypes*, and *CompositeDataTypes*, as given in fragment 4.2.

OCL Fragment 4.2 Recursively Deriving Instance Formula for DataTypes

```
def: count(t:PrimitiveDatatype, t2:PrimitiveDatatype,
             prefix:String) : String
  = if t = t2 then '1' else '0'

def: count(t:PrimitiveDatatype, t2:CollectionDataType,
             prefix:String) : String
  = if t = t2.innerDataType then
     '(' + prefix + '.NoE*' + count(t,t2.innerDataType,prefix+'.INNER')
       + ')'
  else '0'

def: count(t:PrimitiveDatatype, t2:CompositeDataType,
             prefix:String) : String
  = t2.innerDataTypes->iterate(innerDT; result = '0'|
    if t = innerDT.dataType then
      result + '+' + count(t,innerDT.dataType,prefix+'.'+innerDT.name)
    else result)
```

Using the `count` helper, it is easy to define a function which derives the number of instances for each *PrimitiveDatatype* in a marshalling step. Let t be the *PrimitiveDatatype* and *direction* be either IN or OUT depending on whether the call's parameters or its result should be marshalled. Then the OCL function given in fragment 4.3 results in the required stochastic expression to describe the number of occurrences.

OCL Fragment 4.3 Derving the Final Instance Number

```
def: number(sig:Signature, direction:ParameterModifier,
           t:PrimitiveDataType) : String
= if direction = IN then
    p_in->iterate(p; result = '0'|
      result + '+' + count(t,p.dataType,p.name))
  else
    p_out->iterate(p; result = '0';
      result + '+' + count(t,p.dataType,p.name)) +
    if sig.returnType <> null then
      -- Treat the return type as special OUT parameter
      count(t,sig.returnType,'RETURN')
    else
      ''
```

An iteration over all PrimitiveDatatype instances in the PCM yields the needed stochastic expressions to characterise all parameters of the `marshal` function. Note, that the formula generated for *CollectionDataTypes* is an approximation. The exact formula for a parameter named p would be

$$\sum_{i=1}^{p.NoE} count(t, t2.innerDataType, p.name +'.INNER')$$

which is not equal to $p.NoE * count(t, t2.innerDataType, p.name +'.INNER')$ as the expression returned by count may contain random variables, e.g., when describing an array of arrays. These random variables require drawing a new sample each time they are evaluated and hence, their sum does not equal to their multiplication. However, the exact formula might require drawing a lot of random samples which is expensive to compute and lengthens simulation runs which is why the approximation is used currently.

The component modelling the middleware can now contain a RD-SEFF which includes the resource demand caused by serialising the given amount of data and can return a characterisation for the number of bytes in the resulting stream depending on the chosen strategy. For example, serialising 10 integer values using SOAP implies creating 10 nodes in a SOAP XML document which each contains the human-readable form of each integer. Hence, the overall resource demand for serialising the 10 integer is 10 times the resource demand for creating a node and formatting an integer. The resulting byte stream contains the SOAP call overhead and 10 times the average size of a SOAP XML node for an integer value.

After the marshalling action, the generated component calls the next component using the generated extended interface `IA'`. Thus, it delegates the processing of the call to the next component. The derived bytesize resulting from the marshalling step is used to characterise the additional parameter `bytestream` as introduced above. All other parameter characterisations are simply copied so that they do not get lost and become finally available in the RD-SEFF of the called service. Note, that once the parameters have been converted into a bytestream the processing takes place on this stream only. This implies that the transformation needs no additional extended interfaces.

Completion Composition In figure 4.34, an *AssemblyConnector* named `Con1'` remains which further transformations replace recursively with *ConnectorCompletions* in order to model further processing of the message. For example, to include the performance impact of an encryption applied to the communication of the two components according to the features selected in the code transformation's feature configuration the transformation recursively applies the idea of the *ConnectorCompletion* as introduced before. For this, another in-place transformation replaces the *AssemblyConnector* `Con1'` with another *ConnectorCompletion* that deals with encryption/decryption as shown in figure 4.36.

The newly added completion has access to the bytestream's size as produced by the marshalling step. It can use this information to derive the demand for its own processing. For the encryption case, the completion assumes the existence of a middleware service `encrypt` taking a bytestream as input and resulting in a new, encrypted stream. The RD-SEFF of this service contains a size dependent CPU resource demand for the encryption and returns a new bytesize depending on the encryption algorithm. Both can depend on the encryption strength and algorithm used which has been omitted from the feature diagram in figure 4.32, but whose inclusion is easy to integrate in the presented completion method (in analogy to the used protocol in the marshalling case).

Using completion composition the model can be extended with an arbitrary amount of middleware features. For example, adding compression or authentification is similar to the encryption case, authorisation simply adds another post-processor component on the receiver's side. This establishes a direct relationship

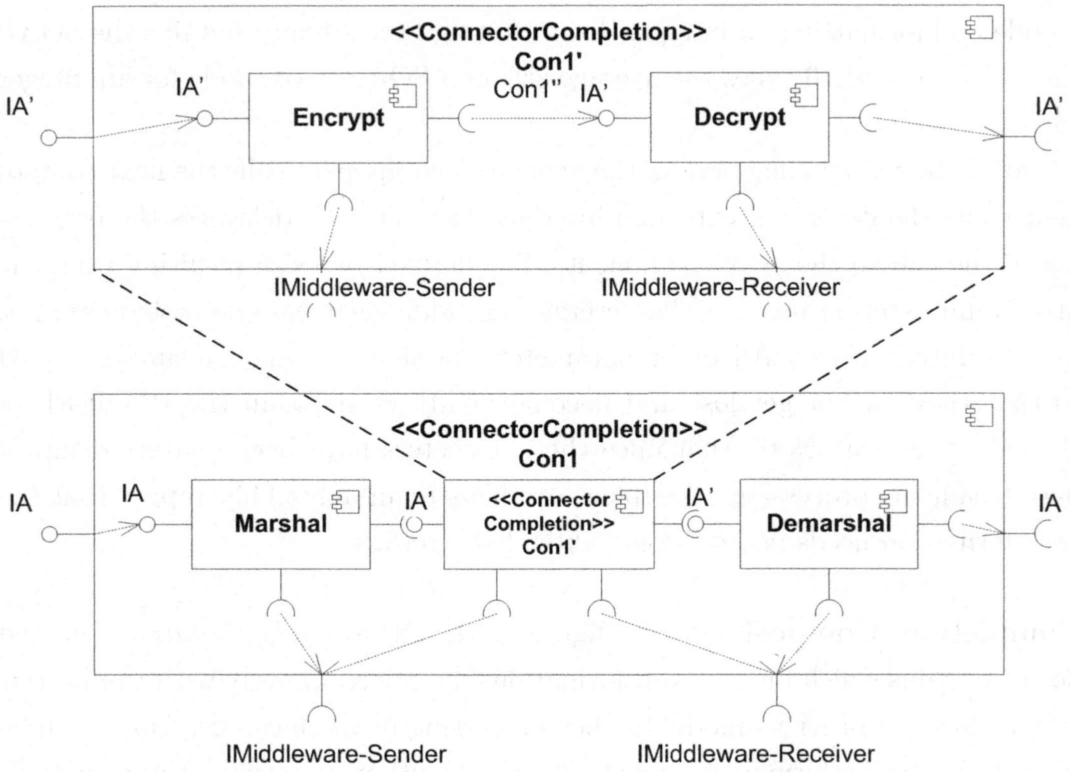

Figure 4.36: Composed Completions

between the selected features and the composed completion components. If the transformation's user chooses a feature, the respective completion component is added to the performance model.

Network Demand The process of adding completions to the model terminates when all middleware features which should be included into the model have been included. A final transformation replaces the last remaining *AssemblyConnector* with a *ConnectorCompletion* having a single *BasicComponent* which adds the network transmission. This is done by a RD-SEFF having a similar structure as the one in figure 4.35. In its pre-processing step it adds a resource demand on the network for the initial message. The bytesize used is the one derived by all the surrounding *ConnectorCompletions*. Then, it delegates the call which is necessary for the simulation to continue. Finally, when the call returns, it adds a network demand with the size of the result on the network.

Resulting Performance Model Impact To illustrate the impact of the connector completion on the performance model, consider figure 4.37 which presents an example connector completion and its deployment. All composite structures have been removed from the figure for reasons of clarity.

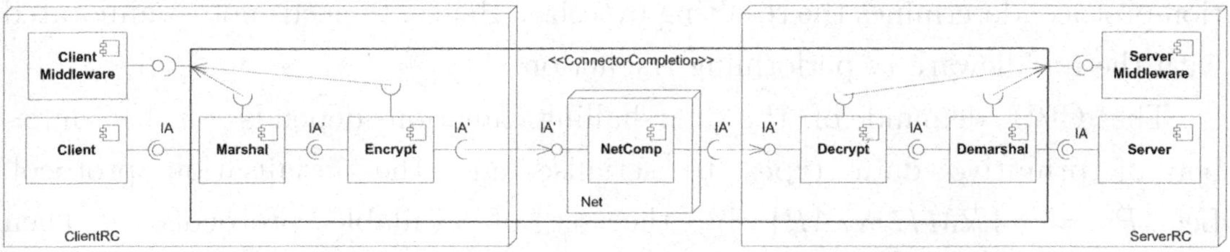

Figure 4.37: Allocated Connector Completion Example

The example depicts a connector with encryption, however, the following discussion regards the general case in which an arbitrary number of processing steps like authentication, compression, etc. may exist. The connector completion's RD-SEFF results from composing the RD-SEFFs of its inner components given in the appendix (see section A.2). Figure 4.38 shows the composed RD-SEFF. Data flow annotations have been omitted from the figure to keep it simple.

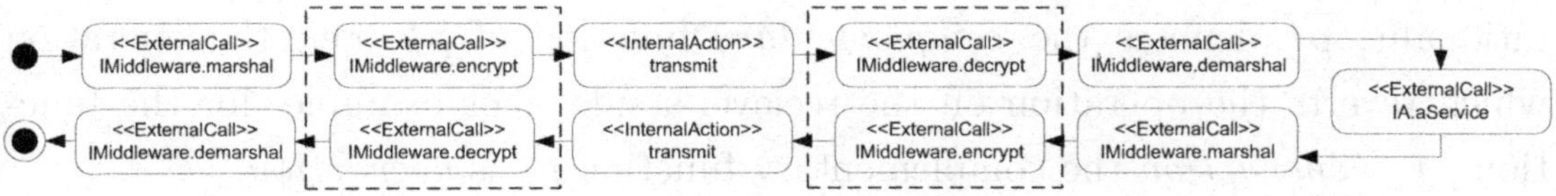

Figure 4.38: Composed RD-SEFF of the Connector Completion

The presented RD-SEFF illustrates how the generated RD-SEFFs of the connector completion's inner components form a processing chain which resembles the processing of an external call on the network. First, the client middleware marshals the parameters, then it processes them (in this case by encrypting them), and hands them to the network for transmission. On the server's side the server's middleware executes the same process in reverse order. After processing the call, the results are returned using the same mechanism. The dashed boxes in figure 4.38 indicate that the contained actions are feature dependent, additional processing steps.

The following aims at deriving a single formulae which represents the time demand for the whole processing chain. For this, several helper functions are introduced. For each of the middleware functions of middleware m, a function $d^m_{function}$ describes the (hardware-dependent) CPU demand of $function$ and

$bs_{function}$ describes the bytesize of the resulting stream. Only the CPU demands depend on the way an actual middleware component m does its processing. For example, the client may use a different middleware than the server or a slower CPU resulting in different processing times. For the bytesizes, solely the interaction protocol determines the resulting bytesize. Hence, bs needs not be annotated with the middleware m performing the action.

The CPU demand of the marshalling function depends on the number of primitive data types to serialise and the serialisation protocol. Let $P = \{RMI, SOAP\}$ be the set of available protocols. Then $d^m_{marshal}(p, ints.NoE, double.NoE, \dots)$ with $d^m_{marshal} : P \times \mathbb{N} \times \dots \mathbb{N} \rightarrow Demand$ describes the CPU demand needed to serialise the given numbers of primitive types using protocol p. Analogue, $bs_{marshal}(p, ints.NoE, double.NoE, \dots)$ with $bs_{marshal} : P \times \mathbb{N} \times \dots \mathbb{N} \rightarrow \mathbb{N}$ describes the resulting bytesize when serialising the given number of primitive types. For example, as integers use 4 bytes in RMI, $bs_{marshal}(RMI, 1, 0, \dots) = 4$.

For other processing functions $pf \in \{encryption, authentication, ..\}$, $d_{pf} : \mathbb{N} \rightarrow Demand$ is the demand caused by processing a bytestream of the given length and $bs_{pf} : \mathbb{N} \rightarrow \mathbb{N}$ gives the size of the stream after processing. Additionally, $\overline{pf}$ denotes the *complementary* function of pf, i.e., the operation which reverts the operation on the reciever's side. For example, for the function $pf = encryption$ the complementary function $\overline{pf}$ is *decryption*.

To model the data flow available in the PCM, causing variables to change their value, the following introduces a notation to model state changes. $[X \leftarrow Y]$ denotes that variable X changes its value to Y in all expressions following the $[X \leftarrow Y]$. For example, $[stream.BS \leftarrow bs_{encrypt}(stream.BS)]$ models the change of the bytestream's size caused by encryption.

Let $p \in P$ be the selected marshalling protocol in the connectors feature configuration. Additionally, let $pf_1, \dots, pf_n$ be the selected additional processing functions, $pf_i \in \{encryption, authentication, ...\}$ and $pf_i \neq pf_j$ for $i \neq j$. Using the introduced helper functions and the function rt (see section 4.4.3), which models the time demand for processing resource demands including resource congestion, and the operator $\oplus$ introduced in section 4.6.1.1 to indicate that demands modelled using the rt function have to be evaluated sequentially, the time needed to transmit a call from the client to the server is:

$$
\begin{aligned}
& rt(Client_{CPU}, d^{Client}_{marshal}(p, ints.NoE, doubles.NoE, ...)) \\
& [stream.BS \leftarrow bs_{marshal}(p, ints.NoE, doubles.NoE, ...)] \\
\oplus\ & rt(Client_{CPU}, d^{Client}_{pf_1}(stream.BS)) \\
& [stream.BS \leftarrow bs_{pf_1}(stream.BS)] \\
\oplus\ & \dots \\
\oplus\ & rt(Client_{CPU}, d^{Client}_{pf_n}(stream.BS)) \\
& [stream.BS \leftarrow bs_{pf_n}(stream.BS)] \\
\oplus\ & rt(net, stream.BS/tp_{net} + l_{net}) \\
\oplus\ & rt(Server_{CPU}, d^{Server}_{\overline{pf_n}}(stream.BS)) \\
& [stream.BS \leftarrow bs_{\overline{pf_n}}(stream.BS)] \\
\oplus\ & \dots \\
\oplus\ & rt(Server_{CPU}, d^{Server}_{\overline{pf_1}}(stream.BS)) \\
& [stream.BS \leftarrow bs_{\overline{pf_1}}(stream.BS)] \\
\oplus\ & rt(Server_{CPU}, d^{Server}_{demarshal}(p, ints.NoE, doubles.NoE, ...))
\end{aligned}
$$

The demand for processing the result is analogous and omitted here. Note, how the feature configuration changes the resource demand. The set of selected additional processing functions $pf_1, \dots, pf_n$ has an impact on the number of processing steps in the given formulae. Additional processing functions add an demand on the client and on the server's side. The chosen serialisation protocol has an impact on the marshalling and demarshalling demands. Additionally, it generates different bytesizes for the processed messages causing a different resource demand on subsequent processing steps and the network.

4.6.4 Add-Ons

The implementation of the transformation of PCM instances to Java EE/EJB realisations supports additional features to make it complete. However, as they have no direct performance impact or do not belong to the application's implementation but to its environment, they are only described briefly here. However, they have an impact on the overall development time when using the model to generate a realisation. It is assumed, that the more code is generated the faster developers can finalise the implementation.

- **Control Flow**: For *BasicComponents* code is generated for their RD-SEFFs. However, due to the abstraction of the RD-SEFF, the generated code is incomplete and has to be completed by the developer. For this, the code is only generated once and not altered on subsequent generator runs. It contains comments for all *InternalActions* giving the developer hints via the name of the action and also via the resource demands from the model. The transformation handles all control flow constructs and generates the respective Java control flow statements, i.e., loops, if-branches, thread starts, etc. Again, parts which depend on variable characterisations like loop iteration counts, or branch conditions are only preserved as comments helping the developer in finally implementing the code.

- **System External Services**: The software architect or the QoS analyst have to add timing information for services which are outside the scope of the system under study. For the generated code to be quickly usable, a mock implementation of the system external services is generated. It can be combined with a mock framework such as EasyMock (Freese, 2002) to build stubs for the external services in order to get a testbed for module testing.

- **Usage Testdriver**: The transformation derives single test scenarios and load test drivers from the usage model. Each *UsageScenario* is transformed into a JUnit (Hunt and Thomas, 2003) test for single execution. Additionally, the transformation generates a workload driver simulating the workload as specified in the *UsageModel* (cf. section 4.4.4 for the workload mapping in SimuCom). The generated code is incomplete in general because parameter values for *EntryLevelSystemCall*s can only be derived from the model if `VALUE` characterisations exist. In other cases, generated comments help the developer to fill in the missing code fragments.

4.6.5 Limitations and Discussion

Some limitations of the transformation of PCM instances and their coupled transformations remain. The following discusses them briefly.

- **Completeness of the Generated Code:** As already mentioned in the previous section, code generation based on the PCM is always incomplete due to the abstraction of the model. As a consequence, the focus has been on mapping the component concepts of the PCM and to use it as demonstration how to realise abstract model concepts (called PIM in OMG's MDA strategy) on a selected implementation platform (called PSM in OMG's

MDA strategy). This mapping has been used to demonstrate the inclusion of the performance impact of code mapping decisions. It is out of the scope of this work to create an industry-style Java EE code generator like AndroMDA which for example also considers generating a Web-GUI. For the PCM the GUI is out of scope, but the database layer can be supported by deriving persistable entities from *CompositeDatatype*. The current implementation does not support this. Nevertheless, the generator served as foundation for some case studies in the PCM's context for fast code generation of Java EE applications from PCM instances whose measured performance could be compared to the predictions done with SimuCom for example.

- **Completeness of the Feature Diagrams:** The given feature diagrams are not complete. For any of the given design decisions there are likely a lot more possible solutions, e.g., further patterns. That's the reason why the code and the prediction transformation are closely coupled. Only features available in the code transformation need to be regarded in the prediction transformation. Additionally, there may be features in the code transformation which do not have a significant performance impact. The prediction transformation can simply ignore such features.

- **Using Resource Types in Transformations:** Whenever a coupled transformation generates an *InternalAction* having *ParametricResourceDemands*, the generated demand specification has to rely on a common understanding of the used *ResourceTypes* and their units between the transformation and the deployer who created the *ResourceEnvironment*. This assumption corresponds to the PCM's assumption that component developer and deployer agree on the used *ResourceTypes*.

- **Inclusion of Non-generated Components** The mapping is distributed among the component developers and the other roles. However, the generated code assumes that the components it uses have been derived by a transformation by the component developer. It is not capable of including manually written components which do not follow the same rules. In order to include these components adapters or wrappers are needed which comply with the naming schema of the transformation. It might be possible to generate these adapters and include their performance impact as well as described in former work (Becker et al. (2006a), Streekmann and Becker (2006)) and realised in a prototypical legacy tool by Krogmann (2004).

4.7 Prototype Mapping

The use of prototypes is common practice in engineering disciplines during the development process of new products. In software engineering, the construction of prototypes is also a recommended practice. It offers early feedback on functional and extra-functional aspects of the software. Especially for the user interface prototypes allow early feedback from customers. But also for performance evaluation prototypes are useeful as Bardram et al. (2005) points out.

The problem with performance prediction models like SimuCom is that they usually rely on assumptions and model abstractions, which are necessary to keep the complexity under control. However, the real software system and its environment is usually much more complex. Because of this, model-based evaluation can help in finding infeasible designs quickly and cost-effective. But they can not assure that a design is feasible given todays complexity of the systems. Having a prototype that can be tested in the destination environment helps to understand system properties under realistic conditions.

However, this comes at the additional cost for setting up this environment which may involve buying hardware, installing operation systems and middleware platforms, setting up networking connections, and finally deploying, executing, and measuring the prototype. As the measurements have to be performed in real-time (compared to simulation time in SimuCom) this consumes additional time and money. In an engineering process, it is desired to combine early model-based predictions and prototyping. First, prototypes can yield important information on the application's environmental characteristics like measured response times of system external calls, middleware delays, etc. Second, models that satisfy the requirements according to the simulation model can be used to validate the results gained in the destination environment. Deriving prototypes automatically from models lowers the cost of prototyping.

This section introduces a mapping of PCM instances to executable prototypes called ProtoCom. It is based on the introduced mappings for SimuCom (described in section 4.4) and the technology mapping to Java EE or POJO components (described in section 4.6). ProtoCom's mapping uses a mixture of the concepts of SimuCom and the code transformation plus a small set of ProtoCom specific mappings. It's realisation is simple by exploiting the modular transformation technique described in section 4.2.

This section is structured as follows. First, section 4.7.1 gives details on ProtoCom's transformation implementation by combining the simulation and the code transformation. Section 4.7.2 describes how ProtoCom mimics resource demands by generating a workload performance equivalent to the PCM's model instance specification. Section 4.7.3 concludes with a list of ProtoCom's assumptions and limitations.

4.7.1 Combining Mappings

As already introduced briefly in section 4.2, ProtoCom uses the code transformation to generate its components and deployment information. For transforming the behaviour part of a PCM instance, i.e., component service implementations or the implementations of workload drivers, it uses the templates of SimuCom. The only exception to this rule is for *InternalActions* and their resource demands. Instead of using SimuCom's resource demand templates, which control SimuCom's queuing network, ProtoCom uses workload generators, which try to mimic realistic resource demands. They are described in section 4.7.2.

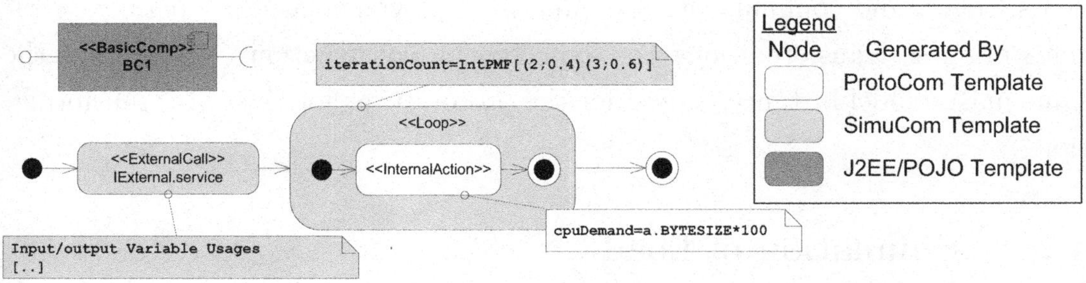

Figure 4.39: An Example for the ProtoCom Mapping Strategy

An example for the combination of the different transformation templates is depicted in figure 4.39. The colouring indicates the origin of the template which is responsible for generating the respective code element: white elements are generated by ProtoCom's own templates, light grey elements are generated by SimuCom templates and dark grey elements are generated by the code transformation. Applying this schema, figure 4.39 shows that the component is generated by the code transformation. Note, that this includes the provided and required ports as well as the communication links between them. This allows deploying the generated components on a Java EE middleware server. For the behaviour of components, SimuCom templates generate most of the control flow logic.

The example contains an *ExternalCall-* and a *LoopAction*. SimuCom templates also generate the code for the variable characterisation handling and the evaluation of stochastic expressions for loop iterations or branch conditions. Note, that due to the fact that SimuCom's transformation generates *ExternalCallActions*, the passing of realistic parameter values is not part of the prototype. Instead it passes simulated stacks, which may have different bytesizes (cf. the corresponding discussion in section 4.7.3).

Finally, a mixture of SimuCom and ProtoCom templates generate the code for *InternalActions*. SimuCom templates generate code for evaluating the resource demand's stochastic expressions. ProtoCom's templates generate code that takes the derived demand and tries to simulate load according to this demand.

Relationship to Coupled Transformations The prototype mapping also has a close relationship to Coupled Transformations. ProtoCom can be seen as prediction transformation which generates a prediction by running a prototype. As such it has to be parameterised by the code transformation as SimuCom had to. However, as it uses the code transformation templates to generate components, ports, and communication as well as deployment aspects, parameterisations of these transformations are respected by construction - given, that the same mark model instance is used for the prototype as for the code transformation.

4.7.2 Simulation of Load

The main difficulty for the ProtoCom mapping is to generate resource demands on the underlying execution environment, which shall be a close approximation of the load generated by the final application. The generated load has to rely on the resource demands defined in the PCM instance and execution environment model only.

The following discusses two issues involved in generating such a resource demand.

Calculation of Hardware-dependent Demands First, the demand as specified in the *InternalAction* is hardware independent, e.g., it is specified in abstract CPU work units. Hence, it has to be transformed into a hardware dependent demand. For example, a demand of 100 abstract CPU work units requires a translation into a certain amount of iterations of a CPU intense algorithm like computing Fibonacci numbers which is expected to cause a performance equivalent CPU load. Two options have been considered for mapping hardware-independent resource demands to hardware-dependent demands. First, support for a number of predefined hardware-independent demand types, e.g., CPU work units, or second, automatic adjusting of ProtoCom to its target environment.

For this option, a constant translation factor for each element of a set of known units to parameters of load simulators would be needed. For example, it could simply be defined that in order to simulate the equivalent of a single work unit, 100.000 Fibonacci numbers need to be calculated. Being rather simple to realise, this approach has some drawbacks. First, it only works for units foreseen by ProtoComs mapping. Second, there is no guarantee, that the selected translation factor matches the assumptions of the developer who specified the PCM instance.

The second option tries to remedy this by attempting to automatically determine the translation factors by executing a small benchmark when starting ProtoCom. The PCM's *ProcessingResourceSpecification* can then be used to estimate translation factors. For example, for a CPU whose processing rate is specified as 1000 work units per second in its *ProcessingResourceSpecification* a translation factor t has to be found for which given a demand of d it takes $d * t/1000$ seconds to compute the respective demand simulation algorithm. Assume a CPU benchmark on the target system yields a response time for a single run of 1 second for calculating 100.000 Fibonacci numbers. Then the factor t is 100.000 FibonacciNo/sec $* \frac{1}{1000}$ sec/work unit = 100 FibonacciNo/work unit. In order to get more reliable factors t, the benchmark is executed several times, outliers are ruled out and an average of all fs is finally used. This option has the advantage that its measurement results can be compared to simulation results. However, as it tries to eliminate the hardware's real processing rate, the physical hardware processing rate is not any longer part of ProtoCom results as it would be for the first option where a twice as fast machine would result in twice as fast results. On the other hand, remaining factors like the operating system's scheduler, cache impact, middleware overhead, etc. are still reflected realistically.

The current implementation supports the second option as ProtoCom mainly served to validate SimuCom's predictions. Nevertheless, adding the first option is easy and part of future improvements.

Selection of the Demand Simulation Strategy The algorithm used to simulate the demand leads to the next issue: the selection of the right algorithm. It is important to select an algorithm which causes a similar resource demand as the final application code. However, the PCM's simplified resource model does not yet contain enough information for this decision. In the PCM, a demand is simply multiplied with the respective processing rate of the corresponding resource to get the demand in time units.

However, in reality, it is not that simple. For example, for a CPU demand it makes a difference whether memory access is involved or not, and if it is involved how the CPU cache is involved in this. For hard-disk accesses it is similar. It makes a difference if data is read in large, continuous chunks or if the disk has to seek a lot and only reads small amounts of data at each location. In order to deal with these issues, ProtoCom supports the selection of a strategy which is used to simulate the resource demand. It contains a central registry for all resource demand strategies which can be used to simulate the demand of a specific resource type like CPU or hard-disk. By varying the resource demand strategies, the software architect can analyse their performance impact. Future versions of the PCM may support additional model elements giving information on memory or disk access which can be used to automatically decide for the most appropriate strategy.

4.7.3 Assumptions and Limitations

There are also assumptions and limitations which have to be made for the transformation of PCM instances to ProtoCom prototypes. The following list summarizes them.

- **Validity of the PCM model Instance:** As the ProtoCom mapping relies on its particular PCM input model, the model has to be valid with respect to the resource demands. The prototype only provides the means to execute a PCM instance in a more realistic execution environment but it cannot provide insights for the question whether the PCM instance's resource demands are valid with respect to the final application.

- **Choosing the Right Load Generation Strategy:** Picking the right resource demand simulation strategy is crucial for the results to be realistic as explained in the previous section. However, currently, there is no guidance for the user helping him to choose the right one. Additionally, ProtoCom's implementation is limited to a global selection of a strategy per *ProcessingResourceType*. However, different *ParametricResourceDemand*s in different *InternalAction*s may be better reflected by different strategies. These improvements are subject to future work.

- **System External Calls:** The code mapping generates only mock stubs for system external services. It is desirable for a prototype to exchange the stub with code calling the real service. However, this also implies specifying parameter values when needed in these calls (see next list item).

- **No Realistic Parameter Passing** ProtoCom relies on PCM's abstraction from the real data and uses parameter characterisations and SimuCom's simulated stack. However, this has several drawbacks.

  First, the network load is not realistic any more as ProtoCom transmits simulated stacks instead of the parameters of the real application. In cases where both differ significantly, ProtoCom's results may be worthless. As a remedy, in future versions of ProtoCom the network load bytesize estimation introduced for *AssemblyConnector*s (cf. section 4.6.3) can help. If the estimation results in a larger bytesize than the size of the serialised simulated stack an additional random payload could be added to the transmitted packages. However, this does not help if the estimated bytesize is smaller than the serialised simulated stack.

  Second, it is difficult to call system external services if this involves parameter passing. In this case, the stub generated for system external services needs manual adjustment and test data has to be used instead of realistic parameter values.

Chapter 5

Validation

The validation of the results presented in sections 3 and 4 is split into several aspects. The overall aim of the approach has been to combine the areas of component-based software development, model-driven software development, and performance prediction. In order to achieve this goal, a meta-model for component-based architectural modelling and performance prediction has been introduced in section 3. Transformations presented in section 4 map instances of this model into a performance simulation, prototype implementation, or code skeletons. The presented Coupled Transformations method exploits the close relationship of the applied transformations to enhance the performance predictions.

These results of prediction methods can be validated on various levels according to Freiling et al. (2008) which introduces three types of validation. As a prerequisite for applying the different validation types, the correctness of the methods realisation and accompanying tool implementations has to be ensured. This step has been incorporated into the method and tool development process and is therefore omitted here. Type I validations demonstrate that predictions made by a prediction method conform to the observed reality given that the method and its tools are applied without making any mistakes. Type II validations show that methods, which depend on human interaction, can be applied by trained users successfully. This is in line with the typical model-driven evaluation criteria that the users for whom a specific DSL (meta-model) has been created should be able to use the modelling language. Type III validations finally seek to validate that the overall approach has benefits over other competing approaches. The last type is extremely hard to show and cost-intensive in larger contexts as it requires to perform projects at least twice - one time using the method under validation and the other time by using competing approaches.

In the context of this thesis and the results given above, Type I validations of the prediction results of the presented simulation. They can be classified in two classes. The first class contains predictions based on the original model instance without respecting Coupled Transformations in order to show that the simulation predicts correctly. Second, Coupled Transformations for the introduced Java EE code mapping should increase prediction accuracy.

A Type II validation should show the appropriateness of the PCM as modelling language, its understandability and the applicability of the developed tool suite accompanying the PCM. For Coupled Transformations it can be quantitatively validated how much it speeds up the construction of accurate prediction models. Additionally, qualitatively questionnaires can yield information on the realisation of Coupled Transformations in the tool suite and whether it meets the user's expectations on its applicability.

Several case studies presented in the following have been performed as joint work with Heiko Koziolek who introduced the usage profile dependent modelling into the PCM's meta-model. The focus of his work has been on the usage profile dependent parts of the PCM, whereas this work focuses on the model-driven aspects especially the transformations and their outputs.

This section is structured as follows. Section 5.1 contains case studies conducted with the PCM to show Type I validity. In the context of this thesis, this means that the PCM's modelling constructs as realised in SimuCom work as expected. Section 5.1.1 shows a successful application of SimuCom without using Coupled Transformations to show its prediction capabilities. Section 5.1.2 shows in a case study how Coupled Transformations significantly increase the prediction accuracy for different *AssemblyConnector* mappings. Section 5.2 presents the results of the Type II validation by presenting the experiment conduced by Martens (2007).

5.1 Type I Validation

This section introduces case studies performed with the PCM and its transformations. First, case studies which did not include mark models are given, second, those which use the additional mark model information as presented for Coupled Transformations.

5.1.1 Mark Model Independent Predictions

Web Audio Store The Web Audio Store has been initially published by Koziolek et al. (2006). Its model was used to integrate initial usage profile modelling concepts into UML and UML-SPT. It has been reused by Becker et al. (2007) and Becker et al. (2008b) to demonstrate the modelling capabilities of the PCM and its performance simulation.

The Web Audio Store is a component-based software system for sharing music like iTunes serving as a representative component-based web application. Users can upload music files to the server and retrieve the files stored later. It is implemented in .NET and based on Microsoft's ASP.NET. The database connected to the system was MySQL. User interaction has been simulated by a manually written HTTP client. An overview on the architecture of the system is given in figure 5.1.

The file upload service has been selected as performance critical use case. As a central aim of the PCM is early design time support for design decisions, an alternative has been introduced into the architecture. For uploaded files there is the option to recode the uploaded file using an OGG encoder before storing it in the database as indicated by the dashed box in figure 5.1. The encoder is able to reduce the size of the music files by a factor of approx. 62%. The reduction in the filesize of the uploaded file causes less load on the network connection to the database but needs an additional CPU demand on the upload server. In the investigated use case, a single user uploads music files in varying numbers according to a given distribution between 8 and 12. Each file's size is either 3.5, 4, or 4.5 MByte. The corresponding usage model is shown in figure 5.2(a) using a syntax close to the PCM tool's concrete graphical syntax.

The Web Audio Store's PCM instance models the middle-tier of the application, i.e., the components `WebUI`, `AudioStore`, `EncodingAdapter`, and `Encoder`. The database interface is modelled as *SystemExternalCall*. Figure 5.2(b) shows the important RD-SEFFs of the `WebUI` component and figure 5.3(a) that of the `EncodingAdapter` component. In contrast to the model published by Koziolek et al. (2006) the model used in Becker et al. (2008b) uses a parametric CPU demand for the encoder (see figure 5.3(b)) and for the time needed to transmit the file over the network. Both dependencies have been roughly estimated based on measured response times in dependence of the filesize.

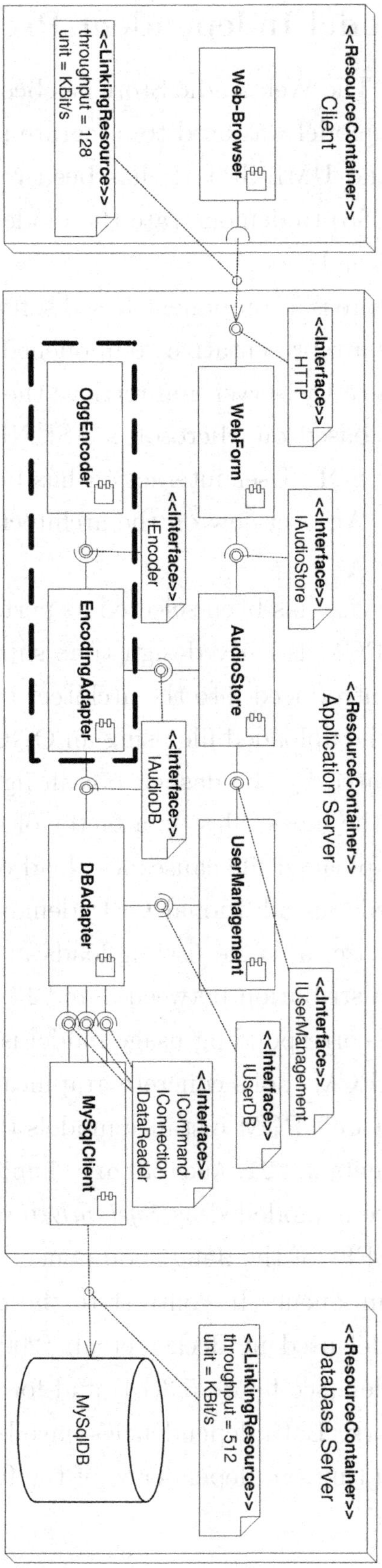

Figure 5.1: Architectural overview on the Web Audio Store (Becker et al., 2007)

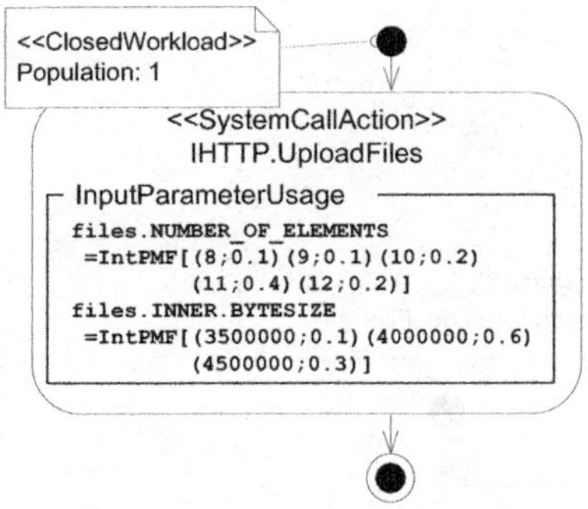

(a) UsageModel

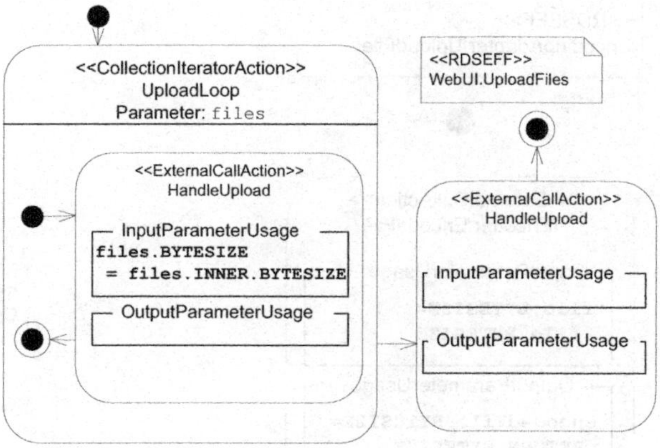

(b) RD-SEFF `WebUI.UploadFiles`

Figure 5.2: Web Audio Store PCM Model

Becker et al. (2007) used a deprecated version of SimuCom which did not use a model transformation but interpreted it. Becker et al. (2008b) use SimuCom as introduced in section 4.4. The following presents the results as gained by the transformation based realisation. Figure 5.4 shows the predicted probability density function and the resulting CDFs as well as the measured values for the architecture alternative without using the encoder component.

Due to the use of measured basic hardware demands, the prediction is close to the measurements. The Kolmogoroff-Smirnov (KS-)statistic (Sachs, 1997) is below 10%, i.e., the maximum difference between the CDFs in figure 5.4(b).

Figure 5.5 shows the predicted and measured response times for the design alternative containing the OGG encoder. As in the other design alternative, prediction and measurements fit well. The KS-statistic is again below 10%. From the predictions, it can be seen, that using the encoder alternative would be the faster alternative under the given usage profile. As measurements and predictions do not deviate much, SimuCom is able to predict the response time correctly.

5.1.2 Mark Model Dependent Predictions

Media Store The Media Store as published by Koziolek et al. (2007) initially served as case study for component parameters and *SetVariableActions*. However, it has been also used as a case study for the Java EE mapping and SimuCom. The Media Store's idea is similar to the Web Audio Store. It represents a multimedia shop suited for MP3 or video files. It supports two use cases, the

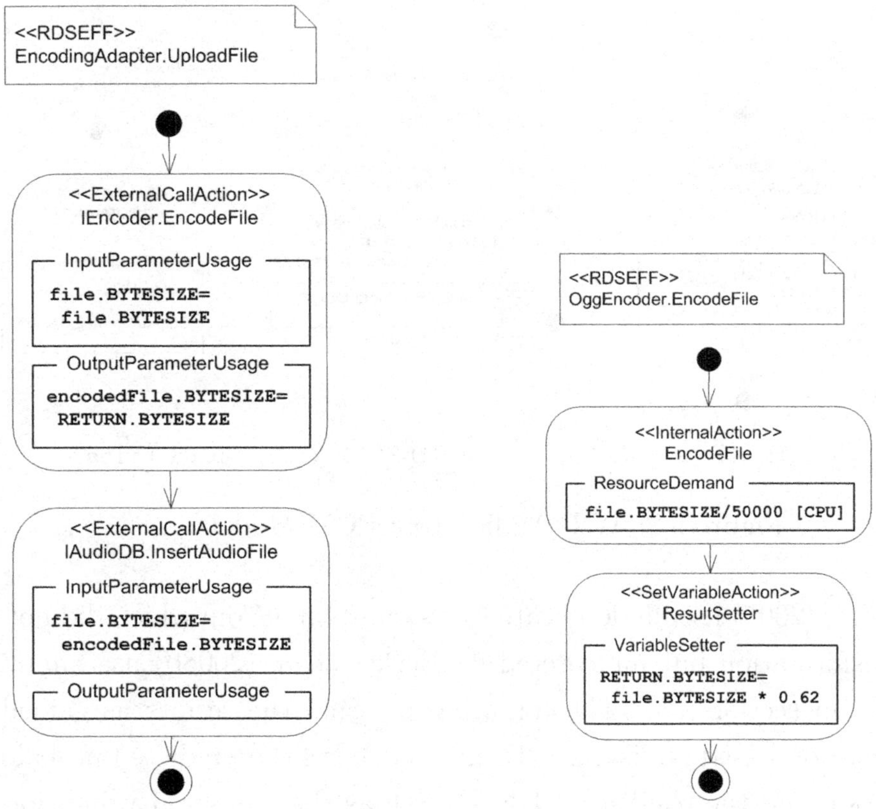

(a) RD-SEFF `EncodingAdapter.UploadFile` (b) RD-SEFF `OggEncoder.EncodeFile`

Figure 5.3: Web Audio Store PCM Model

download of files and their upload. The case study analysed two usage profiles. One for a music web shop and another one for video files. However, these usage dependencies are not of primary interest here. They are covered by Koziolek (2008).

The Media Store's architecture has been modelled directly as PCM instance. The architecture as depicted in figure 5.6 consists of several components from which the case study uses five, i.e., `WebUI`, `MediaStore`, `DBAdapter`, `AudioDB`, and `DigitalWatermark`. The first two components handle client communication, the next two the database interaction and the last one is responsible for adding a digital watermark to the delivered files in order to identify the user if the file should appear illegally somewhere on the Internet.

The Java EE transformation introduced in section 4.6 generated from the Media Store's PCM instance code skeletons. The skeletons lacked the database interaction and an algorithm to do the watermarking. Adding the missing code fragments took about 3-4 person hours. It involved writing classes for the Java

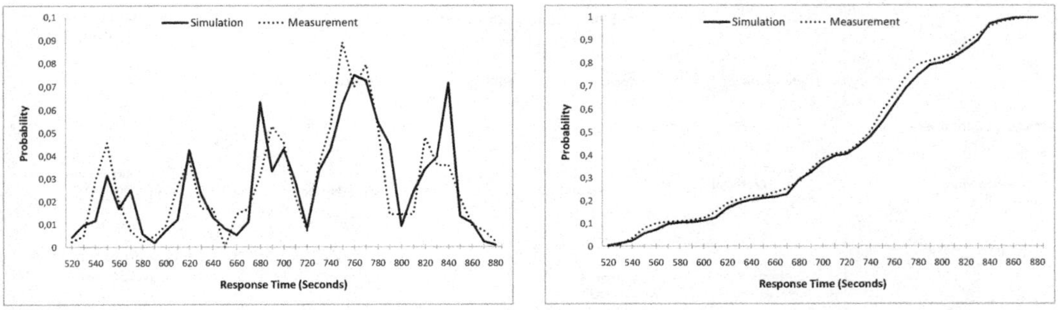

(a) Probability Density (b) Cumulative Distribution Function

Figure 5.4: Prediction and Measurements without Encoder (Becker et al., 2008b)

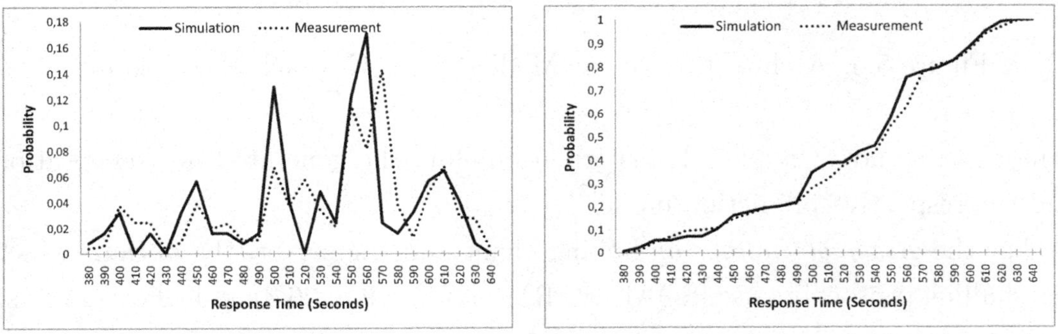

(a) Probability Density (b) Cumulative Distribution Function

Figure 5.5: Prediction and Measurements with Encoder (Becker et al., 2008b)

Persistence API (JPA) for the database interaction and adding a watermarking algorithm. However, all code additions only dealt with the applications business logic. All infrastructure code including build and deployment scripts could be generated by the Java EE mapping demonstrating that the mapping worked. Additionally, to complete the generated test driver (c.f., section 4.6.4) took half an hour for finalising the missing business logic. It downloads randomly selected files from the server and conducts response time measurements.

The Media Store case study as published by Koziolek et al. (2007) forms a solid foundation for an extended case study performed in the context of this thesis as the necessary infrastructure's setup is already available. To demonstrate the validity of Coupled Transformations, a case study in the context of the mapping of *AssemblyConnector*s as introduced in section 4.6.3 has been performed. Focusing on the *AssemblyConnector* linking the client with the server, an investigation of mapping options and their respective performance impact

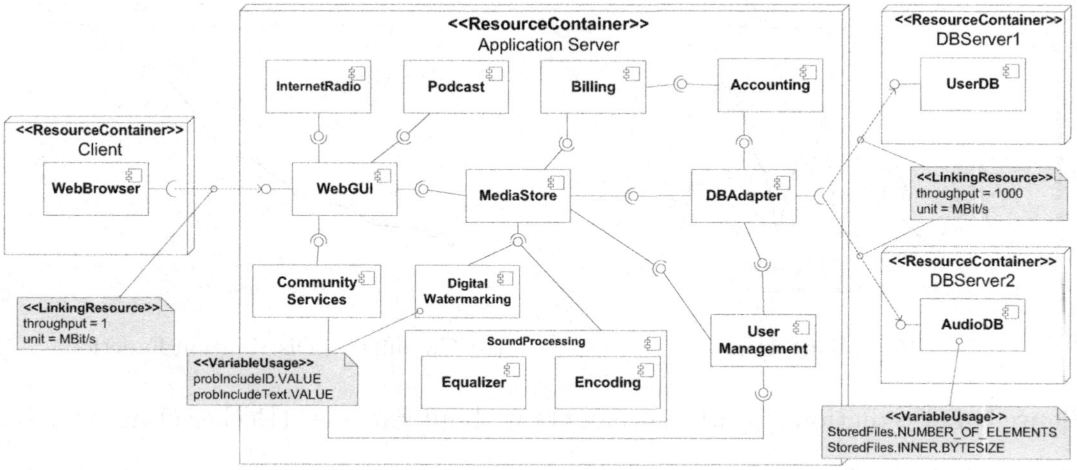

Figure 5.6: Architecture of the Media Store (Koziolek et al., 2007)

demonstrates how Coupled Transformations link the generated implementation and the respective prediction model.

For the *AssemblyConnector* linking client and the server, the options which marshalling protocol to use (SOAP vs. RMI, c.f. section 4.6.3) and whether to use authentication and/or encryption have been selected to validate the automatic inclusion of the respective completions. Note, that the combination of using SOAP and authentication was ruled out due to its unclear configuration in the Glassfish server. For the study, a new method `queryID3` has been added to the interface of the MediaStore. The method takes a list of IDs with the datatype integer and queries the connected database for each of the ID3 tags matching the MP3 file with the respective ID. After collecting the complete set of tags, the server sends the tags back to the client. For all measurements, the client, the Glassfish server, and MySQL run on the same host under Ubuntu Linux 7.10. The host was a laptop with a Core2Duo T7100 CPU and 2GB RAM. During the experiments, only one of the CPU's cores was active. By placing all components on the same host, the network interaction used the local TCP/IP stack instead of using a physical link. The workload was a close workload with a single user and no think time. Altogether, deactivation of a CPU core, not using a physical network, and only using a single user workload, circumvents limitations of the current PCM concurrency modelling (see section 3.10) which would make a comparison of predicted and measured metrics difficult. The measurements used a warmup phase of 20.000 measurements. Afterwards, they collected 20.000 measurements of the overall response time.

To make predictions in the following, measurements taken of the basic functions of the Glassfish server served as basis to create simplified RD-SEFFs for the actions taken by the server. The basic functions include RMI and SOAP marshalling, performing authentication, or performing encryption. The created PCM Glassfish component uses the measured distribution functions directly in its *ParametricResourceDemands*. Using measured data for the basic functions is not a thread to the validity of Coupled Transformations. Measurements mainly capture the execution environment influence factor on performance, however, for Coupled Transformations the important influence factor is the implementation. Thus, fixing the execution environment indeed removes a factor from the prediction which might otherwise make it hard to draw conclusions on the validity of Coupled Transformations.

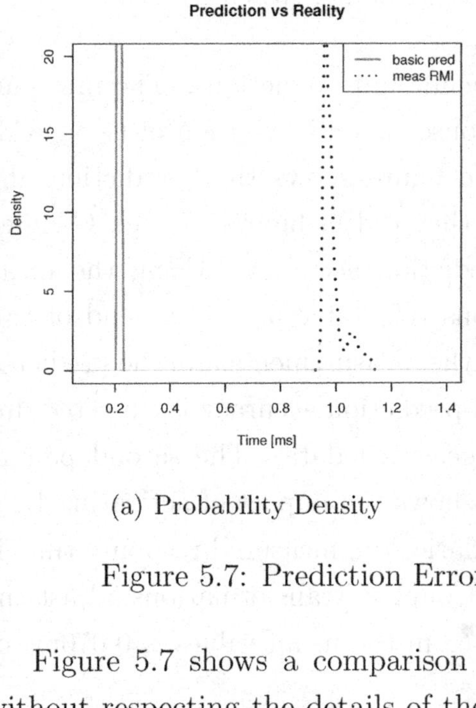

(a) Probability Density

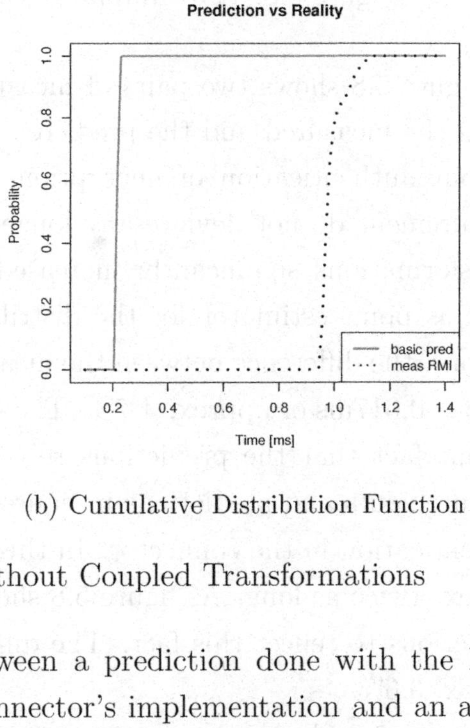

(b) Cumulative Distribution Function

Figure 5.7: Prediction Error without Coupled Transformations

Figure 5.7 shows a comparison between a prediction done with the PCM without respecting the details of the connector's implementation and an actual realisation of the connector using RMI. The figure shows that the prediction deviates from the measurements by around 400%. Also notice the right peek of the measurement's density function. This peek is observable in all subsequent measurements. A possible explanation of these outliers is Java's garbage collection mechnismn which recycles the memory used by the marshaller.

The following demonstrates how Coupled Transformations increase the prediction accuracy using knowledge on the connector's realisation.

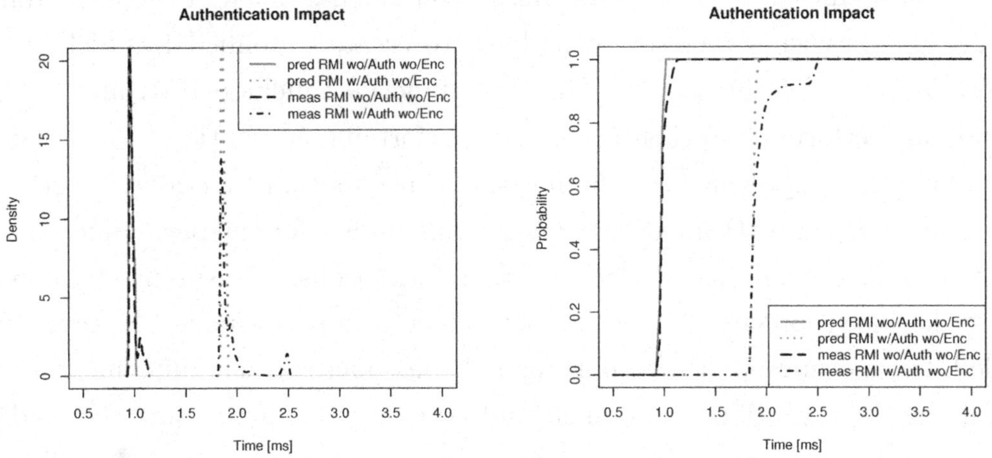

(a) Probability Density (b) Cumulative Distribution Function

Figure 5.8: RMI Mapping with and without Authentication

Figure 5.8 shows two pairs of measurements and predictions. The first pair shows the measured and the predicted response time distribution of using RMI without authentication or encryption. The figure shows that prediction and measurement do not deviate any longer as they did in figure 5.7, i.e., Coupled Transformations significantly increased prediction accuracy. Using the mean value as point estimator for the distributions (cf. table 5.1 at the end of this section), the difference between the mean of the measurements and the predicted mean is 0.017ms or approx. 1.7%. The good prediction accuracy is expected due to that fact that the predictions rely on measured data. The second pair of measurements and predictions in figure 5.8 shows the impact of activating RMI authentication in the connector. In this scenario, the measured response time is approx. twice as long. As figure 5.8 shows, Coupled Transformations adjust the predictions to reflect this fact. The difference in the mean values is 0.070ms or approx. 3.6%.

Figure 5.9 shows the same use case as in figure 5.8. However, this time both pairs additionally use Glassfish's SSL encryption to encrypt the transmitted data. As figure 5.9 shows, the distribution functions match again closely. They are shifted by approximately 0,2ms to the right in comparison to the functions in figure 5.8. This shift is the additional overhead caused by the encryption algorithm. For the use case without authentication the difference between the

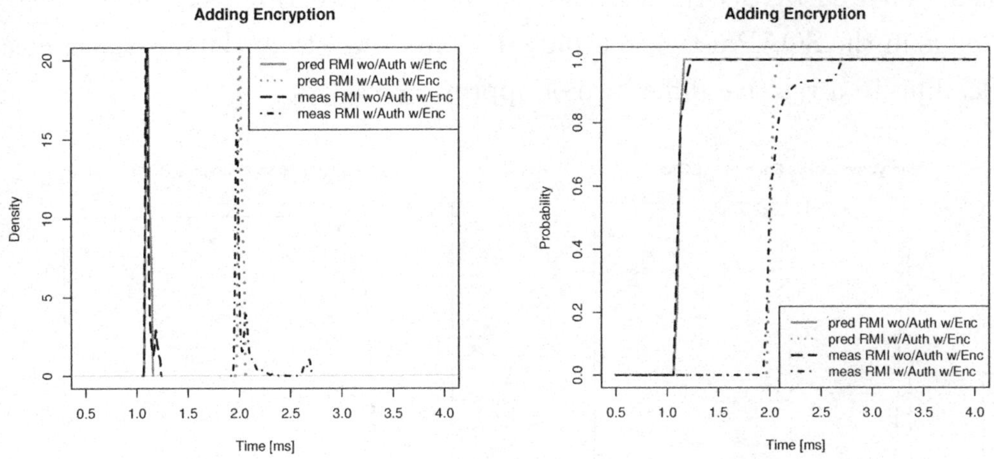

(a) Probability Density (b) Cumulative Distribution Function

Figure 5.9: Adding Encryption to an RMI Connector

measured and the predicted mean value is 0.002ms or approx. 0.2%. For the use case with authentication the difference is 0.049ms or approx. 2.4%.

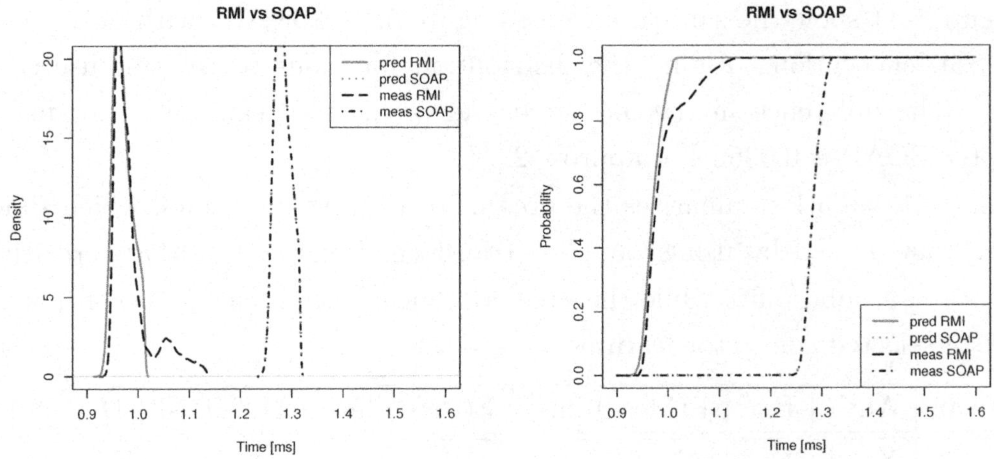

(a) Probability Density (b) Cumulative Distribution Function

Figure 5.10: Different Marshalling Strategies: SOAP vs. RMI

Figure 5.10 shows the impact of using a different marshalling protocol for realising the connector, e.g., a comparison between SOAP and RMI. Both use cases neither use authentication nor encryption. The distribution functions are again close, where SOAP shows a higher response time in the measurements than in the prediction. This is most likely due to the memory overhead of the XML documents created by SOAP not reflected in the PCM. However, the predicted mean value in the SOAP use case is only 0.046ms lower than the measured mean value leading to a relative difference of approx. 3.5%.

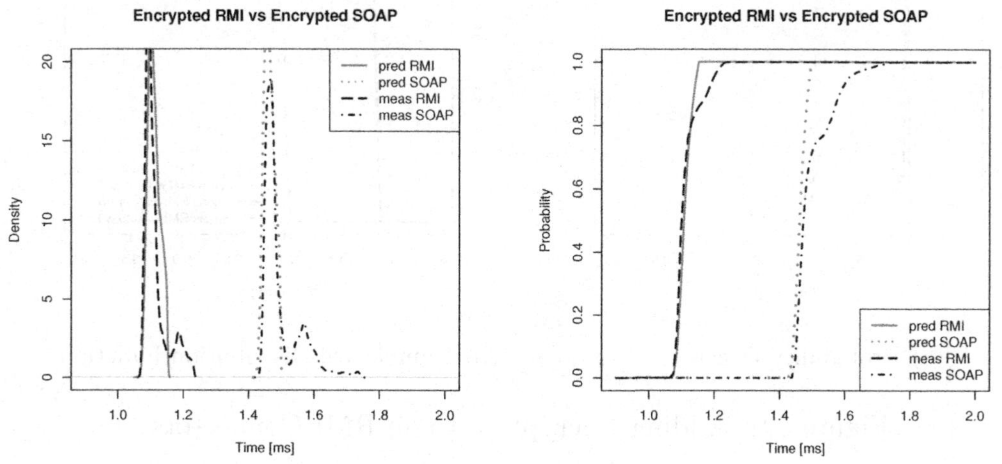

(a) Probability Density (b) Cumulative Distribution Function

Figure 5.11: Adding Encryption to the Comparison of SOAP and RMI

Figure 5.11 show the same use case as figure 5.10, however, with both cases using SSL encryption. Again, the distribution functions reflect this use case closely. The difference in the measured and predicted mean values for using encrypted SOAP is 0.035ms or approx. 2.3%.

Finally, table 5.1 summarizes the presented mean value results, which show the accuracy gained by using Coupled Transformations as the largest relative difference is around 3.6% while the predicted mean values change according to the set of selected connector features.

Protocol	Auth	Enc	E(Meas) [ms]	E(Pred) [ms]	Diff. [ms]	Diff. [%]
none	X	X	n/a	0.215	n/a	n/a
RMI	X	X	0.988	0.971	0.017	1.7
RMI	✔	X	1.941	1.871	0.070	3.6
RMI	X	✔	1.113	1.111	0.002	0.2
RMI	✔	✔	2.060	2.011	0.049	2.4
SOAP	X	X	1.329	1.283	0.046	3.5
SOAP	X	✔	1.498	1.463	0.035	2.3

Table 5.1: Mean Value Comparison

5.2 Type II Validation: Controlled Experiment

The applicability of the PCM and its transformations is subject to a Type II validation. Applicability is subjective and depends on the person using the PCM. Hence, in order to perform a Type II validation an experimental setting involving typical users is needed.

Martens (2007) performed such a study in her master thesis as a controlled experiment. The study investigated the applicability of PCM core concepts, SimuCom, interpretability of simulation results, and the basic applicability of Coupled Transformations.

This section is structured as follows. Section 5.2.1 lists influence factors to the PCM's applicability. Section 5.2.2 gives a description of the PCM's tools from a users point of view. This is important for judging the tools' impact on the results. Section 5.2.3 presents the experimental setting. The results in section 5.2.4 show that the validation was successful. After discussing the experiment's validity in section 5.2.5, a short summary concludes the Type II validation.

5.2.1 Influence factors

When performing a study on the applicability of a model-driven method, several influence factors have an impact on the study's outcome:

- **Meta-Model Complexity:** A major issue in using a modelling language is the meta-model's complexity. The more language concepts and semantic constraints the user has to learn the more likely it is that the modelling language is overly complex. While more complex models usually produce more accurate prediction results, a high complexity can lead to more mistakes made by the users resulting in models which do not adequately reflect the modelled entity.
- **Concrete Syntax:** Up to this point, this thesis did not discuss the issue of a concrete PCM syntax and used either UML-like diagrams with stereotypes or figures exported from the PCM's graphical modelling tool. However, the concrete syntax has a high impact on the applicability of a modelling language. For example, a good concrete syntax can hide meta-model complexity by presenting model information in a compact form like the graphical editor for *ComposedStructure*s which hides several meta-model attributes in simple arrows.

- **Tool Support:** Another major influence factor is the tool support for editing, validating, and analysing model instances. Editors for concrete graphical syntaxes have to present the model instance in a comprehensible way. Features like automatic arranging of diagram elements, tool tips, or modelling suggestions help to use the editor in an effective way. For concrete textual syntaxes established features in programming language editors, such as code highlighting, code completion, and incremental syntax and semantics checks, help in the same way. Tool supported validation of model instances helps to find modelling mistakes. Ideally, suggestions how to fix the issue are already presented. In case of the PCM, which separates the model into sub-models, the validation also ensures that these sub-models form a consistent model when put together. Finally, the configuration and execution of an analysis should be as easy as possible requiring a minimum amount of user interaction.

As a consequence of these influence factors any observations made in an experiment result from a combination of the skills of the participants and the features and quality properties of the tool's implementation. This complicates interpreting the results. It is difficult to judge whether the meta-model is incomprehensible or whether only its implementation is insufficient.

A more detailed description of the PCM's tool suite from a usability perspective compared to the overview given in section 3.9 is needed to help interpreting the case study's results. Therefore, the next section gives details on the tools.

5.2.2 PCM Tool Suite

From a user's point of view, the PCM tools offer three main features: creating and editing model instances, executing analyses, and visualising results for interpretation purposes. In contrast to the prototypical implementation of the concepts sufficient for Type I validations, a Type II validation needs a more sophisticated support as explained in the third bullet point of the enumeration in section 5.2.1. Because of this, the PCM tools have been improved with respect to robustness, usability, and completeness in a five month lasting effort. The following characterises the state of the tools during the experiment.

Editors Graphical editors for the PCM's concepts were available for the *Repository* model, RD-SEFFs, *CompositeStructures*, *Allocation* model, and *UsageSce-*

narios (cf. figure A.3 in the appendix). The editors have been generated to a large extend using the Graphical Modelling Framework 2.0 (GMF), a framework for the definition of concrete graphical syntaxes including the generation of graphical editors for the defined syntax. The diagram elements have a close relationship to UML2's graphical elements. It is expected that this lowers the learning curve for new users. However, it might also lead to confusion between the UML and the PCM's meaning.

Several enhancements have been added to the generated editors. For example, dialogs and property sheets to define *Interfaces* or automatic creation of dependent elements, e.g., start and stop elements for behaviours. For editing stochastic expressions a specialised textual editor has been implemented supporting syntax highlighting, code completion, and on-the-fly error checking for syntactical as well as type system correctness.

There was no specialized editor for instances of the *ResourceEnvironment*. However, it was omitted intentionally because EMF generates basic editors for any EMF based meta-model. This default editor has been considered to be sufficient for the not so complex *ResourceEnviroment*. Additionally, specialised editor support was missing for the specification of component parameters which also had to be done in the generated EMF default editor.

Simulation Execution Andrej (2007) realised a close integration of SimuCom into the model editing environment as a result of his study thesis. It automates checking the model instances for violations of the OCL constraints, the execution of SimuCom's transformation, and running the simulation. The configuration of the simulation including the stop condition and basic feature configuration settings for Coupled Transformations can be edited in a robust configuration dialog.

The automated check of model instances finds violations of the PCM's OCL constraints and additionally SimuCom's generator preconditions. It shows a summarizing dialogue containing all detected constraint violations. It has been introduced after the first experiment session, because many participants had problems with manually executing the model validation. This introduction might have had an impact on the results of the second experiment session as it improved the tool's error reporting. On the other hand, during the first session students also had the possibility to ask the supervisors in case of tool problems. It is arguable that the introduction only automated this process. Furthermore, there were no direct evidence of an influence in the experiment's observations.

Presentation of Simulation Results For the analysis of the simulation results, Andrej (2007) added a visualising GUI for the so called SensorFramework used in SimuCom to collect the results (a screenshot is available in figure 3.20). The SensorFramework offers different types of sensors which can be used to instrument code to measure passage times and state changes. The sensors can be either used to record simulation results, e.g., in SimuCom, or to store measured data, e.g., in ProtoCom or when analysing existing applications. SimuCom's transformation instruments the generated simulation code with sensors which record passage time of *UsageScenario*s and external method calls. For external method calls, it distinguishes the measured passage times using the *AssemblyContext*'s unique identifier which is important if the same component type is used several times in an architecture. That is because the same component might shows different performance measures in different contexts.

Simulated active resources are instrumented with state sensors measuring queue lengths and their changes over time. Additionally, they use passage time sensors to measure wait times of the jobs in the queues.

The developed SensorFramework-GUI can visualise measurements of passage time sensors as histograms and cumulative distribution functions. Using an interface to the statistics package R (R Development Core Team, 2007), users can derive basic point estimators like mean value or standard deviation of measurements. Furthermore, the tool displays queue lengths and the probability distribution of queue lengths as pie charts.

In the Palladio development process, the software architect - supported by the QoS analyst - uses this information to judge design alternatives and choose the alternative best fitting his requirements. As he gets probability density functions as results, it is possible to analyse more sophisticated requirements compared to only mean values. However, additional skills, like deriving distribution quantiles or comparing distributions with intersections, may be needed to interpret the distribution functions correctly. In the experiment presented here, the experiment participants had to perform this task. Evaluating their results and their answers to corresponding questions in the questionnaire helps to gain insights into the interpretation of the results.

5.2.3 Study Design

To perform the Type II validation, Martens (2007) developed a training course for the participants and an experimental setting described in the following. The experiment compares the PCM and its tool to the mature SPE method and its SPEED tool (cf. section 2.3.3). This comparison helps in judging the strength and weaknesses of the approaches and their tools. Additionally, it allows to judge the complexity of the experiment tasks in cases of overly complex tasks.

Preparation The participants in the experiment were trained in applying SPE and Palladio during a course in the summer term covering both theory and practical labs (cf. figure 5.12). For the theory part, there was a total of ten lectures, each of them took 1.5h. The first three lectures were dedicated to foundations of performance prediction and CBSE. Then, two lectures introduced SPE followed by five lectures on the PCM. The three additional lectures on the PCM in comparison to SPE were due to its more complex meta-model which needs more views and different editors to edit its model instances. In parallel to the lectures, eight practical labs took place, again, each taking 1.5h. During these sessions, solutions to the accompanying ten exercises were presented and discussed. Five of these exercises practised the SPE approach and five the Palladio approach.

The exercises had to be solved by the participants between the practical labs. Martens assigned pairs of students to each exercise and shuffled the pairs frequently in order to get different combinations of students working together and exchanging their knowledge. Each exercise took the students 4.75 h in average to complete.

Together, knowledge tests and preparatory exercises were intended to ensure a certain level of familiarity with the tools and concepts, because participants who failed two preparatory exercises or a short tests would have been excluded from the experiment.

Experiment Design To compare Palladio and SPE, Martens (2007) designed modelling tasks for the participants. Each modelling task was executed by a group of participants in which each participant used Palladio and simultaneously by a group of participants in which each participant used SPE. The modelling tasks contained the translation of the design of an example system given as plain text supported by UML diagrams into the input models of the respective method, the execution of the analysis, and the interpretation of the results returned by the respective method's tool. For each system under study, the modelling task involved creating a model for the system's initial design. Additionally, each system had five possible design alternatives. The goal for the participants was to find the alternative that best improved the overall system response time. As such, the modelling task can be considered a typical application scenario for both methods during software design.

Martens (2007) developed a goal-question-metric (GQM (Basili, 1990)) plan to systematically define the evaluation goals, derived questions, and metrics. The overall goal was to judge the applicability of Palladio and SPE. For this, the focus was on two questions. The first question was about the quality of the created models. Note, that quality in this context refers to a correct translation of the given system specifications to input models needed by both methods. The second question asked about the time consumption necessary to create these input models. For both questions, Martens also tried to systematically judge the reasons for the observed results including a questionnaire filled out by the participants after the experiment capturing their subjective impression of both methods.

Martens collected the models created by the participants and analysed them after the experiment. For this analysis, Martens decided to compare the predictions made by the created models to predictions of a so called reference model (Martens, 2007, p.38). The reference model is the solution of the experiment tasks as created by Martens. She used all available information in the task's descriptions to create these models and ensured that they were correctly specified in the experiment's pre-tests.

During the experiment, the participants had to hand in solutions for the system and each design alternative. The experimenters checked the solutions for obvious mistakes. Only when passing this test, the participants were allowed to continue with the experiment task. Martens introduced this so called acceptance test to ensure a minimum quality of the created models. In order to still judge the results later, the experimenters documented the outcome of the acceptance test.

To judge the durations of the activities needed for performing a prediction with both methods, the participants took timestamps whenever they finished an activity from a set of predefined activities. The initial experiment design allocated a maximum of four hours to complete the experiment tasks. However, many participants needed additional time, so the time was extended to six hours during the experiment.

For the experiment, Martens (2007) divided the group of participants into two sub groups and designed two experiment tasks for them. The participants worked on the tasks in a cross-over experiment design. The first group used Palladio for the first task and SPE for the second, the second group did so vice versa (see figure 5.12). The systems under study were the so called MediaStore (MS) in the first experiment session and the WebServer (WS) in the second. The MediaStore is a variant of the system used for Type I validations already introduced in section 5.1.2. The WebServer task deals with a model of a component-based web server.

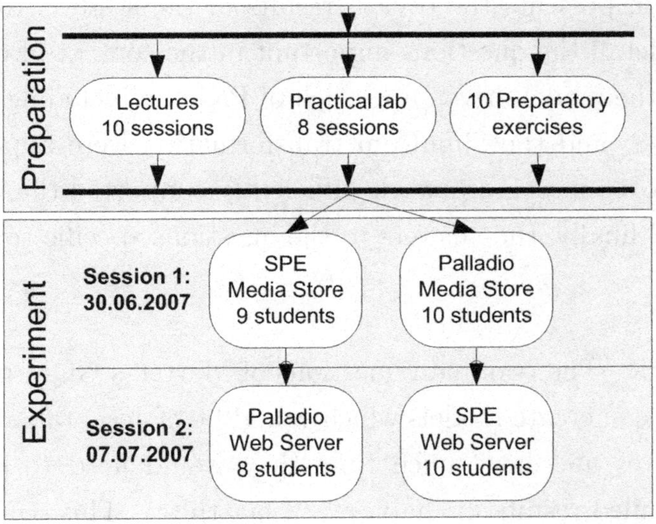

Figure 5.12: Experiment Design (Martens, 2007)

For each system, typical design alternatives exist. For the MediaStore, the design alternatives are adding a cache for frequently requested music files, the use of a database connection pool, allocating some components of the system on a second server, and re-encoding the uploaded files to reduce their size. The WebServer's design alternatives are adding a cache, introducing a thread pool, allocating some components on a second server, and executing the server's logging activities concurrently. Both systems also contain a fifth design alternative specifically designed to test the applicability of Coupled Transformations. This design alternative changes the realisation of looking up required components from dependency injection to broker lookup (cf. section 4.6.1). They question during the experiment was whether all participants would use the automatic model-transformation instead of explicitly modelling the broker interaction and how much time they would save in comparison with SPE which does not offer this automatism.

Additionally, for each system there are two different usage profiles specified. The first usage profile (UP1) is a closed workload with a single user entering the system repeatedly. The second usage profile (UP2) is an open workload with an arrival rate such that multiple users use the systems concurrently. Additionally, UP2 also had different input parameter characterisations than UP1.

5.2.4 Evaluation

First, this section presents the overall results of the study. Afterwards, it discusses in more detail the questions important in the context of this thesis. That is first whether the model-driven approach of Palladio including its meta-model, concrete syntaxes, and the SimuCom transformation were applicable. Second, whether Palladio's SensorFramework sufficiently supported the interpretation of the results. And finally, the answers to the questions specific to Coupled Transformations.

Overall Results The two main questions of Marten's GQM plan are whether the participants can create models which would be of acceptable quality to judge design alternatives and how much time they would need to do so. Martens (2007) gives detailed results in chapter 5 of her thesis. This section only gives a summary of the main results.

	Media Store		Web Server		Average
	$UP1$	$UP2$	$UP1$	$UP2$	
Palladio	4.69%	6.79%	5.47%	10.67%	6.9%
SPE	11.35%	10.21%	2.42%	9.21%	8.3%

Table 5.2: Deviation of the predicted response times (Martens, 2007, p.83 cont.)

Table 5.2 shows the average deviation of the response time as predicted by the models created by the participants and the reference model for both systems and both usage profiles averaged over all design alternatives. In average, prediction results of Palladio models deviated 6.9% and SPE predictions by 8.3%. However, for different design alternatives higher deviations could be found. The maximum deviation of the average of predicting a single design alternative was 20.35% for Palladio and 21.22% for SPE (cf. table A.1 and A.2). Nevertheless, (Martens, 2007, p.109) argues that the participants produced good results with both methods which is a resonable interpretation as most results deviated significantly less than the presented maximum values.

The box-and-whisker diagram in figure 5.13 depicts the duration for completing the experiment tasks, i.e., modelling the system and all design alternatives.

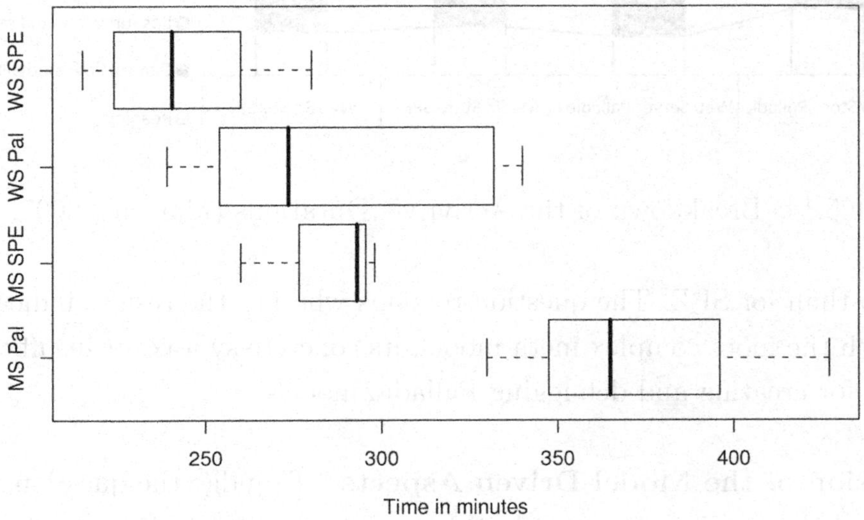

Figure 5.13: Durations for the Complete Task (Martens, 2007, p.102)

Each box in the diagram shows the minimum and maximum value as whiskers, the 25% and 75% quartile (borders of the boxes) and the median value (bold line in the box). Using Palladio it takes longer to complete the experiment tasks. This observation holds for both systems under study. Averaged over both tasks, Palladio took 1.25 times longer to complete than SPE.

Figure 5.14 gives a detailed break down of the durations for completing the modelling and prediction of the initial system model. Figure 5.14 contains at least two important results. First, the accumulated duration of the activities needed to create an initial model, i.e., from reading to UP2 modelling, is larger for Palladio than for SPE. This result is explainable as Palladio models component performance in a reuseable way, i.e., the component models can be used in different assembly, allocation, and usage contexts without the need for adjustment. Creating parameterised models required extra effort for the parameterisation which pays off when reusing the models which was not part of the initial system modelling. Second, the duration for correcting errors is also higher for

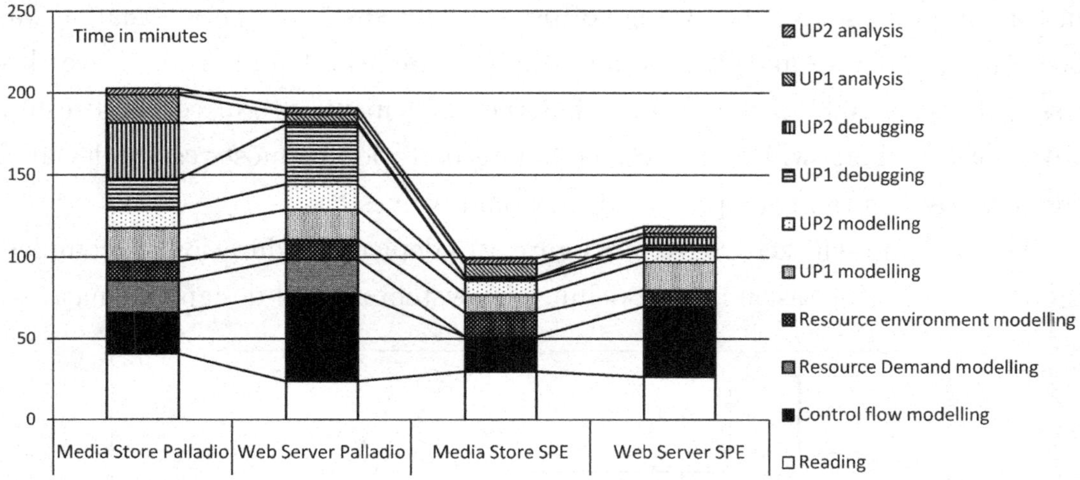

Figure 5.14: Breakdown of the Activity's Durations (Martens, 2007, p.107)

Palladio than for SPE. The question remains whether the results indicate problems with the more complex meta-model, its concrete syntax, or insufficient tool support for creating and debugging Palladio models.

Discussion of the Model-Driven Aspects To judge the question raised at the end of the previous paragraph, this paragraph uses a selection of additional metrics measured by Martens (Martens, 2007, p.89 cont.). These metrics also include the subjective evaluation of Palladio and SPE by the participants in the questionnaire filled out after the experiment.

To evaluate the source of problems, table A.4 gives the average number of problems detected during or after the experiment per participant classified into the most frequent problem classes. The table shows that in average most problems with Palladio had their cause either in a wrong usage of the PCM's tool, or due to bad error messages or bugs of the tool (in average 2.27 per participant). This indicates that for Palladio the tool even after its five month of development still was a major source of problems.

Looking at the detailed problem descriptions (Martens, 2007, p.CCLXII cont.) almost all of these problems relate to insufficient support for entering values on the GUI of the PCM's tool or its insufficient robustness against model instances containing errors. An analysis of the latter reveals a set of missing OCL constraints in the PCM meta-model's static semantics. Additionally, also the preconditions of the SimuCom transformation were incomplete causing additional problems. Therefore, it is expected that spending more time for making the meta-model, the transformation, and the tool more robust will significantly reduce the class of tool related problems.

Problems that occurred second most were related to parameterisations of the components. For method parameters, in average 1.1 problem per participant occurred and 0.69 for component parameters. From the collected metrics, it is hard to derive the cause for these problems. One aspect might be the concrete syntax of the stochastic expression language as it is mainly used to specify parametrisations. The hypothesis, that the concrete textual syntax of the stochastic expressions and its corresponding editing dialog, caused the problems, cannot be invalidated based on the experiment results. However, a lack of understanding and training in the use of parameters is also possible. As Koziolek (2008) introduced the parameterisation into the PCM, his PhD thesis discusses possible explanations and ideas for further studies to learn more about the parameter related problems.

As a comparison, SPE had a comparable amount of problems per participant like Palladio. However, the amount of problems directly related to SPE's methodology was significantly larger (in average 4.21) than the amount of tool related problems (in average 0.24) (Martens, 2007, p.93).

The subjective evaluation of the questionnaire further supports the impression that more problems related to the PCM's tool than to its meta-model. Note, that the following needs careful interpretation due to the subjectiveness of the results. 17 of 18 participants stated that Palladio's process- and meta-model was comprehensible. Only a single participant found it overly complex. Additionally, the grades the participants gave to single concepts of the meta-model show a good acceptance. The grades ranged from -2 to +2. Besides the parameterisation (also matching the previous discussion) all other PCM concepts got an average grade above 1.0 (see table A.3). Overall, taking the subjective evaluation of the PCM's concepts, there is no indication for the hypothesis that the PCM's meta-model is hard to comprehend. Also in the comparison to SPE, the evaluation of the PCM by the participants showed a significant trend towards the PCM as 12 participants claimed that Palladio was easier to understand and only 4 participants favoured SPE. The result of a comparison of the SPE and the PCM's tools yielded similar results. 10 participants favoured the PCM's tool and 4 favoured SPEED.

A final question focused on the appropriateness of the concrete graphical syntax of the PCM and whether using a textual syntax would be preferable for some parts of the model. Only 5 participants found a textual syntax more useful with no significant preference for a certain part of the meta-model. However, it may remain questionable whether all participants understood the meaning of the respective question in the questionnaire.

Prediction Results Interpretation For Palladio, the SensorFramework supported the interpretation of SimuCom's results as introduced in section 5.2.2. After the experiment, the participants were asked whether it was harder to interpret the distribution functions than using mean values as given by SPE. Only 4 participants ranked interpreting distribution functions harder than mean values, 15 participants denied this. 18 participants judged distribution functions to be a more reliable foundation for making a design decision.

Additionally, among the answers to the question what should be improved in the PCM's tool, only one participant named the SensorFramework and requested a specific presentation of the results to compare the results.

Despite the fact, that this amount of available data might not be sufficient to draw conclusions, at least it does not indicate that the SensorFramework causes problems in its application.

Coupled Transformations Part of the experiment was a design alternative (broker lookup) explicitly designed to learn about the applicability of Coupled Transformations. The first question was whether all participants would use the automatic transformation instead of explicitly modelling the broker lookup. The result was that all participants realised it and used the transformation. However, the Coupled Transformation in the experiment only supported this design alternative, so it might have been too easy for the participants to detect it (see section 6.3 for further experiment ideas).

The second question was about the time savable by the automatic transformation. The duration for analysing this alternative was approximately equal to the duration it took for SimuCom to simulate the model and produce the result which was approximately 5 minutes in the experiment. For SPE it took approximately the same time, however, in SPE the participants spent the 5 minutes to model the alternative. Overall, in the case studied in the experiment, the automatic transformation saved the modelling time which otherwise had to be spent by the participants. As the broker design option was quite simple compared to more complex cases presented in section 4.6.3 it is expected that even more time can be saved in these cases.

In the questionnaire filled out by the participants after the experiment, a question dealt with the subjective evaluation of the possibility to use Coupled Transformations to solve the broker design alternative using Palladio. Table 5.3 shows a summary of the answers given by the participants.

Advantages (No. of participants)	**Disadvantages (No.)**
Easy to model (5)	Not so precise (1)
Fast (5)	Loss of control (1)
Transparency during modelling (2)	Less flexible (3)
Elegant (1)	Not applicable for complex cases (1)
Not manually (1)	Unclear what happens (1)
	Less practical relevance (1)

Table 5.3: Subjective advantages and disadvantages of the automated transformation (Martens, 2007, p.108)

As expected, the named number of advantages was higher than the named number of disadvantages. The two main advantages named were the ease of modelling and the fast modelling. The answers for the advantages do not contain any unexpected results.

The most important named disadvantages are a reduction in flexibility and the loss of control on how the transformation changes the model. The latter was rather unexpected and thus more interesting. Not knowing what happens inside an automatic transformation seems to lower the trust the participants had in the final result. They wanted to know, how the transformation alters the model. The same was partially true for SimuCom's transformation for which several participants claimed in the questionnaire that their trust in the transformation was higher due to the fact that they were able to look inside the generated Java simulation code. A hypothesis is that access to a good documentation of transformations and the output of (immediate) transformations increases the trust in the transformation.

The second most named disadvantage was the reduced flexibility which was indeed an issue with the implementation of Coupled Transformations in the experiment tools where only the option was available to use the broker lookup or dependency injection for all connectors, i.e., the global setting. Adding the ability to adjust the feature settings on a more fine granular level as described in section 4.5.2 to the PCM tool's GUI might resolve this issue as it increases the flexibility by offering more options than the simple coupled transformation used in the experiment.

5.2.5 Validity

After presenting the experiment's results in the previous section, this section summarizes important threats to validity of the experiment's results and the interpretations based on it. The complete list is given by (Martens, 2007, p.117 cont.).

Internal Validity The internal validity is the degree to which changes in the dependent variables of an experiment are indeed results of changing the independent variables (Wohlin et al., 2000, p.68). The independent variable in the experiment described here was the method (Palladio or SPE) and the dependent variables the quality of the models and the duration for finishing the experiment's tasks.

- **Different Capabilities of the Students**: Martens controlled this influence factor by using the cross-over experiment design and by forming the two groups of participants based on their performance in the preparatory exercises.
- **Biased Opinion of the Participants**: The participants might have favoured the Palladio approach because of the influence of the experimenters which were the developers of the Palladio approach. Especially, for the subjective answers to the questions in the questionnaire, participants might have reproduced an opinion told them before during the theoretical lectures. However, (Martens, 2007, p.118) found no strong evidence for the assumption that the participants were biased.
- **Influence of the Experimenters Help**: As the experimenters helped the participants during the acceptance test and also when they had problems with the tools or the experiment task, they might have had an impact on the observed results. Martens used protocols for all activities of the experimenters to make this influence transparent as good as possible.

External validity The external validity is the degree to which the results of an experiment can be generalised to other, in particular practical, situations (Wohlin et al., 2000, p.72). Mainly the size and complexity of the experiment's systems is a thread to external validity as real industrial systems usually are larger. Whether the results are valid in such a setting is unknown.

However, both systems are representatives of typical industrial applications as targeted by the Palladio approach. Looking at such systems on an architectural level might also lead to a rather low number of components. The architecture of business information systems often consists of components for database interaction and components containing the business logic. Both types of components were also present in the systems under study.

5.2.6 Summary

The experiment results showed no major problems threatening the applicability of Palladio. Conceptionally, only the parametric component specifications introduced by Koziolek (2008) caused some problems. The contributions of this thesis, e.g., the model-driven approach followed by Palladio, the concrete syntaxes as implemented in the PCM's tool, and the application of Coupled Transformations revealed only minor problems. Here, the robustness of the PCM's tool and the transformations caused the most problems. However, this is acceptable given the fact that the tool is a scientific prototype and not industrially developed and tested.

Chapter 6

Conclusions

This section first gives a summary of the contributions presented in this thesis. Afterwards, it discusses open questions in section 6.3 and points to application scenarios of the PCM and Coupled Transformations in areas different to performance prediction of component-based systems (Section 6.4) like additional quality attributes or other options to couple transformations.

6.1 Summary

In this thesis, I present two contributions to model-driven component-based software engineering. First, the PCM, which is a meta-model specifically designed to support model-driven component-based software development including early design-time performance prediction. Second, I introduce Coupled Transformation in this thesis, which allows using knowledge on a parametrisable transformation A in another transformation B that depends on the output of A. In this thesis, I apply Coupled Transformations in transformations based on the PCM to increase performance prediction accuracy.

The Palladio Component Model The PCM is a meta-model for component-based software development. It respects the developer roles taking part in a component-based software development process. It especially supports a strict separation between component developers and software architects, deployers, and domain experts. To enable this separation, the PCM clearly separates components on the type level, i.e., component implementations, and component usages. To enable this separation it uses its context concept where the context stores all usage dependent information while the type stores all implementation dependent information. This explicitly introduced component context allows to derive context dependent component properties like performance. The contexts available in the PCM are *AssemblyContext* to characterise component bindings via connectors, *AllocationContext* to characterise component allocation on different soft- and hardware execution environments, and the *UsageContext* to characterise the influence of different call frequencies or service parameters on component properties. To describe the behaviour parameterised by these contexts, the PCM uses the *ResourceDemandingSEFF*s. RD-SEFFs allow the specification of context dependent resource demands, loop iteration counts, branch conditions, etc. The usage parameterisation is part of an extension of the PCM's meta-model in collaboration with Koziolek (2008).

The PCM's meta-model explicitly supports model-driven transformations. The avoidance of ambiguities in the control flow of its RD-SEFF is an example for this. This makes it easier to query and transform PCM instances than for example instances of UML2 activities. Another example is the availability of the stochastic expressions language as EMOF model which allows easier access to performance annotations compared to string-based tagged values as used in UML2 profiles.

The PCM supports general distributed random variables for its performance and data flow annotations. While restricting analytical solutions of PCM instances, this avoids making assumptions on components and their composition. Such assumptions like exponential distributed resource demands can not be checked or guaranteed by any of the roles participating in the CBSE development process. Component developers can not check them as they do not know how their components will behave in different contexts, e.g., if a branch condition depends on the result of an external call, and software architects do also not know how the system behaves in detail as they should not need to know internal details of components due to their black-box nature. Despite the former issues, even if software architects could detect violations of assumptions, they could not correct such problems, as they can not change components or their specifications. Only component developers can do this.

The PCM helps component developers and software architects.

- **Component developers**: Component developers can specify their components parameterised by the context of the components allowing the specifications to be used in different contexts and thus, making them more reusable. Additionally, they can use the PCM's component type hierarchy to derive their components by refining them from *ProvidesComponentTypes* to *ImplementationComponentTypes*.

- **Software architects**: Software architects can assemble components into systems and evaluate the performance of the composition. They can systematically experiment with different design alternatives each having different components or connectors. The results of these experiments can be used for checking whether the system's performance requirements are fulfilled. For design alternatives not violating these requirements the predicted performance differences help in making cost-benefit analyses.

Coupled Transformations The second major contribution of this thesis is a method that allows to exploit situations where model transformations map an abstract model to an implementation and where analyses should be performed on the abstract model to predict properties of the *resulting* system. An important application scenario for this situation is model-driven prediction of Quality of Service properties such as performance or reliability at system design time. In this case, a transformation can generate code skeletons from architectural models while another generates prediction models for the aforementioned extra-functional properties.

The method I developed exploits the strong relationship between the model and the generated implementation, which is defined by the transformations that map the model to an implementation. In contrast to a manual translation of the abstract model into an implementation, for automated transformations the result is deterministic and hence, can be foreseen. Knowing the result of the implementation transformation allows the creation of a second transformation which alters the prediction model such that it reflects the generated implementation more accurately. As this second transformation is coupled to the implementation transformation it is called a coupled transformation.

I included an abstract, formal description of coupled transformations to capture the central idea of Coupled Transformation independent of the application scenario. Coupled Transformations also deal with *parameterisable* transformations using mark models as parameters as envisioned in the OMG's MDA guide (Object Management Group (OMG), 2006c). Coupled Transformations use the same mark models as the transformations they are coupled to, i.e., they are parameterised with the same set of parameters. This allows using the selected parameters also in the coupled transformation.

In this thesis, I apply the method to component-based software development where the PCM serves as abstract software and performance prediction model. To predict the performance of instances of the PCM, I developed a transformation, which maps PCM instances to an event-driven Java simulation code based on Desmo-J. The transformation and its accompanying PCM simulation framework are called SimuCom. Because SimuCom is a simulation, it is able to deal with the full complexity of PCM instances, i.e., general distributed random variables, stochastic dependent variables as needed for *CollectionIteratorActions*, or arbitrary stochastic expressions. As such, it is currently the only solver for PCM instances which deals with all concepts of the PCM's meta-model. However, this flexibility comes at the price of longer execution times and huge amounts of measured data during simulation runs.

Furthermore, I developed a mapping of PCM instances to Java EE/EJBs or optionally plain old Java objects (POJOs). This mapping preserves the semantics of the respective PCM entities by applying patterns like the component context pattern. The transformation accepts parameters via a mark model based on feature diagrams. The mark model allows fine grained control of the available mapping options. For each option, I discuss the performance impact and define the necessary coupled transformation which changes the prediction model to reflect the selected options. The main issues bridged by the mapping is the realisation of required roles and assembly connectors.

To reflect the impact of different connector mapping options, I adapted the completion concept presented by Woodside et al. (2002) and by Wu and Woodside (2004) to component-based performance prediction in the PCM by introducing *completion components*. Completion components are special components in the PCM which reflect the performance of the application's interaction with lower application layers like the middleware. I present a transformation that replaces assembly connectors in PCM instances by these completion components which then add the impact of using the middleware for call processing. The inner structure of the generated completions depends on the features selected in the mark model instance of the implementation transformation.

As an additional transformation, I developed ProtoCom as a combination of SimuCom and PCM2EJB. It generates prototypes from PCM instances which generate performance equivalent resource demands. These prototypes can serve as a further validation for the predictions made under more realistic conditions as they are not restricted by assumptions on the execution environment, e.g., the scheduling discipline of the CPU, the behaviour of hard-disks, or network links. The prototype transformation is also coupled to the implementation transformation as it uses the same target environment (EJBs) and the same mark model.

In this specific application of Coupled Transformations they help the software architect to include his implementation mapping into the prediction model. Thus, the prediction model becomes more accurate allowing better estimates of design decisions.

Validation I validated the contributions on two levels. A Type I validation shows that using Coupled Transformations increased prediction accuracy by comparing measurements made on a generated implementation with the corresponding predictions. The results show that in the investigated cases a significant increase in prediction accuracy is reached. A Type II validation shows that the model-driven approach of the PCM is applicable by third parties. In this thesis the main focus of the Type II validation lied on the evaluation of the PCM's concrete syntaxes, their realisation in tools, and the applicability of Coupled Transformations when they are embedded in the prediction process.

6.2 Limitations

Limitations have been discussed already in sections at the end of each contribution of this thesis. Hence, this section only gives references to the respective sections. Section 3.10 discusses various PCM limitations and assumptions. Besides the overall PCM limitations, each of the presented transformations has its own assumptions and limitations. Section 4.4.10 presents the limitations of SimuCom, section 4.6.5 discusses limitations of the mapping of PCM instances to an implementation, and section 4.7.3 presents ProtoCom's assumptions and limitations.

6.3 Open Questions and Future Work

The following gives an overview on open questions and opportunities for future work.

Extending the PCM Section 3.10 lists the assumptions and limitations of the version of the PCM as introduced in this thesis. The list contains two main classes of limitations. First, limitations with close relationship to CBSE, like the missing support for dynamic architecture, i.e., architectures in which connectors change at run-time, or the missing support for stateful components. The other class of limitations are general issues for performance prediction approaches, i.e., they also apply to performance predictions of other types of systems, e.g., monolithic systems. This class contains issues like dealing with missing support for predicting the performance impact of memory consumption, more accurate models for the execution environment, or limited support for exception handling.

For both classes there is always the trade-off between model accuracy and model analysability. The more accurate a model reflects reality the larger becomes the analysis model's state space. For such models, analytical as well as simulation solvers might fail. The former fail due to extremely large state-spaces the latter fail or become impractical because of their time and memory consumption.

Despite the complexity issue, the class of issues related to CBSE may be supportable by extending the PCM's context concept to run-time contexts. A run-time context then stores the state of the component, including the bindings of the required roles. A specification based on state-machines attached to the run-time context defines how the component changes it state. These state changes may be based on random variables or on events occurring at the component like calling component services. However, for stateful components it is also important to specify the visibility of the state, i.e., whether all clients of the component modify a single state (singleton semantics) or whether each client has its own state associated to its communication with a server component (session based state).

The second class of limitations requires additional research in performance prediction methods on how to specify and analyse these factors in a way which keeps the analysis models both accurate and solvable. The completion components introduced in this thesis can help in modelling lower layers of software systems more accurately, thus, improving the software execution environment model. They are especially useful when transformations add them to the analysis model automatically. Model libraries of completion components can help to reflect different implementations of the same functionality, e.g., different middleware completions based on different implementation of an application server by different vendors. The parameterised specification of components in the PCM is extremely useful for completion components in model libraries as they are reused in a broad range of different contexts.

Extending the PCM's Tools The controlled experiment revealed several issues with the robustness of the PCM's tool and parts of the used concrete syntax. However, as these factors do not influence the Type I validity of the Palladio method, they are usually ignored when creating new prediction approaches. But, as the controlled experiment showed, these factors are important for the applicability and acceptance of a method by third parties. For future experiments with the PCM tools it is advisable to deal with these factors early during experiment design. An interesting question is whether making the tool more robust and changing the concrete syntax will lead to a different outcome of the experiment.

In analogy, a remaining question is whether a more comprehensive support for Coupled Transformations in the PCM tool will lead to different results of the questions dealing with Coupled Transformations in the experiment. A hypothesis is that having more Coupled Transformations available makes them harder to identify in the experiment task. Additionally, choosing the right transformation among a larger set of choices might also be more difficult. However, for more complex Coupled Transformations the difference in modelling speed with and without them is also expected to increase in favour of using Coupled Transformations.

Systematic Discovery of the Simulation's Limits All case studies which used SimuCom had no problems with long simulation runs. However, some had problems with memory consumption for collecting data. The memory consumption issue is primarily a technical issue because using the hard-drive as background storage device allows to store much more data than using memory. Additionally, adding the ability to aggregate data already during simulation runs will also help resolving these issues.

After sorting them out, the question remains, how large a PCM instance can get for SimuCom to produce useful results in acceptable time spans. To systematically investigate this, a generator should create random PCM instances with a configurable amount of components, RD-SEFFs, or stochastic expressions. Additionally, the envisioned investigation should deal with different types of stop conditions for the simulation, containing confidence intervals of point estimators like the mean value, or on characteristics of the distribution like the KS-statistic. The latter needs adoption, as its corresponding test (the KS-test (Sachs, 1997)) is sensitive to the number of observations. The higher the number of observations, the more likely it is, that the test rejects the hypothesis. This is a bad property, as the simulation produces a high number of observations. If the simulation would use a stop condition based on an unmodified KS-test, it is likely that it never ends.

Heuristically Determine the Necessary Completions Adding completions or using coupled transformations to enrich the prediction model with additional model elements, increases on the one hand the accuracy of predictions but on the other hand it comes at the cost of longer simulation runs. However, an observation is that the increase in accuracy highly depends on the context of the additional model elements.

Consider for example the additional *InternalAction* added to the model to reflect querying a broker to look up a component's required role (cf. section 4.6.1). Let the time needed for this lookup be around 20 microsecond which is a realistic value for a LAN if there is no contention on the network. Assume that the called service computes a complex mathematical operation which takes several minutes. In this setting the increase in accuracy gained is marginal and can be neglected. But when assuming that the called service only performs a quick memory lookup which takes less than a microsecond then the increase in accuracy gained by adding the broker lookup is significant. The issue is that with arbitrary composed black-box components you do not know in advance which parts of the system have a significant impact on the performance.

An idea to deal with this issue is to apply a heuristic which tries to estimate at simulation run time which completions increase the accuracy significantly. For example, one approach might be to simulate for a short time without using any completions or coupled transformations. Based on this simulation run, a heuristic determines the bottlenecks of the system and decides based on rules which completions to add or which coupled transformations to execute.

Taking the idea a step further, it could also help reducing the specification needs for the software architect. Imagine that it is not a binary decision of adding a completion or a coupled transformation, but that they exist in different variants with different accuracies and specification needs. For example, instead of deciding whether to use an accurate completion for the middleware, there is a set of middleware completions requiring different amounts of specifications. One completion might not be able to distinguish between different marshalling protocols and only take a single scale factor to do a rough estimate of the transmitted bytes while another completion is able to model the difference between protocol like SOAP or RMI more accurately (like to one presented in section 4.6.3). In this case the simulation can start with the simple model and ask the software architect for a more accurate completion only if the utilisation on the network indicates a possible performance bottleneck. In case of coupled transformations, the simulation starts by not using all information available in a mark model and successively adds more information if the heuristic indicates problems with elements added by the respective coupled transformation.

Experiment with a Component Scenario The PCM explicitly supports different CBSE developer roles including the fact that they might be physically distributed. The experimental setting in section 5.2.3 had to assign all developer roles to a single student in order to fulfil SPE's preconditions. However, having distributed roles, the workload which needs to be handled by a single role is significantly smaller. Hence, the interesting question here is to empirically evaluate how much time each developer role spends for creating its part of a PCM instance. This distribution of workload makes it more realistic that the extra time needed for creating PCM models is feasible.

An additional question in the distributed setting is also to learn whether software architects can compose the component models produced by different people and still analyse the performance. A situation which might cause a mismatch arises if the different roles do not agree on common *ResourceTypes* or parametric usage annotations, i.e., a component requires a characterisation of a variable not being provided by the component connected to it.

Broad Scale Industrial Applicability The performed validations only demonstrate that the PCM makes correct predictions in cases where its assumptions fit the regarded case. Additionally, they show that third parties are able to apply the PCM. However, this does not validate whether the PCM will prevail in a large scale industrial context. In such contexts, a larger group of developers works on a large system. In order to investigate the industrial applicability, different companies in Karlsruhe apply the PCM in case studies in their projects. The results gained will improve the PCM and direct it to additional issues.

Type III Validation Besides the validations done in this thesis and the ones missing as described in the previous paragraphs, the Type III validity (Freiling et al., 2008) remains an open question. Type III validity investigates whether a newly introduced method improves the whole software development process. A way to show this would be to execute a single software development project in an industrial setting twice - one time with applying the method, the other time without applying the method. In the end, the durations and costs occurred show whether the method helped. However, this kind of validation is expensive and hard to perform in practice.

Instead of showing the Type III validity in a controlled experiment, Williams and Smith (2003) simply *argued* on the benefit of using SPE based on their project experiences. While this approach is questionable because of the missing controlled conditions and the hypothesis that their experiences might be biased towards SPE, the study at least gives an estimation of the advantage of using the SPE method. A same approach would be feasible for the PCM. Based on the experiences gained in industrial case studies, evidences can be collected for the hypothesis that applying the PCM during software design lowers development costs caused by performance issues in the developed system.

(Semi-)Automatic Recovery of Coupled Transformations In the current state of the Coupled Transformations method, an expert has to create a coupled transformation based on a thorough analysis of the code transformation. If the transformation is executed frequently, the extra effort pays off. However, the manual creation of the coupled transformation limits the applicability of Coupled Transformations. An idea to improve the situation is to automatically analyse the rules encoded in the code transformation. Based on such an analysis it might be possible to create parts of a coupled transformation automatically.

In this context, there is also a close relation to transformation traceability. Traces store the information which parts of a source model generated which parts of a target model (Object Management Group (OMG), 2007a, p.5). As modern model transformation languages and their engines, e.g., QVT, generate such traces automatically, they are available at no additional cost. Combining the information on the rules of a transformation and a set of example traces might result in enough information to derive a coupled transformation for a specific QoS attribute at least semi-automaticly.

6.4 Visions

The following lists further application areas for both, the PCM and Coupled Transformations.

Applying the PCM to other QoS Attributes The PCM with its current state of the RD-SEFF focuses on performance prediction and code generation. However, the PCM's core concepts like interfaces, protocols, component types, composite structures, different types of component contexts, or the stochastic expressions package are independent of performance prediction. Thus, applying them to other application areas is possible.

Reussner's parameterised contracts for protocol adaptation can serve as an example for a functional component property. Hence, including them into the PCM and storing the adapted protocols in a derived assembly context should be not difficult. The PCM could support interoperability checking for *Assembly-Connectors*. Additionally, if these checks detect mismatches in component interactions, component adapter generators with predictable QoS impact (Becker et al., 2006a) can also be included in the PCM.

For extra-functional properties PCM extensions for reliability and maintainability are planned. For reliability, the aim is to reuse many concepts also used for performance like the RD-SEFF and its annotations. However, reliability might involve the development of a new set of analysis methods. This is due to the fact that reliability is difficult to evaluate with simulation-based approaches as the rate of failure occurrences is usually very low, i.e., the desired events happen seldomly causing long simulation runs to observe a significant amount of them. The latter might be especially true, if Performability (Haverkort et al., 2001), i.e., a combination of performance and reliability models, is of interest. In this case, the simulation has to simulate the performance for a long time until a failure occurs. As a consequence, abstractions of such detailed analysis methods are needed for the analysis to remain feasible.

Maintainability is an extra-functional property which is not a QoS attribute. As such, it might indeed need different concepts like those already present in the PCM's core concepts. For example, it is questionable whether the concept of component contexts helps in evaluating the maintainability of component assemblies.

Using Coupled Transformations in other Application Scenarios The central idea of Coupled Transformations is independent of the prediction of performance properties. It may be applied to any situation where additional coupled transformations may benefit from information on the generated realisation.

As for the PCM, applying Coupled Transformation to other QoS attributes like reliability is a reasonable extension. For example, as discussed in section 4.6.1 mapping component required roles using the Broker pattern also has an impact on the reliability of the system. While the Broker allows switching to a different component if a component fails thus increasing reliability, it is also a single point of failure, i.e., if it fails the whole system is unable to provide its services any longer.

Besides extra-functional properties Coupled Transformations can also help in other areas. Recent ideas include but are not limited to run-time performance monitoring, documentation generation, or generated test cases. For model-driven run-time performance monitoring, a transformation adds probes into the generated code which monitors the behaviour of the system at run-time (Duzbayev and Poernomo, 2006). Based on this information a prediction is made on the performance behaviour in the near future. Currently, the probes are defined on the model level, however, the transformation into code might violate assumptions made on the model level. In this situation, a coupled transformation can adjust values measured by the generated probe based on the architectural model *and* the generated code.

For documentation generation, Coupled Transformations can include specific details of a particular implementation in a documentation which is otherwise generated from the architectural model. For example, it can include the implementation detail that a specific connector uses RMI in a concrete realisation. The generated documentation would contain the architectural information and implementation details in contrast to the usual way of extracting Javadoc from the generated code which usually lacks the abstract structure available at the architectural level.

A last example is model-based generation of test drivers. As coupled transformations can include details on the realisation, using them for test case generation might help to generate test drivers which explicitly test details of particular realisation. For example, such a transformation can generate a test driver to test a Broker interaction only if the Broker interaction has been selected as realisation.

Domain Specific Languages As already mentioned, the more abstract the initial source model is, the more information is encoded into the transformation. Domain specific languages commonly fulfil this criteria as they aim at abstracting from realisation details by specifying software systems on abstract, conceptual levels.

When MDSD matures in the near future, the use of DSLs will increase. With an increasing use of DSLs the relationship between the requirements (expressed in a DSL instance) and the code resulting from this instance becomes more and more explicit (by the transformation rules) increasing the predictability of the resulting system. Coupled Transformations can help to exploit the increased determinism in the created software artefacts for prediction methods.

Appendix A

A.1 Contributions and Imported Concepts

Figure A.1 shows the PCM's package structure and denotes for each package, who mainly created the package and its contents. Becker refers to this thesis, Koziolek to Koziolek's PhD thesis (Koziolek, 2008) and Krogmann to Krogmann's master thesis (Krogmann, 2006).

Figure A.2 shows the transformations available in the context of the PCM. Stereotypes indicate which elements represent meta-models, transformations, or conceptual ideas. Additionally, the indicate which parts are results of master theses. Additionally, they indicate the input and output meta-model of each transformation. The larger boxes give the borderline of the PhD thesis of Krogmann, Koziolek, and myself.

Figure A.3 gives an overview on the PCM's editor support. Stereotypes indicate whether the editor uses a graphical or a textual concrete syntax. Additionally, they show whether the editors have been generated by a MDSD framework like GMF or whether they have been created manually.

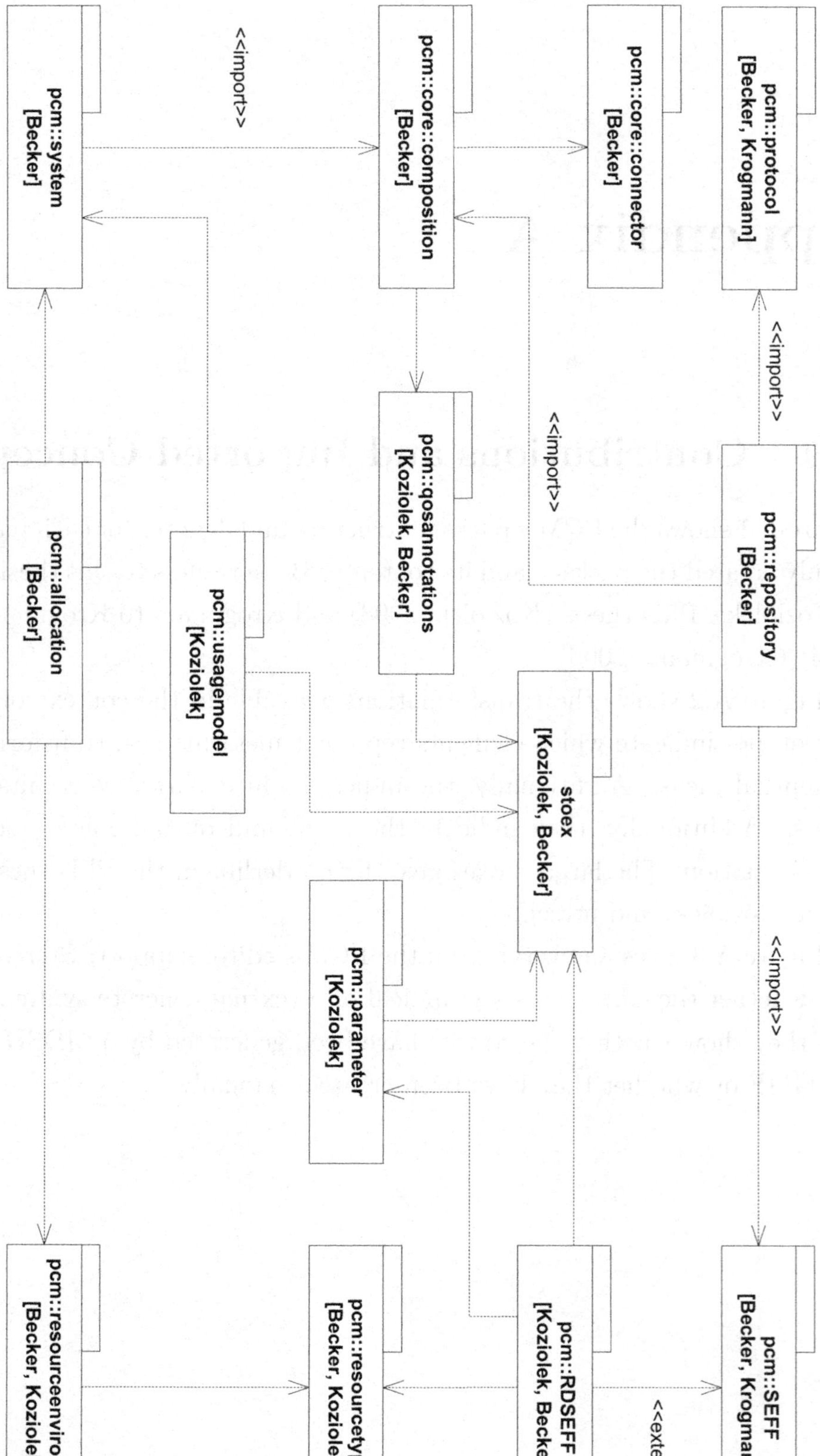

Figure A.1: PCM Packages and their Creators

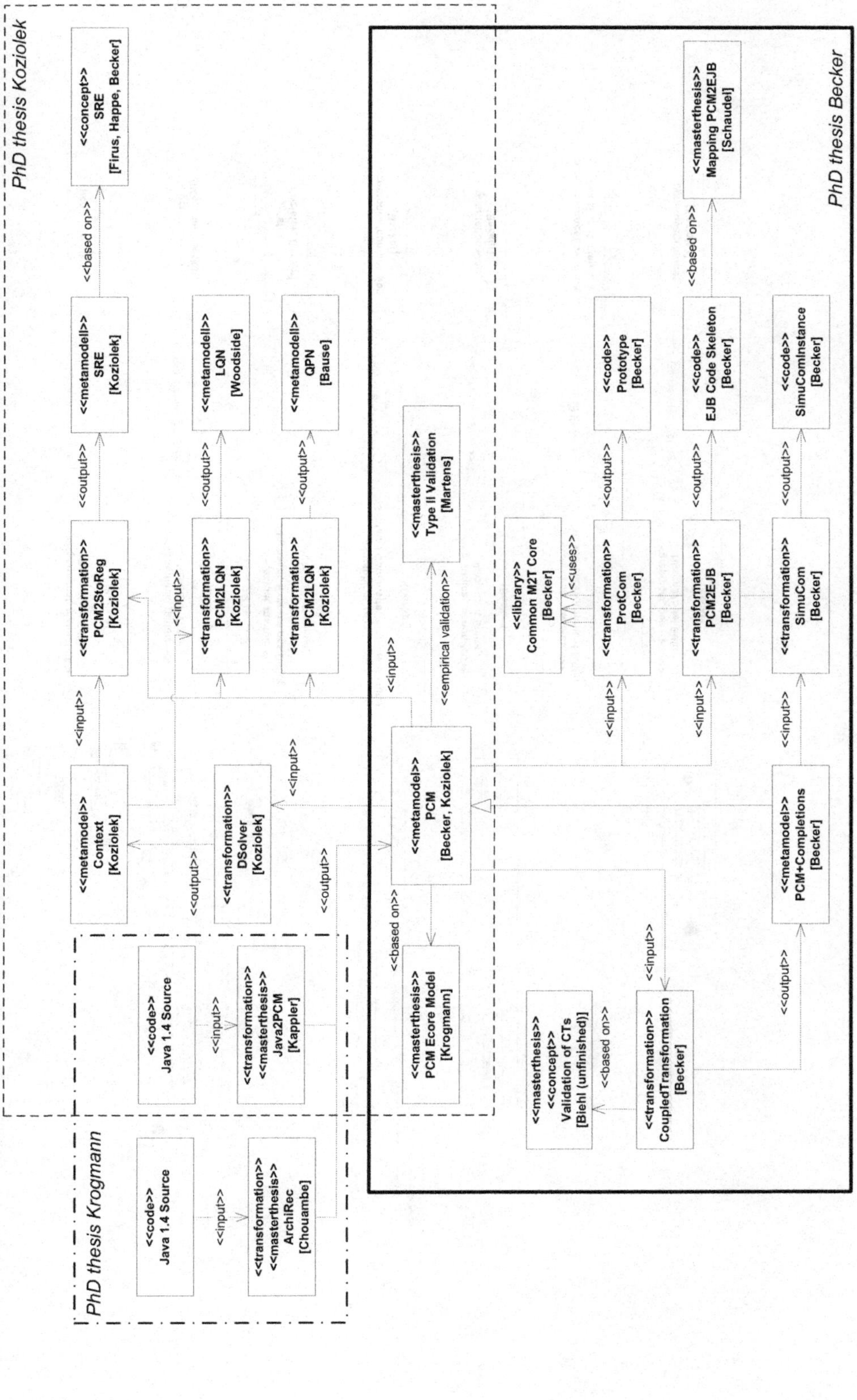

Figure A.2: PCM Transformations and their Creators

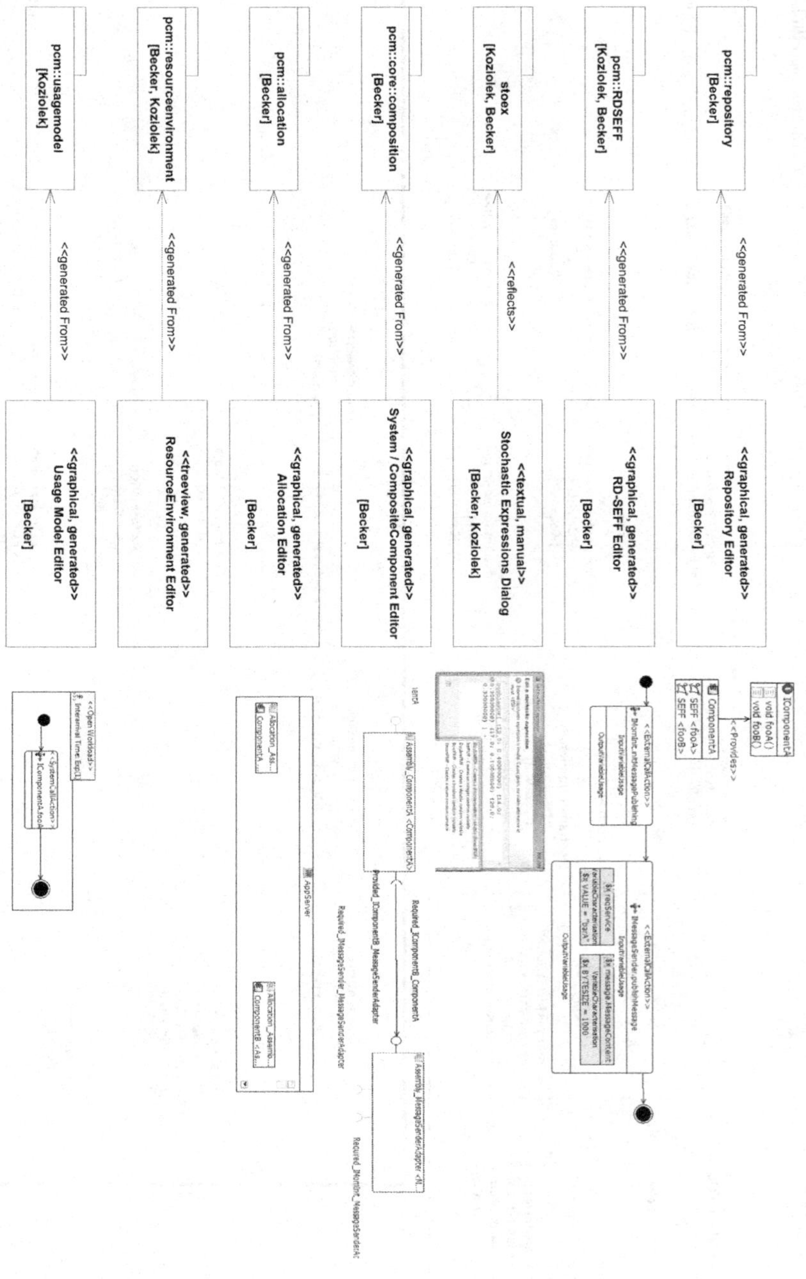

Figure A.3: PCM Editor Support and their Creators

A.2 Generated RD-SEFFs for Connector Completions

Figure A.4: Generated RD-SEFFs in Connector Completions

A.3 Detailed QVT Transformations

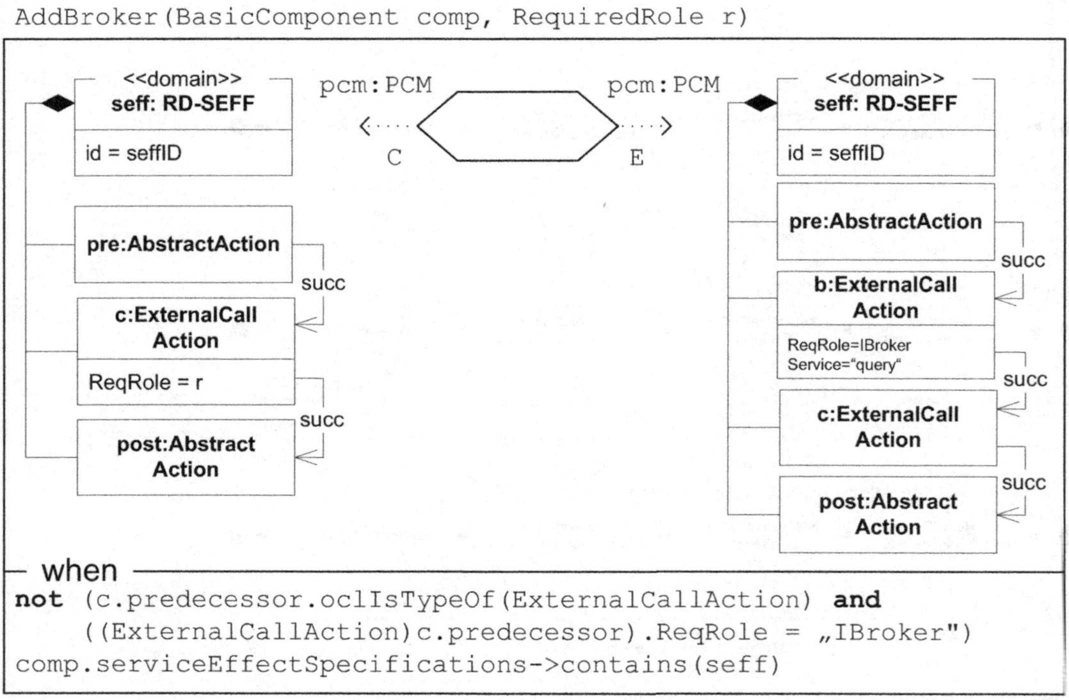

Figure A.5: Adding Broker Calls

A.4 Detailed Experiment Results

All tables presented in the following are taken from the master thesis by Martens (2007). Therefore, the tables captions give the page number of the originating page in Marten's thesis instead of repeating the full reference each time.

		v_0^s	v_1^s	v_2^s	v_3^s	v_4^s	v_5^s	Avg
Media Store	$UP1$	1.93%	0.90%	0.49%	20.08%	3.02%	1.69%	4.69%
	$UP2$	13.21%	2.20%	4.15%	13.23%	4.42%	3.51%	6.79%
Web Server	$UP1$	1.00%	11.07%	1.94%	4.23%	4.55%	9.40%	5.47%
	$UP2$	15.92%	20.35%	10.87%	10.67%	2.57%	3.64%	10.67%
Overall $propDevMeanResp_{Pal}$								6.90%

Table A.1: Relative deviation of the predicted response times for Palladio (p.83)

		v_0^s	v_1^s	v_2^s	v_3^s	v_4^s	v_5^s	Avg
Media Store	$UP1$	8.31%	9.58%	13.18%	11.59%	15.49%	9.95%	11.35%
	$UP2$	4.10%	9.49%	5.74%	21.22%	12.54%	8.17%	10.21%
Web Server	$UP1$	0.34%	1.28%	2.83%	2.15%	6.33%	1.56%	2.42%
	$UP2$	1.01%	1.22%	8.29%	4.47%	37.92%	2.33%	9.21%
Overall $propDevMeanResp_{SPE}$								8.3%

Table A.2: Relative deviation of the predicted response times for SPE (p.84)

Concept	**Average grade**	**Standard deviation**
Repository model	1.84	0.37
SEFF specification	1.74	0.45
System	1.61	0.50
Allocation	1.53	0.61
Resource environment	1.21	1.13
Usage Model	1.58	0.51
Parametrisation	0.58	1.02
Visualisation of the results	1.32	0.58
Distributions	1.32	0.48

Table A.3: Subjective evaluation of the comprehensibility of the Palladio concepts (p.96)

	Tool				Methodology						
	Usage	Error	Bug	Sum	Parameters	Component parameters	Types and units	Assembly	Usage model	Sum	Sum
Media Store											
minor	0.00	0.00	0.00	0.00	0.00	0.43	0.14	0.00	0.00	0.57	0.57
intermediate	0.43	0.43	0.14	1.00	1.00	0.29	0.57	0.00	0.00	1.86	2.86
major	0.14	0.00	0.14	0.29	0.57	0.29	0.00	0.00	0.00	0.86	1.14
Sum	0.57	0.43	0.29	1.29	1.57	1.00	0.71	0.00	0.00	3.29	4.57
Web Server											
minor	0.25	0.00	0.25	0.50	0.00	0.25	0.00	0.00	0.00	0.25	0.75
intermediate	0.88	0.38	0.13	1.38	0.63	0.13	0.38	0.00	0.00	1.13	2.50
major	1.13	0.00	0.25	1.38	0.00	0.00	0.25	0.13	0.13	0.50	1.88
Sum	2.25	0.38	0.63	3.25	0.63	0.38	0.63	0.13	0.13	1.88	5.13
Both systems											
minor	0.13	0.00	0.13	0.25	0.00	0.34	0.07	0.00	0.00	0.41	0.66
intermediate	0.65	0.40	0.13	1.19	0.81	0.21	0.47	0.00	0.00	1.49	2.68
major	0.63	0.00	0.20	0.83	0.29	0.14	0.13	0.06	0.06	0.68	1.51
Sum	1.41	0.40	0.46	2.27	1.10	0.69	0.67	0.06	0.06	2.58	4.85

Table A.4: Relative number of Palladio related problems (p.92)

Bibliography

A. V. Aho, R. Sethi, and J. D. Ullman. *Compilers & Principles, Techniques, and Tools.* Addison-Wesley, Reading, MA (1986).

M. Ajmone Marsan, G. Balbo, A. Bobbio, G. Chiola, G. Conte, and A. Cumani. *The Effect of Execution Policies on the Semantics and Analysis of Stochastic Petri Nets.* IEEE Transactions on Software Engineering, 15(7):832–846 (1989).

R. Andrej. *Entwurf und Implementierung eines GUI-Simulationsframeworks für das Palladio Komponentenmodell auf Basis der Eclipse Rich Client Platform.* Study thesis, University of Karlsruhe (2007).

AndroMDA.org. *AndroMDA Homepage* (2007). Last retrieved 2008-01-06.
URL `http://galaxy.andromda.org`

Apache Software Foundation. *Apache Axis 2* (2008). Last retrieved 2008-01-06.
URL `http://ws.apache.org/axis2/`

L. B. Arief and N. A. Speirs. *A UML Tool for an Automatic Generation of Simulation Programs.* In *Proceedings of the Second International Workshop on Software and Performance*, pages 71–76. ACM Press (2000).

ATLAS Group. *Atlas Transformation Language (ATL) Homepage* (2007). Last retrieved 2008-01-06.
URL `http://www.eclipse.org/m2m/atl/`

S. Balsamo, A. Di Marco, P. Inverardi, and M. Simeoni. *Model-Based Performance Prediction in Software Development: A Survey.* IEEE Transactions on Software Engineering, 30(5):295–310 (2004a).

S. Balsamo and M. Marzolla. *A Simulation-Based Approach to Software Performance Modeling.* In *Proceedings of the 9th European Software Engineering*

Conference held jointly with 11th ACM SIGSOFT international symposium on Foundations of Software Engineering, pages 363–366. ACM Press (2003).

S. Balsamo, M. Marzolla, A. Di Marco, and P. Inverardi. *Experimenting different software architectures performance techniques: a case study.* In *Proceedings of the fourth international workshop on Software and performance*, pages 115–119. ACM Press (2004b).

J. E. Bardram, H. B. Christensen, A. V. Corry, K. M. Hansen, and M. Ingstrup. *Exploring Quality Attributes Using Architectural Prototyping.* In R. Reussner, J. Mayer, J. A. Stafford, S. Overhage, S. Becker, and P. J. Schroeder, editors, *Quality of Software Architectures and Software Quality, First International Conference on the Quality of Software Architectures, QoSA 2005 and Second International Workshop on Software Quality, SOQUA 2005, Erfurt, Germany, September 20-22, 2005, Proceedings*, volume 3712 of *Lecture Notes in Computer Science*, pages 155–170. Springer-Verlag, Berlin, Germany (2005).

V. R. Basili. *Viewing Maintenance as Reuse-Oriented Software Development.* IEEE Software, 7:19–25 (1990).

L. Bass, P. Clements, and R. Kazman. *Software Architecture in Practice, Second Edition.* Addison-Wesley, Reading, MA, USA (2003).

F. Bause and P. S. Kritzinger. *Stochastic Petri Nets: An Introduction to the Theory.* Vieweg-Verlag (1996).

F. Bause and P. S. Kritzinger. *Stochastic Petri Nets.* Vieweg, 2nd edition (2002).

S. Becker. *Coupled Model Transformations.* In *Proceedings of the 7th International Workshop on Software and Performance (WOSP2008).* ACM Sigsoft (2008). To Appear.

S. Becker, A. Brogi, I. Gorton, S. Overhage, A. Romanovsky, and M. Tivoli. *Towards an Engineering Approach to Component Adaptation.* In *Architecting Systems with Trustworthy Components*, volume 3938 of *Lecture Notes in Computer Science*, pages 193–215. Springer (2006a).

S. Becker, T. Dencker, and J. Happe. *Model-Driven Generation of Performance Prototypes.* In *Proceedings of the SPEC International Performance Evaluation Workshop 2008* (2008a). To Appear.

S. Becker, L. Grunske, R. Mirandola, and S. Overhage. *Performance Prediction of Component-Based Systems: A Survey from an Engineering Perspective.* In R. Reussner, J. Stafford, and C. Szyperski, editors, *Architecting Systems with Trustworthy Components*, volume 3938 of *LNCS*, pages 169–192. Springer (2006b).

S. Becker, J. Happe, and H. Koziolek. *Putting Components into Context - Supporting QoS-Predictions with an explicit Context Model.* In R. Reussner, C. Szyperski, and W. Weck, editors, *Proceedings of the Eleventh International Workshop on Component-Oriented Programming (WCOP'06)* (2006c).

S. Becker, H. Koziolek, and R. Reussner. *Model-based Performance Prediction with the Palladio Component Model.* In *Proceedings of the 6th International Workshop on Software and Performance (WOSP2007).* ACM Sigsoft (2007).

S. Becker, H. Koziolek, and R. Reussner. *The Palladio Component Model for Model-Driven Performance Prediction.* Journal of Systems and Software (2008b). In Press, Accepted Manuscript.

S. Becker, S. Overhage, and R. Reussner. *Classifying Software Component Interoperability Errors to Support Component Adaption.* In I. Crnkovic, J. A. Stafford, H. W. Schmidt, and K. C. Wallnau, editors, *Component-Based Software Engineering, 7th International Symposium, CBSE 2004, Edinburgh, UK, May 24-25, 2004, Proceedings*, volume 3054 of *Lecture Notes in Computer Science*, pages 68–83. Springer, Berlin, Heidelberg (2004).

S. Becker, R. H. Reussner, and V. Firus. *Specifying Contractual Use, Protocols and Quality Attributes for Software Components.* In K. Turowski and S. Overhage, editors, *Proceedings of the First International Workshop on Component Engineering Methodology* (2003).

M. Bernardo and R. Gorrieri. *A tutorial on EMPA: A theory of concurrent processes with nondeterminism, priorities, probabilities and time.* Theoretical Computer Science, 202(1–2):1–54 (1998).
URL `http://www.cs.unibo.it/~gorrieri/Papers/tcs202.ps.gz`

M. Bertoli, G. Casale, and G. Serazzi. *The JMT Simulator for Performance Evaluation of Non-Product-Form Queueing Networks.* In *Annual Simulation Symposium*, pages 3–10. IEEE Computer Society, Norfolk,VA, US (2007).

A. Bertolino and R. Mirandola. *CB-SPE Tool: Putting Component-Based Performance Engineering into Practice.* In I. Crnkovic, J. A. Stafford, H. W. Schmidt, and K. C. Wallnau, editors, *Proc. 7th International Symposium on Component-Based Software Engineering (CBSE 2004), Edinburgh, UK*, volume 3054 of *Lecture Notes in Computer Science*, pages 233–248. Springer-Verlag, Berlin, Germany (2004).

A. Beugnard, J.-M. Jézéquel, N. Plouzeau, and D. Watkins. *Making Components Contract Aware.* Computer, 32(7):38–45 (1999).

H. C. Bohnenkamp, P. R. D'Argenio, H. Hermanns, and J.-P. Katoen. *MODEST: A Compositional Modeling Formalism for Hard and Softly Timed Systems.* IEEE Transactions on Software Engineering, 32(10):812–830 (2006).

G. Bolch, S. Greiner, H. de Meer, and K. S. Trivedi. *Queueing Networks and Markov Chains.* John Wiley & Sons Inc. (1998a).

G. Bolch, S. Greiner, K. S. Trivedi, and H. de Meer. *Queueing Networks and Markov Chains: Modeling and Performance Evaluation With Computer Science Applications.* Wiley & Sons, New York, NY, USA (1998b).

G. Bolch and M. Kirschnick. *PEPSY-QNS - Ein Programmsystem zur Leistungsanalyse von Warteschlangennetzwerken.* In *Messung, Modellierung und Bewertung von Rechen- und Kommunikationssystemen ; Kurzberichte und Werkzeugvorstellungen zur 7.ITG/GI-Fachtagung Aachen, 21.-23. Sep. 1993; Aachener Beiträge zur Informatik (Bd. 2)*, pages 216–220. Verlag der Augustinus Buchhandlung, Aachen (1993).

E. Bondarev, M. Chaudron, and P. de With. *A Process for Resolving Performance Trade-Offs in Component-Based Architectures.* In *Proceedings of the 9th International Symposium on Component-based Software Engineering (CBSE2006)*, volume 4063 of *Lecture Notes in Computer Science*, pages 254–269 (2006).

E. Bondarev, P. de With, M. Chaudron, and J. Musken. *Modelling of Input-Parameter Dependency for Performance Predictions of Component-Based Embedded Systems.* In *Proceedings of the 31th EUROMICRO Conference (EUROMICRO'05)* (2005).

E. Bondarev, P. H. N. de With, and M. Chaudron. *Predicting Real-Time Properties of Component-Based Applications.* In *Proc. of RTCSA* (2004).

A. D. Brucker and B. Wolff. *HOL-OCL: Experiences, Consequences and Design Choices.* In J.-M. Jézéquel, H. Hussmann, and S. Cook, editors, *UML 2002: Model Engineering, Concepts and Tools*, number 2460 in Lecture Notes in Computer Science, pages 196–211. Springer-Verlag, Dresden (2002).
URL `http://www.brucker.ch/bibliography/abstract/brucker.ea-hol-ocl-2002`

F. Budinsky, D. Steinberg, E. Merks, R. Ellersick, and T. J. Grose. *Eclipse Modeling Framework.* Eclipse Series. Prentice Hall (2003).

F. Buschmann, R. Meunier, H. Rohnert, P. Sommerlad, and M. Stal. *Pattern-Oriented Software Architecture – A System of Patterns.* Wiley & Sons, New York, NY, USA (1996).

Carnegie Mellon University. *Website on Published Software Architecture Definitions* (2007). Last retrieved 2008-01-06.
URL `http://www.sei.cmu.edu/architecture/published\_definitions.html`

J. Cheesman and J. Daniels. *UML Components: A Simple Process for Specifying Component-based Software.* Addison-Wesley, Reading, MA, USA (2000).

P. C. Clements, F. Bachmann, L. Bass, D. Garlan, J. Ivers, R. Little, R. Nord, and J. Stafford. *Documenting Software Architectures.* SEI Series in Software Engineering. Addison-Wesley (2003).

V. Cortellessa. *How far are we from the definition of a common software performance ontology?* In *WOSP '05: Proceedings of the 5th International Workshop on Software and Performance*, pages 195–204. ACM Press, New York, NY, USA (2005).

V. Cortellessa, P. Pierini, and D. Rossi. *Integrating Software Models and Platform Models for Performance Analysis.* IEEE Transactions on Software Engineering, 33(6):385–401 (2007).

G. Coulouris, J. Dollimore, and T. Kindberg. *Distributed Systems - Concepts and Design, 3rd Ed.* Addison Wesley (2000).

K. Czarnecki and U. W. Eisenecker. *Generative Programming.* Addison-Wesley, Reading, MA, USA (2000).

K. Czarnecki and S. Helsen. *Classification of Model Transformation Approaches.* In *OOPSLA 2003 Workshop on Generative Techniques in the context of Model Driven Architecture* (2003). Last retrieved 2008-01-06.
URL `http://www.softmetaware.com/oopsla2003/czarnecki.pdf`

M. de Miguel, T. Lambolais, M. Hannouz, S. Betge-Brezetz, and S. Piekarec. *UML extensions for the specification and evaluation of latency constraints in architectural models.* In *WOSP '00: Proceedings of the 2nd International Workshop on Software and Performance*, pages 83–88. ACM Press, New York, NY, USA (2000).

DESMO-J. *The DESMO-J Homepage* (2007). Last retrieved 2008-01-06.
URL `http://asi-www.informatik.uni-hamburg.de/desmoj/`

A. Di Marco and P. Inveradi. *Compositional Generation of Software Architecture Performance QN Models.* In *Proceedings of WICSA 2004*, pages 37–46 (2004).

A. Di Marco and R. Mirandola. *Model Transformations in Software Performance Engineering.* In C. Hofmeister, I. Crnkovic, R. Reussner, and S. Becker, editors, *Quality of Software Architectures, 2nd International Conference, QoSA 2006, Västerås, Sweden, June 27 - 29, 2006, Proceedings*, volume 4214 of *Lecture Notes in Computer Science*, pages 95–110 (2006).

B. P. Douglass. *Real-Time Design Patterns.* Object Technology Series. Addison-Wesley Professional (2002).

N. Duzbayev and I. Poernomo. *Runtime Prediction of Queued Behaviour.* In C. Hofmeister, I. Crnkovic, and R. Reussner, editors, *Quality of Software Architectures, Second International Conference on Quality of Software Architectures, QoSA 2006, Västerås, Sweden, June 27-29, 2006 Revised Papers*, volume 4214 of *Lecture Notes in Computer Science*, pages 78–94. Springer (2006).

Eclipse Foundation. *The Eclipse Modelling Project* (2006). Last retrieved 2008-01-06.
URL `http://www.eclipse.org/modeling/`

Eclipse Foundation. *EMF-based OCL Implementation* (2007a). Last retrieved 2008-01-06.
URL `http://www.eclipse.org/modeling/mdt/?project=ocl`

Eclipse Foundation. *Graphical Editing Framework Homepage* (2007b). Last retrieved 2008-01-06.
URL `http://www.eclipse.org/gef/`

Eclipse Foundation. *Graphical Modeling Framework Homepage* (2007c). Last retrieved 2008-01-06.
URL `http://www.eclipse.org/gmf/`

EJB. *Sun Microsystems Corp., The Enterprise Java Beans homepage* (2007). Last retrieved 2008-01-06.
URL `http://java.sun.com/products/ejb/`

M. A. Ellis and B. Stroustrup. *The Annotated C++ Rerenence Manual.* Addison–Wesley, Reading, MA (1990).

E. Eskenazi, A. Fioukov, and D. Hammer. *Performance Prediction for Component Compositions.* In *Proceedings of the 7th International Symposium on Component-based Software Engineering (CBSE7)*, volume 3054 of *Lecture Notes in Computer Science*, pages 280–293. Springer-Verlag, Berlin, Germany (2004).

V. Firus, S. Becker, and J. Happe. *Parametric Performance Contracts for QML-specified Software Components.* In *Formal Foundations of Embedded Software and Component-based Software Architectures (FESCA)*, volume 141 of *Electronic Notes in Theoretical Computer Science*, pages 73–90. ETAPS 2005 (2005).

M. Fowler. *Inversion of Control Containers and the Dependency Injection pattern* (2004). Last retrieved 2008-01-06.
URL `http://martinfowler.com/articles/injection.html`

T. Freese. *EasyMock - Dynamic Mock Objects for JUnit.* In M. Marchesi, editor, *Proceedings of the 3rd International Conference on Extreme Programming and Agile Processes in Software Engineering*, pages 1–5 (2002).

F. Freiling, I. Eusgeld, and R. Reussner, editors. *Dependability Metrics*. Lecture Notes in Computer Science. Springer-Verlag, Berlin, Germany (2008). To appear.

E. Gamma, R. Helm, R. Johnson, and J. Vlissides. *Design Patterns: Elements of Reusable Object-Oriented Software*. Addison-Wesley, Reading, MA, USA (1995).

R. L. Glass. *Software Runaways: Monumental Software Disasters*. Prentice Hall, Englewood Cliffs, NJ, USA (1998).

Gorilla Logic Inc. *Gorilla Logic Homepage* (2007). Last retrieved 2008-01-06. URL `http://www.gorillalogic.com/`

N. Götz, U. Herzog, and M. Rettelbach. *TIPP - Introduction and Application to Protocol Performance Analysis*. In H. König, editor, *Formale Methoden für verteilte Systeme, GI/ITG-Fachgespräch, Magdeburg, 10.-11. Juni 1992*, pages 105–125. K. G. Saur Verlag (1992).

V. Grassi, R. Mirandola, and A. Sabetta. *From Design to Analysis Models: a Kernel Language for Performance and Reliability Analysis of Component-based Systems*. In *WOSP '05: Proceedings of the 5th international workshop on Software and performance*, pages 25–36. ACM Press, New York, NY, USA (2005).

V. Grassi, R. Mirandola, and A. Sabetta. *A Model Transformation Approach for the Early Performance and Reliability Analysis of Component-Based Systems*. In I. Gorton, G. T. Heineman, I. Crnkovic, H. W. Schmidt, J. A. Stafford, C. A. Szyperski, and K. C. Wallnau, editors, *Component-Based Software Engineering, 9th International Symposium, CBSE 2006, Västerås, Sweden, June 29 - July 1, 2006, Proceedings*, volume 4063 of *Lecture Notes in Computer Science*, pages 270–284. Springer (2006).

D. Hamlet, D. Mason, and D. Woit. *Component-Based Software Development: Case Studies*, volume 1 of *Series on Component-Based Software Development*, chapter Properties of Software Systems Synthesized from Components, pages 129–159. World Scientific Publishing Company (2004).

J. Happe. *Concurrency Modelling for Performance and Reliability Prediction of Component-Based Software Architectures.* Ph.D. thesis, University of Oldenburg (2008). To appear.

J. Happe, H. Koziolek, and R. Reussner. *Parametric Performance Contracts for Software Components with Concurrent Behaviour.* In F. S. de Boer and V. Mencl, editors, *Proceedings of the 3rd International Workshop on Formal Aspects of Component Software (FACS06), Prague, Czech Republic*, Electronical Notes in Computer Science (2006).

P. G. Harrison and B. Strulo. *SPADES - a Process Algebra for Discrete Event Simulation.* Journal of Logic and Computation, 10(1):3–42 (2000). URL `http://pubs.doc.ic.ac.uk/spades/`

B. R. Haverkort, R. Marie, G. Rubino, and K. S. Trivedi. *Performability Modelling : Techniques and Tools.* Wiley & Sons, New York, NY, USA (2001).

H. Hermanns, U. Herzog, and J.-P. Katoen. *Process Algebra for Performance Evaluation.* Theoretical Computer Science, 274(1–2):43–87 (2002).

J. Hillston. *A Compositional Approach to Performance Modelling.* Cambridge University Press, New York, NY, USA (1996).

S. A. Hissam, G. A. Moreno, J. A. Stafford, and K. C. Wallnau. *Packaging Predictable Assembly.* In J. M. Bishop, editor, *Component Deployment, IFIP/ACM Working Conference, CD 2002, Berlin, Germany, June 20-21, 2002, Proceedings*, volume 2370 of *Lecture Notes in Computer Science*, pages 108–124. Springer (2002).

G. Hohpe and B. Woolf. *Enterprise Integration Patterns: Designing, Building, and Deploying Messaging Solutions.* Addison-Wesley Longman, Amsterdam (2003).

A. Hunt and D. Thomas. *Pragmatic Unit Testing in Java with JUnit.* The Pragmatic Programmers (2003).

HyPerformix Inc. *Hyperformix Homepage* (2007). Last retrieved 2008-01-06. URL `http://www.hyperformix.com`

A. Kostian. *Vergleich der Performance-Auswirkungen generierter Adaptoren.* Diplomarbeit, University of Oldenburg (2005).

S. Kounev. *Performance Modeling and Evaluation of Distributed Component-Based Systems Using Queueing Petri Nets.* IEEE Transactions on Software Engineering, 32(7):486–502 (2006).

S. Kounev and A. Buchmann. *SimQPN: a tool and methodology for analyzing queueing Petri net models by means of simulation.* Performormance Evaluation, 63(4):364–394 (2006).

H. Koziolek. *Parameter Dependencies for Reusable Performance Specifications of Software Components.* Ph.D. thesis, University of Oldenburg (2008).

H. Koziolek, S. Becker, and J. Happe. *Predicting the Performance of Component-based Software Architectures with different Usage Profiles.* In *Proc. 3rd International Conference on the Quality of Software Architectures (QoSA'07)*, volume 4880 of *LNCS*, pages 145–163. Springer (2007).

H. Koziolek, S. Becker, J. Happe, and R. Reussner. *Model-Driven Software Development: Integrating Quality Assurance*, chapter Evaluating Performance and Reliability of Software Architecture with the Palladio Component Model, page To appear. IDEA Group Inc. (2008).

H. Koziolek and V. Firus. *Parametric Performance Contracts: Non-Markovian Loop Modelling and an Experimental Evaluation.* In *Proceedings of FESCA2006*, Electronical Notes in Computer Science (ENTCS) (2006).

H. Koziolek and J. Happe. *A Quality of Service Driven Development Process Model for Component-based Software Systems.* In I. Gorton, G. T. Heineman, I. Crnkovic, H. W. Schmidt, J. A. Stafford, C. A. Szyperski, and K. C. Wallnau, editors, *Component-Based Software Engineering*, volume 4063 of *Lecture Notes in Computer Science*, pages 336–343. Springer-Verlag, Berlin, Germany (2006). URL `http://dx.doi.org/10.1007/11783565\_25`

H. Koziolek, J. Happe, and S. Becker. *Parameter Dependent Performance Specification of Software Components.* In *Proceedings of the Second International Conference on Quality of Software Architectures (QoSA2006)*, volume 4214 of *Lecture Notes in Computer Science*, pages 163–179. Springer-Verlag, Berlin, Germany (2006).

K. Krogmann. *Generierung von Adaptoren.* Individual project, University of Oldenburg, Germany (2004).

K. Krogmann. *Entwicklung und Transformation eines EMF-Modells des Palladio Komponenten-Meta-Modells.* Master's thesis, University of Oldenburg, Germany (2006). Last retrieved 2008-01-06.
URL `http://www.kelsaka.de/kelsaka/extra/content/Diplomarbeit%20Entwicklung%20und%20Transformation%20eine%20EMF-Modells%20des%20Palladio%20Komponenten-Meta-Modells.pdf`

K. Krogmann. *Reengineering of Software Component Models to Enable Architectural Quality of Service Predictions.* In R. Reussner, C. Szyperski, and W. Weck, editors, *Proceedings of the 12th International Workshop on Component Oriented Programming (WCOP 2007)* (2007).

K. Krogmann and S. Becker. *A Case Study on Model-Driven and Conventional Software Development: The Palladio Editor.* In W.-G. Bleek, H. Schwentner, and H. Züllighoven, editors, *Software Engineering 2007 - Beiträge zu den Workshops*, volume 106 of *Lecture Notes in Informatics (LNI) - Proceedings*, pages 169–176. Series of the Gesellschaft für Informatik (GI) (2007).

K. Krogmann and R. Reussner. *Palladio - Prediction of Performance Properties.* In *The Common Component Modelling Example: Comparing Software Component Models*, volume To Appear of *To Appear in LNCS*. Springer-Verlag, Berlin, Germany (2008).

K.-K. Lau. *Software Component Models.* In *Proceedings of the 6th International Conference on Software Engineering (ICSE06)*, pages 1081–1082. ACM Press (2006).

K.-K. Lau and Z. Wang. *A Taxonomy of Software Component Models.* In *Proceedings of the 31st EUROMICRO Conference*, pages 88–95. IEEE Computer Society Press (2005).

K.-K. Lau and Z. Wang. *A Survey of Software Component Models.* Technical report, School of Computer Science, The University of Manchester (2006). Second edition, Pre-print CSPP-38, Last retrieved 2008-01-06.
URL `http://www.cs.man.ac.uk/cspreprints/PrePrints/cspp38.pdf`

A. M. Law and W. D. Kelton. *Simulation, Modelling and Analysis.* McGraw-Hill, New York, 3rd edition (2000).

E. Lazowska, J. Zahorjan, G. S. Graham, and K. C. Sevcik. *Quantitative System Performance - Computer System Analysis Using Queueing Network Models.* Prentice-Hall (1984).

P. L'Ecuyer and E. Buist. *Simulation in Java with SSJ.* In *WSC '05: Proceedings of the 37th conference on Winter simulation*, pages 611–620. Winter Simulation Conference (2005).

K. Lee, K. C. Kang, and J. Lee. *Concepts and Guidelines of Feature Modeling for Product Line Software Engineering.* In C. Gacek, editor, *Software Reuse: Methods, Techniques, and Tools, 7th International Conference, ICSR-7, Austin, TX, USA, April 15-19, 2002, Proceedings*, volume 2319 of *Lecture Notes in Computer Science*, pages 62–77. Springer (2002).

Y. Liu, A. Fekete, and I. Gorton. *Design-Level Performance Prediction of Component-Based Applications.* IEEE Transactions on Software Engineering, 31(11):928–941 (2005).

R. G. M. Bravetti, M. Bernardo. *Towards Performance Evaluation with General Distributions in Process Algebras.* In D. Sangiorgi and R. de Simone, editors, *Proceedings of the 9th International Conference on Concurrency Theory (CONCUR '98)*, volume 1466 of *LNCS*, pages 405–422 (1998a).

F. Marinescu. *EJB Design Patterns.* John Wiley & Sons (2002).

A. Martens. *Empirical Validation of the Model-driven Performance Prediction Approach Palladio.* Master's thesis, Universität Oldenburg (2007).
URL `http://sdq.ipd.uka.de/diploma\_theses\_study\_theses/completed\_theses`

N. Medvidovic and R. N. Taylor. *A classification and comparison framework for software architecture description languages.* IEEE Transactions on Software Engineering, 26(1):70–93 (2000).

metamodel.com. *metamodel.com, Community site for meta-modeling and semantic modeling: What is metamodeling, and what is it good for?* (2007). Last retrieved 2008-01-06.
URL `http://www.metamodel.com/staticpages/index.php?page=20021010231056977`

B. Meyer. *Object-Oriented Software Construction.* Prentice Hall, Englewood Cliffs, NJ, USA, 2nd edition (1997).

Microsoft Corporation. *The DCOM homepage* (2007). Last retrieved 2008-01-06. URL `http://www.microsoft.com/com/default.mspx`

R. Milner. *A calculus of communicating systems.* Lecture Notes in Computer Science, 92 (1980).

ModelWare. *ModelWare Information Society Technologies (IST) Sixth Framework Programme: Glossary* (2007). Last retrieved 2008-01-06. URL `http://www.modelware-ist.org/index.php?option=com\_rd\_glossary\&Itemid=55`

S. S. Muchnick. *Advanced Compiler Design and Implementation.* Morgan Kaufmann Publishers, San Mateo, CA, USA (1997).

.NET. *Microsoft Corp., The .NET homepage* (2007). Last retrieved 2008-01-06. URL `http://www.microsoft.com/net/default.aspx`

Object Management Group (OMG). *IDL to Java Language Mapping Specification (formal/02-08-05)* (2002). URL `http://www.omg.org/docs/formal/02-08-05.pdf`

Object Management Group (OMG). *UML Profile for Modeling Quality of Service and Fault Tolerance Characteristics and Mechanisms* (2005a). URL `http://www.omg.org/cgi-bin/doc?ptc/2005-05-02`

Object Management Group (OMG). *UML Profile for Schedulability, Performance and Time* (2005b). URL `http://www.omg.org/cgi-bin/doc?formal/2005-01-02`

Object Management Group (OMG). *Unified Modeling Language Specification: Version 2, Revised Final Adopted Specification (ptc/05-07-04)* (2005c). URL `http://www.uml.org/\#UML2.0`

Object Management Group (OMG). *CORBA Component Model, v4.0 (formal/2006-04-01)* (2006a). URL `http://www.omg.org/technology/documents/formal/components.htm`

Object Management Group (OMG). *Meta Object Facility (MOF) 2.0 XMI Mapping Specification, v2.1 (formal/05-09-01)* (2006b).
URL http://www.omg.org/cgi-bin/apps/doc?formal/05-09-01.pdf

Object Management Group (OMG). *Model Driven Architecture - Specifications* (2006c).
URL http://www.omg.org/mda/specs.htm

Object Management Group (OMG). *MOF 2.0 Core Specification (formal/2006-01-01)* (2006d).
URL http://www.omg.org/cgi-bin/doc?formal/2006-01-01

Object Management Group (OMG). *Object Constraint Language, v2.0 (formal/06-05-01)* (2006e).
URL http://www.omg.org/cgi-bin/doc?formal/2006-05-01

Object Management Group (OMG). *UML Profile for Modeling and Analysis of Real-Time and Embedded systems (MARTE) RFP (realtime/05-02-06)* (2006f).
URL http://www.omg.org/cgi-bin/doc?realtime/2005-2-6

Object Management Group (OMG). *Meta Object Facility (MOF) 2.0 Query/View/Transformation Specification (ptc/07-07-07)* (2007a).
URL http://www.omg.org/docs/ptc/07-07-07.pdf

Object Management Group (OMG). *MOF Models to Text Transformation Language, Beta 2* (2007b).
URL http://www.omg.org/docs/ptc/07-08-16.pdf

Object Web. *The Fractal Project Homepage* (2006). Last retrieved 2008-01-06.
URL http://fractal.objectweb.org/

openArchitectureWare (oAW). *openArchitectureWare (oAW) Generator Framework* (2007). Last retrieved 2008-01-06.
URL http://www.openarchitectureware.org

S. Overhage. *Vereinheitlichte Spezifikation von Komponenten: Grundlagen, UnSCom Spezifikationsrahmen und Anwendung*. Ph.D. thesis, Augsburg University (2006).

B. Page and W. Kreutzer. *The Java Simulation Handbook. Simulating Discrete Event Systems with UML and Java.* Shaker Verlag GmbH, Germany (2005).

C. A. Petri. *Kommunikation mit Automation.* Schriften des Rheinisch-Westfälischen Institutes für Instrumentelle Mathematik an der Universität Bonn, Bonn FRG (1962).

D. C. Petriu and H. Shen. *Applying the UML Performance Profile: Graph Grammar-based Derivation of LQN Models from UML Specifications.* In *Computer Performance Evaluation – Modelling Techniques and Tools*, volume 2324 of *Lecture Notes in Computer Science*, pages 159 – 177. Springer (2002).

D. C. Petriu and X. Wang. *From UML Description of High-level Software Architecture to LQN Performance Models.* In M. Nagl, A. Schürr, and M. Münch, editors, *Proc. of AGTIVE'99 Kerkrade*, volume 1779. Springer (2000).

G. Pietrek, J. Trompeter, J. C. F. Beltran, B. Holzer, T. Kamann, M. Kloss, S. A. Mork, B. Niehues, and K. Thoms. *Modellgetriebene Softwareentwicklung - MDA und MDSD in der Praxis.* entwickler.press (2007).

F. Plasil and S. Visnovsky. *Behavior Protocols for Software Components.* IEEE Transactions on Software Engineering, 28(11):1056–1076 (2002).

R Development Core Team. *R: A Language and Environment for Statistical Computing.* R Foundation for Statistical Computing, Vienna, Austria (2007). ISBN 3-900051-07-0, Last retrieved 2008-01-06.
URL `http://www.R-project.org`

A. Rentschler. *Model-To-Text Transformation Languages.* In *Seminar: Modellgetriebene Software-Entwicklung Architekturen, Muster und Eclipse-basierte MDA.* Fakultät für Informatik, Universität Karlsruhe (TH), Germany (2006).

R. H. Reussner. *Parametrisierte Verträge zur Protokolladaption bei Software-Komponenten.* Logos Verlag, Berlin (2001).

R. H. Reussner, S. Becker, and V. Firus. *Component Composition with Parametric Contracts.* In *Tagungsband der Net.ObjectDays 2004*, pages 155–169 (2004).

R. H. Reussner, S. Becker, H. Koziolek, J. Happe, M. Kuperberg, and K. Krogmann. *The Palladio Component Model.* Interner Bericht 2007-21, Universität Karlsruhe (TH), Faculty for Informatics, Karlsruhe, Germany (2007).

R. H. Reussner and W. Hasselbring. *Handbuch der Software-Architektur.* dPunkt.verlag, Heidelberg (2006).

R. H. Reussner, H. W. Schmidt, and I. Poernomo. *Reliability Prediction for Component-Based Software Architectures.* Journal of Systems and Software – Special Issue of Software Architecture – Engineering Quality Attributes, 66(3):241–252 (2003).

J. Ritter. *Prozessorientierte Konfiguration komponentenbasierter Anwendungssysteme.* Ph.D. thesis, Universität Oldenburg, Universität Oldenburg (2000). Dissertation, Universität Oldenburg, Fachbereich Informatik. URL `http://docserver.bis.uni-oldenburg.de/publikationen/dissertation/2000/ritpro00/ritpro00.html`

L. Sachs. *Angewandte Statistik: Anwendung statistischer Methoden.* Springer-Verlag, Berlin, Germany, 8th edition (1997).

R. Schaudel. *Modellgetriebene Transformation von Instanzen des Palladio Komponentenmodells in eine ablauffähige J2EE Realisierung.* Master's thesis, University of Karlsruhe (TH) (2007).

M. Shaw and D. Garlan. *Software Architecture: Perspectives on an Emerging Discipline.* Prentice Hall, Englewood Cliffs, NJ, USA (1996).

M. Sitaraman, G. Kuczycki, J. Krone, W. F. Ogden, and A. Reddy. *Performance Specification of Software Components.* In *Proceedings of the 2001 symposium on Software reusability: putting software reuse in context*, pages 3–10. ACM Press (2001).

C. U. Smith. *Performance Engineering of Software Systems.* Addison-Wesley, Reading, MA, USA (1990).

C. U. Smith and L. G. Williams. *Performance Engineering Evaluation of Object-Oriented Systems with SPEED.* In R. Marie, editor, *Computer Performance Evaluation: Modelling Techniques and Tools*, volume 1245 of *Lecture Notes in Computer Science.* Springer-Verlag, Berlin, Germany (1997).

C. U. Smith and L. G. Williams. *Performance Solutions: A Practical Guide to Creating Responsive, Scalable Software.* Addison-Wesley (2002).

Spring. *The Spring Framework Homepage* (2006).
URL `http://www.springframework.org/`

H. Stachowiak. *Allgemeine Modelltheorie.* Springer Verlag, Wien (1973).

N. Streekmann and S. Becker. *A Case Study for Using Generator Configuration to Support Performance Prediction of Software Component Adaptation.* In C. Hofmeister, I. Crnkovic, R. Reussner, and S. Becker, editors, *Short Paper Proceedings of the Second International Conference on Quality of Software Architectures (QoSA2006), Västerås, Sweden, June 27 - 29, 2006, TR 2006-10, University of Karlsruhe (TH)* (2006).

Sun Microsystems Corp. *Java Platform, Enterprise Edition (Java EE) Specification, v5* (2006). Last retrieved 2008-01-06.
URL `http://jcp.org/aboutJava/communityprocess/final/jsr244/index.html`

C. Szyperski, D. Gruntz, and S. Murer. *Component Software: Beyond Object-Oriented Programming.* ACM Press and Addison-Wesley, New York, NY, 2nd edition (2002).

A. S. Tanenbaum. *Modern Operating Systems.* Prentice Hall, Englewood Cliffs, NJ, USA, 2nd edition (2001).

K. S. Trivedi. *Probability and Statistics with Reliability, Queuing and Computer Science Applications.* Wiley & Sons, New York, NY, USA, 2nd edition (2001).

M. Uflacker. *Design of an Editor for the model-driven Construction of Component Based Software Architectures.* Master's thesis, University of Oldenburg, Germany (2005).

A. Uhl. *Model-Driven Architecture, MDA.* In *Handbuch der Software-Architektur*, chapter 6, pages 106–123. dPunkt.verlag, Heidelberg (2007a).

A. Uhl. *Model-Driven Development in the Enterprise* (2007b). Last retrieved 2008-01-06.
URL `https://www.sdn.sap.com/irj/sdn/weblogs?blog=/pub/wlg/7237`

R. van Ommering, F. van der Linden, J. Kramer, and J. Magee. *The Koala Component Model for Consumer Electronics Software.* Computer, 33(3):78–85 (2000).

T. Verdickt, B. Dhoedt, F. Gielen, and P. Demeester. *Automatic Inclusion of Middleware Performance Attributes into Architectural UML Software Models.* IEEE Transactions on Software Engineering, 31(8):695–711 (2005).

T. Verdickt, B. Dhoedt, F. D. Turck, and P. Demeester. *Hybrid Performance Modeling Approach for Network Intensive Distributed Software.* In *Proceedings of the 6th International Workshop on Software and Performance (WOSP2007)*, ACM Sigsoft Notes, pages 189–200 (2007).

M. Völter and T. Stahl. *Model-Driven Software Development.* Wiley & Sons, New York, NY, USA (2006).

L. G. Williams and C. U. Smith. *Making the Business Case for Software Performance Engineering.* In *Proceedings of the 29th International Computer Measurement Group Conference, December 7-12, 2003, Dallas, Texas, USA*, pages 349–358. Computer Measurement Group (2003).

C. Wohlin, P. Runeson, M. Höst, M. C. Ohlsson, B. Regnell, and A. Wesslén. *Experimentation in Software Engineering: an Introduction.* Kluwer Academic Publishers, Norwell, MA, USA (2000).

C. M. Woodside, J. E. Neilson, D. C. Petriu, and S. Majumdar. *The Stochastic Rendezvous Network Model for Performance of Synchronous Client-Server-like Distributed Software.* IEEE Transactions on Computers, 44(1):20–34 (1995).

M. Woodside, G. Franks, and D. C. Petriu. *The Future of Software Performance Engineering.* In *Proceedings of ICSE 2007, Future of SE*, pages 171–187. IEEE Computer Society, Washington, DC, USA (2007).

M. Woodside, D. C. Petriu, H. Shen, T. Israr, and J. Merseguer. *Performance by unified model analysis (PUMA).* In *WOSP '05: Proceedings of the 5th International Workshop on Software and Performance*, pages 1–12. ACM Press, New York, NY, USA (2005).

M. Woodside, D. C. Petriu, and K. H. Siddiqui. *Performance-related Completions for Software Specifications.* In *Proceedings of the 22rd International Confer-*

ence on Software Engineering, ICSE 2002, 19-25 May 2002, Orlando, Florida, USA, pages 22–32. ACM (2002).

X. Wu and M. Woodside. *Performance Modeling from Software Components.* SIGSOFT Softw. Eng. Notes, 29(1):290–301 (2004).

Made in the USA
Monee, IL
08 November 2026

68033803R00175